Spiritually Oriented Psychotherapy for Trauma

Spiritually Oriented Psychotherapy for Trauma

EDITED BY
Donald F. Walker, Christine A. Courtois,
and Jamie D. Aten

American Psychological Association • Washington, DC

Published by
American Psychological Association
750 First Street, NE
Washington, DC 20002
www.apa.org

To order
APA Order Department
P.O. Box 92984
Washington, DC 20090-2984
Tel: (800) 374-2721; Direct: (202) 336-5510
Fax: (202) 336-5502; TDD/TTY: (202) 336-6123
Online: www.apa.org/pubs/books
E-mail: order@apa.org

In the U.K., Europe, Africa, and the Middle East, copies may be ordered from
American Psychological Association
3 Henrietta Street
Covent Garden, London
WC2E 8LU England

Typeset in Goudy by Circle Graphics, Inc., Columbia, MD

Printer: Maple Press, York, PA
Cover Designer: Mercury Publishing Services, Inc., Rockville, MD
Cover Art: Marietje B. Chamberlain, Marsh Light, 2013, oil on linen, 32″ × 48″

The opinions and statements published are the responsibility of the authors, and such opinions and statements do not necessarily represent the policies of the American Psychological Association. Any views expressed in chapter 11 do not necessarily represent the views of the United States government, and the author's participation in the work is not meant to serve as an official endorsement.

Library of Congress Cataloging-in-Publication Data

Spiritually oriented psychotherapy for trauma / [edited by] Donald F. Walker, Christine A. Courtois, and Jamie D. Aten. — First edition.
     p. ; cm.
  Includes bibliographical references and index.
  ISBN 978-1-4338-1816-5 — ISBN 1-4338-1816-7
  I. Walker, Donald F. (Donald Franklin), editor. II. Courtois, Christine A., editor.
III. Aten, Jamie D., editor. IV. American Psychological Association, issuing body.
  [DNLM: 1. Stress Disorders, Traumatic—therapy. 2. Psychotherapy—methods. 3. Religion and Psychology. 4. Spirituality. WM 172.5]
  RC489.B48
  616.89'166—dc23
                                        2014014699

British Library Cataloguing-in-Publication Data
A CIP record is available from the British Library.

Printed in the United States of America
First Edition

http://dx.doi.org/10.1037/14500-000

This book is dedicated to my parents, Alice and John Walker, who in addition to loving me, taught me to persevere in the midst of adversity, to find meaning in service, and to go the second mile. I also dedicate this book to my students in the Child Trauma Institute at Regent University, to whom I hope to impart these lessons. You honor me with your service to our clients.
—*Donald F. Walker*

To my parents, Normand and Irene Courtois, who taught me about faith, morality, and trust, and to my husband, Tom, who puts all three into practice every day. I'm grateful beyond words for your love and support. Damaged spirituality is at the core of traumatic injury. I hope this book provides a resource as well as recourse for therapists and clients alike.
—*Christine A. Courtois*

To Dr. I. Michael Shuff. I am grateful to have had you as a mentor and for all I learned from you. You taught me much about compassion and about the importance of finding opportunity even in the most difficult of times.
—*Jamie D. Aten*

CONTENTS

CONTRIBUTORS

Meline A. Arzoumanian, MA, Trauma Research Institute, San Diego, CA

Jamie D. Aten, PhD, The Humanitarian Disaster Institute, Wheaton College, Wheaton, IL

Michael E. Berrett, PhD, Center for Change, Orem, UT

David Boan, PhD, The Humanitarian Disaster Institute, Wheaton College, Wheaton, IL

Christine A. Courtois, PhD, ABPP, private practice, Washington, DC; National Clinical Training Consultant, Elements Behavioral Health/ Promises, Malibu and Los Angeles, CA

Kristen Dahlin, MA, Trauma Research Institute, San Diego, CA

Constance Dalenberg, PhD, Trauma Research Institute, San Diego, CA

Jillian DeLorme, MA, Trauma Research Institute, San Diego, CA

Kent D. Drescher, PhD, National Center for PTSD: Dissemination and Training Division, VA Palo Alto Health Care System, Menlo Park, CA

Jan E. Estrellado, MA, Trauma Research Institute, San Diego, CA

David W. Foy, PhD, Pepperdine University, Encino, CA

Mary Gail Frawley-O'Dea, PhD, Presbyterian Psychological Services, Charlotte, NC

Sue Grand, PhD, New York University Postdoctoral Program
   in Psychotherapy and Psychoanalysis, New York
Randy K. Hardman, PhD, Brigham Young University, Rexburg, ID
Emily Hennrich, MA, Trauma Research Institute, San Diego, CA
Sharon G. Horne, PhD, University of Massachusetts Boston
Katlin R. Knodel, MA, Virginia Beach, VA
Troy Lea, Brigham Young University, Provo, UT
Heidi M. Levitt, PhD, University of Massachusetts Boston
Kerry L. McGregor, MA, Regent University, Virginia Beach, VA
Glen Milstein, PhD, City College of New York, City University of New York,
   New York
Kari A. O'Grady, PhD, Loyola University Maryland, Columbia
Crystal L. Park, PhD, University of Connecticut, Storrs
David Quagliana, PhD, Cleveland, TN
P. Scott Richards, PhD, Brigham Young University, Provo, UT
Heather E. Rodriguez, MA, Trauma Research Institute, San Diego, CA
Alice Schruba, MA, Wheaton College, Wheaton, IL
Jeanne M. Slattery, PhD, Clarion University, Clarion, PA
Melissa A. Smigelsky, MA, The University of Memphis, Memphis, TN
Rachel L. Stephens, MA, Regent University, Virginia Beach, VA
Jessica M. Stevens, MA, Trauma Research Institute, San Diego, CA
Stephanie Van Deusen, PhD, LPC, STAGES Counseling Center,
   Lancaster, PA
E. Grace Verbeck, MA, Trauma Research Institute, San Diego, CA
Donald F. Walker, PhD, Regent University, Virginia Beach, VA
Mei-Chuan Wang, PhD, Fayetteville State University, Fayetteville, NC
Isaac Weaver, MA, Wheaton College, Wheaton, IL
Emily E. Wheeler, MS, University of Massachusetts Boston

Spiritually Oriented Psychotherapy for Trauma

INTRODUCTION

DONALD F. WALKER, CHRISTINE A. COURTOIS,
AND JAMIE D. ATEN

Though He slay me, yet will I trust in Him.
—Job 13:15 (King James Version)

Introducing a book about spirituality and trauma is a daunting task. To say that both of these topics are immensely personal in nature is a profound understatement. Consider the fact that all major world religions include some basic commandment to love other people, yet wars have been repeatedly fought throughout human history over differing views of the divine. In a similar vein, traumatic experiences are also intensely private in nature. Dalenberg (2000) reminded us that trauma is simultaneously difficult for clients to speak about aloud and for psychotherapists and others to hear about. When it comes to describing the emotional and spiritual meaning of child abuse, rape, or torture, words simply fall short.

At the same time, the observations of many trauma experts and the clinical experience of many psychotherapists, including the three coeditors of this text—and the findings of our own independent research programs— suggest that spirituality and trauma are often inextricably intertwined. Trauma affects the individual and his or her beliefs in the divine and the

http://dx.doi.org/10.1037/14500-001
Spiritually Oriented Psychotherapy for Trauma, D. F. Walker, C. A. Courtois, and J. D. Aten (Editors)

sacred in ways that may interrupt or sever these beliefs or, simultaneously or alternatively, in ways that strengthen them. As a result, we believe that trauma work is inherently spiritual and must include a focus on the client's belief system. Although much of the research and practice content of this volume is based on theistic belief systems, other nontheistic systems of belief or concepts of the sacred can also be considered part of a client's spirituality. The three of us, and many psychotherapists with whom we have worked, experience the feeling of working against evil on some level when working with our traumatized clients. We have the sense that something good and redemptive is happening when we help victims of battering, rape, torture, or other forms of traumatization to face what was inflicted on them. In addition to processing traumatic memories, over time, we work to help survivors of such experiences find their courage, regain hope, and become whole again. This is a spiritual process.

Engaging with spiritual issues in trauma psychotherapy is not, however, an easy process. Consider the experience and writings of Elie Wiesel, a Holocaust survivor and Nobel Prize winner. Wiesel is a Jewish man who was sent to Auschwitz, lost most of his family to the Nazis, and survived the Holocaust. In his autobiographical book *Night* (1972), he provided an account of his nightmarish experience of being separated from family members who were killed and then being forced to work in a camp at Auschwitz. Throughout his account of the Holocaust, he discussed the nature of his spiritual struggle on multiple levels, first in talking about the event and then in coming to grips with the spiritual meaning of the suffering. Early in his internment, he described the efforts of other prisoners to cling to their faith:

> Some of the men spoke of God: His mysterious ways, the sins of the Jewish people, and the redemption to come. As for me, I had ceased to pray. I concurred with Job! I was not denying His existence, but I doubted His absolute justice. (p. 45)

Later, on the eve of Rosh Hashanah, Wiesel (1972) expressed his reaction to a service taking place at the camp:

> Blessed be God's name. . . . Thousands of lips repeated the benediction, bent over like trees in a storm. Blessed be God's name? Why would I bless Him? Every fiber in me rebelled. Because He caused thousands of children to burn in His mass graves? Because He kept six crematoria working day and night, including Sabbath and the Holy Days? Because in His great might, He had created Auschwitz, Birkenau, Buna, and so many other factories of death? How could I say to Him: Blessed be thou, Almighty, Master of the Universe, who chose among all nations to be tortured day and night, to watch as our fathers, our mothers, our brothers end up in the furnaces? Praised be Thy Holy Name, for having chosen us

to be slaughtered on Thine altar? I listened as the inmates' voice rose: it was powerful yet broken, amid the weeping, the sobbing, the sighing of the entire "congregation": All the earth and universe are God's! (p. 67)

Wiesel's (1972) experience was unique as a Holocaust survivor. Unfortunately, the kinds of spiritual issues and doubts that he described are not uncommon for survivors of traumatic events who are religiously committed people. As the chapters in this book discuss in detail, survivors of child abuse and other traumatic events often experience spiritual struggles in the course of healing. Many trauma survivors try to come closer to God on the one hand while simultaneously questioning how God could allow the event to happen on the other hand. Other survivors struggle with specific and more personalized issues of spirituality, religion, or their relationship to God. In listening to clients and helping them process trauma, psychotherapists too may experience spiritual struggles, such as questions on the existence of evil or why so many people suffer.

SPIRITUALITY AND RELIGION IN PSYCHOLOGY AND AS EXPERIENCED BY PSYCHOLOGISTS

Psychologists have typically considered spirituality and religion (and religious practice and religiousness) to be separate but related concepts that are not necessarily within the domain of either psychology or psychotherapy. Over the past 20 years or so, however, psychotherapists have increasingly recognized the relevance of these issues as essential dimensions of human experience and therefore as pertaining to psychology and psychotherapy.

Surveys have suggested that psychologists experience spirituality and religion in several ways that differ from the experience of the American public whom they serve (Delaney, Miller, & Bisono, 2007; Walker, Gorsuch, & Tan, 2004). In a meta-analysis involving 26 studies and over 5,000 therapists, Walker et al. (2004) found that most psychotherapists considered spirituality important to their personal lives but rarely engaged in spiritual practices or corporate religious worship. Shafranske (2001) found that 58% of the general public in a national sample reported that religion was very important versus 26% of counseling and clinical psychologists. Over 90% of the U.S. general population reported belief in a personal god, whereas only 24% of the psychologist sample endorsed this belief. These disparities in beliefs between psychologists and clients, as well as the view of some psychologists that spirituality is often more of a problem than a resource in the lives of many clients, have resulted in an absence of focus on the spiritual in psychotherapy. An additional factor has been a lack of emphasis on spirituality and religion in clinical training programs across the United States, the result being that psychologists (as well as psychotherapists from other disciplines) may not know how to approach issues of spirituality and religion over the course of psychotherapy. Despite these factors, to provide a more holistic and integrated experience for the client, psychologists often need to address spiritual issues in the treatment process.

Within the American Psychological Association (APA), Division 36 (Society for the Psychology of Religion and Spirituality) has been active in encouraging research, theory, and practice in the psychology of religion and related areas. Two division journals—*Psychology of Religion and Spirituality* and *Spirituality in Clinical Practice*—and a number of books, including this one, have been published on the topic of spiritually oriented interventions in psychotherapy for adults and for children and adolescents, including the two-volume handbook of psychology, religion, and spirituality published early in 2013 (Pargament, 2013).

In parallel, until the past decade or so, the curricula of professional psychologists (and other mental health and medical professionals) have not included attention to traumatic life experiences, including their psychological impact initially, later, and across the life span; their relationship to the development of psychological symptoms; or approaches to treatment. As a result, many psychologists do not understand the role of trauma in their clients' lives, nor do they know how to approach or treat these issues when they are disclosed (Courtois & Gold, 2009). They may actively avoid following up on trauma revelations for fear of hurting their clients or simply because of their own discomfort or avoidance. As a result, issues that are almost always relevant to the presenting concerns and symptoms of the traumatized client are left unaddressed. For many, experiences of trauma have been treated as unspeakable and subjected to active silencing by perpetrators and others for whom silence provides protection. A psychotherapist's avoidance or nonrecognition leaves a traumatized client further silenced or isolated or both and fails to assist in making the connection between symptoms and the trauma. As can be seen, this becomes an issue involving ethics. On the other end of the spectrum, an exclusive emphasis on trauma to the exclusion of other life issues also raises ethical concerns.

As with issues of spirituality, this professional lacuna regarding human traumatization is now changing as the field of traumatic stress has expanded dramatically over the course of the past several decades. APA Division 56 (Trauma Psychology) was founded within the past 10 years and has actively encouraged attention to the impact of psychological trauma on clients' lives. A division journal, *Psychological Trauma: Theory, Research, Practice, and Policy*, is now in its fifth year of publication, and a number of books and monographs on a variety of trauma-related topics have been published by division members. This volume is the first published by APA to directly address the spiritual issues involved in traumatization and spiritually oriented interventions in trauma recovery.

PURPOSE AND MAJOR THEMES

This book is intended for psychotherapists working with traumatized clients in a range of settings. We focus on recent developments that have fostered greater sensitivity to spirituality in the ways psychotherapists understand and treat trauma. For many years, clinicians neglected the links between religion, spirituality, and trauma or, worse, viewed religion and spirituality stereotypically as forces that interfered with health and well-being. This book helps to provide an important corrective to that bias.

This volume has several themes. First, the chapters integrate research and practice. Throughout, we highlight emerging empirical literature that underscores how trauma can affect people not only psychologically, socially, and physically but spiritually as well. In doing so, chapter authors provide case examples and clinical illustrations that bring the empirical findings into sharper, more human focus. Second, the book is balanced, pointing to both the potentially helpful and harmful ways in which religion and spirituality can affect adjustment to trauma. Finally, we attempt to avoid the kind of spiritual reductionism that has plagued work in the field (i.e., spirituality is merely a source of anxiety reduction, social connectedness, control, meaning).

A number of the chapters focus on the impact of trauma on spirituality as an important issue in itself and as a target for change. In doing so, we acknowledge that there are both healthy and unhealthy aspects to spirituality. In differentiating between these two aspects, Zinnbauer (2013) cited Pargament (2007):

> At its best, spirituality is defined by pathways that are broad and deep, responsive to life's situations, nurtured by the larger social context, capable of flexibility and continuity, and oriented toward a sacred destination that is large enough to encompass the full range of human potential and luminous enough to provide the individual with a powerful guiding vision. At its worst, spirituality is dis-integrated, defined by pathways that lack scope and depth, fail to meet the challenges and demands of life events, clash and collide with the surrounding social system, change and shift too easily or not at all, and misdirect the individual in the pursuit of spiritual value. (p. 136)

Our hope is to help clinicians differentiate between healthy and unhealthy forms of spirituality across different populations of traumatized clients. Toward that end, the chapters cut across a broad cross section of presenting problems, with specific focus on relational forms of trauma, such as sexual abuse, partner violence, and other familial forms of trauma. Although the chapter authors have unique theoretical backgrounds, there is some emphasis on psychodynamic treatment for adults as well as cognitive behavior therapy for children throughout the book. In compiling the chapters, we sought case studies reflecting a range of racial and ethnic backgrounds, as well as varying spiritual and religious traditions. Though we were largely successful in this regard, there is some emphasis on Christian religious traditions, broadly speaking, because many of the authors and much of the research in this area are from this tradition. Our hope is that this book will help move spirituality from a peripheral interest at best among mainstream trauma researchers and practitioners to a construct and process of central value.

KEY TERMS AND CONCEPTS

Starting with William James and his contemporaries over a century ago, psychologists have considered spirituality and religion as highly relevant to the discipline of psychology. James (1902) considered religion the "feelings, acts, and experiences of individual men in their solitude, so far as they apprehend themselves to stand in relation to whatever they may consider the divine" (pp. 31–32).

In the last century, psychologists often separated religion from spirituality conceptually. *Spirituality* is considered as the personal, affective, and experiential involving a quest or search for the sacred or divine (Pargament, 1999; Richards & Bergin, 2005). In contrast, *religion*, or *religiousness*, is broadly defined as more corporate or organization-oriented and as a cognitive set of beliefs and practices usually associated with an organized faith tradition (Richards & Bergin, 2005). The theoretical and practical utility of distinguishing spirituality and religion has been supported by some yet questioned by others (e.g., Hill & Pargament, 2003; Worthington & Sandage, 2001), with Hill and Pargament (2003) directly asserting that theoretical distinctions between both constructs are artificial. They also reported that the majority of the American public does not differentiate between the two concepts and that most practice their personal spirituality in the context of a faith tradition or organized religion.

Two aspects of personal spirituality and religiousness seem particularly pertinent in addressing faith in the context of trauma psychotherapy. The first issue concerns the nature of spiritual struggle, a phenomenon of increasing interest to psychologists in the past several years. Exline (2013) defined *religious or spiritual struggle* as a form of distress in the religious or spiritual realm. Pargament (2007) suggested that spiritual struggles may take several forms, including divine, intrapersonal, and interpersonal. Divine struggles, as the name implies, involve struggles specifically in one's relationship with God or a higher power. In the context of trauma psychotherapy, clients who are survivors of abuse may question why God allowed the abuse to occur or express chronic anger toward God about their abuse. Intrapersonal spiritual struggles involve struggles internal to one's person. For example, some adolescent female survivors of rape struggle with perceptions of their own sexuality and purity afterward. Finally, interpersonal struggles are related to struggles with other people. For instance, in trauma treatment, some survivors of intimate partner violence struggle over whether to forgive their abuser and remain in abusive relationships or to leave for their own safety.

A related area of spirituality and religion that is relevant to trauma treatment involves God images and God concepts. According to Davis, Moriarty, and Mauch (2013), *God images* refer to internal working models of attachment to specific divine figures (e.g., God, Jesus, Allah, Buddha) and the self in relationship to that divine figure. Davis et al. further suggested that God images involve implicit relational knowing at a "gut level" of one's relationship with their divine attachment figure. God images are dealt with extensively in several chapters of this book, particularly Chapter 8, which describes working with God images among survivors of clergy sexual abuse. In general, previous research has found that survivors of abuse experience God as more distant, punitive, angry, and wrathful than do people who have not been abused (see Chapter 7, this volume, for further review).

Conversely, *God concepts* refer to people's theological set of beliefs about a divine attachment figure, including the nature of that figure, how that figure relates to humanity, and how human beings should relate to the divine attachment figure (Davis et al., 2013). God concepts usually develop from what people of various faith traditions are taught in their churches, synagogues, or mosques. Many people who have experienced traumatic events struggle to reconcile their God concepts, grounded in religious teachings, with their lived experience of God that forms their God images. In the context of trauma psychotherapy, therapists may sometimes use God concepts grounded in sacred writings to counter negative God images that clients have developed as a result of past abuse. We explore these and related issues throughout the book.

A final concept pertinent to our introduction concerns the use of the term *survivor* as opposed to *victim*. As Campbell (2001) noted, some advocates and researchers have suggested important distinctions between the two terms in trauma research: Some have called for the use of *survivor* as a term to emphasize the individual's personal strength necessary to recover from rape. Others have differentiated the two terms on the basis of the time involved since the rape occurred—those researchers suggested using the term *victim* to refer to individuals who have recently been assaulted, and the term *survivor* to refer to people further along in the process of recovery. We prefer the term *survivor* to emphasize the strength and resiliency of women and men who have survived traumatic events and continue to actively engage in the process of recovery. Thus, we use the term *survivor* throughout the book.

STRUCTURE OF THE BOOK

The first four chapters of this book provide a foundation and context for more specific inclusion of spirituality in trauma psychotherapy. In Chapter 1, we summarize the basics of working with spiritual issues in trauma psychotherapy. In Chapter 2, Van Deusen and Courtois consider in more detail the complex relationship among spirituality, religion, and complex developmental trauma. In recent years, the field of trauma psychology has given increased attention to the damaging effects of complex trauma that occur at different developmental stages. Some authors (e.g., Ford & Courtois, 2009) have also described the effects of multiple, repetitive traumas on one's spiritual life as creating spiritual alienation from self, others, and God images. This chapter discusses the effects of complex trauma at different stages of development on one's spirituality, morality, and religious faith. In addition, the authors describe treatment strategies designed to restore the client's sense of religious and spiritual identity at different developmental stages.

Trauma cases often involve legal and/or ethical issues, such as when child abuse is suspected or reported. Quite separately, psychotherapy involving religion and spirituality also brings ethical issues to the forefront, for example, when clients receive spiritual direction as part of therapy and a third party payer is involved. In Chapter 3, Courtois discusses legal and ethical issues at the intersection of trauma psychotherapy involving religion and spirituality.

Richards and Bergin (2005) described a two-tiered approach to assessing the potential role of religion and spirituality in psychotherapy. In Chapter 4, Richards, Hardman, Lea, and Berrett discuss this two-level approach along with the religious and spiritual domains that may be relevant to psychotherapy with trauma survivors.

The rest of the chapters of this book consider the process of addressing spiritual issues in trauma psychotherapy. In Chapter 5, Verbeck and her colleagues consider ways in which the spirituality of the client and psychotherapist affects the working alliance with trauma survivors. Discussing traumatic experiences is difficult for both client and psychotherapist. This chapter considers the process of managing countertransference related to religion, spirituality, and trauma. It illustrates critical events in psychotherapy, as well as therapeutic responses that serve to foster or repair the therapeutic alliance.

A substantial body of research has demonstrated that people use meaning-making systems (including spirituality) to make sense of traumatic events. In Chapter 6, Slattery and Park consider survivors' attempts to draw meaning from traumatic events and the role spirituality plays in this process.

In Chapter 7, Walker, McGregor, Quagliana, Stephens, and Knodel discuss ways for psychotherapists to understand and respond to changes in clients' personal spirituality and religion after trauma. People respond to traumatic events in a variety of ways. Some turn to God or a higher power for support, whereas others completely turn away from any religious or spiritual faith. Still others maintain a personal faith somewhere in between, uncertain of what to make of the experience. In this chapter, Walker and coauthors discuss such changes and describe various domains of religious and spiritual experience (i.e., spiritual struggles involving questioning one's faith, distorted religious beliefs resulting from religion-related abuse).

Many survivors of sexual abuse experience profound damage to their image of God. Some come to view God as more punitive, demanding, abandoning, and angry than do men and women who have not been abused. Other victims of abuse report believing that God could not love them because He allowed the abuse to occur. In Chapter 8, Frawley-O'Dea considers ways psychotherapists can help clients repair God images after they have experienced abuse.

In Chapter 9, Aten and his colleagues examine ways for psychotherapists to work with religious and spiritual clients and communities after natural disasters. This chapter outlines how to work with the unique spiritual and psychological challenges that often emerge after mass traumas such as Hurricane Katrina in 2005 and the Haiti Earthquake in 2010. The chapter also addresses mass trauma with human origins such as terrorist attacks and technical disasters. Readers will learn approaches for addressing religious and spiritual issues across disaster phases and diverse disaster scenarios.

In Chapter 10, Levitt, Horne, Wheeler, and Wang describe the religious and spiritual dynamics involved in intimate partner violence against women. Although religion is often a source of healing and comfort, it may also provide a context supporting the abuse of women in intimate relationships, particularly in fundamentalist religious communities. For example, some religious communities explicitly teach that husbands are the leaders in their families and wives are to submit to their authority. Indeed, in both Western and Middle Eastern religions, religious tradition is sometimes used to support the abuse of women, even to the point of maiming and death. Religious pressure on the part of one's family of origin, one's religious community, or one's clergy member may also play a role in keeping these spiritually oriented women in abusive relationships.

In Chapter 11, Foy and Drescher describe means of addressing spiritual issues involving faith and honor in trauma treatment for military personnel and their families. War is a profound experience that can challenge or strengthen one's faith before, during, and after deployment. For example, when facing personal injury or the death of friends around them, combat troops may experience spiritual struggles involving the trauma or turn to God or a higher power for support. Spirituality may also be an important resource for remembering fallen friends or family members among military families.

In Chapter 12, Grand considers the problem of evil and suffering in trauma psychotherapy and presents options for responding to clients who are grappling with this dilemma. Any survivor of a traumatic experience that was perpetrated by another human being (e.g., incest, rape, assault, harassment, genocide) has to decide how to respond to the trauma. Some religiously and spiritually committed men and women may attempt to do so by considering forgiveness in psychotherapy. Others may attempt to avenge or work against what happened to them in an attempt to make the world a better place for other people affected by similar forms of trauma.

In the afterword, the coeditors reflect on the themes considered throughout the book. We discuss the future of spiritually oriented trauma psychotherapy, including clinical practice, training, and research. We call for a greater integration of spirituality in trauma treatment to provide a more inclusive treatment for the victimized.

CONCLUSION

We began this book with a quote from Job in the Hebrew Bible. In addition to reflecting the lived spiritual experience of many trauma survivors, this quote also reflects our own spiritual faith as well as our professional therapeutic commitment to working to preserve the spiritual and religious faith of men, women, and children after traumatic events. The work that we do is challenging but is also immensely rewarding. We continue to be amazed by the spiritual resources and beliefs exhibited by our clients—often those who are most wounded. Somehow through "the grace of God" they have developed or retained a capacity for empathy toward others that they never experienced in their interactions with their abusers. We consider it a privilege to engage in this journey with you, the reader, throughout the pages of this book. We hope that the chapters will not only enrich your clinical practice but also encourage you to persevere in your work.

REFERENCES

Campbell, R. (2001). *Mental health services for rape survivors: Current issues in therapeutic practice*. Retrieved from Minnesota Center Against Violence Against Women Electronic Clearinghouse website: http://www.mincava.umn.edu/documents/commissioned/campbell/campbell.html

Courtois, C. A., & Gold, S. N. (2009). The need for inclusion of psychological trauma in the professional curriculum. *Psychological Trauma: Theory, Research, Practice, and Policy, 1*, 3–23. doi:10.1037/a0015224

Dalenberg, C. (2000). *Countertransference and the treatment of trauma*. Washington, DC: American Psychological Association. doi:10.1037/10380-000

Davis, E. B., Moriarty, G. L., & Mauch, J. C. (2013). God images and god concepts: Definitions, developments, and dynamics. *Psychology of Religion and Spirituality, 5*, 51–60. doi:10.1037/a0029289

Delaney, H. D., Miller, W. R., & Bisono, A. M. (2007). Religiosity and spirituality among psychologists: A survey of clinician members of the American Psychological Association. *Professional Psychology: Research and Practice, 38*, 538–546. doi:10.1037/0735-7028.38.5.538

Exline, J. J. (2013). Religious and spiritual struggles. In K. I. Pargament, J. J. Exline, & J. W. Jones (Eds.), *APA handbook of psychology, religion, and spirituality: Vol. 1. Context, theory, and research* (pp. 459–475). Washington, DC: American Psychological Association.

Ford, J. D., & Courtois, C. A. (2009). Defining and understanding complex trauma and complex traumatic stress disorders. In C. A. Courtois & J. D. Ford (Eds.), *Treating complex traumatic stress disorders: An evidence-based guide* (pp. 13–30). New York, NY: Guilford Press.

Hill, P. C., & Pargament, K. I. (2003). Advances in the conceptualization of and measurement of religion and spirituality: Implications for physical and mental health research. *American Psychologist, 58*, 64–74. doi:10.1037/0003-066X.58.1.64

James, W. (1902). *The varieties of religious experience*. New York, NY: Random House. doi:10.1037/10004-000

Pargament, K. I. (1999). The psychology of religion and spirituality? Yes and no. *International Journal for the Psychology of Religion, 9*, 3–16. doi:10.1207/s15327582ijpr0901_2

Pargament, K. I. (2007). *Spiritually integrated psychotherapy: Understanding and addressing the sacred*. New York, NY: Guilford Press.

Pargament, K. I. (2013). (Ed.). *APA handbook of psychology, religion, and spirituality*. Washington, DC: American Psychological Association.

Richards, P. S., & Bergin, A. E. (2005). *A spiritual strategy for counseling and psychotherapy* (2nd ed.). Washington, DC: American Psychological Association. doi:10.1037/11214-000

Walker, D. F., Gorsuch, R. L., & Tan, S. Y. (2004). Therapists' integration of religion and spirituality in counseling: A meta-analysis. *Counseling and Values, 49*, 69–80. doi:10.1002/j.2161-007X.2004.tb00254.x

Wiesel, E. (1972). *Night*. New York, NY: Hill & Wang.

Worthington, E. L. Jr., & Sandage, S. J. (2001). Religion and spirituality. *Psychotherapy: Theory, Research, Practice, Training, 38*, 473–478. doi:10.1037/0033-3204.38.4.473

Zinnbauer, B. (2013). Models of healthy and unhealthy religion and spirituality. In K. I. Pargament, A. Mahoney, & E. P. Shafranske (Eds.), *APA handbook of psychology, religion, and spirituality: Vol. 2. An applied psychology of religion and spirituality* (pp. 71–89). Washington, DC: American Psychological Association.

1

BASICS OF WORKING ON SPIRITUAL MATTERS WITH TRAUMATIZED INDIVIDUALS

DONALD F. WALKER, CHRISTINE A. COURTOIS, AND JAMIE D. ATEN

Darkness cannot drive out darkness, only light can do that.
—Martin Luther King Jr.

In this chapter, we begin by highlighting (a) spirituality as a diversity variable that should be addressed in case conceptualization and treatment (Brown, 2008) and (b) the particular damage to relational spirituality as a consequence of complex interpersonal trauma (Courtois & Ford, 2009). We then provide an overview of models for addressing spiritual issues in psychotherapy. We conclude this chapter by presenting an overview of spiritually oriented trauma-focused cognitive behavior therapy (SO–TF–CBT; Walker, Reese, Hughes, & Troskie, 2010), an example of a secular trauma treatment that has been adapted to include spiritual content.

UNDERSTANDING SPIRITUALITY AS A DIVERSITY VARIABLE

It is only in the relatively recent past that psychologists and other mental health professionals have been mandated to consider, assess, and value various aspects of the client's context and issues of diversity (i.e., age, gender,

http://dx.doi.org/10.1037/14500-002
Spiritually Oriented Psychotherapy for Trauma, D. F. Walker, C. A. Courtois, and J. D. Aten (Editors)
Copyright © 2015 by the American Psychological Association. All rights reserved.

sexual orientation and identity, race and ethnic group, culture, political group, capacity and incapacity). This must include attention to the client's spirituality, belief system, and faith tradition, as emphasized in the *Ethical Principles of Psychologists and Code of Conduct* of the American Psychological Association (2010) and the *Resolution on Religious, Religion-Based and/or Religion-Derived Prejudice* (American Psychological Association, 2007). Brown (2008), Bryant-Davis (2008), and other writers have called for the inclusion of spirituality, religiosity, and faith traditions as diversity and multicultural issues within the psychotherapist's purview. This is especially salient given the results of a number of research studies suggesting that psychologists as a group are less spiritually oriented and less involved in formal religion or religious activities than their clients and that little or no attention has been given in their professional training with regard to their clients' religious traditions, beliefs, and spiritual lives. This is now changing because some programs are explicitly organized around these issues and offer specialized degrees or areas of emphasis, and others address religious or spiritual issues as part of the emphasis on diversity and multiculturalism.

As a consequence of the lack of attention, some traditionally trained psychologists have assumed that spirituality is not within the domain of psychotherapy. In the best case, this stance was due to a lack of focus, ignorance, or indifference; in the worst, it was due to biases toward conventional religion or active hostility toward addressing such issues as part of psychotherapy (Hathaway, 2011), making it an ethics issue. This lack of attention to the spiritual has changed considerably in recent years as more psychotherapists have become attuned to spirituality and spiritually based practices including but not limited to the practices of the major religious faith traditions and to yoga, meditation, mindfulness, and acceptance of self and others. Yet, a psychologist recently published a book, *Adieu to God: Why Psychology Leads to Atheism* (Power, 2012), in which he acknowledged the many psychological benefits of religion while questioning the validity of its supernatural belief systems. He suggested atheist alternatives to a fulfilling life and reminded us that atheism is, in fact, a spiritual belief system for some (Power, 2012). In a related vein, Hathaway (2011) offered the perspective that an overly pro-religious stance and proselytizing on the part of a psychotherapist can also be an ethical violation.

In her 2008 book on cultural competence in trauma therapy, Laura Brown recognized the diversity factors (including age, gender, culture/phenotype, religious beliefs and faith tradition, ethnicity, disabilities, social class, and systems of meaning, among others) that affect both the experience of and response to trauma. She proposed using spirituality and religion as a diversity variable in conceptualizing and treating trauma victims and survivors, and she emphasized the complexity of the relationship between faith, spirituality, and trauma. As a foundation, Brown suggested that clinicians attend to issues of meaning and existential questions that arise because of traumatization, specifically "in the risk for trauma exposure; the ways in which trauma assaults those systems; and . . . in the healing process" (p. 229). Trauma of all kinds—but especially of the types that shatter or obstruct the concept of a merciful, just, and loving God and that call into question the goodness and trustworthiness of other humans—have special capacities to interfere with systems of meaning. Brown approached the issue from many different perspectives, several of which we have selected for inclusion here.

Belief in the Divine (or Not)

There are innumerable ways that humans understand the sacred or divine. Some religions identify and worship more than one god figure, whereas others focus on only one. Religious beliefs and practices range from those that are highly organized, ritualized, widely observed, and embedded within cultures and cultural traditions to those that are more personal, much less organized, and practiced alone or in small groups. Another alternative involves individuals who are atheist but claim a belief system that shapes their lives. As an aspect of diversity, some psychotherapists share the same faith tradition of their clients and yet, given the many ways that the same tradition can be organized and practiced in different branches and denominations, they may have little more in common with their clients' beliefs than the name of the religion. In working with their clients, therapists may discover that they hold highly similar or dissimilar beliefs, or that they are somewhere in between. They might find themselves aligned with the stance of a client's religion or offended or put off by it. In any event,

> Whatever the psychotherapist's own meaning-making systems might be, culturally competent work with trauma survivors requires respect for those used by clients in their healing processes. When clients have not yet explored a meaning-making system or are struggling with finding helpful those systems and traditions that they perceive to be available, psychotherapists should invite clients to appreciate that some system of meaning may be helpful in their recovery but never be prescriptive as to which system that might be. Psychotherapists also need to be careful not to assume that simply because persons identify as adherents of a particular meaning-making system that they will find assistance for their trauma recovery process in that system. One of the most painful disruptions that trauma can and does engender is a disruption with spiritual and religious belief systems that served a person well until then. (Brown, 2008, p. 232)

In addition, despite little or no attention having been paid to comparative religions or to spiritual and religious issues in the majority of mental health training programs, at a minimum, cultural competence in spirituality and religion involves a basic awareness of the religious beliefs and doctrine of various major religious groups, namely, Christianity, Judaism, Islam, Hinduism, Buddhism, as well as the range and diversity that exists within each of them. Furthermore, when a client holds a spiritual or religious belief that is less mainstream and more idiosyncratic or is associated with a particular cultural tradition, following Brown's (2008) counsel, it behooves the therapist to get to know something about the belief system and the culture within which it operates.

This point was illustrated in a recently published case description of a Malaysian adolescent who was abused by a religious leader who had also taken on the role of traditional healer (Chan, Tan, Ang, Kamal Nor, & Sharip, 2012). The authors discussed assessment, case conceptualization, and treatment issues in the context of the client's cultural and belief systems. In this case, in the Malaysian Islamic faith tradition, the victim resisted reporting because of the identity of her perpetrator and his role and status in the community, her deference to him, and her fear of being disbelieved. Her family was highly shamed by her disclosure and sought to minimize the severity of the event and its impact and to blame her for its occurrence. The family sought out another traditional healer rather than mental health treatment for their daughter, with deleterious consequences for her.

Spirituality and Religion as a Source of Anxiety or Comfort

Brown (2008), like many of the writers and the authors of the chapters in this volume, recognized that spirituality and religion may be either a source of anxiety and distress or of comfort and solace for believers, in life in general and during times of trauma and crisis. Although we concur with this opinion, we also draw attention to our own research findings that have demonstrated that spirituality and religion may be a simultaneous source of comfort and stress following traumatic events (Walker, Reid, O'Neill, & Brown, 2009). Religious beliefs and practices may be comforting by providing sustenance, explanation, and organization following the upheaval of the trauma. Frankl's (1968) discussion of the role of making meaning in coping with traumatic events is an example of comfort. He found meaning in acts of kindness among inmates in Auschwitz while he was incarcerated there—being able to witness resistance to his Nazi captors' attempts to dehumanize the inmates created meaning and purpose for him, supporting his will to survive. However, an individual's foundational beliefs may have been shattered by the trauma, especially if these or other religious tenets were used to justify or excuse interpersonal violence (especially spouse abuse and other forms of domestic or community violence) causing betrayal and mistrust. More fundamentalist religions that are highly rigid and controlling and that promote religious dogma as something that must be accepted without question may, on the one hand, be comforting in terms of clarity and boundaries, and on the other, may be toxic and damaging when an adherent is terrified into submission or when dogma is used to excuse, rationalize, or support abuse or violence.

Religious Wounding and Persecution

When wounding and persecution occur, the religion itself may be a source of trauma. Brown (2008) noted that religion can damage and even destroy the individual adherent and entire congregations and communities rather than provide them with a source of security or a resource in adversity. To wit: Religious faith and zealotry have been the cause of some of the most egregious behaviors and events in human history, providing the rationale for far-reaching persecution, warfare, terrorism, torture, and colonization in the name of God and a particular set of religious beliefs. Examples of past history-changing events include the Inquisition of the Middle Ages and religious warfare and eradication of infidels over the course of decades and centuries. Contemporary examples include the attacks of 9/11 by Muslim jihadists and the resultant warfare in the Middle East, and the sexual abuse of children by clergy and other members of religious institutions. When abuse or trauma occurs in the name of God or is carried out by religious leaders, religious beliefs and impact are crucial factors to consider in case conceptualization and treatment.

Brown (2008) recommended some helpful stances for psychotherapists faced with clients struggling with spiritual and religious issues stemming from trauma, whether the trauma originated in religious belief or practice or not. She suggested that when these clients ask questions such as "What was God thinking?" or "Why did God let this happen?" culturally competent trauma psychotherapists refrain from answering, instead empowering trauma survivors to self-explore to find their own answers. Often, this involves clients struggling with their own spiritual beliefs in the context of and apart from their religious tradition and determining what makes sense or is meaningful to them. This is a highly individualistic process for which there is no right or wrong answer. It is recommended that therapists address questions such as these within and as part of the treatment. Responding in this way to spiritual questions involves hearing them as not about God per se or God alone but as a faith-informed version of the existential question "Why me?"

In a related vein, Brown (2008) suggested that therapists not automatically refer clients who are struggling with their spiritual beliefs and understanding to clergy. To begin with, clients who are part of a large congregation or who do not attend any institution may not have a relationship with clergy members. Clients may distrust clergy (especially if a client has been abused by a clergy member or another religious figure). Also, clergy members often have little or no training in or understanding of trauma. Yet, there are times when the involvement of clergy or a referral to a clergy member is quite appropriate, as is the case when particular points of doctrine or belief are involved or when a clergy member has the capacity to offer spiritual counsel or solace or a spiritual ritual or practice that can alleviate the abused client's distress. Such was the case in Croatia when Muslim women who had been raped as spoils of war and who believed (as part of the cultural or religious and community belief) they were permanently defiled and unable to marry were "made whole" in a religiously based healing ritual. Another example from our clinical experience involves a client who was unable to forgive herself for extensive self-harm, including several suicide attempts, as an adolescent and young adult and who benefited from confessing to a clergy member who forgave her for her sins and in the process relieved her of her shame and self-blame.

Differential Diagnosis

A number of authors writing about spiritually oriented psychotherapy have noted that cultural competence involving spirituality includes the ability of therapists to recognize the difference between adherence to religious doctrine and symptoms of a diagnosable condition (Griffith, 2010). Some similarity between the two may be evident, and it is the psychotherapist's job to determine whether a particular behavior is the result of a religious belief or whether it is a symptom of an emotional or psychiatric condition in need of treatment. Obsessive–compulsive disorder, mania or hypomania or other mood disorder, major anxiety, and psychotic delusions are among the conditions that might be misinterpreted as religious practice. These call for detailed assessment to determine differential diagnosis and treatment tailored to the diagnosis. Spiritual and religious issues may or may not be part of the treatment.

DAMAGED SPIRITUALITY AS A SEQUELA OF COMPLEX TRAUMA

Related to spiritual meaning-making and religious beliefs, schemas about self and others are highly vulnerable to disturbance as a consequence of trauma, especially trauma that is interpersonal in causation and implementation and that occurs repeatedly over the course of significant developmental epochs (as opposed to other more impersonal types that are usually one-time occurrences or of short duration; Courtois & Ford, 2009; McCann & Pearlman, 1990; van der Kolk, Roth, Pelcovitz, Sunday, & Spinazzola, 2005). Recognition of the deleterious effects of trauma increased significantly when the diagnosis of posttraumatic stress disorder (PTSD) was first included in the *Diagnostic and Statistical Manual of Mental Disorders* in 1980 (3rd ed., American Psychiatric Association). At that time, the three signature criteria of the newly codified diagnosis (re-experiencing alternating with numbing of memories of the trauma, and physiological hyperarousal) were largely, if not exclusively, based on the study of the effects of war trauma on adolescent and adult males, whose personalities were developed and bodies mature. It soon became apparent to those studying and treating child abuse in particular (and other forms of domestic and community violence as well) that the fit was not an exact one for these other traumas because many involved children whose personalities and bodies were under development during the time of the trauma (see Chapter 2, this volume, for a more extensive review).

In 1992, Judith Herman proposed the diagnosis of complex PTSD (CPTSD) to account for the differences that had been identified and suggested seven additional criteria sets derived from the study of child abuse and neglect and other forms of domestic violence and entrapment trauma. These included alterations in (a) emotional regulation, (b) identity and self-worth, (c) dissociation, (d) relationships with others, (e) relationship with the perpetrator, (f) somatic and medical conditions, and (g) systems of meaning. Recently, these have been distilled to five primary domains: (a) emotion dysregulation, (b) loss of self-integrity, (c) loss of self-integration (dissociation), (d) compromised relationships with others, and (e) somatic reactions and medical conditions (see Courtois & Ford, 2009, for a review). CPTSD is related to such factors as the age of onset of first trauma; its repetition and chronicity; its occurrence within the family, the social group, or larger community; and the degree of relationship (and betrayal) between perpetrator and victim, such that those with early life trauma that meet these additional dimensions are more likely to have CPTSD rather than PTSD alone. This suggests that individuals who experienced early life child abuse and other forms of interpersonal trauma are at particular risk of this symptom profile.

Attachment and child development researchers investigating trauma in children have routinely identified psychophysiological and behavioral differences between samples of abused or traumatized and nonabused children. In attachment parlance (and in highly simplified form), *secure attachment* between parent or caregiver and child results in a stable and positive identity and self-esteem and the ability to trust others, whereas *insecurity* (demonstrated by overanxiety on one hand or nonresponse regarding the child's needs on the other) typically results in less stable identity and positive self-esteem and anxiety or detachment in interaction with others. A third and by far the most debilitating style of insecure attachment is termed *disorganized*, consisting of grossly opposite forms of behavior (ranging from attentive and responsive to neglectful and highly abusive, involving one or more forms of physical, sexual, emotional, or verbal abuse and neglect or nonprotection) on the part of the parent or caregiver with little or no consistency in the behavior. Disorganized children and adults tend to be highly dysregulated emotionally, behaviorally, and interpersonally; they tend to be dissociative and to experience dissociative disorders and major degrees of distress in many life domains.

Although complex trauma has been most associated with childhood onset, other forms have been identified in recent years. Complex trauma can occur over the course of adulthood, sometimes layered on past childhood abuse and trauma (as seen in victims of domestic and spousal violence who were previously victimized as children). Kira (2010) has been particularly instrumental in documenting additional types of complex trauma: (a) identity, the largely immutable characteristics of the individual victim's identity (e.g., gender, skin color, ethnicity and related phenotypes, sexual orientation) that make him or her susceptible in some way to being discriminated against or otherwise victimized; (b) community, membership in a group (e.g., family, ethnic or cultural, religious, political) whose status or power vis-à-vis other groups also causes susceptibility to discrimination, victimization, and even annihilation; and (c) continuous, cumulative, or lifelong. Trauma can be intergenerational and can span decades and even centuries in cases of conflict between warring groups (usually on the basis of domination of one group by the other, often because of different systems of belief, including religious and spiritual beliefs). Historical trauma, colonialism, and genocide are now viewed as forms of complex trauma. All types of complex trauma within families and across cultures can have intergenerational impact on the individual, the family, the community, and the society at large.

On average, trauma that is interpersonal and deliberate in causation has a negative impact beyond trauma that is impersonal or accidental, especially with regard to schema about self and others and as related to spirituality and religious beliefs. Because most abuse and victimization is perpetrated by those related to or known to the victim, relational betrayal is often a salient characteristic. Freyd (1996) pioneered the study of betrayal trauma and found that the degree of betrayal has been a long-hidden dimension related to the severity of reaction and to personal and interpersonal impact. It causes a more complicated circumstance for the victim who was hurt and exploited not by a stranger but a relative or acquaintance who used the relationship for access and exploitation rather than for protection and nurturance. Betrayal is often a prominent dimension of the spiritual angst experienced by victims regarding their own spirit and worthiness and the trustworthiness and beneficence of others (including their God figure or higher power). Van Deusen (n.d.) and other researchers have studied how the effects of childhood trauma affect the individual's views and attachment to God, how that God is represented, the influence of the attachment on subjective well-being, and how the type and severity of childhood trauma influence attachment to God and subjective well-being (see Chapter 3, this volume, for a review). Early research documented that child abuse survivors experience more anger and distrust of God than nonsurvivors (Elliott, 1994), in a further permutation of the feeling that God is ashamed of them for feeling this anger (Kane, Cheston, & Greer, 1993), a likely projection of their own feelings of shame. Another study found that women survivors with the most severe trauma histories reported experiencing God as "absent," "unloving," and "wrathful" (Doehring, 1993). These women may ask why God allowed such a thing to happen or consider that they are cursed by its occurrence (and recurrence) and are thus deserving of abuse. Alternatively, other studies of individuals from insecure traumatic backgrounds related to the unavailability or loss of a principal attachment figure have found that these individuals may seek out God as a substitute attachment figure (Kirkpatrick, 1999).

Including attention to spirituality in complex trauma treatment and conceptualizing the treatment as involving a quest for spirituality can help address issues of meaning, in the process providing mechanisms for reconciliation and reconnection with self, others, and God (or a God figure or representation). Although the objective dimensions of the trauma remain the same, the victim's or survivor's subjective view and understanding change, in the process allowing a change in the perception of self, others, and the world, and in reconciling the events and their implications. Moving beyond despair and hopelessness are important goals that are attained through transformations in understanding and purpose, often including a reconfiguration of and an attachment to a God figure.

GENERAL MODELS FOR ADDRESSING SPIRITUALITY IN PSYCHOTHERAPY

In recent years, psychologists have expanded their consideration of spirituality in trauma psychotherapy beyond case conceptualization to actual treatment models. In this section, we briefly review different paradigms for addressing spiritual issues in psychotherapy. Afterward, we highlight SO–TF–CBT as an adaptation of a gold standard secular trauma treatment.

Implicit–Explicit Continuum

Approaches to the inclusion of spirituality in psychotherapy have evolved over time. Nearly 20 years ago, Tan (1996) proposed that all methods for addressing spirituality in psychotherapy could be conceptualized along a continuum according to how explicit or implicit psychotherapists were with respect to spirituality. According to Tan, psychotherapists practice at the explicit end of the continuum when they openly discuss spiritual issues, and/or when they draw on spiritual resources such as prayer or reference to sacred texts in session. Conversely, Tan proposed that psychotherapists practice from an implicit approach to psychotherapy when they do not openly discuss spirituality and do not openly engage spiritual resources, but continue to operate out of their own spiritual values with respect for the spiritual values of their clients. Psychotherapists practicing from the implicit end of the continuum might refrain from suggesting psychotherapy interventions that they know are incongruent with the religious values of the clients they are treating. For example, a couples therapist treating a religiously committed married couple might refrain from suggesting divorce, especially if the clients have noted that divorce is incompatible with their religious beliefs.

It is important to note that psychotherapists frequently move along the implicit–explicit continuum. Tan (1996) suggested that movement along the continuum be determined by several factors, including (a) the degree to which the client wishes to discuss spiritual and religious issues in psychotherapy; (b) the presenting problem of the client; (c) the degree of religious commitment or salience on the part of the client; (d) the setting in which the client is being seen; (e) the psychotherapist's familiarity with the religious beliefs, values, and practices of the client; and (f) the psychotherapist's comfort in explicitly including discussions of spirituality in psychotherapy. This list is not meant to be exhaustive. Rather, it illustrates the complex "wheel" of factors involved in deciding when and how to explicitly or implicitly engage spirituality in treatment. Tan's model has been a useful one for helping psychotherapists to understand and categorize their approaches to addressing spirituality in psychotherapy.

Categorization of Spiritual Interventions in Psychotherapy

More recently, Aten, McMinn, and Worthington (2011) suggested that explicit use of spiritual interventions in psychotherapy can be categorized in three ways. First, some approaches to psychotherapy use secular interventions to help meet spiritual goals. For example, a highly religiously committed adult client might seek outpatient cognitive behavior therapy for depression. Seeing their problems through a religious lens, they might identify "regaining their joy" as a treatment goal. Secular cognitive behavior therapy could be used to not only reduce irrational beliefs related to depression but also to evaluate thoughts that are interfering with their experience and expression of joy, even in a religious context.

Second, some approaches to spiritual interventions adapt secular interventions to include spiritual content. Propst, Ostrom, Watson, Dean, and Mashburn (1992) published a religion-accommodative approach to cognitive therapy of this sort. They adapted Beck's (1967) cognitive therapy (CT) to include religious imagery and references to Scripture as part of the treatment for highly religiously committed clients. In conducting outcome research, they found that religiously accommodative CT was more effective in reducing depression among adult psychotherapy clients than secular CT.

Third, a number of spiritual interventions involve spiritual practices without any incorporation of secular treatment protocols. For example, yoga, delivered as a stand-alone spiritual intervention, has been found to be effective in reducing anxiety, depression, and chronic pain in samples of adults (Tekur, Nagarathna, Chametcha, Hankey, & Nagendra, 2012). Other examples of spiritual practices that can be used apart from secular content include the use of prayer or forgiveness (for a review, see Walker, Doverspike, Ahmed, Milevsky, & Woolley, 2013).

SPIRITUALLY ORIENTED TRAUMA-FOCUSED COGNITIVE BEHAVIOR THERAPY: AN EXAMPLE OF ADDRESSING SPIRITUALITY IN TRAUMA PSYCHOTHERAPY

In this section, we briefly review SO–TF–CBT (Walker et al., 2010) as an exemplar adaptation of secular TF–CBT (Cohen, Mannarino, & Deblinger, 2006). Readers who work primarily with children and adolescents are undoubtedly already familiar with TF–CBT. In its secular form, this therapy is a gold standard, empirically supported treatment for children and teens who have experienced physical or sexual abuse or other traumatic events. SO–TF–CBT was developed to help children from various faith backgrounds work through spiritual issues that are inextricably intertwined both with various traumatic events as well as the psychological sequelae stemming from such occurrences.

For example, Walker et al. (2010) presented the case study of Kristy, a 7-year-old Caucasian girl who was sexually abused by her biological father, a lay leader in the church where she worshipped.[1] In attempting to intimidate her into silence, her father told that she would go to hell and God would hate her if she ever told anyone about the abuse. Afterward, Kristy's faith was shaken and, quite understandably, she came to view God as angry and frightening. Kristy's case illustrates the need for a spiritually oriented approach to TF–CBT on several levels. First, some children are exposed to religion-related forms of abuse in which religious and spiritual faith is in some way part of the abuse itself. It was difficult for Kristy to separate her relationship

---

[1]The details of the clinical cases have been changed to preserve the anonymity of the individuals involved.

with God from her father's abuse, given that he was a church leader. Second, as we discussed earlier in this chapter, personal spirituality and religion are often damaged by abuse. In Kristy's case, her personal relationship with God was wounded by both the abuse and the threats.

In SO–TF–CBT, a multilevel assessment of client personal spirituality and religion is conducted and repeated (see Chapter 4 for further discussion of assessment in trauma psychotherapy). As part of that assessment, children's spiritual and religious background generally, including religious affiliation and level of religious commitment, is evaluated. In addition, the ways in which spirituality may be a source of pain as well as a potential resource for healing following abuse are considered. Clients are subsequently reassessed over time to determine changes in personal faith. After an initial assessment, children's psychotherapy is carefully crafted on the basis of the ways in which personal spirituality and religiousness may be either a source of pain or of healing or both simultaneously. Some abused children with a preexisting personal spirituality may not question their faith in the abuse aftermath but instead use their faith for coping and meaning making. For these children, psychotherapists use spiritual resources in an explicit fashion throughout treatment. For example, during the relaxation module early in treatment, psychotherapists might teach clients to pray while engaging in deep breathing or, alternatively, recommend a contemplative form of prayer as an adjunct for treatment. Later in treatment, while engaging in the trauma narrative, psychotherapists might pray with their clients prior to their clients beginning the narrative process. In the past, when supervising student psychotherapists, I (DFW) have encouraged trainees to pray that God would be with them and their clients in session, that He would give their clients courage to complete the narrative, and help the psychotherapist to hear the client and be there for him or her.

Other clients, like Kristy, might experience damage to their spirituality that would make explicit forms of spiritual intervention counterproductive initially. For these clients explicit integration of spirituality is not recommended until formal trauma narration is initiated. Then, in the trauma narrative module, children are asked whether they believed God was present when the event abuse occurred and if they have ever talked to God about it. If they say no, they are encouraged to talk to God about it, either in or outside of session, or both. Psychotherapists then attempt to facilitate such conversations in session, sometimes with an empty-chair technique. After the use of such an approach, many children who have experienced damage to their spiritual faith report feeling closer to God, and the therapist may engage in more explicit forms of spiritual intervention throughout the rest of the TF–CBT modules. For a complete description of ways to apply SO–TF–CBT, see Walker et al. (2010).

REFERENCES

American Psychiatric Association. (1980). *Diagnostic and statistical manual of mental disorders* (3rd ed.). Washington, DC: Author.

American Psychological Association. (2007). *Resolution on religious, religion based, and/or religion derived prejudice.* Retrieved from https://www.apa.org/about/policy/religious-discrimination.pdf

American Psychological Association. (2010). *Ethical principles of psychologists and code of conduct (2002, Amended June 1, 2010).* Retrieved from http://www.apa.org/ethics/code/principles.pdf

Aten, J. D., McMinn, M. M., & Worthington, E. L., Jr. (Eds.). (2011). *Spiritually oriented interventions for counseling and psychotherapy.* Washington, DC: American Psychological Association. doi:10.1037/12313-000

Beck, A. T. (1967). *The diagnosis and management of depression.* Philadelphia: University of Pennsylvania Press.

Brown, L. S. (2008). *Cultural competence in trauma psychotherapy: Beyond the flashback.* Washington, DC: American Psychological Association. doi:10.1037/11752-000

Bryant-Davis, T. (2008). *Thriving in the wake of trauma: A multicultural guide.* Lanham, MD: AltaMira Press.

Chan, L. F., Tan, S. M., Ang, J. K., Kamal Nor, N., & Sharip, S. (2012). A case of sexual abuse by a traditional faith healer: Are there potential preventions? *Journal of Child Sexual Abuse, 21,* 613–620. doi:10.1080/10538712.2012.719597

Cohen, J. A., Mannarino, A. P., & Deblinger, E. (2006). *Treating trauma and traumatic grief in children and adolescents.* New York, NY: Guilford Press.

Courtois, C., & Ford, J. (Eds.). (2009). *Treating complex traumatic stress disorders: An evidence-based guide.* New York, NY: Guilford Press. doi:10.1037/e608902012-109

Doehring, C. (1993). *Internal desecration—Traumatization and representations of God.* Lanham, MD: University Press of America.

Elliott, D. M. (1994). The impact of Christian faith on the prevalence and sequelae of sexual abuse. *Journal of Interpersonal Violence, 9,* 95–108. doi:10.1177/088626094009001006

Frankl, V. (1968). *Man's search for meaning.* New York, NY: Pocket Books.

Freyd, J. J. (1996). *Betrayal trauma: The logic of forgetting childhood abuse.* Cambridge, MA: Harvard University Press.

Griffith, J. (2010). *Religion that heals, religion that harms: A guide for clinical practice.* New York, NY: Guilford Press.

Hathaway, W. L. (2011). Ethical guidelines for using spiritually oriented interventions. In J. D. Aten, M. R. McMinn, & E. L. Worthington (Eds.), *Spiritually oriented interventions for counseling and psychotherapy* (pp. 65–81). Washington, DC: American Psychological Association. doi:10.1037/12313-003

Kane, D., Cheston, S., & Greer, J. (1993). Perceptions of God by survivors of childhood sexual abuse: An exploratory study in an underresearched area. *Journal of Psychology and Theology, 21,* 228–237.

Kira, I. A. (2010). Etiology and treatment of post-cumulative traumatic stress disorders in different cultures. *Traumatology, 16*, 128–141. doi:10.1177/1534765610365914

Kirkpatrick, L. A. (1999). Toward an evolutionary study of religion and personality. *Journal of Personality, 67*, 921–952. doi:10.1111/1467-6494.00078

McCann, I. L., & Pearlman, L. A. (1990). Vicarious traumatization: A framework for understanding the psychological effects of working with victims. *Journal of Traumatic Stress, 3*, 131–149. doi.org/10.1007/BF00975140

Power, M. (2012). *Adieu to God: Why psychology leads to atheism.* New York, NY: Wiley. doi:10.1002/9781119950868

Propst, L. R., Ostrom, R., Watson, P., Dean, T., & Mashburn, D. (1992). Comparative efficacy of religious and nonreligious cognitive behavioral therapy for the treatment of depression. *Journal of Consulting and Clinical Psychology, 60*, 94–103. doi:10.1037/0022-006X.60.1.94

Tan, S. Y. (1996). Religion in clinical practice: Implicit and explicit integration. In E. P. Shafranske (Ed.), *Religion and the clinical practice of psychology* (pp. 365–387). Washington, DC: American Psychological Association. doi:10.1037/10199-013

Tekur, P., Nagarathna, R., Chametcha, S., Hankey, A., & Nagendra, H. R. (2012). A comprehensive yoga program improves pain, anxiety and depression in chronic low back pain patients more than exercise: An RCT. *Complementary Therapies in Medicine, 20*, 107–118. doi:10.1016/j.ctim.2011.12.009

van der Kolk, B. A., Roth, S., Pelcovitz, D., Sunday, S., & Spinazzola, J. (2005). Disorders of extreme stress: The empirical foundation of a complex adaptation to trauma. *Journal of Traumatic Stress, 18*, 389–399. doi.org/10.1002/jts.20047

Van Deusen, S. (n.d.). *Childhood trauma, attachment to God and psychological well-being* (Unpublished doctoral dissertation). Loyola University, Baltimore, MD.

Walker, D. F., Doverspike, W., Ahmed, S., Milevsky, A., & Woolley, J. (2013). Prayer. In D. F. Walker & W. L. Hathaway (Eds.), *Spiritual interventions in child and adolescent psychotherapy* (pp. 181–207). Washington, DC: American Psychological Association. doi:10.1037/13947-009

Walker, D. F., Reese, J. B., Hughes, J. P., & Troskie, M. J. (2010). Addressing religious and spiritual issues in trauma-focused cognitive behavior therapy with children and adolescents. *Professional Psychology: Research and Practice, 41*, 174–180. doi:10.1037/a0017782

Walker, D. F., Reid, H., O'Neill, T., & Brown, L. (2009). Changes in personal religion/spirituality during and after childhood abuse: A review and synthesis. *Psychological Trauma: Theory, Research, Practice, and Policy, 1*, 130–145. doi:10.1037/a0016211

2

SPIRITUALITY, RELIGION, AND COMPLEX DEVELOPMENTAL TRAUMA

STEPHANIE VAN DEUSEN AND CHRISTINE A. COURTOIS

The purpose of this chapter is to describe the effects of multiple, repetitive traumas occurring primarily over the course of childhood on an individual's spiritual development. We begin by describing the effects of complex trauma, with a focus on spiritual problems stemming from trauma of this type. Then, using the lens of the work of Erik Erikson and James Fowler, we provide a developmental framework to set out a number of identifiable steps leading to healthy faith development. With a fixed developmental trajectory in place, we are able to assess how and when experiences of complex trauma affect standard developmental trajectories. We review how the five primary domains of complex posttraumatic stress disorder (CPTSD) influence a survivor's ability to develop a healthy sense of faith that fosters positive identity and hope. We present the case of a client with dissociative identity disorder, including some of her artwork and writings, to illustrate how extreme emotional dysregulation and trauma-related expectations of relationships affect spirituality, attachment to God, and faith development. Finally, this chapter

http://dx.doi.org/10.1037/14500-003
Spiritually Oriented Psychotherapy for Trauma, D. F. Walker, C. A. Courtois, and J. D. Aten (Editors)

highlights specific strategies for integrating issues of spirituality into each of the three main phases of treatment for CPTSD.

A METAPHOR FOR THE EFFECTS OF COMPLEX TRAUMA: HOMELESSNESS

Complex trauma encapsulates a recurrent experience of deprivation (and at times overstimulation or the often unpredictable alternation between the two) that leads victims and survivors to feel ensnared by a sense of imminent danger. It challenges their identity and self-worth, causes a disconnection from primary support systems and community, and often results in despair. One of our clients described the experience as being analogous to being cut out of her family picture and left homeless, an apt metaphor that conveys some of the disconnection and dis-identification experienced by survivors of complex trauma. This client's sense of being "without an identity or a home" speaks not only to her place in the world but also to another fundamental "home base" loss, that of a self and of positive identity: "Who am I?" "Am I a reflection of what was done to me?" "Do I have a place where I fit?" "Do I deserve good attention?"

Having a spiritual home and faith in a beneficent God are also issues that are affected, causing survivors of complex trauma to ask additional questions such as, "Is there a God?" "If so, where is He or She?" "Why was this allowed to happen?" "Is God punishing me?" "Has God abandoned me?" The cumulative ruptures specific to this type of interpersonal trauma most often involve primary caregivers and others in close relationships who, rather than nurturing and supporting the development of the child, commit layered affronts to that growing child's basic self-capacities, in the process tainting the ability to develop trusting relationships with others. In a complex trauma scenario, the victim can experience one or more types of abuse (physical, sexual, and emotional), neglect, exploitation, betrayal, rejection, antipathy, and abandonment (Courtois & Ford, 2013). In turn, these create situations of *betrayal trauma*, in which those who are supposed to be trustworthy and safe are not and have violated their roles and responsibilities (Freyd, 1998).

Trauma survivors as well as the larger culture, including faith communities, often answer these questions about personal worthiness in the negative, by way of disparaging labels bred in a failure to understand an individual who has been profoundly injured in relationship to others and who is in the throes of emotional (and sometimes physical) survival. I (SVD) can remember having a discussion with a pastor and his wife about how the church could best respond to traumatized individuals. As some of the difficulties of working with survivors were discussed, particularly the distrust of their pastoral care and God's sovereignty, the pastor's wife abruptly ended the conversation with the pronouncement, "People don't change or heal not because they were injured as children but because their hearts are not open to God." The implication that a survivor's profound disconnection and distrust is about a "hardening heart" is a Christian reference to rebelliousness and dishonoring of God that unfortunately does not take into account the defenses that are mounted to protect a damaged heart and spirit. Often, disparaging labels have come out of other biblical references used out of the appropriate context, for example, asking a woman in a domestic violence situation to "turn the other cheek" or challenging a person to repent for a set of behaviors that allowed him or her to survive the deprivation and overstimulation of complex trauma. These create yet another betrayal or secondary trauma because they are other reminders of misunderstanding, and they lack empathy and validation of the injustice or abuse.

Survival is the most basic task of human development, initially requiring a relationship with a caregiver who provides essentials such as safety, shelter, food, clothing, physical proximity, and sufficient responsiveness to adequately stimulate the child's developing brain. Erikson (1993) defined the developmental task of the stage of infancy and early childhood as one of *trust versus mistrust*. In optimal conditions, trust builds on a foundation of security and responsiveness provided in early life by a competent or "good enough" caregiver (Winnicott, 1963). In contrast, when such a foundation is lacking, the relational breach (usually referred to as *relational* or *attachment trauma;* Schore, 2003) breeds insecurity in the child who internalizes distrust of others coupled with personal shame and a sense of contamination. This sense of being unvalued and not being seen as unique or precious nor being positively responded to heightens insecurity and becomes an implicit memory that lives in the child's psyche and soma. Moreover, and unfortunately, when interpersonal trauma occurs so early in life, the child is left vulnerable to additional mistreatment and exploitation (revictimization) both within and outside the family (Duckworth & Follette, 2012). Such recurrence creates a condition of layered and cumulative trauma (hence, complex trauma) over the course of childhood and adolescence. Anodea Judith (2004) identified the paradoxical nature of the fear response in circumstances such as these:

> If danger was a frequent presence growing up, then fear pervades our baseline program for survival. The sense of fear brings a feeling of safety, as paradoxical as that might sound. We feel safe only because we are hyper-vigilant and become even more uncomfortable when we try to relax. (p. 59)

Attachment

From infancy to approximately 18 months of age, children form attachment styles that are in keeping with their earliest experiences with their parents and other caregivers (Bowlby, 1969). A *secure attachment style* results from a safe haven created by "good enough" attunement by a parent who provides basic security and responsiveness. The child is free enough to explore the world and to return to a responsive caregiver when overwhelmed, frightened, or in need of reassurance, soothing, and nurturance. In contrast, *insecure attachment styles* result from inadequate safety or responsiveness, overstimulation, or danger from the caregiver and/or the environment, often without needed regard and protection. Circumstances such as these are traumatic for developing infants and young children who are physically and emotionally immature and dependent on their caregivers for modulating overstimulation and for nurturance (i.e., for their very survival). It takes much less to traumatize an infant or toddler than it does an older and more mature child or an adult. Depending on the intensity and severity of these forms of attachment or relational trauma and whether other caregivers are available to mitigate some of the trauma or its effects, *preoccupied* (child anxious or fearful), *detached* (child dismissive and self-sufficient), or *disorganized attachment styles* (child disoriented and shifting between positions of anxiety and fear, indifference, control and caretaking, and other strategies) emerge as a consequence. These attachment styles have been found to remain relatively stable over the life span (Main, Hesse, & Kaplan, 2005) until such time as the child or adult is in a relationship with someone with a secure style who creates conditions within which an *earned secure style* can develop.

We note that although our focus here is on complex developmental trauma in childhood, additional forms have been identified that can build on and further exacerbate and confound the aftereffects. A number of theorists (Brown, 2008; Carter, 2007; Pole & Triffleman, 2010; Triffleman & Pole, 2010) have noted that characteristics of an individual's identity (e.g., gender, age, ability, skin color, ethnicity, sexual orientation) or community (e.g., kinship group, clan, tribe, race, political, national, religious tradition) in themselves can cause discrimination and conflict that are traumatic. At times, these circumstances and other forms of complex trauma begin in adulthood rather than in childhood or adolescence. Despite adults' better capacity to cope with adversity and their superior access to resources, the effect of adult-onset trauma may be severe enough to cause a regression in personal development in addition to existential and spiritual crises. When one or more of these types of trauma coalesce, as is often the case, another form of *layered* or *cumulative trauma* is created. Multiple traumatizations can be so constant and never-ending for some unfortunate humans that Kira et al. (2013) identified trauma of this type as *continuous* and *lifelong*.

Five primary domains of aftereffects resulting from complex trauma over the course of childhood have been identified (Cloitre et al., 2012; Courtois & Ford, 2013): (a) emotional dysregulation, (b) identity, (c) dissociation, (d) relations with others, and (e) somatization. To these we add a sixth, *systems of meaning* (as originally articulated by Herman, 1992, in her conceptualization of CPTSD), to capture some of the spiritual, religious, and faith-based elements and some of the existential questions resulting from the highly dispiriting traumatic events that survivors have endured. We address the developmental impact of complex trauma on each of these domains using Erikson's developmental framework in the following sections and note that these domains are interconnected and not mutually exclusive.

Domain 1: Emotional Dysregulation

Emotional dysregulation is now identified as the hallmark of insecure and—especially—disorganized attachment (Hesse & Main, 2000). A responsive caregiver attunes to and coregulates with the child, in the process teaching autoregulation skills (Schore, 2003). In contrast, caregivers who are abusive and unresponsive do not attune to the child, nor do they name or help to regulate their child's emotional states, leaving a significant developmental deficit. In addition, traumatized children have posttraumatic responses—fear or terror-based *hyperarousal* (exhibited in flashbacks, startle responses, sleep disturbance, nightmares, externalizing behaviors) alternating with *hypoarousal* (dissociation or other forms of emotional shutdown) and avoidance that become part of and compound this dysregulation, leaving child victims—and later adult survivors—in a whirlwind of unpredictability that brings into focus the extreme dysregulation seen in their affect and in their behavior as well, because children's symptoms are more likely to be exhibited behaviorally.

Learning how to identify, tolerate, and express emotions without feeling overwhelmed or numb or without automatically exhibiting emotions through behavior is a significant challenge at the onset and often throughout the course of treatment (Courtois & Ford, 2013). It also requires reworking expectations of others, especially people who are available for support and caring. Survivors with insecure attachment styles have learned that emotions were either too much, unacceptable, or inconsistently received by their primary caregivers. This loss of an available and safe attachment figure positions emotional distress as an obstacle that leads to more suffering rather than as a piece of their story that creates dimensionality. For many survivors of complex trauma, emotional distress becomes the whole story, permeating their identity and existence.

In a recent book on complex trauma Courtois and Ford (2013) used the metaphor of being "imprisoned" by anger, grief, alienation, distrust, confusion self-esteem, loneliness, shame, self-loathing, and emotional distress. This picture of being held captive by the disrupted psychology and biology of this form of trauma illustrates the complexities of establishing a secure attachment. Consequently, these clients feel danger not only in relation to an external threat but also to the internal threat of being unable to self-regulate, self-organize, or draw on relationships to regain self-integrity (Courtois & Ford, 2009, 2013). Erikson's (1993) psychosocial conflicts of *trust versus mistrust* and *autonomy versus shame and doubt* are encompassed within this domain. The capacity to self-regulate thus has widespread significance for the child's and later the adult's positive identity and capacity to be in personal control.

Domains 2 to 5: Identity, Dissociation, Relation With Others, and Somatization

The process of hypoarousal, or what ethologists have called a default state of physical shutdown and paralysis referred to as *tonic immobility* and what Porges (2011) identified as related to the polyvagal nervous system, is also relevant to understanding the process of faith development in a complex trauma population. What many survivors describe as the void in self describes the subjective feelings associated with a voided or absent self and an absence of emotion and the capacity for vitality. The mind and body protest any new information or connection, thereby adding to the avoidance process. One of our clients actually got so lost in this process that she literally experienced herself as being invisible. In bearing witness to her story of the terror of her abuse, her psychotherapist observed her body's frozen posture, her shallow breathing, and vacant eyes. For her, being invisible was an attempt to remain hidden from the predator. The problem was that the past had become the present and she had no sense that she was no longer the prey.

When dissociation becomes primary in keeping the perceived threat at bay, it limits exposure to other information. Furthermore, it has the effect of positioning all relationships (including relationship with God) as enactments of victim, perpetrator, nonprotector bystander, or rescuer. As noted previously, their psychological and relational responses often mirror those of their physiology. In terms of attachment status, a condition of hyper- and hypoattachment that parallels hyper- and hypoarousal enters the relational domain and can be observed: Insecurely attached children tend toward *hyperattachment* (or anxious preoccupation) on one hand and to *hypoattachment* (avoidance and detachment) on the other, or a confusing blend of both, especially when attachment to caregivers has been of the disorganized/disoriented/dissociative type. Thus, survivors are overly trusting and vulnerable or overly mistrusting and suspicious of others and rarely get what they need with either strategy.

Chronic heightened stress also has somatic and health implications, and survivors experience a wide variety of psychosomatic manifestations. They have been found to have a multitude of physiological reactions leading up to illness and disease in all major body systems, and they are especially susceptible to autoimmune disorders due to their bodies' chronic dysregulation and allostatic stress load (Kendall-Tackett, 2013).

Impact on Spirituality and God Image

This brief review of the impact of complex trauma provides an infrastructure to grasp how a layered assault of this type affects an individual's overall sense of spirituality and God image. Shengold (1999) used the term *soul murder* to describe the impact of complex trauma on development in general, but we emphasize its spiritual dimension and allusion to the murder of the self and of the spiritual. This term was originally coined by a 19th century playwright who defined it as "the destruction of another human being's love for life" (Ibsen, 1896, p. 246). Doehring (1993) described the impact of complex trauma as an internal desecration, a scriptural reference to the temple, a holy place, being irreverently disrespected. This image fits into other references in the Christian faith tradition of the body being the temple, thereby emphasizing that an individual's experience of God is felt in his or her body. *Merriam-Webster's Collegiate Dictionary* (n.d.) defines the soul as "the spiritual principle embodied in human beings, all rational and spiritual beings, or the universe." In the book *Eastern Body Western Mind*, Judith (2004) described the soul as an entity "that coalesces toward the body, leaning toward form, attachment, and feeling" (p. 13). To understand the connection between spirituality and complex trauma, it is important to underscore the concept of *embodiment*—specifically, that spirituality and faith involve a connection to one's body, relationships, and personal narratives. This is a significant detail given the propensity for survivors of complex trauma to dissociate and maintain an almost phobic reaction to being in their bodies.

COMPLEX TRAUMA AND FAITH DEVELOPMENT

The description of complex trauma and its effects provided earlier in this chapter informs how spiritual struggle—including image of God and attachment to God—gets exhibited and is assessed in survivors. In this section, we consider ways in which these struggles or symptoms can be understood developmentally. In his seminal work on faith development, *Stages of Faith*, Fowler (1981) offered a description of faith as a "force field of life" that he proposed evolved through seven developmental stages (p. 4). Like those of other developmental theories, these stages progress in a step-wise fashion and incorporate biological maturation, emotional and cognitive development, and psychosocial experiences. In addition, Fowler elaborated on the role of religio–cultural symbols, meanings, and practices to provide an understanding of how individuals conceptualize God or a higher power and how those concepts affect core values, beliefs, meanings, and relationships (Fowler, 1993; Fowler & Dell, 2004). In Exhibit 2.1 Fowler's model of spiritual development is outlined to provide a framework to conceptualize how traumatic

EXHIBIT 2.1
Fowler's Stages of Faith Development

Stage One: Primary Faith
- First 2 years of life
- Undifferentiated self
- Balancing trust versus mistrust
- Implicit attachment memories
- First symbols of faith develop on the basis of a primal sense of goodness and badness of self and the surrounding world

Stage Two: Intuitive/Projective Faith
- Children 4 to 8 years of age
- Child projects the visible faith of their parents and significant others
- Faith is affect driven
- Knowledge and feelings are fused together
- Symbols are taken literally
- Faith is a reflection of the child's imagination
- There is an awareness of an independent self
- Constructs of faith are drawn around symbols and stories of good and evil, power and size

Stage Three: Mythic/Literal Faith
- Children 8 to 12 years of age
- Organize their belief about God's rule or control of the universe around fairness and moral reciprocity
- Belief that goodness is rewarded and badness is punished
- The child begins to take on and own the stories, beliefs, and practices that symbolize their faith community
- Identification with other people who are seen as similar
- Aligning with deep feelings of terror and guilt, as well as of love and companionship

Stage Four: Synthetic/Conventional Faith
- People from approximately 12 years of age to early adulthood
- Young people begin to reflect on their own stories and name and synthesize meaning into those narratives
- People develop a personal myth about themselves
- Meaning is prescribed by personal relationships is dominated by a conformist mentality thus lacks a third-person perspective
- The vulnerability of this stage is dependency on external referencing

Stage Five: Individuative/Reflective Faith
- Young adulthood
- There is an ability to reflect critically on one's story, values, and relationships and dismantle the personal myths about self, others, God, and the world
- A person begins to differentiate and develop a sense of self and others that are more reflective of personal values and beliefs as opposed to absorbing the values of a social group or institution

Stage Six: Conjunctive Faith
- Individuals experience an increased ability to hold two differing beliefs without judging or fearing the implications of those differences
- Paradoxes and polarities are embraced and held in creative tension with each other

EXHIBIT 2.1
Fowler's Stages of Faith Development   *(Continued)*

- There is an ambiguity in the meaning-making process allowing autonomous commitment to their own tradition while respecting and being genuinely open to the truth in other positions.

Stage Seven: Universalizing Faith
- A person in this stage of faith development makes a radical commitment to transform the world
- Culminates in the practice of inclusiveness, justice, and compassion
- Identifies with God ways of knowing and valuing others
- Examples: Gandhi, Mother Theresa, Lincoln, Martin Luther King, Jr.

injuries create developmental ruptures in a survivor's sense of spirituality. We also overlay these in Table 2.1 with the conflicts identified in Erikson's model described earlier.

Understanding that complex trauma stifles early development and a normative trajectory, it is important to listen for the themes highlighted in both Fowler's and Erikson's early stages of development. Are the schematic themes affect driven? Are there ideas surrounding good and evil, power and size? Can the psychotherapist identify attachment themes that reflect primary attachment relationships? How do the stories of betrayal trauma play out in the imagery described by the client or produced in artwork or writing? Next, we present the artwork of Gigi, a client with a complex trauma history, and a format of early recollections in which the client described subjective impressions of each memory using the format "I am _____. Other people are _____. God is _____. The world is _____. Therefore, I will _____" to illustrate the internal working models of a client with complex trauma. For the purpose of protecting this client's privacy, the author is using the fictitious name "Gigi" when referencing the details of this client's history.

CASE STUDY: GIGI

Gigi grew up in a home in which both her parents contended with adverse childhood experiences. Her primary description of her mother was "stoic"; Gigi described her as being a woman who pushed away any emotional expression with a dismissive Pollyannaism. She reported that the few times she did see her mother cry, it was shut down with an apology or hidden behind her bedroom door. Gigi also described her father as being dismissive of any emotional expression to the point where he was not open to saying "I love you" to his own children. She was a tender and emotional child who grew up in an emotional vacuum.

TABLE 2.1
Erikson and Fowler Developmental Models

Age	Womb to 2 years	3 to 7 years	7 to 12 years	Adolescence	Early adulthood	Middle adulthood	Late adulthood
Fowler	Primal faith	Intuitive–projective faith (impulsive self)	Mythic–literal faith (imperial self)	Synthetic–conventional faith (interpersonal self)	Individuative–reflective faith (institutional self)	Conjunctive faith (interindividual self)	Universalizing faith (God-grounding self)
Erikson	Trust vs. mistrust	Autonomy vs. shame and doubt	Initiative vs. guilt	Industry vs. inferiority	Identity vs. identity role confusion	Intimacy vs. isolation	Generativity vs. self-absorption; integrity vs. despair

Her mother was religious woman who attended church and believed in a high moral standard but who experienced her faith from the vantage point of an avoidant attachment style. Gigi described her father as being in and out of various faith traditions until she was a teenager, at which point he stepped away from any formal church involvement. Gigi's perspective on her father's childhood was that he was "left alone a lot" by his mother, who had to work, and he was "unwanted" by his stepfather. It appears that her father's faith journey mimics that lack of attachment or wandering that is consistent with a person who grew up feeling like they did not belong anywhere. Gigi grew up with two parents who walled off their emotional experiences and dismissed the need to deal with painful life experiences. So when Gigi was sexually abused, starting in early childhood, her parents were either too shut down affectively to recognize the signs the she was being abused or they saw her as being "too sensitive."

Gigi's history of multiple types of abuse began when she was 5 years old and continued throughout her adolescence. The abuse and its impact on top of the earlier relational trauma that resulted in an insecure (fearful/avoidant) dissociative attachment style were severe enough to result in dissociative identity disorder. According to Wilson (2006), dissociation that occurs during a specific stage of identity formation can be considered a traumatic *mile marker* because it "marks" the age, stage, and nature of the traumatic injury (p. 95). In Gigi's drawing, generated in therapy when she was 35 years old, can be seen questions of faith and spirituality, splintered into varying inquiries by different self-states regarding God's choice or ability to protect her from being abused (see Figure 2.1). For her, Jesus was experienced as the grim reaper, an image representing death or annihilation, whereas nature or God's creation was a place of safety. This is further represented in her subjective impressions of those abuse experiences listed next.

Childhood Memories of Sexual Trauma

Gigi reported being sexually abused for approximately one year from the ages of 5 to 6 by a customer at a family-owned business. She also reported being sexually abused at the age of 7 during a public event where several boys turned off the lights and conned her into grabbing one of the boys' penises while the other boys laughed at her.

In response to the prompts, "I am _____. Other people are _____," and so on, she wrote, "I am <u>trapped in plain sight</u>. Other people are <u>around</u>. God is <u>somewhere</u>. The world is <u>uncaring or blind</u>. Therefore, I will be <u>a good girl and listen to adults</u>."

One of the client's dissociative self-states wrote a letter referencing this specific time frame (see Figure 2.2). This artwork and writing illustrate the child-self of Gigi grappling with the implications of attachment ruptures. Her

Figure 2.1. Artwork created by a client to process childhood memories of sexual trauma.

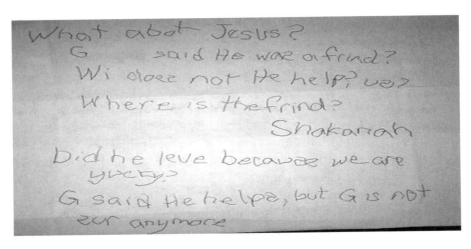

Figure 2.2. Letter written by a client's dissociative self-state.

attachment pleas, "Help," "Hide," "Listen," or the questions, "Where are you," "When are you coming," and "Why is this happening?" along with the singular response illustrated by the grim reaper God image, "Just follow," illustrate the traumatic mile markers (Wilson, 2006) in Fowler's (1981) intuitive/projective stage. She transfers her dismissive attachment figures and the abusers onto her God image. Gigi's pronouncement that she is going to be a "good girl" appears to indicate a developmental rupture in Fowler's mythical/literal stage in which she hopes to be rewarded with validation and protection from further abuse. Like many complex trauma survivors, she arrived at the conclusion that God and others abandoned her because there was something wrong with her. This sense of abandonment was exacerbated during Gigi's adolescence as she experienced additional interpersonal trauma. Next, we describe a memory highlighting the recurring experiences of being victimized by bullies and the onset of tension-reduction behaviors as a way of managing the emotional and physical pain.

Adolescent Memories of Interpersonal Violence (Bullying)

Gigi described being bullied physically, emotionally, and verbally at a Christian school from the seventh through the 12th grade. During this period, she attempted suicide and began to self-harm to numb the pain. Repeating the "I am _____" exercise, she wrote,

> I am being laughed at by Christians. Other people are cruel. God is supposed to be here. The world is not helpful. Therefore, I will not trust "it" or "Christians." I am not like them and I don't want to be alive or feel.

There is a sense in Gigi of being abandoned and that God is supposed to be different. According to Fowler (1981), the initial stage of faith development involves assimilating the symbols of good and evil and power and size into the internal working models (IWMs) of what faith is and the associated images of God. For this client, the recurrent experiences of others' cruelty and sadism and the sense of being abandoned are the deeply rooted introjects that underlie her sense of faith. The tension of needing a safe community and perceiving others as dangerous pushed this client inward, in the process creating a pseudo-community of internal self-states that became a "force field" of its own that protected her but also separated her from life.

Dissociation and Faith Development

The activation of the stress response system signaling that self-preservation requires shutdown and invisibility to survive is one of the ways that dissociation works to protect a child in the throes of chronic abuse and entrapment.

In the context of normative development, Fowler (1981) theorized that there is a mythic/literal stage of faith development in which children begin to align with others who are similar and develop deep feelings of love and companionship as they take on and own the stories and practices of their faith community. For Gigi and other complex trauma survivors, the stories they align with instead leave them with a perpetual sense of abandonment, alienation, terror, guilt, and personal contamination that forces them to be disembodied and to feel, as referenced earlier, without a home. This creates what Fowler and other developmental theorists have identified as a *personal mythology*. This synthesis of ideas, values, and images provides a primary schema for faith and personal ideology. The following is a more crystallized subjective impression Gigi wrote as the caption of a picture she drew of herself sitting in nature with tears running down her face as she held on to her cat: "I am sad and alone. Other people are absent. God is in nature. The world is beautiful with no people. Therefore, I can be safe and emotional in nature without people."

Gigi found safety outside relationships. She connected with nature and her animals. The trauma-related and despairing expectations of people and God coupled with the unresolved emotional pain and injury became the lens of her faith. Her IWM fluctuated from a dismissive or avoidant attachment dynamic with others and in her attachment to God. He was seen as distant and unreliable to the point of being withholding and sadistic in allowing her to be hurt. In both cases Gigi was locked into what Hesse and Main (2000) called the *fright without solution dilemma*, in which the potential protective attachment figures—God, her primary caregivers, and the surrounding Christian community—were complicit in her being abused, thereby creating a major betrayal trauma and an unsolvable dilemma. Like other complex trauma survivors, this dilemma created for Gigi a breakdown in the development of organized strategies to use toward any attachment figure when distressed. For many, this dynamic is further compounded by the abstract nature of the God–person relationship. A person has to be able to sense the presence of God to experience comfort and security, which is more difficult when there are ruptures in early development, specifically around the responsiveness and permanence of caregivers. It is the proverbial peek-a-boo game that launches clients into the abandonment crisis—"I don't see you; you don't exist." The opportunity to rework those IWMs of God require a secure attachment with a psychotherapist who is sensitive to issues of faith and trauma and is able to enter that inner void to create a transitional space where those flawed attributions can be challenged.

A Pastor Entered the Void: The Power of Validation

The final subjective impression of this particular client highlights how a therapeutic relationship offered a new opportunity for her as a survivor of repeated interpersonal trauma to reframe her identity and self-worth in the context of relationships that offered the reparative dimensions lacking in her upbringing. When Gigi was 21 years old, she risked disclosing the abuse and her resultant despair to a pastor, who responded by empathizing with her and validating her story. He referred her to psychotherapy and later made himself available to help her disclose her experiences to her parents. The attachment experiences with her psychotherapist and pastor provided her with a different model for relationships and for a faith community. This illustrates the restorative value of receiving attunement and caring within a real relationship from someone who is trustworthy and who can validate and help process the myriad emotional, cognitive, relational, and spiritual wounds that attend complex trauma. Gigi's new phrases indicated her changing view of God and the world: "I am <u>family</u>. Other people are <u>mostly helpful</u>. God is <u>questionable</u>. The world is <u>friendly</u>. Therefore, I will <u>be helped</u>."

THE FIRST PHASE: THE THERAPEUTIC ALLIANCE

The first phase of psychotherapy with clients with complex trauma has as its foundation the establishment of safety. During this phase the psychotherapist continually assesses with the client his or her environmental and emotional safety and collaborates in developing a customized treatment plan. This phase also provides the client with skills to manage symptoms and stabilize daily life. The most important foundational skills are the ability to identify and regulate emotional responses. Establishing a therapeutic relationship that provides a "safe haven" from which the client can engage in self-exploration is another focal point of this first phase of treatment. A core issue in establishing a therapeutic relationship during this initial phase is to reframe what it means to trust and for others to be trustworthy (Courtois & Ford, 2013). Understanding that trust is the implicit ingredient of faith, this process of establishing a baseline for trust is a key element in assessing how the client's faith development has been affected by complex trauma. It is also important for psychotherapists to understand that the therapeutic relationship can serve as a place to help complex trauma survivors rework faith and reclaim a healing relationship with God. One of our clients wrote about how the therapeutic relationship provided a secure base that shifted her IWM of God and community:

> When I first went to therapy I had a strong painful energy field that I carried around in my chest in the location of my fourth chakra, the heart chakra. After years of therapy where I have felt loved, the pain has subsided and the chance for power has presented itself. Recently, I have been able to move forward and become open enough to discover love and support from friends, church, and God.

The therapeutic relationship equipped this client to move through the intense distrust she felt toward people, God, and her community because of the severe neglect and abuse of her childhood to a place where she was able to risk hoping for a different experience. Hope and determination are ego strengths acquired as a client works through the early developmental crises, or traumatic mile markers specific to Erikson's first two stages of development, trust versus mistrust and autonomy versus shame and doubt (Wilson, 2006, p. 73). As she stated, it was the sense of being liked for herself and being "loved" that provided her with the courage to explore new relationships and revise her personal mythology related to faith and her image of God. Her attachment to God also changed as she began to experience God in that same place in her body where she felt painful energy.

Early in treatment an 18-year-old male complex trauma survivor wrote the following trust statement in his Sexual Addiction Anonymous second step journal:

> Is the God I thought I believed in the one who sends men to rape kids and then string them along for years without providing an escape? I believe God prescribed the abuse to teach me to trust Him and to more fully rely on Him.

Understanding that the affect-driven interpretation of God's role in the abuse is indicative of an early developmental rupture in which the story of an extremely sadistic sexual assault and a naive and helpless 11-year-old boy got reformulated to position God as the perpetrator. Clients who have adopted a Christian image of God often find it hard to trust God because He did not prevent the abuse from happening. This perspective of self-in-relationship-to-God fuels a fearful/avoidant attachment to God that needs to be identified and deconstructed (Griffith, 2010). Table 2.2 highlights the emotional qualities and beliefs associated with different attachment styles.

In the qualitative assessment section of the dissertation on attachment to God in a clinical sample of complex trauma survivors mentioned earlier, 80% of the 243 participants identified God as a trustworthy attachment figure; yet, the quantitative assessment revealed that 30% met criteria for a dismissive/avoidant attachment to God subtype and 64% met criteria for a fearful/avoidant attachment to God subtype (Van Deusen, n.d.). One might infer from this finding that complex trauma survivors either experience closeness with God as frightening or actively avoid a connection with God as they do with other people. Instead, they develop extreme forms of self-sufficiency and self-reliance. These results also show that a complex trauma survivor may present as spiritually knowledgeable and connected to God as an expression of the "as-if" or "apparently normal" defense to keep this pain or ruptured relationship "invisible." This may serve, as illustrated in Gigi's drawing, as

TABLE 2.2
Attachment Styles Toward a Personal God

Attachment style	Emotional quality of personal relationship with God	Associated beliefs about God
Secure	"God feels close, loving, and compassionate toward me."	"God is a being who is loving and reliably present."
Anxious	"I feel unworthy of God's love."	"God is a loving being, but His love for me is conditional or unreliable."
Dismissive/avoidant	"I feel that I can rely only on myself."	"God is a distant and unreliable being—A relationship with God counts for little."
Fearful/avoidant	"I feel unworthy of God's love, and I fear God may punish me."	"God is a distant being who can be threatening."

Note. From *Religion That Heals, Religion That Harms: A Guide for Clinical Practice* (p. 108), by J. L. Griffith, 2010, New York, NY: Guilford Press. Copyright 2010 by Guilford Press. Adapted with permission.

a means to hold the grim reaper God image privately and to minimize the rejection of a larger faith community.

Developing a secure base within psychotherapy provides a new context to experience relational safety and protection. The attuned, responsive psychotherapist teaches the client how to reflect on his or her story, identify and manage the emotional experience of being traumatized, and find meaning in the events. This process brings to light what it felt like to be helpless and objectified and who is held responsible for these offenses. This process of addressing the trauma narrative by increasing the survivor's basic self-capacities to tolerate and narrate the story repositions the focus on how the primary caregivers and other abusers violated and abandoned the survivor. Having the real story in the therapy room allows the psychotherapist to address the IWMs of God and the ruptures in faith development in the second phase as a grief-related wound. It also shifts God and faith as a resource for anchoring the survivor as he or she reconstructs what it means to be safe and connected in relationships.

In a poem titled "But God," used here with permission, one of our clients wrote about how her relationship with God served as an anchor that provided what Fowler (1981) called a *third person perspective* in which she experienced God seeing her in her pain. You will notice in the poem that her belief that God was there but did not lessen the impact of the domestic violence, poverty, neglect, and multiple types of abuse, *But*, the conjunction she used throughout her poem, it did offer her a deeply felt presence that carried her.

But God

Little girl wants to be heard. She wants to be known. No, you have to go away. You have to be silent! But the little girl wants to be heard. She wants to be known.

So tired of the struggle

So tired of the noise

Clamoring voices inside refuse to cease.

Hear me. Listen. I have something to say.

No shut up! She has something to say!

The little girl is still there locked away walls erected, prison chains.

Love and hatred, how can that be?

Listen to me Mami. Why can't you listen to me? Here I am. Don't you see me? Oh, Mami, please stop the hatred. Please stop the fighting, chaos and confusion.

What's with the Hail Marys?

Heartfelt prayers to a powerless savior? Cold nights, hungry days

Mami, can I have some coffee? In the bottle please.

Little girl hears a voice inside that says,

But God.

Would it have made a difference?

Broken girl. Who can put her back together? The pieces don't fit. Someone please finish this puzzle. Pieces are missing.

Have you ever tried to do a puzzle?

Frustrating isn't it?

Almost done. Anticipation builds. Huge letdown when you realize something is missing.

It's got to be somewhere. Walk away. Screw it. Let it be.

Can't resist the urge to search for that missing piece.

But God.

This poem illustrated the client's readiness to move on to the next phase of treatment that involves helping the client use faith as a resource to facilitate the process of meaning-making. It also involves collaborating with her to gather those lost pieces to grieve the experiences she did not have—that all children deserve—and to work through the ambiguous losses associated with multiple, repetitive traumas.

THE SECOND PHASE: REMEMBRANCE AND MOURNING

This phase requires the psychotherapist and the client to hold on to ambiguity, as exemplified in the client's poem: God was there, but He did not stop the perpetrator who sexually terrorized Gigi; God was there, but He did not stop the 11-year-old boy from being raped and cajoled in a way that led to a horrifying sexual addiction; God was there, but He did not provide a safe home for the client who was living in constant terror, who felt invisible and broken by the chaos of domestic violence. He was there, but the abuse still happened. In this context, it can be helpful to emphasize that faith is about ambiguity. In Kathleen Norris's (1998) book, *Amazing Grace*, she asserted that faith is not about certainty; rather, it is a decision to "keep your eyes open" (p. 169). When doing exposure-related work with clients (whether with formal exposure techniques such as prolonged exposure or more graduated and narrative-based exposure), during this phase of treatment the psychotherapist has to help the client hold that ambiguity as he or she tolerates the emotional pain of having eyes open. This phase of treatment is about finding, feeling, and reconstructing the trauma story.

Interventions that address the spiritual ruptures during this phase of treatment include the following: (a) Identifying the developmental trauma markers embedded in the client's images, stories, and metaphor. For example, the clinician may see a symbiotic coupling in the client's image of God, where God is all they need and there is minimal room for self-reflection or interpersonal relationships. This undifferentiated God–person relationship is a window into a detached/avoidant internal working model that prevents the client from being able to use relationships to work through the early developmental crisis of trust versus mistrust and subsequently creating a traumatic mile marker in the primary faith stage. This rupture presents itself symptomatically as a chronic state of hopelessness or helplessness that is rooted in distrust and a lack of safety. The fact that at this early stage of emotional, cognitive, and faith development there is no solidified sense of self to interact with God to promote change, the solution is often an affect-driven fixation or primary fantasy of God being a rescuer who will take away all the pain and replace that "missing piece" with a bulletproof armor that will shield the client from grief and more pain. The clinician should use the therapeutic dyad to offer a mirror that challenges this dissociative process while providing opportunities to use new resources to manage the pain behind that defense structure. Providing the client with resources will allow the clinician to move the client toward understanding the story embedded in their symbols and recurring metaphors.

(b) Managing the posttraumatic avoidance is another key intervention to facilitate trauma memory and emotional processing. This may include purposeful or more automatic evasion of emotions, thoughts, and physical symptoms. Or it may involve a broader form of overgeneralization where symbols, interpretations (e.g., God sends children to be raped to glorify Him), or a client's perception that God is withholding or sadistic become a foundational personal mythology (Courtois & Ford, 2013). This process involves a structured exposure exercise in which the client shares, and often reexperiences, the details of trauma narrative with the clinician.

In the case of Gigi, the clinician used a specific sequence of questions following each memory to understand how she experienced herself, other people, God, and the world as a result of the trauma ("I am _____. Other people are _____. God is _____. The world is _____. Therefore, I will _____."). This framework gave her a chance to revisit and reexamine the trauma memories. Helping Gigi understand and tolerate the story and the intense fear embedded in the grim reaper God image facilitated her understanding that she did not have to live under that reign of fear now. Titrating this exposure process to invite Gigi to move into her immobilizing fear challenges the body–brain registry that is indicating through sensations that there is danger. Levine (2010) identified this process as "uncoupling fear from immobility" (p. 86) so that the appropriate posttraumatic response of fear and helplessness can be differentiated from the biological response of immobility. The clinician should create a space where the client can organize the fragmented and painful life events into a coherent narrative that offers a picture of what was taken from him or her by the abuse in order to move through the pain toward a sense of personal meaning and purpose.

(c) Repositioning God as an ally or witness who grieves their pain is a necessary part of reconstructing the trauma narrative to facilitate opportunities to accelerate faith development and transform the damage trauma (soul murder) did to a survivor's spirit. What if God could function alongside the psychotherapist as an attachment figure who offered the client permission to "speak the unspeakable" (Herman, 1992, p. 175), a phrase Herman used to describe the psychotherapist role in this phase of treatment, without judgment?

The trauma-based expectations transferred onto the client's sense of faith and image of God create an IWM of personal unworthiness and fear of being punished by God. Courtois and Ford (2013) described transference issues as reactions originating from formative relational experiences with caretakers that have been internalized. This projection offers the psychotherapist a picture of a relational dilemma that occurred implicitly earlier in life that is outside of the client's awareness (p. 299). Those implicit messages or beliefs transferred onto the psychotherapist and God communicate important elements of the trauma story that may be too threatening to voice or unavailable because of dissociation. Just as the psychotherapist should expect to be drawn into posttraumatic and related abandonment and rejection reenactments, so is God.

The majority of complex trauma survivors have a fearful/avoidant attachment dynamic, both to people and to God, in which they vacillate along the stress response continuum of hyperarousal or fight–flight stress response to hypoarousal, an emotional deadness, or what Courtois and Ford (2013) metaphorically described as a breach or "void of the self" (p. 236) is important for psychotherapists as they work with clients to reconstruct and transform what sometimes seems like memory that is "wordless and static" (Herman, 1992, p. 175). On the low end of the spectrum, clients who are dealing with hypoarousal may experience emotional numbness and a disconnection from the felt experience of faith. If the breach or void is somatic, the client does not have the ability to feel or experience God enough to hear the internal whisper "But God" or, as another one of our other clients put it, the comforting energy that replaced the pain she felt in her heart. Consistent with the notion that faith is a visceral experience, Norris (1998) contended that faith is a constant energy that manifests with different degrees of intensity. For the client who lives in an emotional void, this energy can be a source of distress rather than an opportunity to connect to God or find another dimension to the story.

The other extreme of the spectrum involves hyperarousal, a scary place described by several authors as the "black hole" of trauma in which the survivor is stuck in a cycle of intense arousal in which escape is perceived as impossible, exacerbating feelings of fear and helplessness, and if not interrupted by a new action, bounces the nervous system back into hypoarousal (Levine, 2010; van der Kolk, 1996). Neuroscience has clearly linked this reactivity to a sensitized nervous system tasked with survival, but it is also a somatic narrative that paints a graphic picture of what it was like for the client to be imprisoned, trapped, and lost in the "breach." Feeling at the mercy of this terror is at the heart of the trauma. The critical clinical question here is how the client perceives God fitting into this horrifying narration. Does He fit into the part of the cycle where the client feels trapped or helpless, or is He part of the story that offers hope?

In Gigi's picture, the grim reaper is scary, a definitive symbol connected to her arousal and sense of entrapment, but that projection belongs somewhere else. Living with the reality that the person who inflicted this soul murder is not a sadistic God carrying a large scythe, clothed in a black cloak with a hood, but someone who was supposed to love and protect the client is a horrifying psychological and spiritual death that survivors have to grieve—it is much more horrifying than a fictive character created by a dissociative child self-state.

THE THIRD PHASE: THE THREE Rs OF RECONNECTION— REDEEMING, RECLAIMING, AND RECREATING

Judith Herman (1992) described this phase of treatment as *reconnection*, a place in recovery where survivors "come to terms with" (p. 196) their traumatic past and are able to envision a future that is separate and different from the past. This phase of treatment is about reclaiming what was taken by the trauma and developing a home base of self and with others; it is about learning to assert oneself and fight; it is about having a sense of self that is not defined by the trauma; it is being able to distinguish between healthy and unhealthy relationships and taking risks to be intimate with a person and God;

and finally, it is about the survivor discovering a personal calling that turns their personal hell into a source of hope and social advocacy (Herman, 1992).

Redemption: Connecting to a Larger Story

During this stage of healing, the individual trauma story connects to a more universal story. In the Christian faith tradition, the Easter story models this progression from undeserved pain and betrayal to an unspeakable and humiliating death to a transformed life that offered hope and transformation. Most faith-based clients have a person or a story in their theology that offers a picture of hope and healing. Maybe it is Gandhi, Martin Luther King, Jr., Mother Theresa, or a character from the Bible such as Mary, King David, or the Samaritan woman who connected to Jesus while embroiled in shame. Connecting our clients to these stories offers a larger perspective to understand that there is a beginning, middle, and end to a story that at some point arrived at, but also departed from, that heart-wrenching question of "Why?" Maybe it is a specific question directed to God, as it was for many of the previously mentioned clients, or a general inquiry regarding suffering that is more existential but just as developmentally derailing if there is not an expectation of redemption.

Redemption is a process of moving from something to something else; it is the act of taking back something that was wrongly taken from you (Wilkerson, 2011). The variable that drives this progression from slavery to freedom, an Old Testament analogy that parallels the complex trauma survivor's journey from experiencing life as a person who has been objectified to being someone who is able to hold the ambiguity embedded in the healing process, is community. Clinicians who can elicit faith-based stories from their clients can facilitate a broader perspective of what healing looks like for them. Some of our clients who are involved in 12-step fellowships and who are spiritual but not aligned with a specific faith tradition find this future-oriented focal point in the Alcoholics Anonymous promises, which begins with the statement, "If we are painstaking honest, we will be amazed by a new freedom and happiness, less regret and shame, more serenity and peace, less fear and economic security" (Wilkerson, 2011, pp. 83–84), and so forth. There is an emphasis on community ("we") and a focal point that inspires recovering people to actively move toward a healthy life.

Recreating Safety in Communities: "Tamar Speaks"

Several years ago in a training session of the Air Force Chaplain Corp on the impact of sexual assault, one of the officers challenged the notion that we have to work toward connection; he proposed that we begin the process of treatment by creating a community, a modern day church, that could surround survivors and *recreate* what it means to belong and have value. In my clinical practice, I (SVD) run a monthly community group called Tamar Speaks. The group was named after the biblical character Tamar, the daughter of King David, who was subjected to incest by her stepbrother and left without a voice. The story progressed with the family crumbling because of this violation while Tamar, the victim, was never heard from again. Her grief, like so many of the individuals we sit with, was disenfranchised. This community group offers women a space to reclaim their voice and in that process discover that they have something to offer other women. The group incorporates ritual, specific spiritual practices such as prayer and worship, movement, community activism, mentoring, and monthly discussion groups focused on a topic that integrates faith and trauma. Being a part of this process illustrates what is redemptive about community. These women are moving from isolation and despair to a place of perspective and hope. It is like Gigi said in her final statement after experiencing the validation of a pastor: I am family, people are mostly helpful, and although God remains questionable, I believe that I can be helped. Creating a Phase Three ritual that models what a healthy community can be offers a space where faith-based questions can be heard and the client's developing faith can tolerate both the grief embedded in the "But God" concept and the hope from other women who have walked through those stories but have experienced the freedom of recovery. We need to create an "And God" paradigm in which faith becomes a connector that brings community and survivors together in a way that is restorative.

Reclaiming the Sacred: Using Rituals to Symbolize Transformation

As a part of the Tamar Speaks program, we sponsored a 1-day retreat in the spring to bring survivors together to reflect on the impact of complex trauma. The clinician facilitating the retreat created a "wailing wall" for each of the women to memorialize the harm done by sexual violence and mourn the losses felt by those violations. This ritual symbolized bringing their hurt and questions to God. At the end of the ritual, the women had the opportunity to silently witness what other women wrote by walking from one end of the wall to other. The silence created a reverence and visibility for the wounds that survivors carry. The participants were a part of faith-based community that offered a positive identity or "home base" to struggle with those questions of personal worthiness while participating in a sacred ritual that highlighted stories of redemption that started with pain but were moving toward restoration. At the conclusion of the retreat, the women came together in small groups and wrote a prayer. The following is a prayer that Gigi wrote with two other women:

Changing Seasons
Just as the seasons change we recognize our own movement through the rhythms of life.
There is time for introspection and regeneration
There is time to push forward and acknowledge the sacredness and beauty of life.
Our hope is that we find healing in each other and the gathering here today.
We celebrate that life is a gift to be cherished
We have faith that healing is possible through patience and perseverance, through rain and sun.

REFERENCES

Bowlby, J. M. (1969). *Attachment*. New York, NY: Basic Books.

Brown, L. S. (2008). *Cultural competence in trauma therapy: Beyond the flashback*. Washington DC: American Psychological Association.

Carter, R. T. (2007). Racism and psychological and emotional injury: Recognizing and assessing race-based traumatic stress. *The Counseling Psychologist, 35,* 13–105. doi:10.1177/0011000006292033

Cloitre, M., Courtois, C. A., Ford, J. D., Green, B. L., Alexander, P., Briere, J., . . . Van der Hart, O. (2012). *The ISTSS expert consensus treatment guidelines for complex PTSD in adults*. Retrieved from http://www.istss.org/AM/Template.cfm?Section=ISTSS_Complex_PTSD_Treatment_Guidelines&Template=%2FCM%2FContentDisplay.cfm&ContentID=5185

Courtois, C. A., & Ford, J. D. (2009). *Treating complex traumatic stress disorders: An evidenced-based guide*. New York, NY: Guilford Press.

Courtois, C. A., & Ford, J. D. (2013). *Treatment of complex trauma: A sequenced, relationship-based approach*. New York, NY: Guilford Press.

Doehring, C. (1993). *Internal desecration—Traumatization and representations of God*. Lanham, MD: University Press of America.

Duckworth, M. P., & Follette, V. M. (Eds.). (2012). *Retraumatization: Assessment, treatment, and prevention*. New York, NY: Routledge, Taylor & Francis Group.

Erikson, E. H. (1993). *Childhood and society*. New York, NY: Norton.

Fowler, J. W. (1981). *Stages of faith: The psychology of human development and the quest for meaning*. San Francisco, CA: HarperCollins.

Fowler, J. W. (1993). Alcoholics Anonymous and faith development. In B. S. McCrady & W. R. Miller (Eds.), *Research on Alcoholics Anonymous: Opportunities and alternatives* (pp. 113–135). New Brunswick, NJ: Rutgers Center for Alcoholism Studies.

Fowler, J. W., & Dell, M. L. (2004). Stages of faith and identity: Birth to teens. *Child and Adolescent Psychiatric Clinics of North America, 13,* 17–33. doi:10.1016/ S1056-4993(03)00073-7

Freyd, J. (1998). *Betrayal trauma: The logic of forgetting childhood abuse.* Cambridge, MA: Harvard University Press.

Griffith, J. L. (2010). *Religion that heals, religion that harms: A guide for clinical practice.* New York, NY: Guilford Press.

Herman, J. L. (1992). *Trauma and recovery: The aftermath of violence from domestic abuse to political terror.* New York, NY: Basic Books.

Hesse, E., & Main, M. (2000). Disorganized infant, child, and adult attachment: Collapse in behavioral and attentional strategies. *Journal of the American Psychoanalytic Association, 48,* 1097–1127. doi:10.1177/00030651000480041101

Ibsen, H. (1896). *Works of Henrik Ibsen* (W. Archer, Trans.). New York, NY: Scribner.

Judith, A. (2004). *Eastern body, Western mind: Psychology and the chakra system as a path to the self.* New York, NY: Crown.

Kendall-Tackett, K. (2013). *Treating the lifetime health effects of childhood victimization* (2nd ed.). Kingston, NJ: Civic Research Institute.

Kira, I. A., Ashby, J. S., Lewandowski, L., Alaweh, A. W. N., Mohanesh, J., & Odnat, L. (2013). Advances in continuous traumatic stress theory: Traumatogenic dynamics and consequences of intergroup conflict: The Palestinian adolescents case. *Psychology, 4,* 396–409.

Levine, P. (2010). *In an unspoken voice: How the body releases trauma and restores goodness.* Berkeley, CA: North Atlantic Books.

Main, M., Hesse, E., & Kaplan, N. (2005). Predictability of attachment behavior and representational processes at 1, 6, and 19 years of age. In K. E. Grossmann, K. Grossmann, & E. Waters (Eds.), *Attachment from infancy to adulthood: The major longitudinal studies* (pp. 245–304). New York, NY: Guilford Press.

Norris, K. (1998). *Amazing grace: A vocabulary of faith.* New York, NY: Riverhead Books.

Pole, N. E., & Triffleman, E. (2010). Introduction to the special issue on trauma and ethnoracial diversity. *Psychological Trauma: Theory, Research, Practice, and Policy, 2,* 1–3. doi:10.1037/a0018979

Porges, S. W. (2011). *The polyvagal theory: Neurophysiological foundations of emotions, attachment, communication, self-regulation.* New York, NY: Norton.

Schore, A. N. (2003). *Affect regulation and the repair of the self.* New York, NY: Norton.

Shengold, L. (1999). *Soul murder revisited.* New Haven, CT: Yale University Press.

Soul. (n.d.) In *Merriam-Webster's online dictionary* (11th ed.). Retrieved from http:// www.merriam-webster.com/dictionary/soul

Triffleman, E. G., & Pole, N. (2010). Future directions in studies of trauma among ethnoracial and sexual minority samples: Commentary. *Journal of Consulting and Clinical Psychology, 78,* 490–497. doi:10.1037/a0020225

Van der Kolk, B. A. (1996). The body keeps score: Approaches to the psychology of posttraumatic stress disorder. In B. A. Van der Kolk, A. McFarlane, &

L. Weisaeth (Eds.), *Traumatic stress: The effects of overwhelming experience on mind, body and society* (pp. 214–241). New York, NY: Guilford Press.

Van Deusen, S. (n.d.). *Childhood trauma, attachment to God and psychological well-being* (Doctoral dissertation). Loyola University.

Wilkerson, M. (2011). *Redemption—Freed by Jesus from the idols we worship and the wounds we carry*. Wheaton, IL: Crossway.

Wilson, J. P. (2006). *The posttraumatic self: Restoring meaning and wholeness to personality*. New York, NY: Routledge.

Winnicott, D. W. (1963). *The maturational processes and the facilitating environment: Studies in the theory of emotional development*. London, England: Hogarth Press.

3

FIRST, DO NO MORE HARM: ETHICS OF ATTENDING TO SPIRITUAL ISSUES IN TRAUMA TREATMENT

CHRISTINE A. COURTOIS

Because most trauma involves an assault on the victim's spirit, identity, and self-worth, healing from trauma is fundamentally a spiritual process or a quest for spirituality involving a deep need for meaning and value (Barrett, 1999). Many traumatized individuals are dispirited by the assaults, abuses (i.e., physical, sexual, verbal, emotional), and the neglect and indifference they endured (or continue to endure) at the hands of other humans, some of whom are related to them as parents or through other blood ties or kinship, friendship, or professional and fiduciary associations. The latter group includes clergy and other representatives of faith traditions, and teachers, coaches, therapists, doctors, military commanders, and supervisors.

In consequence of their traumatic experiences, many victimized clients despair at ever being understood or being able to heal. Attention to how their spirit and spiritual beliefs were altered by the trauma is therefore well within the domain of their psychotherapy and is in the interest of healing, renewal,

http://dx.doi.org/10.1037/14500-004
Spiritually Oriented Psychotherapy for Trauma, D. F. Walker, C. A. Courtois, and J. D. Aten (Editors)

and transformation. Trauma-informed care has been developed and advocated in recent years, and attention to spiritual issues is overtly included. Evidence-based strategies are now available for the treatment of trauma symptoms. These can and should be applied with attention to the type of trauma and the treatment guidance for symptoms of classic and complex posttraumatic stress disorder (PTSD; Foa, Keane, Friedman, & Cohen, 2008; International Society for Traumatic Stress Studies, 2012) that is now available, as well as with attention to the *Preliminary Religious and Spiritual Intervention Guidelines* (Hathaway, 2009).

The focus of this chapter is twofold: (a) to present the ethical impera-tive to "do no more harm," and to include within it the necessity for includ-ing attention to spiritual issues, spirituality, and religion in the treatment of traumatized individuals; and (b) to describe some of the ethical risks and dilemmas that are relatively unique in trauma treatment and that can chal-lenge the psychotherapist's competence and personal worldview, including faith and spiritual beliefs. The essential intersection between the two areas of interest is explicitly acknowledged.

THE ETHICS OF DOING NO HARM AND PROVIDING TRAUMA-INFORMED CARE

Within psychology and allied helping professions, the process of how ethical principles are applied has been in flux, with more attention now given to contextual and situational or personal factors (Bennett et al., 2006). Attention to characteristics of the psychotherapist, taking account of per-sonal history (including the history of the trauma and whether it has been addressed and resolved), training, mental health and values (including spiri-tual beliefs and beliefs regarding attention to spiritual issues as a valid part of psychotherapy), and the need for mindfulness about the impact of these char-acteristics on ethical decision making are increasingly emphasized in ethics discussions. There is also a broad-based understanding that most psychother-apists want to engage in ethical practice. Yet, because ethics codes do not provide clear answers in all circumstances, psychotherapists can face many dilemmas about what is a best and least harmful course of action. What's more, there are times when ethics and legal obligations and advice are at odds with one another and it may be necessary to determine whether one is prominent over the other. I was once faced with my corporate attorney's objection to my providing information to a credentialing body about a psychotherapist's sexual transgression and subsequent plea of nolo contendere to second-degree sexual abuse. When informed about the ethical obligation to provide the informa-tion, the attorney yielded.

Within the subfield of traumatic stress, the vulnerability of traumatized clients to additional victimization outside and even within psychotherapy (as well as within other professional and social service contexts, including pastoral counseling and in religious congregations and communities) is now recognized. Therefore, to provide ethical treatment and do no more harm, psychotherapists and other professionals must be mindful of their own strengths and vulnerabilities as well as those of their traumatized clients, taking special care to consider contextual and situational or personal variables. These can create spiritual and value crises for the psychotherapist just as they can for the client, and these too require recognition and focus lest they lead the psychotherapist into as much despair as the client and result in major boundary violations.

In recognition of the number of survivor clients in the health care system and the transgressions that have so routinely attended their treatment, reform initiatives led by both consumer–client or survivors and professionals who have studied trauma and treated traumatized individuals have consolidated in recent years, all under the general rubric of trauma-informed care (Bloom, 2013; Bloom & Farragher, 2010, 2013; Harris & Fallot, 2001; Jennings, Morford, & Tregerman, 2007; Kezelman & Stavropoulos, 2012; Poole & Greaves, 2012). As the name suggests, *trauma-informed care* refers to mental health and medical care that includes knowledge and appreciation of traumatic experiences as highly relevant and influential in the development of many behavioral, mental health, and medical conditions. Treatment should be attuned to the needs of traumatized individuals whose presentation style and symptoms must not be stigmatized. Instead, the professional (along with support staff) is expected to approach clients from a position of respect and openness, with an understanding that symptoms may reflect the best attempt to cope with and to adapt to traumatic situations and relationships.

Attention is also given to the environment with the specific intention of providing as much safety, comfort, and stability as possible under the circumstances. In recognition that the traumatized have been "done to" by others in authority and are often deferential to them in a conditioned self-protective response, clients are encouraged to collaborate in their treatment through informed consent (and refusal) documents and detailed explanations of procedures before and as they are undertaken. In particular, any medical treatment that is invasive or causes physical pain should be undertaken with attention to the client or patient's comfort and well-being, at times involving modification of procedures and protocols. Trauma-informed care is a recommended approach to all clients and not only the traumatized; however, for the traumatized, its application is likely to make a major difference to how they are treated and how they respond.

FIVE ISSUES IN TRAUMA TREATMENT AND ETHICAL AND SPIRITUAL IMPLICATIONS

Five issues common to trauma treatment have been selected for discussion in general and with respect to their intersection with spiritual issues, with recommendations for their ethical management: (a) the competence and personal wellness of the psychotherapist, with attention to the spiritual impact, benefits, challenges, and consequences of working with trauma and the traumatized on the psychotherapist; (b) the psychotherapist's willingness to treat traumatized individuals, in general and with regard to their spiritual concerns, including his or her willingness to seek additional knowledge and consultation, supervision, and support as needed; (c) maintenance of professional boundaries and attention to issues of dual relationships, including attention to value conflicts, informed consent, and appropriate and considered self-disclosure on the part of the psychotherapist; (d) safety, risk management, and harmful religiosity, including how and when some of a client's religious beliefs or tenets are in conflict with personal safety and well-being; and (e) evidence-based practices and the available clinical consensus regarding the treatment of trauma and spirituality and spiritually based interventions.

Competence and Personal Wellness of the Psychotherapist

Because of the lack of inclusion of trauma in professional training curricula, psychologists and other professionals may not have the necessary knowledge, skill, or attitudinal competence to treat traumatized clients (per sections 2.01–2.06 of the *Ethical Principles of Psychologists and Code of Conduct* of the American Psychological Association, 2010). In the absence of formal training and under the press of caseloads that are replete with the traumatized, many have had to learn by "flying by the seat of their pants," a notoriously poor and inefficient way to learn that puts both client and psychotherapist at risk. Many practicing psychotherapists have recognized the need for additional training and have sought out specialized reading, consultation, and continuing education. Moreover, as discussed by Barrett (1999), Saakvitne, Gamble, Pearlman, and Lev (2000), and others who routinely treat trauma and provide training to psychotherapists, attention to its spiritual dimensions and impact on both the client and the psychotherapist is needed for comprehensive treatment because these issues are so prominent.

A similar situation within the professional training curriculum has occurred regarding attention to spiritual issues in general and in psychotherapy. Although still not included on a routine or requisite basis, attention to issues of spirituality and religiosity among psychotherapists has greatly increased in recent years because many have sought resources for their own spiritual development. Those treating trauma who recognized its personal impact on their worldview and life meaning (e.g., vicarious traumatization, described later) also sought out resources for themselves as they sought more holistic ways to treat clients. The focus on spirituality and religion is finding its way into education and training in a number of ways in specialized training programs or areas of emphasis and in continuing education offerings.

Barrett (1999) described the personal spiritual challenges she faced in the early years of her career specializing in treating traumatized individuals and their families. She first sought help for herself from clergy and other therapists and developed and deepened her own spiritual practice. She conducted exit and follow-up interviews with clients who had completed treatment, querying them about what was most helpful and what they would recommend for the continued development of her treatment model. Many spoke of the importance of discussing existential issues and concerns and making personal meaning of their adversities, of being with others (including the psychotherapist) who cared about them and did not hurt or use them and who offered support and community, and of personal transformation involving the resolution of spiritual dimensions of their injuries. With the information gleaned from her former clients and her own deepened spirituality, Barrett changed the orientation of her treatment model to explicitly (and with informed consent) incorporate discussion of spiritual issues and a number of spiritually oriented practices.

Challenges to the Psychotherapist's Competence

In treating complexly traumatized clients, psychotherapists are typically confronted with their many symptoms, including degree of life disruption, danger and chaos; emotional dysregulation and a lack of life skills; negative identity to the point of self-loathing and extreme shame; degree of emotional and spiritual pain, including despair and hopelessness; the maladaptive ways used to manage pain (e.g., addictions and compulsions; risky and dangerous behavior and personal disregard, personal and social alienation; violence or other means of harming others, self-injury, suicidality, being the most common); chronic sense of entrapment and personal disempowerment; multiple (and sometimes ongoing and escalating) revictimization (e.g., repeat victimizations by the original abuser, domestic violence, community assaults, torture); posttraumatic and dissociative symptoms; and lack of relational trust, resources, and supports. In addition, psychotherapists are emotionally challenged when they hear clients' often horrific stories of abuse and mistreatment, especially when committed by parents and others of significance.

If these were not enough, Loewenstein (1993) articulated some of the unique process and transference or relational challenges, including atypical (and often quite spontaneous) events, symptoms, and personal and interpersonal processes that occur within what he termed the *posttraumatic and dissociative matrices* of the treatment relationship. Clients can exhibit flashbacks and other reexperiencing phenomena; extreme numbing and dissociation, at times verging on catatonia; somatic symptoms associated with physiological hyperarousal, including agitation, startle responses, and conversion reactions; extreme mistrust (verging on paranoia) of the psychotherapist and other authority figures; extreme avoidance, hypoarousal, and splitting off of reality; anger and rage reactions; and idiosyncratic alterations in memory, identity, or personal consciousness, among many other manifestations.

In turn, these challenges can lead to a wide variety of countertransference responses, which when used productively can assist in understanding the client and when problematic can cause damage. Even experienced psychotherapists may find themselves feeling startled, shocked, powerless and overwhelmed, and unskilled (or "de-skilled") when faced with these stressful client processes and events. Psychotherapists who have little or no preparation, training, or experience with such posttraumatic and dissociative phenomena are often hard-pressed to remain steady and on-track in the treatment. Instead, they may overrespond by becoming enmeshed and doing too much, engaging in rescue behaviors, and not having appropriate boundaries and limitations in place. This has the often inadvertent effect of encouraging overdependence while not respecting or promoting the client's resilience, autonomy, or authority. The overinvolved response is especially likely in novice psychotherapists who feel compelled to help. Turkus (personal communication, 2012) labeled this process *vicarious indulgence*. It usually backfires when the psychotherapist becomes exhausted and depleted, resents the client's overdemands, and feels powerless. He or she may then act out in directly hostile or passive–aggressive ways.

In an alternative response, some psychotherapists underrespond by distancing, blaming, shaming, and ultimately rejecting the client, or by behaving aggressively in other ways (e.g., direct criticism and hostility, abandonment), in the process causing additional interpersonal and spiritual damage (Dalenberg, 2000; Wilson & Lindy, 1994; Wilson & Thomas, 2004). Psychotherapists are advised to be neither overindulgent nor underresponsive while maintaining awareness that their clients (even those who have detached/avoidant or fearful/avoidant attachment styles that obscure their attachment needs) are emotionally needy and dependent because of insecure early attachment relationships and subsequent abuse and neglect (Steele, Van der Hart, & Nijenhuis, 2001). Psychotherapists must provide their clients with a relational and emotional "safe haven" (Bowlby, 1988) from which to learn about themselves and their worlds (inner and outer). This does not require psychotherapists to be perfect but to be "good enough," as advised by Winnicott (1963) in his comments with regard to mothering. They must have some flexibility with regard to getting close, but not too close, to their clients—what has been called the *transference–countertransference dance* by some authors (Baker, 2003; Courtois & Ford, 2013). Psychotherapists' interactions with and attunement to their clients provide both a context and a catalyst for exploration of all issues (Kinsler, Courtois, & Frankel, 2009), including those having to do with spiritual beliefs and practices (whether these protected against or intensified the trauma) and the effect the trauma may have had on them in turn.

Challenges to the Psychotherapist's Self

Thus far, we have primarily discussed challenges to psychotherapists' technical competence in working with highly traumatized individuals within the relational matrices that are cocreated. Of course, competence does not only relate to professional training and proficiency but also to overall mental health status, emotional health, and personal wellness (including broad-based spiritual health, whatever the therapist's religious orientation and spiritual beliefs), including the ability to emotionally regulate and remain attuned and responsive when faced with the client's dysregulation or with other disruptions and challenges typical of this treatment. Psychotherapists' self-care has received considerable professional attention in recent years, and steps and strategies to maintain the psychotherapist's own physical and emotional health or wellness are now viewed as ethical imperatives that work against becoming burned-out and also against impairment (Baker, 2003; Norcross & Guy, 2007). Psychotherapists are advised to be attentive to life-stage and transition issues as they affect and are affected by professional roles and responsibilities and to make special self-care efforts when in the throes of personal or professional crises (especially in the case when a major loss is involved, including a significant illness or death or the breakup of a significant relationship or a marriage). Times of personal vulnerability require additional support and consultation, possibly including personal therapy, major schedule reduction or even a leave of absence, retirement, or the closing of a practice.

On another and related matter, psychotherapists have been found to undergo their own personal and worldview transformations in response to being shocked and overwhelmed as a result of exposure to traumatized client experiences, stories, symptoms, and relational processes. McCann and Pearlman (1990) were the first to discuss what they labeled *vicarious traumatization*. Per their constructivist self-development theory, they proposed that psychotherapists experience changes in their views of self and others (including frame of reference regarding worldview, identity, and spirituality) and in several primary domains of psychological needs (safety, trust, esteem, intimacy, and control) in parallel to the changes experienced by their traumatized clients. Pearlman and Caringi (2009) specifically mentioned challenges to psychotherapists' personal spirituality. Other writers have described similar responses as *secondary traumatization* or *secondary traumatic stress reactions* (Stamm, 1995), *compassion fatigue* (Figley, 1995), and *empathic strain* (Wilson & Lindy, 1994), which might involve or invoke challenges to spiritual beliefs and spiritual transformations, including cynicism and dispiritedness in reaction to exposure to exploitation and evildoing. Although McCann and Pearlman (1990) and Pearlman and Saakvitne (1995) regarded personal changes such as these as inevitable in work with trauma and as relatively permanent transformations, other writers are not as definite. All, however, write that it is helpful for psychotherapists to consider and anticipate changes such as these before they occur and to develop strategies for their management lest they change from being reactions to symptoms. Attention to spiritual health (broadly defined) as well as emotional health can serve to somewhat desensitize and immunize psychotherapists to the toll of working with trauma and the traumatized.

Secondary reactions can challenge psychotherapists' ability to function with appropriate empathy and to provide secure attachment for clients, with healthy boundaries in place (Wilson & Lindy, 1994; Wilson & Thomas, 2004). Like unmanaged countertransference (and in conjunction with it), unrecognized and unmanaged secondary reactions can negatively affect psychotherapists' judgment, causing them to make mistakes they might not make under different circumstances. These mistakes can subsequently lead to actions and reactions that are harmful to clients. Strategies for specifically identifying and dealing with vicarious trauma responses are available in Saakvitne and Pearlman (1996) and in other self-help resources such as those listed earlier.

One other personal reaction on the part of psychotherapists who work with traumatized populations deserves mention: posttraumatic growth and positive transformation. Some psychotherapists (especially those who are more experienced in their work with chronic and developmental trauma) have expressed feelings of gratitude, humility, and satisfaction, especially as clients recover (Sanness, 2012). Some have also expressed how their own capacity for tolerance and compassion and for resilience increased as a result (Werdel & Wicks, 2012) and how their spiritual beliefs and/or beliefs in the goodness of humans and the divine were strengthened (Barrett, 1999).

Empathy and Willingness to Treat

Unwillingness to treat the traumatized might be due to lack of information and training, as discussed earlier; however, it can also be the result of feelings of fear, horror, discomfort, aversion, and avoidance, all common societal reactions to which psychotherapists are not immune. As noted, a spectrum of countertransference responses have been identified, ranging from distancing, stigmatizing, and hostility, on the one hand, to overinvolvement, voyeurism or curiosity, intrusion, and enmeshment, on the other (Dalenberg, 2000; Pearlman & Saakvitne, 1995; Wilson & Lindy, 1994). Another issue of significance is that many psychotherapists have their own trauma histories, something that has not been sufficiently recognized or attended to until fairly recently (Pope & Feldman-Summers, 1992). Such a history can be an asset if the psychotherapist has addressed and resolved its aftereffects, yet it can be a serious impediment if he or she has not (Little & Hamby, 1996).

Still another issue resulting in aversion and unwillingness to treat has to do with the interpersonal and spiritual challenges presented by the traumatized. The ability to empathize with victims and survivors is essential to effective treatment (Wilson & Thomas, 2004), as is the ability to tolerate their stories and modes of interaction. If, for any reason, a psychotherapist cannot start from or return to a basis of empathy and general goodwill, becomes embroiled in an ongoing impasse, or has personal (including spiritual or faith-based) factors that impede his or her ability to continue treatment and to adequately maintain the relationship, expert consultation and supervision should be sought (Pearlman & Saakvitne, 1995). It is important for psychotherapists to self-assess (or to seek the assessment of trusted others) regarding their willingness or ability to treat. As noted, this is particularly crucial when they are dealing with serious and ongoing life stresses (e.g., illness, death or other losses, "sandwich generation" issues) or other matters (e.g., financial problems, addictions, compulsions) in their own lives. Their personal mental health and spiritual foundations might be shaken to the core in some circumstances. When this is the case, it may be necessary and the most ethical course of action to not treat a particular trauma client or client population, to stop a particular psychotherapy that has become problematic, or to take a sabbatical or leave of absence. Whatever course is chosen, suspension or termination of a treatment must be handled with great care so as not to cause additional distress (Saakvitne, Pearlman, & Courtois, 2008).

Psychotherapists are charged with not abandoning clients, and guarding against doing so is an ethical imperative. Problematic countertransference responses can result in treating clients with indifference and hostility, including but not limited to ending treatment abruptly without explanation or in ways that shame or blame, in the process causing additional distress as their most available resource is withdrawn. Psychotherapists do have the prerogative to end treatments that in their judgment are not effective or that involve major transgressions of the treatment contract and expected behavior or lack of motivation or responsibility on the part of the client; however, ending a treatment ethically is different from abandoning the client. Guidelines are available for terminating treatment in ways that are organized, transparent, and timely and that attend to the client's welfare, including detailed explanation of the reason for the termination and the provision of other resources.

Boundaries and Multiple Relationships

It is now well-recognized that working with survivors of interpersonal trauma presents more opportunities for boundary transgressions than with a more general treatment population (Bennett et al., 2006); thus, the maintenance of appropriate boundaries is essential. Trauma, by definition, violates the individual's psychological and physical boundaries, thereby disrupting personal security and safety. Individuals whose trauma symptoms are active and as yet unresolved are prone to illogically repeating or reenacting their trauma in an attempt at mastery and resolution. This occurs in psychotherapy as well as in other relationships (Chu, 1998). The adult survivor of childhood abuse (incest in particular) is especially at risk of multiple and/or abusive relationships, especially with authority figures. Paradoxically, yet understandably, survivors may play out a variety of conditioned roles because their experience has taught them that dual relationships are the norm and to be expected. They might even expect exploitation as an inevitable part of what is supposed to be a helping relationship (Courtois, 2010).

Attachment Difficulties and Boundary Challenges

Together with posttraumatic and dissociative symptoms, psychotherapists treating interpersonally traumatized clients should anticipate the playing out of a variety of attachment difficulties, relational styles, reenactments, and boundary challenges. These occur almost as a coded transmission of the "messages of abuse" learned by the client (Davies & Frawley, 1994; Pearlman & Courtois, 2005). Most often, trauma survivors approach relationships from a position of profound mistrust, wariness, and alienation, even when they are seemingly compliant and deferential. This can be disconcerting to the psychotherapist who is devoted to being a healer and, indeed, who has invested considerable time, energy, and expense in learning the skills and earning the credentials to be a helping professional. Psychotherapists should therefore be informed about challenges of this sort before they have to face them so as not to take them in an overly personal way. They should also be prepared to explain these relational stances and discuss them with the client in a joint effort to understand and interpret their emergence in enactments or other behaviors.

Multiple and Dual Relationships

Most important of all, psychotherapists must be prepared to avoid the potential harm and misuse involved in multiple or dual relationships (e.g., becoming friends and socializing, doing business with a client, accepting expensive gifts from a client, having a sexual relationship with a client, entering into a professional or close relationship with a client's friend or family member) by scrupulously maintaining appropriate professional boundaries. When psychotherapists provide a responsive and nonexploitive relationship in which clients can explore past and present, they simultaneously model and provide the conditions for personal and relational healing. In keeping with contemporary perspective on ethics, however, psychotherapists might engage in the occasional boundary crossing (as distinguished from boundary violation) with careful consideration of its potential impact and with open discussion with the client before and after it occurs (Bennett et al., 2006; Gutheil & Brodsky, 2008). For example, a psychotherapist might agree to attend a medical appointment with a phobic and terrified client after having discussed the implications of changing the usual treatment frame and setting. As with other interventions, the client should receive informed consent and the right to decide, and the intervention should be documented in the record.

A Well-Thought-Out Treatment Frame

The therapy frame ought to receive careful consideration and explanation at the start of treatment as it is used to establish its foundation. With regard to boundaries and limitations, it is recommended that psychotherapists start with tighter rather than looser boundaries, because it is easier to loosen them gradually over time as both parties get to know each other rather than having to tighten them up after they have been breached in some problematic way. A treatment contract that is organized around the treatment frame and includes information about mutual responsibilities, informed consent, confidentiality and its limitations, assessment and the development of treatment goals, therapist availability outside of session, scheduling, safety, and business issues is recommended by many professional organizations. In it, psychotherapists can also include information about their training, therapeutic orientation, experience, and how they work. This could incorporate such issues as the psychotherapist's religious affiliation or spiritual perspective and other issues of diversity and how they are brought to bear in treatment (see Chapter 5, this volume, for further discussion). These may be new areas for psychotherapists and trainees to consider. Supervisors might bring these issues to trainees' attention as they develop treatment contracts. The document is signed by the client to indicate agreement and understanding of its provisions and by the psychotherapist to indicate a clear mutual understanding that can be returned to in the event that questions arise.

Self-Disclosure by the Therapist

In many ways, personal self-disclosure by the psychotherapist is a boundary issue. Although some psychotherapists are more comfortable with self-disclosure than others (a stance that might be in keeping with and supported by their orientation and training as well as their personal preference and sense of privacy), caution regarding overdisclosing personal details is advised in most cases, particularly at the start of treatment. This may be especially pertinent in the treatment of trauma survivors because there are many hidden relational treatment traps and dilemmas involved in this issue, some of which involve ethics. Because dual relationships were the norm as part of the abuse, some clients start treatment with the expectation that, as they self-disclose, so will the therapist. They expect that as they learn all about the therapist's life and become involved in it, they and the therapist will become "best friends," a dual relationship at odds with ethics codes.

The disclosure of some information by the psychotherapist (e.g., training and credential or licensing status, treatment orientation, level of experience, and name, license number, and contact information of supervisor, in the event he or she is still under supervision) is a general requirement. Regarding other and more personal self-disclosure, it is helpful for psychotherapists to predetermine their general stance and comfort with various topics before they are asked about them. Areas of personal disclosure that psychotherapists can anticipate include but are not limited to the following: the quality of their upbringing and any personal abuse or trauma history; sexual orientation and functioning; relationship status; medical status; addiction history or recovery status; religious beliefs and spiritual orientation; name of partner or spouse sex; names and ages of children; home address; location of upcoming vacation; and a wide variety of other personal issues and preferences. Several guiding rules in making disclosures include determining whether doing so is in the interest of the client and is generally therapeutic, knowing that information once disclosed cannot be taken back, and assessing how the client asks for information and for what reason (e.g., with genuine curiosity and for a valid reason or with hostility, a sense of entitlement, a nonappreciation of boundaries, or as a way to "get at" the psychotherapist). Psychotherapists have to be especially circumspect and cautious in what they disclose when they feel pressured in either a hostile or a dependent way (or both).

Challenges of the Internet and Social Media

Over the past few years, additional challenges have emerged with the wealth of information now available on the Internet and on social media sites. Psychotherapists might anticipate these issues by addressing them in their treatment contract. It is worthwhile for them to consider a priori how they might nondefensively and educationally discuss boundaries and their management. In the digital age, younger clients in particular may have very different concepts of privacy (including no expectation of having any), and psychotherapists now face the prospect that their clients can learn a lot about them—including things they consider private and would not disclose—from online sites. Of course, the reverse is also true, and psychotherapists too can seek information on clients by conducting web searches. This has recently led to discussions in professional circles as to whether it is ethical for psychotherapists to seek information from outside sources apart from what is provided directly by the client and whether any searches and their results ought to be disclosed. A related issue has to do with what personal information psychotherapists post online. The current recommendation is for them to exercise discretion and to occasionally "Google" themselves to find out what is accessible on the Internet about them.

Dalenberg (2000) brought to light another aspect of psychotherapist self-disclosure in trauma treatment. She surveyed individuals who had completed trauma treatment to determine what aspects of treatment advanced it and what detracted from it. Volunteer respondents reported that they were most assisted when psychotherapists offered emotional self-disclosure "in the moment." Because many developmentally traumatized clients have had little by way of emotional education—including encouragement to feel, identify, name, and regulate feelings on the basis of attunement by and reflection of primary attachment figures—they may be greatly confused about their own feelings and those of others. What's more, the accuracy or reality of their feelings may have been challenged or suppressed as part of their dysfunctional environment, so they cannot rely on their feelings or easily read those expressed by others, including psychotherapists.

Emotional openness and a willingness to share and discuss feelings on the therapist's part can be helpful in reversing past (and sometimes present) invalidation and in encouraging clients to explore their feelings and their authenticity and to express them. This then extends to the impressions they have regarding the feelings of others, including the psychotherapist's. Having a therapist who is available "in the moment" and who shares his or her responses and feelings can provide valuable modeling and in vivo experiencing. On the basis of this and similar findings, Dalenberg (2000) and other writers have suggested that, in the treatment of developmental trauma in particular, the psychotherapist show a degree of emotional transparency to assist the client in learning about personal emotions and responses and accurately reading those of others.

Unmet Dependency Needs and Individuation

Psychotherapists must take care not to impose their values or orientations (spiritual or otherwise) on their clients as part of the process. Because some of these clients have an external locus of control, including a highly honed recognition of how to please or be acceptable to others as well as high level of unmet dependency needs, they may comply with the perspective and values of others without regard to their own. Psychotherapists must respect their clients' viewpoints, beliefs, and diversity and seek to assist in clarifying them when there is uncertainty. Also, as many traumatized clients are dissociative, a process that can make them more prone to suggestion, psychotherapists must scrupulously avoid using approaches that are controlling, authoritarian, intimidating, or overly directive (Courtois, 1999). Only if the client is in some sort of severe danger would the psychotherapist be justified in being highly directive, yet it still behooves them to resist an authoritarian approach and to maintain as much collaboration with the client as possible.

From another perspective, Knapp, Lemoncelli, and VandeCreek (2010) discussed the ethical challenges that can occur when clients' religious beliefs appear to harm their well-being. Griffith (2010) also wrote about how religion can harm as well as heal, and provided guidance for clinical practice. Research studies have generally found that religious beliefs, values, and practices are associated with good mental health (Galen & Kloet, 2011), so it may not be typical for them to be associated with distress and dysfunction. However, as previously noted, they may contribute to family or social problems in a number of ways by being at odds with client well-being or the welfare of children or other vulnerable persons. Knapp and colleagues recommended responses in such circumstances, including engaging in respectful conversations with clients about their religious beliefs (with the recognition that some may resist discussing their beliefs in any detail because they do not trust psychotherapists to understand or accept them), clarifying them, and at times challenging them by discussing their implications or outcomes or by providing expanded or alternative perspectives. This may be especially important for clients who were raised or remain in highly rigid fundamentalist religions that limit relativistic thinking and perspectives and that emphasize obedience and unquestioning acceptance.

Safety and Risk Management

It is tragic that victims of interpersonal trauma (especially when it occurs over the course of childhood and/or involves rape and other forms of sexual assault) are much more vulnerable than the general population to repeat harm and revictimization, both from self and from others. A serious trauma history and diagnoses of PTSD and dissociative disorders along with the various common comorbidities, particularly major and recurrent depressive disorder, may create a "perfect storm" for self-injury and suicidality as well as for many other problems. In some cases, in identification with the perpetrator, some clients pose emotional and physical danger to others, including psychotherapists (see Chapter 12 for a case description of such a client). In consequence, clients with trauma histories carry above average risk, of which the treating psychotherapist ought to be generally aware and prepared for. This suggests the need for skills in the assessment and management of crises and in ongoing safety planning (Brand, 2001). To work with this population and issues of violence and life threat, psychotherapists must have some degree of desensitization to and tolerance of these issues, be able to conduct risk and violence assessments, and know when and how to appropriately and sensitively intervene, including when to hospitalize or to call the police. The psychotherapist must maintain awareness that, although he or she is responsible for identifying and managing the client's risk, it is the client who is ultimately responsible for the maintenance of personal safety, for the decision to stay alive, and for not aggressing against others (Chu, 1988). Specialized and updated information on suicide and other forms of risk and their management is a necessity for any psychotherapist working with traumatized clients.

Pertaining to the focus of this chapter on spirituality and spiritual issues as they relate to treatment of traumatized individuals, psychotherapists should ascertain whether anything in the client's faith tradition or its teachings is related to ongoing risk. Griffith (2010) described a number of ways that religious life can propel suffering and be destructive. Additional examples are given throughout this volume of how religious teachings and beliefs can be used to support spouse abuse and other forms of violence and mistreatment. When religion is misused in this way, the client must be assisted in ascertaining whether safety is possible and in weighing options. Involving clergy can be helpful as long as he or she does not endorse the use of religious beliefs or tenets in support of violence and does not counsel that the victim should stay in an abusive relationship no matter what.

The loss of sustaining beliefs (e.g., in the goodness of others, in spiritual and faith traditions, or in a beneficent God, or the loss of belief in and connection to a deity) that accompanies traumatization for some victims or the development of beliefs that bad things happened because God was punishing the individual for his or her transgressions or badness can be debilitating. For some clients, it fuels their shame, guilt, despair, and hopelessness that undergird suicidality and risk taking. For others, religious beliefs and spirituality offer protective factors against suicide or contribute to the process of healing following a suicide attempt (Colucci & Martin, 2008). Engaging the client in discussions about spiritual and existential issues and challenging maladaptive or erroneous patterns of thinking can enable the client to develop a different meaning (see Chapter 6, this volume), something that might in turn undercut his or her suicidality. As they feel better about themselves and others, and as they otherwise come to a new understanding of what happened to them and why and resolve the associated shame and self-blame, their symptoms may abate and their anguish diminish.

Application of Evidence-Based Approaches in Treating Traumatized Patients

Increasingly, psychotherapists are called on to be knowledgeable about and to apply evidenced-based treatments, that is, those that rely on research findings, clinical consensus, and client values (American Psychological Association Presidential Task Force on Evidence-Based Practice, 2006). An evidence base is now available and growing for the treatment of the symptoms of PTSD (Foa et al., 2008) and complex traumatic stress disorders (Courtois & Ford, 2009, 2013) and for spiritually oriented interventions (Richards & Worthington, 2010), although much research is still needed. Concerning the treatment of trauma and related symptoms of PTSD, cognitive behavior therapy (CBT; particularly prolonged exposure), cognitive processing therapy (Resick & Schnicke, 1993), and eye-movement desensitization and reprocessing (Shapiro, 2001) have the highest degree of endorsement to date. Despite this, their wholesale applicability across different types of trauma response has been questioned by psychotherapists who have suggested that, for complex trauma in particular, these techniques may be overwhelming for the client, especially if applied prematurely in the early stage of treatment without adequate attention to safety and capacity for self-regulation or if applied by a therapist without appropriate clinical training and experience.

The implication for the ethical treatment of survivors is that the psychotherapist must stay up-to-date with treatment guidelines and treatment efficacy studies and carefully consider various available techniques and whether they are effective for their particular client as they plan and implement treatment. Books such as *Effective Treatments for PTSD: Treatment Guidelines From the International Society for Traumatic Stress Studies* (Foa et al., 2008) and *Treating Complex Traumatic Stress Disorders: An Evidence-Based Guide* (Courtois & Ford, 2009) and guidelines for trauma treatment now available from a variety of major professional organizations (American Psychiatric Association, 2004; Institute of Medicine of the National Academies, 2006; International Society for the Study of Dissociation, 2005 [http://www.isstd.org]) should be consulted as treatment foundations. Specific strategies and procedures should be applied according to the needs and capacities of the client and the training and experience of the psychotherapist.

This same guidance pertains to spiritually oriented practices or interventions (e.g., spiritual assessments; see Chapter 4, this volume)—consulting with or referring to spiritual leaders, teaching spiritual concepts, encouraging forgiveness, discussing scriptures, teaching mindfulness meditation, praying with or privately for clients—that respect the healing potential of clients' spiritual beliefs and faith traditions. A number of different psychological orientations have been integrated with spiritual perspectives and interventions (Sperry &

Shafranske, 2005). Richards and Worthington (2010) surveyed six available outcome reviews of research. They concluded that the six reviews were consistent in finding specific support for Christian and Muslim forms of cognitive (and rational emotive) psychotherapy for depression and anxiety and that preliminary evidence supports the efficacy of a variety of other types of spiritually oriented psychotherapies. It is heartening to see more research on spiritual issues as related to psychotherapy in professional journals; yet more is needed pertaining to spiritual treatments for the traumatized, especially traumatized children (Bryant-Davis et al., 2012). Some therapists have been creatively integrating treatments that have an established evidence base (e.g., trauma-focused CBT; Cohen, Deblinger, & Mannarino, 2005) with spiritual issues and practices (Walker, Reese, Hughes, & Troskie, 2010), a likely forerunner of similar efforts in the future.

In providing spiritually oriented treatment for trauma, psychotherapists should be aware that little evidence is as yet available but that these issues are on researchers' radars because the need is clear. In terms of ethical behavior regarding treatment of traumatized individuals, psychotherapists must take it on themselves to stay abreast of the emerging literature on innovative treatments and their empirical support. The use of any technique, whether supported by research or not, requires that the client be given information on which to base informed consent and refusal, including information about its evidence base.

REFERENCES

American Psychiatric Association. (2004). *Practice guideline for the treatment of patients with acute stress disorder and posttraumatic stress disorder*. Washington, DC: Author.

American Psychological Association. (2010). *Ethical principles of psychologists and code of conduct (2002, Amended June 1, 2010)*. Retrieved from http://www.apa.org/ethics/code/principles.pdf

American Psychological Association Presidential Task Force on Evidence-Based Practice. (2006). *Evidence-based practice in psychology*. Retrieved from http://www.apa.org/practice/resources/evidence/evidence-based-statement.pdf

Baker, E. K. (2003). *Caring for ourselves: A therapist's guide to personal and professional well-being*. Washington, DC: American Psychological Association.

Barrett, M. J. (1999). Healing from trauma: The quest for spirituality. In F. Walsh (Ed.), *Spiritual resources in family therapy* (pp. 135–150). New York, NY: Guilford Press.

Bennett, B. E., Bricklin, P. M., Harris, E., Knapp, S., VandeCreek, L., & Youngren, J. N. (2006). *Assessing and managing risk in psychological practice: An individualized approach*. Rockville, MD: American Psychological Association Insurance Trust. doi:10.1037/14293-000

Bloom, S. L. (2013). *Creating sanctuary: Toward the evolution of sane societies*. New York, NY: Routledge. doi:10.1093/acprof:oso/9780199796366.001.0001

Bloom, S. L., & Farragher, B. (2010). *Destroying sanctuary: The crisis in human service delivery systems*. New York, NY: Oxford University Press.

Bloom, S. L., & Farragher, B. (2013). *Restoring sanctuary: A new operating system for trauma-informed systems of care*. New York, NY: Oxford University Press. doi:10.1093/acprof:oso/9780199796366.001.0001

Bowlby, J. (1988). *A secure base: Clinical applications of attachment theory*. London, England: Routledge.

Brand, B. (2001). Establishing safety with patients with dissociative identity disorder. *Journal of Trauma & Dissociation, 2*(4), 133–155. doi:10.1300/J229v02n04_07

Bryant-Davis, T., Ellis, M. U., Burke-Maynard, E., Moon, N., Counts, P. A., & Anderson, G. (2012). Religiosity, spirituality, and trauma recovery in the lives of children and adolescents. *Professional Psychology: Research and Practice, 43*, 306–314. doi:10.1037/a0029282

Chu, J. A. (1988). Ten traps for psychotherapists in the treatment of trauma survivors. *Dissociation: Progress in the Dissociative Disorders, 1*(4), 24–32.

Chu, J. A. (1998). *Rebuilding shattered lives: The responsible treatment of complex posttraumatic and dissociative disorders*. New York, NY: Wiley.

Cohen, J., Deblinger, D., & Mannarino, A. (2005). *Trauma-focused cognitive-behavioral therapy*. New York, NY: Guilford Press.

Colucci, E., & Martin, G. (2008). Religion and spirituality along the suicidal path. *Suicide and Life-Threatening Behavior, 38*, 229–244. doi:10.1521/suli.2008.38.2.229

Courtois, C. A. (1999). *Recollections of sexual abuse: Treatment principles and guidelines*. New York, NY: Norton.

Courtois, C. A. (2010). *Healing the incest wound: Adult survivors in therapy* (2nd ed.). New York, NY: Norton.

Courtois, C. A., & Ford, J. D. (Eds.). (2009). *Treating complex traumatic stress disorders: An evidence-based guide*. New York, NY: Guilford Press. doi:10.1037/e608902012-109

Courtois, C. A., & Ford, J. D. (2013). *Treatment of complex trauma: A sequenced, relationship-based approach*. New York, NY: Guilford Press.

Dalenberg, C. J. (2000). *Countertransference and the treatment of trauma*. Washington, DC: American Psychological Association. doi:10.1037/10380-000

Davies, J., & Frawley, M. G. (1994). *Treating the adult survivor of childhood sexual abuse: A psychoanalytic perspective*. New York, NY: Basic Books.

Figley, C. R. (Ed.). (1995). *Compassion fatigue: Coping with secondary traumatic stress disorder in those who treat the traumatized*. Philadelphia, PA: Brunner/Mazel.

Foa, E., Keane, T. R., Friedman, M. J., & Cohen, J. A. (2008). *Effective treatments for PTSD: Practice guidelines from the International Society for Traumatic Stress Studies* (2nd ed.). New York, NY: Guilford Press.

Galen, L. W., & Kloet, J. D. (2011). Mental well-being in the religious and the non-religious: Evidence for a curvilinear relationship. *Mental Health, Religion & Culture, 14*, 673–689. doi.org/10.1080/13674676.2010.510829

Griffith, J. L. (2010). *Religion that heals, religion that harms: A guide for clinical practice.* New York, NY: Guilford Press.

Gutheil, T. G., & Brodsky, A. (2008). *Preventing boundary violations in clinical practice.* New York, NY: Guilford Press.

Harris, M., & Fallot, R. D. (2001). *Using trauma theory to design service systems.* San Francisco, CA: Jossey-Bass.

Hathaway, W. L. (2009, October). *Proposed practice guidelines for clinical work with religious and spiritual issues.* Paper presented at the Annual Convention of the American Psychological Association, Toronto, Ontario, Canada.

Institute of Medicine of the National Academies. (2006). *Posttraumatic stress disorder: Diagnosis and assessment.* Washington, DC: The National Academies Press.

International Society for the Study of Dissociation. (2005). Guidelines for treating dissociative identity disorder in adults. *Journal of Trauma & Dissociation, 6*(4), 69–149.

International Society for Traumatic Stress Studies. (2012). *The ISTSS expert consensus treatment guidelines for complex PTSD in adults.* Retrieved from http://www.istss.org/AM/Template.cfm?Section=ISTSS_Complex_PTSD_Treatment_Guidelines&Template=%2FCM%2FContentDisplay.cfm&ContentID=5185

Jennings, A., Morford, K., & Tregerman, R. (2007). *Models for developing trauma-informed behavioral health systems and trauma-specific services.* Bethesda, MD: National Center for Trauma-Informed Care, Center for Mental Health Services, Substance Abuse and Mental Health, U.S. Department of Health and Human Services.

Kezelman, C., & Stavropoulos, P. (2012). *"The last frontier": Practice guidelines for treatment of complex trauma and trauma informed care and service delivery.* Kiribilli, Australia: Adults Surviving Child Abuse.

Kinsler, P. J., Courtois, C. A., & Frankel, A. S. (2009). Therapeutic alliance and risk management. In C. A. Courtois & J. D. Ford (Eds.), *Treating complex traumatic stress disorders: An evidence-based guide* (pp. 183–201). New York, NY: Guilford Press.

Knapp, S., Lemoncelli, J., & VandeCreek, L. (2010). Ethical responses when patients' religious beliefs appear to harm their well-being. *Professional Psychology: Research and Practice, 41*, 405–412. doi:10.1037/a0021037

Little, L., & Hamby, S. L. (1996). Impact of a psychotherapist's sexual abuse history, gender, and theoretical orientation on treatment issues related to childhood sexual abuse. *Professional Psychology: Research and Practice, 27*, 617–625. doi:10.1037/0735-7028.27.6.617

Loewenstein, R. J. (1993). Posttraumatic and dissociative aspects of transferences and countertransference in the treatment of multiple personality disorder.

In R. P. Kluft & C. G. Fine (Eds.), *Clinical perspectives on multiple personality disorder* (pp. 51–86). Washington, DC: American Psychiatric Association.

McCann, I. L., & Pearlman, L. A. (1990). Vicarious traumatization: A framework for understanding the psychological effects of working with victims. *Journal of Traumatic Stress, 3,* 131–149. doi:10.1007/BF00975140

Norcross, J. C., & Guy, J. D. (2007). *Leaving it at the office: A guide to therapist self-care.* New York, NY: Guilford Press.

Pearlman, L. A., & Caringi, J. (2009). Living and working self-reflectively to address vicarious trauma. In C. A. Courtois & J. D. Ford (Eds.), *Treating complex traumatic stress disorders: An evidence-based guide* (pp. 202–224). New York, NY: Guilford Press.

Pearlman, L. A., & Courtois, C. A. (2005). Clinical applications of the attachment framework: Relational treatment of complex trauma. *Journal of Traumatic Stress, 18,* 449–459. doi.org/10.1002/jts.20052

Pearlman, L. A., & Saakvitne, K. W. (1995). *Trauma and the psychotherapist: Countertransference and vicarious traumatization in psychotherapy with incest survivors.* New York, NY: Norton.

Poole, N., & Greaves, L. (2012). *Becoming trauma informed.* Toronto, Ontario, Canada: Centre for Addiction and Mental Health.

Pope, K. S., & Feldman-Summers, S. (1992). National survey of psychologists' sexual and physical abuse history and their evaluation of training and competence in these areas. *Professional Psychology: Research and Practice, 23,* 353–361. doi:10.1037/0735-7028.23.5.353

Resick, P. A., & Schnicke, M. K. (1993). *Cognitive processing therapy for rape victims: A treatment manual.* Thousand Oaks, CA: Sage.

Richards, P. S., & Worthington, E. L. Jr. (2010). The need for evidence-based, spiritually oriented psychotherapies. *Professional Psychology: Research and Practice, 41,* 363–370. doi:10.1037/a0019469

Saakvitne, K. W., Gamble, S. G., Pearlman, L. A., & Lev, B. T. (2000). *Risking connection: A training curriculum for working with survivors of childhood abuse.* Lutherville, MD: Sidran Press.

Saakvitne, K. W., & Pearlman, L. A. (1996). *Transforming the pain: A workbook on vicarious traumatization.* New York, NY: Norton.

Saakvitne, K. W., & Pearlman, L. A., & Courtois, C. A. (2008, August). *Termination in long-term trauma treatment.* Paper presented at the 116th Annual Convention of the American Psychological Association, Boston, MA.

Sanness, K. J. (2012). *Predictors and moderators of difficulties and coping for trauma therapists* (Unpublished doctoral dissertation). The George Washington University, Washington, DC.

Shapiro, F. (2001). *Eye movement desensitization and reprocessing: Basic principles, protocols, and procedures* (2nd ed.). New York, NY: Guilford Press.

Sperry, L., & Shafranske, E. P. (Eds.). (2005). *Spiritually oriented psychotherapy*. Washington, DC: American Psychological Association. doi:10.1037/10886-000

Stamm, B. H. (Ed.). (1995). *Secondary traumatic stress: Self-care issues for psychotherapists, researchers, and educators*. Baltimore, MD: Sidran Press.

Steele, K., Van der Hart, O., & Nijenhuis, E. R. S. (2001). Dependency in the treatment of complex posttraumatic stress disorder & dissociative disorders. *Journal of Trauma & Dissociation, 2*(4), 79–116. doi:10.1300/J229v02n04_05

Walker, D. F., Reese, J. B., Hughes, J. P., & Troskie, M. J. (2010). Addressing religious and spiritual issues in trauma-focused cognitive behavior therapy for children and adolescents. *Professional Psychology: Research and Practice, 41*, 174. doi:10.1037/a0017782

Werdel, M. B., & Wicks, R. J. (2012). *Primer on posttraumatic growth: An introduction and guide*. New York, NY: Wiley.

Wilson, J. P., & Lindy, J. D. (Eds.). (1994). *Countertransference in the treatment of PTSD*. New York, NY: Guilford Press.

Wilson, J. P., & Thomas, R. B. (2004). *Empathy in the treatment of trauma and PTSD*. New York, NY: Routledge.

Winnicott, D. W. (1963). The development of the capacity for concern. *Bulletin of the Menninger Clinic, 27*, 167–176.

4

RELIGIOUS AND SPIRITUAL ASSESSMENT OF TRAUMA SURVIVORS

P. SCOTT RICHARDS, RANDY K. HARDMAN, TROY LEA,
AND MICHAEL E. BERRETT

The purpose of this chapter is to describe a rationale and approach for assessing religion and spirituality in trauma psychotherapy. We begin by discussing why the assessment of the spiritual dimension of trauma survivors' lives is crucial for effective treatment. Next, we describe a multilevel, multi-dimensional approach to assessment and offer some process suggestions and clinical questions that can facilitate a spiritual assessment. We then discuss spiritual issues that may be relevant in the treatment of trauma survivors, as well as several standardized religious and spiritual measures that can be helpful in assessment and outcome research. We conclude with a case study that demonstrates the significance of assessing religion and spirituality in trauma psychotherapy.

http://dx.doi.org/10.1037/14500-005
Spiritually Oriented Psychotherapy for Trauma, D. F. Walker, C. A. Courtois, and J. D. Aten (Editors)

RATIONALE FOR CONDUCTING A SPIRITUAL ASSESSMENT

Assessment is an important first step in the treatment of traumatized individuals. A general spiritual assessment should be included as part of the overall psychosocial assessment. With clients with established religious beliefs and faith traditions and those who indicate a desire or need to work on spiritual issues in treatment, a much more detailed assessment is in order and is discussed in the remainder of this chapter. Whether more general or more detailed, the spiritual assessment should be conducted with attention to the guidance on trauma assessment provided by various authors (Briere, 2004; Carlson, 1997; Wilson & Keane, 2004) and in the recently completed guidelines provided by the Division of Psychological Trauma (Division 56) of the American Psychological Association (2009). This guidance stresses the need for awareness of the vulnerability of trauma survivors.

Assessment (like treatment) must be conducted with sensitivity to the pain and other emotions that are often unearthed when asking about trauma. Some individuals can describe what happened to them without a great deal of emotion, whereas others may decompensate because of the intensity of their emotional response. As a result, careful pacing and assessment of ongoing response is recommended—including stopping if the client cannot be restabilized. Assessors should also be knowledgeable about the possibility of delayed reactions to disclosures made as part of the assessment; they should advise the client about them at its conclusion and about how to reach the assessor in the event that the reactions become overwhelming. Finally, to determine symptoms and diagnosis, assessment might include the use of psychological instruments, measures, and interviews. The assessor should be familiar with the more established instruments such as the Minnesota Multiphasic Personality Inventory—2 (Butcher, Dahlstrom, Graham, Tellegen, & Kaemmer, 1989) and the Millon Clinical Multiaxial Inventory–III (Millon, 1994) and be aware that these were not normed on trauma survivors; thus, their use should be supplemented with those more specifically normed—for example, the Trauma Symptom Inventory (Briere, 1995). Short, specialized instruments are also available for the screening and diagnosis of posttraumatic stress disorder and other trauma-related disorders (e.g., the Clinician-Administered Posttraumatic Stress Disorder Scale [Blake et al., 1995]; Dissociative Experiences Scale [Bernstein & Putnam, 1986]).

A spiritual assessment, as the term implies, can help therapists determine whether the client has a particular religion or faith tradition while assessing its significance, including the ways in which the trauma may have injured the client's spirituality and their posttraumatic spiritual needs. Moreover, it can help identify ways that clients' spirituality may be a resource in treatment and healing. Richards and Bergin (2005) suggested five additional reasons why psychotherapists should conduct a spiritual assessment. All of these suggestions are applicable when working with trauma survivors. A spiritual assessment can help psychotherapists

- better understand clients' worldviews, including their religious affiliation if they have one, thereby enabling them to treat clients in a more culturally sensitive and ethical manner;
- understand in what ways clients' spiritual beliefs are congruent, or in conflict, with those of the therapist;
- clarify whether religion and associated beliefs have a healthy or unhealthy influence in clients' lives and what impact they have on their presenting problems and disturbance;
- ascertain whether clients have unresolved spiritual doubts, concerns, or needs they wish to address in therapy;
- find out whether clients' religious and spiritual beliefs and community can offer help and support during treatment and recovery; and
- decide whether there are spiritual interventions that can be used in the course of treatment.

A spiritual assessment is an essential ingredient in establishing a spiritually safe and open therapeutic environment because many religious clients distrust mental health professionals and fear that they will fail to understand and respect their religious beliefs and values (Richards & Bergin, 2000; Worthington, Kurusu, McCullough, & Sanders, 1996). They also often do not know whether it is appropriate and safe to discuss religious and spiritual issues as a part of psychotherapy (Richards & Bergin, 2005). For these reasons, we recommend that psychotherapists explicitly inform clients during intake procedures that it is appropriate to discuss religious and spiritual issues during treatment, should they desire. Psychotherapists can also help create a safe environment for discussions about spirituality by including questions about clients' religious backgrounds and spirituality during the assessment process. Conducting a sensitive and effective spiritual assessment provides psychotherapists with an opportunity to affirm the relevance and value of clients' religion and spirituality for the therapeutic process. In the next several sections, we describe the process of conducting detailed spiritual assessments with trauma survivors. We illustrate the process with the case study of Rebecca.

CREATING A SAFE CONTEXT FOR A SPIRITUAL ASSESSMENT

The assessment and treatment phases of psychotherapy, along with the establishment of the treatment relationship, are interconnected, complementary, and nonlinear (see Courtois & Ford, 2013). From the time of the first contact and the preliminary assessment, efforts are directed toward establishing a trusting and safe therapeutic relationship to counteract the effects of the trauma, especially important when it was interpersonal and involved betrayal (see Chapters 1 and 2, this volume). In treating traumatized individuals, the processes of relationship establishment and assessment can be therapeutic in themselves. They also create the context for the implementation of ethically sensitive and therapeutically effective interventions. In addition, they establish the basis for conducting a spiritual assessment after determining its importance to the client and ascertaining that the client is open to discussing spiritual issues during treatment.

Conducting a spiritual assessment also gives psychotherapists opportunities to listen to the language of clients' spirituality, crucial for understanding their spiritual framework. We have been fascinated with the words and language clients use when describing their spirituality; thus, we recommend paying special attention to this dimension when conducting a spiritual assessment in order to more fully understand clients' worldviews, personal values, and sense of identity. Such understandings are essential for establishing a trusting and positive working alliance.

Conducting a spiritual assessment that shows an interest in clients' spiritual beliefs also gives psychotherapists an opportunity to communicate their desire to understand their clients and to let their clients know that they care about all aspects of their lives. Caring should be expressed carefully, however, because it is contrary to what clients experienced during their trauma, when they may have been objectified or depersonalized, and they may have great difficulty accepting it, at least initially. In contrast, the psychotherapist's caring and concern demonstrate to clients that how they feel, what they think, and what the trauma means to them are important. These are healing messages, the cornerstone of a therapeutic alliance. Even when asking assessment questions, psychotherapists can communicate caring and compassion. We recommend that, rather moving from question to question in a rote manner, psychotherapists on occasion might linger a bit, process a little deeper, and communicate empathy and caring. By taking the time to express empathy, psychotherapists foster a climate and a relationship that both convey emotional safety and healing. This approach takes time but opens the door to explorations of sacred spiritual matters that are relevant to trauma survivors' healing and growth.

When psychotherapists conduct spiritual assessments, we recommend that they seek and remain open to spiritual impressions and insights about their clients. *Meta-empathy* is the capacity to receive impressions and insights about clients that go beyond ordinary clinical hypothesizing or hunches (Richards & Bergin, 2005). Psychotherapists from a variety of spiritual traditions have reported that they at times experience intuitive, inspirational insights that deepen and clarify their understandings of clients' presenting problems and clinical issues (Chamberlain, Richards, & Scharman, 1996; O'Grady & Richards, 2010; West, 2000). In this sense, therefore, conducting a spiritual assessment involves much more than simply asking diagnostic questions and administering and interpreting standardized measures of client functioning. It also involves using one's own sense of spirituality as another tool to promote healing. During sessions therapists who are in tune with their own spirituality may have intuitive insights from moment to moment about assessment questions that are important to ask clients. Nonreligious therapists may find that tuning into their own personal sense of compassion, respectfulness, and kindness helps them better understand and validate the spiritual importance of clients' stories.

During a spiritual assessment, psychotherapists can also help clients learn to listen to and access their own spiritual wisdom. Often it is hard for clients to connect with their sense of spirituality. In those cases, psychotherapists can access this knowledge by using "the heart" as an access point. We believe that the heart is a conduit for spiritual impressions and insights (Richards, Hardman, & Berrett, 2007). When clients talk about feelings and impressions of their hearts, they are connecting to a powerful form of spiritual language that might otherwise elude them. We ask clients questions such as "How did your heart speak to you during the traumatic experience?" "How has your heart spoken to you since?" "What have been consistent messages from the heart to you?" "What have you come to know in your heart?" and "What are some of the quiet answers that seem to have come to your heart?"

Sometimes clients are not in touch with such "heart impressions" because they have been too preoccupied in coping with the pain and emotional survival. But often clients do know what their hearts have been telling them. Such clients will say, "I really felt this" or "I knew that." Identifying and validating clients' spiritual impressions during the assessment process can provide valuable information and be therapeutic. Doing so can help theistically oriented clients see that the divine has been helping them or that they still have a spiritual connection, even though they have been engulfed with emotional pain.

A MULTILEVEL, MULTIDIMENSIONAL ASSESSMENT STRATEGY

The overarching goal of a spiritual assessment is to gain an understanding of whether a client has a religious background and current spiritual framework in order to implement a comprehensive treatment plan that is sensitive to the client's belief system. As we recommended previously (Richards & Bergin,

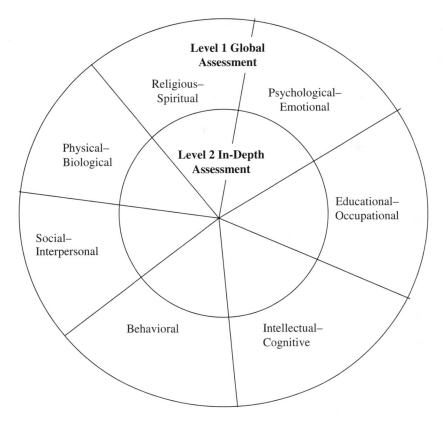

Figure 4.1. A multilevel, multidimensional assessment strategy. Adapted from *A Spiritual Strategy for Counseling and Psychotherapy* (2nd ed., p. 235), by P. S. Richards and A. E. Bergin, 2005, Washington, DC: American Psychological Association. Copyright 2005 by the American Psychological Association.

2005), we conduct a spiritual assessment within the context of a multilevel, multidimensional assessment strategy, illustrated in Figure 4.1. The circle represents the client, and the divisions within the circle represent the different systems or dimensions within the client that psychotherapists assess: physical, social, behavioral, intellectual, educational–occupational, psychological–emotional, and religious–spiritual. When we begin working with a new client, we do a brief global assessment of all the major dimensions. Richards and Bergin (2005) called this a *Level 1 multisystemic assessment,* which is represented in Figure 4.1 by the outer ring of the circle.

Level 1 assessment relies primarily on clients' perceptions and self-descriptions of how they are functioning in each dimension of their lives. During a Level 1 religious–spiritual assessment, it is helpful to ask general questions relevant to clients' religious and spiritual background and current functioning to ascertain how important discussing spiritual issues in treatment is to them and how relevant religion and spirituality may be to their trauma and to the treatment goals and process. For example, we ask questions such as "Is religion or spirituality important in your life?" "Do you wish to discuss religious or spiritual issues during counseling?" "Are you aware of any religious or spiritual resources in your life that could be used to help you?" and "How do you think your spirituality can help you in your therapy goals?" Such questions can be asked during the assessment interview or on written intake questionnaires (Richards & Bergin, 2005).

Depending on the client's presenting problems and goals, along with the information obtained during the Level 1 multisystemic assessment, a more in-depth assessment is undertaken (referred to as a *Level 2 assessment* by Richards & Bergin, 2005), when it seems clinically warranted. Psychotherapists can pursue Level 2 assessments in as much depth as is indicated by the client's symptoms. For example, if a client reports that he or she is not experiencing any significant physical health concerns, we would not do any further assessment in this realm of the client's life. If the client reported experiencing significant religious concerns (e.g., anger at God for allowing sexual abuse to occur), a more in-depth assessment of the client's perceptions of God and the spiritual meaning of the abuse would be warranted. We tend to ask more focused, probing questions during our clinical interviews, and on occasion we might ask the client to complete some standardized religious–spiritual assessment measures. We mention several of these measures later in the chapter.

With trauma survivors, we have found that it is important to be specific in our questioning and also to ask variations of the same question. Because it may be extremely threatening to disclose or discuss, information about the trauma often does not come out all at once. We often find it helpful to ask open-ended questions such as "What else needs to be said that you have not yet expressed?" Even if clients have talked to others about issues related to their trauma, we often find it helpful to say, "Can you tell me what you have not yet discussed with anyone that we now can talk about to help you reach your goals for recovery and healing?" In the section that follows we provide additional examples of Level 2 assessment questions we might ask.

PROCESS SUGGESTIONS FOR CONDUCTING A SPIRITUAL ASSESSMENT

At the start of the assessment process, we invite clients to tell their story about their trauma. As clients recount their experience, they can be asked whether and how the trauma affected them spiritually. We ask questions such as "How do you feel this traumatic experience has affected your spiritual and religious life?" "Did this trauma cause any spiritual damage in your life?" "Has this trauma caused any confusion, questions, or changes in your religious or spiritual beliefs?" and "What kind of spiritual needs do you have now in the aftermath of this trauma?" Therapists should not assume that the experiencing of a traumatic event always damages spirituality. To the contrary, it may have awakened or even strengthened the client's sense of spirituality. If this is the case, psychotherapists can validate and affirm the role spirituality has played, and can continue to play, in coping and healing.

The assessment process can also help psychotherapists and clients identify available religious and spiritual resources and strengths clients possess that may be of assistance during treatment and recovery. Relevant questions here include "What are some of your spiritual strengths that you still have, even after this traumatic experience?" "In what ways has your religious community and/or your spiritual beliefs helped you cope with the trauma you have experienced?" and "What are some of the spiritual resources in your life that can help you recover?" Identifying the spiritual resources available in clients' lives is an important goal of a spiritual assessment because such resources often play a crucial role in treatment and recovery (Richards et al., 2007).

Spiritual assessment can also identify what meaning clients ascribe to their traumatic experience and its impact. We ask questions such as "What does the trauma you have experienced mean to you or about you?" "What can you take from this difficult and hurtful experience that will help you (and possibly others) in your life now and in the future?" "Did you learn anything about compassion from this traumatic experience? If so, how could that compassion be a blessing to you and others?" and "Can your experience help you become a stronger person?" These are all questions about meaning making (see Chapter 6). Helping clients begin to search for and identify meaning in the traumatic event can not only help psychotherapists understand more fully the impact of the trauma but it is also an intervention itself that can assist in the healing process.

During the assessment process, psychotherapists can also help clients begin to look at issues involved in healing and recovery. Often we ask questions such as "Do you believe that healing can or will happen?" "Has your spirituality already helped you deal with the traumatic experiences you have been through?" and "What role might your religious beliefs and personal spirituality play in your treatment and recovery?" It is important for psychotherapists to keep in mind that asking assessment questions represents an opportunity to engage in some indirect teaching and planting of therapeutic seeds. Messages that we try to send our clients include "You get to decide," "You do have power," "Healing is possible," "You can find positive meaning in tragedy," "Perhaps there is something you can learn from the trauma," "There is a way to move on from the trauma," "Recovery is not about what happened—it is about now," "Recovery is about deciding what you are going to do now and in the future with the traumatic experience," and "Recovery is about deciding how you going to heal." If clients have a better understanding of the impact of the trauma and if they help their psychotherapists understand that impact, the treatment relationship can be an important support in healing. The assessment questions psychotherapists ask can convey hope and teach principles of recovery.

It is important that psychotherapists not only help clients see the possibilities for healing and recovery but also affirm clients' strength and resilience and any progress they have already made. We ask questions such as "What, if any, healing has already occurred?" and "How did you accomplish that?" Many times when psychotherapists tell clients what they still need to work on during recovery, it serves to remind them that they are not where they need to be and can make them feel like a failure. They might tell themselves, "I haven't done a good job," I need to have more faith," "I need to have more courage," and "I need to heal more." Thus, it can be helpful for psychotherapists to help clients notice their strengths and their progress by saying things such as "You do have faith," "You do have courage," "You are already progressed in your recovery," "You have taken some big steps," and "Your spirituality has played a role in the healing you have enjoyed and experienced." Focusing on clients' strengths and what they have already achieved rather than on what remains to be done is empowering. It increases clients' hope and self-efficacy. Encouraging and affirming clients' strengths and positive efforts is an important intervention that can flow naturally from the spiritual assessment process.

SPIRITUAL ISSUES FOR ASSESSMENT THAT ARE RELEVANT TO TRAUMA WORK

Spiritual issues may be intertwined with clients' emotional, physical, and relationship concerns in complex ways, and thus they should be explored as part of the assessment. In the next section, we briefly touch on various spiritual issues about which to gather more information. From our experience, it is typical for clients to need therapeutic attention to a few spiritual issues; however, it is rare that they need to work on all of the issues discussed here. Therefore, it is necessary to discover which spiritual domains are most relevant and necessary for healing and recovery.

Spiritual Crisis

A *spiritual crisis* occurs when someone's previously held religious and spiritual beliefs are called into question or abandoned completely. Not uncommonly, spiritual crises occur as a result of a specific traumatic exposure or experience. Victims and survivors often perseverate on such questions as "Why did this happen?" and "Why would God let this happen?" If they are unable to make sense of the traumatic event within their existing spiritual belief system, their whole spiritual worldview can be threatened to the point of collapse, provoking an abandonment of, and a complete loss of faith in, their previously held beliefs. When this occurs, it may rob survivors of a powerful support system and recovery tool. Furthermore, it may undermine clients' sense of meaning, order, and purpose, while triggering feelings of hopelessness and shame. Often, spiritual crises are also accompanied by emotional and relationship crises that in turn may severely undermine the ability to function (Seirmarco et al., 2012).

Psychotherapists should not assume that a traumatic event always triggers a spiritual crisis. Traumatic events can have the opposite effect, serving as catalysts that can increase observance and spiritual awareness. A brief spiritual crisis is sometimes followed by increased faith or spiritual resolve or understanding. If, however, a spiritual crisis has been triggered, the psychotherapist must assess its severity because it may trigger anxiety, depression, hopelessness, and suicide risk. It may further undermine the survivor's functioning in multiple life domains, including family, work, school, church, and relationships with others in one or all domains. In some cases, survivors withdraw from all of their spiritual practices and involvement in their religious community, leaving them with a serious, even life-threatening, void, underscoring the importance of carefully assessing the severity of the spiritual crisis and its impact.

The severity of a spiritual crisis depends in part on what meaning the individual has made of the traumatic experience and possibly the messages he or she receives from significant others, friends and colleagues, and even strangers. For example, beliefs that they have let God down, that they are not doing their part, that they are unworthy, or that they are not living up to God's expectations for them or are deserving of punishment can undermine survivors' hope and contribute to feelings of shame and depression. If clients believe their trauma experiences mean that God does not love them or has abandoned them, it can greatly intensify their emotional and spiritual pain.

The nature of the traumatic experience can also influence the severity of a spiritual crisis. When the trauma itself is religious or spiritual in nature or the perpetrator is someone in a position of religious authority, it may be more likely to provoke a spiritual crisis. Take, for example, the woman who experienced two traumas in a short period of time. Her husband died, and afterward she was sexually assaulted by a religious leader who was in a position of trust in her church. When the trauma occurs within a religious context, it makes it difficult to separate the abuse or trauma from spiritual beliefs. Such betrayal trauma (Gobin & Freyd, 2013) is more likely to provoke a spiritual crisis and, potentially, a more serious one.

The client's ego strength is another determinant of the severity of a spiritual crisis. Clients with low ego strength are often more ashamed and self-critical, making them especially vulnerable to a spiritual and emotional crisis in trauma's aftermath. If, however, they are resilient and capable of kindness and compassion toward themselves, their ability to cope with the trauma will be greater (see Chapter 8, this volume).

Metaphysical Worldview

A *metaphysical worldview* refers to the beliefs people have about the universe and the nature of reality. Does the client have spiritual beliefs? If so, what do they mean? Are the beliefs theistic? New age? Eastern? Do they include a higher power of any kind? If so, in what form or entity? Within that, do they include the theistic idea that there is a divine being greater than humans? Is it a personage? If so, what kind? A man? A woman? Does the client believe he or she can interact with this deity?

Just as psychotherapists should not assume their clients are nontheistic, they should also not assume that all of them are going to be theistic. If they are not, it may be more difficult to assess and understand their spirituality because it may be less defined. Clients who grew up in an organized religion or in religious homes often have a more defined spirituality. Many clients without such traditions or environments often have less of a spiritual language to talk about their beliefs and, as a result, may talk about their spirituality in more abstract terms. For example, one client said,

> I finally figured out there is something greater than I am. As I watched the waves come crashing in on the beach, I realized that there is something greater or more powerful than me. I don't know what it is yet, but there is something.

As psychotherapists seek to understand these worldviews, they can learn the language of their clients' spiritual beliefs. Some clients say that they do not know what they believe in, but somehow they believe that things happen for a reason, so perhaps the trauma or the abuse happened for a reason. This may be all they can articulate about their beliefs, and it is their starting point.

God Image

God image refers to clients' perceptions of a Supreme Being or higher power. Do clients view God as angry? detached? vengeful? loving? merciful? Research has shown that perceptions of God are influenced by a variety of things, including relationships with parents or other primary caregivers, self-esteem, religious instruction, religious practices, and spiritual or mystical experiences (Moriarty & Hoffman, 2007; O'Grady & Richards, 2008).

Trauma certainly can affect people's perceptions of God, sometimes calling into question previous beliefs. For trauma survivors who are, or previously were, theistic in their religious beliefs, we have found it essential to assess and explore how the trauma may have affected or changed their beliefs about God and their relationship with the divine. Such an assessment can illuminate maladaptive religious beliefs that need to be addressed in therapy in order for clients to heal fully.

It is important to explore the origins of clients' perceptions about God. An understanding of where their negative perceptions of God originated can enhance the likelihood that those perceptions can be changed. For example, if a client's perceptions of God originated in his or her relationship with an angry, judgmental, or critical father, psychotherapists can ask questions such as "Is God like your dad?" "Is your dad like God?" "Could God be different from your dad and have a different way, a different presence, a different understanding?" and "Is God willing to be there for you?" Pondering such questions can help clients realize that perhaps their view of God is not accurate or healthy and is in need of updating. They can experiment and find out who God is instead of holding onto old, maladaptive, and often unconscious notions or traditions about what God is like (O'Grady & Richards, 2008).

Some survivors of sexual and/or emotional abuse find their perceptions of the perpetrator and their perceptions of God to be similar (i.e., incestuous abuse by fathers, grandfathers, uncles, or clergymen may make God the father unacceptable and untrustworthy; by association, they may not be sure they can trust God either because the trauma is connected directly to the God image). In such a situation, they may pull away both from their religious community and from a God they perceive as untrustworthy and exploitive.

Clients might be asked about renewing a relationship with God. In a previously prayerful person, we seek to understand how the trauma has affected the ability to pray. We might ask, "How has the trauma affected how you talk to yourself, to others, and to God?" "What are your prayers like now?" "Do you now talk to God?" Such questions elicit information about how clients are feeling about their relationship with God and their perceptions of themselves in that relationship.

Spiritual Coping Style

Assessment of clients' spiritual coping style can help determine whether spirituality is a coping resource. Pargament et al. (1988) described three styles of spiritual coping:

- in the *self-directing style*, people do not seek God's help, believing that their problems are their own responsibility to resolve;
- in the *deferring style*, they do not take personal responsibility for solving their problems, but wait for God or another higher power to fix things for them;
- in the *collaborative style*, they believe they are responsible for doing their best to solve their problems, but they believe that God will assist them in their efforts.

Clients who defer responsibility and believe that God will take care of everything may use such a belief to avoid their issues and taking responsibility for resolving them. Such avoidance should be examined and confronted so that clients can face and resolve their personal problems.

Some clients, most often those who are obsessive–compulsive and perfectionistic (or who have a detached/avoidant attachment style), believe they must be self-sufficient, something they likely learned over the course of their upbringing. They do not believe that anyone will be there to respond to or support them, and they tend to believe that if God or other people have to help them, then they must be weak, undisciplined, or flawed. In consequence, they have to prove they are not deficient by doing it all by themselves. In taking this stance, they do not leave room for God's love and guidance or help from others. They may be exhausted and in crisis when they finally reach out for assistance. Thus, they may be most in need of the psychotherapist's help in opening up to the support and guidance from God and others who care about them.

Rigidity of the Religious Belief System

We have found that the more complex and stressful people's problems are, the more rigid they tend to become. The more out of control, vulnerable, hurt, and hopeless they feel, the more rigid they become in an effort to regain control or gain a sense of stability in their life. Thus, some people who are rigid tend to get more so when traumatized, and if they are religious, this can affect their religious and spiritual thinking and behavior, at times creating a roadblock to treatment progress and recovery. We have observed that personal rigidity can result in unrealistic expectations of God and related beliefs (i.e., if they live their lives in a certain religiously orthodox way, God will reward them in kind and God's blessings will show up in certain predictable ways). They think and say things such as "If God is in my life it will look just like this"; "If it is a blessing from God, it will show up like this"; and "God rewards the righteous." When such expectations are not perfectly confirmed, their faith may waver and a spiritual crisis can ensue. Rather than understanding that life is not subject to such control, they take this disappointment as proof that God is not there or does not love them or that they are unworthy or defective. Because trauma can challenge anyone's faith and spiritual framework, those who start with a rigid belief system may find it especially difficult to accommodate and make sense of their experiences in a manner that allows them to hold onto a sense of spiritual meaning, fulfillment, and purpose.

Another way that the rigidity issues come into play for clients who are in a state of "emotional survival" is that they may find it difficult to honor all their religious values and they may struggle to maintain their religious observances as fully as they have in the past. For those with rigid self-expectations and religious standards who fail in their normal observances, intense feelings of shame and spiritual deficiency can result. They may find it difficult to remain involved in their religious community because they no longer feel that they are living up to the standards and expectations of their faith tradition. With such clients we sometimes ask, "Are your spiritual beliefs going to guide you in your life and support you, or are they going to control, punish, and hurt you?" Such a question can assist clients in noticing and changing the ways they use their spiritual beliefs against themselves. When previously traumatized clients get into rigid thinking and a perfectionistic style, they may need assistance in learning how to be more self-understanding and compassionate.

Spiritual Identity and Purpose

Spiritual identity and purpose refers to how people see themselves and their place in the universe. Who are they? What is their purpose? What is the meaning of life? Are they of spiritual value and worth? People who enjoy a positive sense of spiritual identity and purpose believe they have worth and potential and have a purpose, mission, or calling to fulfill during their lives. Those who believe in God can feel God's love and support for them. They often believe that their spirit or soul is eternal and that their identity and consciousness will persist beyond the death of their physical body (Richards & Bergin, 2005).

Severe trauma may have a negative impact on their sense of spiritual identity and purpose. We have found that personalizing the trauma (i.e., feeling responsible for its occurrence, feeling to blame, or feeling that it defines them and their worth) intensifies a loss of positive spiritual identity. We have witnessed this with sexual abuse victims, with those in abusive marriages, and with soldiers who have experienced severe combat trauma. Such clients often think and say, "I am bad," "I am to blame," "I caused this terrible thing to happen," "This is who I am," and "I deserve it." They may even think,

"This is how God made me, and there is no hope of changing it." Their sense of identity is shamed, and their behavior is entangled in their identity. Such harsh self-judgment can have devastating effects. As we seek to understand the impact of trauma on clients' sense of spiritual identity and purpose, we ask questions such as "Has your trauma changed your sense of who you are or your beliefs about your value or worth?" and "What do you feel is still spiritually intact about you in spite of what you have been through?"

Relationship With One's Religious Community and Spiritual Leaders

Many people seek support and guidance from their religious community and spiritual leaders during times of trauma and stress (Richards & Bergin, 2005) instead of, or before, turning to mental health professionals (Worthington et al., 1996). When conducting a spiritual assessment, it is helpful to ascertain the degree to which clients feel connected to a religious community and supported by their religious leaders and whether these groups or individuals do or can function as resources. Are they a source of comfort, or have they created alienation and pain? Some clients feel estranged from their religious community and have no desire to reach out or to reconnect. Not all religious leaders are helpful, and some use shame, guilt, and other coercive tactics in their attempts to influence followers. Some clients have unresolved anger toward religious authorities and institutions and would understandably react negatively to efforts to involve them in their treatment. Yet, clients who have positive connections with their religious community and leaders may benefit from their emotional and spiritual support and guidance. For those abused by religious leaders or others in the church setting, attempts to involve clergy in treatment would likely be inappropriate and harmful, especially early in treatment (although some clients prefer to be counseled by someone from their same faith tradition). The selection of a clergy member should to be done with great sensitivity to and in collaboration with the client and with attention to the clergy member's integrity and knowledge of and sensitivity to issues of trauma. This individual must also be able to tolerate hearing about abuse perpetrated by other members of the clergy or religious community; she or he must not disbelieve the client, minimize their abusive events or their consequences, or defend their colleagues or the church.

Because trauma can have a negative impact on victims' ability and desire to show love to others, the traumatized may also get to the point in their recovery when they benefit by giving service back to others, both within and outside their religious community. Finding ways that clients can serve others or a cause can help them find meaning and purpose in what they have experienced and in their lives. Often the client's religious community can facilitate this kind of service, helping them begin to take down the walls they have put up to protect themselves.

Shame and Guilt

Many trauma survivors, particularly those who have been sexually abused, feel a deep sense of shame and guilt, feeling unworthy, bad, flawed, evil, contaminated, and/or defective. If they believe in God, they most often believe that God views them negatively. They tend to be harsh critics of themselves and to feel guilty for even minor shortcomings and mistakes. Spiritual assessment can seek to determine whether and to what degree clients are shamed and what associated beliefs and behaviors they might have that are emotionally and spiritually destructive. We raise questions concerning the degree to which clients felt (and continue to feel) responsible for the traumatic event and explore why or how they feel this way. Ultimately we find that most clients have taken on too much responsibility for what happened (often and paradoxically exonerating the perpetrator in the process), and we seek to increase their awareness so that they can begin to let go of misplaced responsibility, unnecessary shame, and guilt. To accomplish this, we may ask questions such as "What were you thinking and feeling when the trauma occurred?" "If you could have ended the abuse, would you have?" "What, if anything, could you do now if that happened that you could not have done then?" and "Despite what happened, and what the abuser did, did you stay true to yourself and your beliefs during the traumatic experience?" Asking such questions can give clients an opportunity, in the safe, nonjudgmental context of the therapeutic relationship, to acknowledge ways they may feel like they failed to live in accordance with their values and principles and to explore their powerlessness.

Normalizing of all feelings, particularly shame, regarding the loss of previously held values or principles during or after the trauma—a time that is inherently stressful and destabilizing—can be especially crucial. During times of desperation and terror individuals do things in the interest of survival, at times violating their own moral codes. Psychotherapists can communicate understanding and compassion as they explore the specifics with clients, hopefully in ways that allow them to give up destructive shame and irrational guilt. This process can support them in owning and affirming what they did right and in learning self-compassion.

Existential Anxiety and Doubt

Many individuals with histories of severe trauma struggle with existential anxiety and doubt. Trauma challenges a sense of security and order, leaving survivors feeling unsafe, powerless and abandoned, afraid of life and an uncertain future. This can result in the belief that their life is futile, and they sometimes express thoughts such as "Terrible things happened and so what is the point?" "What's the use?" "Whatever I do doesn't really matter." This can be different from what psychotherapists normally hear when treating depressive disorders. When clients are depressed, they often view themselves as the problem and have associated self-contempt and self-directed anger. But with existential doubt, the problem is externalized to life or the universe, beyond the client's control. When clients have an underlying futility, chronic disempowerment, hopelessness, or a sense that their choices do not matter, even contemplating change may be difficult.

Giving attention to clients' beliefs about the meaning or purpose of their traumatic experience can help them begin to examine their existential anxiety. Many clients are searching for a "why" to their trauma and for associated meaning and understanding. They ask questions such as "Why did it happen?" "Why did it happen to me?" and "Why did it happen to a child?" "Why would God let this happen?" In our experience, most clients believe that things happen for a reason. For example, some Christian clients may have religious beliefs about divine justice and grace, or some Hindu clients may have beliefs about karma that give meaning to their experiences. Such spiritual beliefs in themselves can take clients a long way in their healing. During spiritual assessment, psychotherapists can ask questions such as "What difficulties or adversities have you experienced in your life in the past and now?" "Why do you think you have had to experience this adversity?" "What do you think it means about you that you have suffered so?" "What do you think you have or can learn from these trials?" "What are you going to do with these experiences?" and "What are you going to take away from this that may help you in your life?" When psychotherapists ask such questions, they endorse the idea that the individual can decide or find meaning in their adversities and that doing so can be healing.

Forgiveness

During a spiritual assessment, it is essential to explore the topic of forgiveness of self and others. The question of whether and how to forgive themselves and those who have hurt them often requires difficult therapeutic work.

Research supports the idea that forgiveness promotes emotional and spiritual healing (Enright & Fitzgibbons, 2000; Worthington, 1998). Some clients, however, have unrealistic expectations about forgiveness and about what is expected of them, believing that God (or their religion and the congregation) wants or expects them to forgive others who have transgressed against them. Such a belief may pressure them to forgive too quickly out of religious obligation without adequate consideration or preparation, in the process, short circuiting the emotional healing. This also keeps them from truly going to God with any struggles they have with forgiveness. In a desire to please God and others, they may be afraid to be honest about how hurt and angry they really are.

We encourage clients to be more authentic in their feelings and more honest with God and with others about any difficulties they have with forgiveness. We also suggest that a process rather than an outcome approach to forgiveness may be more helpful and achievable. Questions such as "What would you have to do if you felt obligated to forgive this person right away?" often lead them to respond that they would have to bury their feelings of anger, hurt, and pain. If they were unable to forgive, they would have to pretend otherwise and bury these feelings right away. We attempt to validate what clients are feeling in the moment, encouraging them to take the time needed to work their issues through. We teach that forgiveness is a process that often takes time, intention, and effort. We remind them that anger is not a lack of forgiveness, but one step in the process. We might help clients understand the steps in forgiveness to determine where they are in the process.

Other issues that may need to be explored include helping clients forgive themselves; decide whether to forgive the abuser; and work through concerns they may have about whether the abuser is being held accountable, showing remorse, and/or seeking to repent and whether he or she merits forgiveness. In some cases, victims feel they cannot forgive and choose not to. When this occurs, we encourage them in the process of self-forgiveness.

SPIRITUAL ASSESSMENT AND OUTCOME MEASURES

Researchers in the psychology of religion have developed numerous measures of religiousness and spirituality during the past few decades (Gorsuch, 1984; Hill & Hood, 1999); however, few of these have been validated for use in clinical settings and, in most cases, their value for non-Christian clients is unclear. With these limitations in mind, we have found that several of these measures are at times useful in working with trauma survivors; these include measures of intrinsic religious commitment (Worthington et al., 2003), spiritual well-being (Paloutzian & Ellison, 1991), God image (Lawrence, 1991), and religious problem-solving (Pargament et al., 1988). Although they are not validated for diagnostic purposes and may not have adequate normative data for comparison purposes, these instruments can be used for promoting clients' spiritual self-exploration and insight. More theoretical and research work is needed on spiritual assessment and outcome measures across all religious beliefs and faith traditions.

The Religious Commitment Inventory (RCI-10; Worthington et al., 2003) may be the measure of intrinsic and extrinsic religious orientation that is most useful in treatment. It is a 10-item measure regarding "the degree to which a person adheres to his or her religious values, beliefs, and practices and uses them in daily living" (Worthington et al., 2003, p. 85). The RCI-10 is composed of two subscales: (a) Intrapersonal and (b) Interpersonal Religious Commitment. Considerable evidence has accumulated to support the reliability, validity, and clinical usefulness of the RCI-10 with both Christian and non-Christian and client and nonclient samples.

The Spiritual Well-Being Scale (SWBS; Paloutzian & Ellison, 1991) was developed to measure individuals' overall spiritual well-being. It has two subscales: (a) Religious and (b) Existential Well-Being. The SWBS has several assets: It is nondenominational, easy to understand, brief, and easy to score. The instrument was normed on a large diverse sample, has adequate reliability and validity, and has been used in clinical settings (Hill & Hood, 1999; Paloutzian & Ellison, 1991).

Although there are a number of standardized instruments that measure concepts and images of God, we recommend the God Image Inventory (Lawrence, 1991), which was developed for research and for clinical and pastoral use. God image is defined as an individual's inner or intuitive sense of God. This measure consists of six principle (Influence, Providence, Presence, Challenge, Acceptance, and Benevolence) and two control scales (Faith and Salience). It was standardized with a national sample of 1,580 respondents and has shown adequate reliability and validity. It has 136 questions and takes about 20 minutes to complete.

The Religious Problem-Solving Scale assesses three styles (Pargament et al., 1988). The full form of this paper-and-pencil measure has 36 items (12 per subscale) and also takes about 20 minutes to complete. It is easy to interpret and has strong reliability, validity, and usefulness among Presbyterian and Lutheran samples. Normative data need to be collected from a greater diversity of religious orientations and ethnic backgrounds to increase its scope.

As psychotherapists monitor treatment progress, where warranted, we recommend including assessment of spiritual outcomes. The SWBS (Paloutzian & Ellison, 1991) has been used as a therapy outcome measure in a number of studies. It is brief, and it correlates positively with a variety of physical and mental health indicators, making it appealing as an outcome measure. To help meet the need for brief, sensitive spiritual outcome measures, we developed the Theistic Spiritual Outcome Survey (TSOS; Richards et al., 2005). It is theoretically grounded in a theistic view of spirituality and includes several dimensions or components: (a) faith in God's existence and loving influence; (b) awareness of one's spiritual identity and purpose as a creation of God; (c) love for other people, including a desire to promote their welfare; and (d) feelings of moral congruence, worthiness, and self-acceptance. A 17-item version of the TSOS was found to have adequate reliability and validity in client and student samples (Richards et al., 2005). It can be administered on a weekly basis.

CASE STUDY: REBECCA

The following case study illustrates how a spiritual assessment can facilitate the processes and outcomes of psychotherapy with traumatized clients. The client's name and identifying details have been changed to disguise her identity.

Rebecca sought treatment because she was experiencing high levels of chronic anxiety daily, along with periodic panic attacks that were affecting her ability to function as a college student and in her marriage. She was completing her senior year and had been married for 15 months and, at the onset of therapy, had no children. She was the fourth of five children and had grown up in a small city in the western United States. Rebecca is a member of the Church of Jesus Christ of Latter-day Saints and served for 18 months as a missionary at age 21. She reported no previous psychotherapy or use of medication. She indicated that she had experienced mild to moderate bouts of depression since she was a young teenager. She was concerned that an episode of depression would return because of her current anxiety and stress levels.

Gathering background information and history regarding this client's life and presenting problems included global, Level 1 spiritual-based assessment questions and clarifications, as well as more denominationally specific Level 2 questions tailored to Rebecca's Latter-day Saint tradition. Rebecca reported a long history of anxiety, worry, fear, and stress that started in childhood and became constant during junior high school. She started to experience intense bouts of anxiety in high school that continued into college, with periodic panic attacks during the last 2 years of college escalating to one or two episodes each week for several months before she sought treatment.

Rebecca described a history and symptoms consistent with posttraumatic stress disorder. She disclosed that an older adolescent male cousin had sexually abused her when she was in the first grade, an experience she downplayed and minimized by stating that she was "over it" and just "needed to do everything right so nothing bad happens again." She had told no one of the childhood abuse. She had always been a good student, with high grades and academic success, but functioning had become more difficult and stressful over time. She no longer felt as capable of channeling the anxiety (in a form of dissociation) into school and studies as she had been in the past. She shared some information regarding intense phobic-like fears that created high levels of anxiety.

She reported a somewhat close relationship with her father, but her personal connection with him was limited due to his long work hours as a small business owner. He often came home late from work and would become easily angered and yell at the children for "not doing things," or he would have arguments with his wife over the children, finances, and the lack of order in and cleanliness of the home. These arguments were upsetting to Rebecca because, as a child, she felt guilty and bad about herself and wanted to make things better for her parents by being extra good and not adding to their distress. Rebecca felt increased pressure to be perfect and to do everything right when an older sister rebelled and acted out as a teenager. Her inability to help her parents' relationship despite her hundreds of daily repetitive prayers and private pleadings for divine assistance left her feeling ineffective and unworthy of God's help or blessings.

Rebecca reported having experienced an extremely negative and painful relationship with her mother since childhood. The lack of warmth and a caring connection had a negative spiritual impact, especially given that she was so desperate for approval and encouragement. Unfortunately, her mother had experienced depression, low self-esteem, and chronic medical issues, which often left her irritable, critical, moody, or nonresponsive to the needs or feelings of her daughter. Throughout Rebecca's life, she felt that she was on her own because "my mother wasn't there for me when I needed her the most." She had a deep and painful sense or feeling of being abandoned and being not good enough for her mother's love. Over the years, these beliefs and feelings had gradually translated into a spiritual sense that somehow she was also the exception to God's love because she was not being good enough or acceptable to God. She did not feel angry toward God but rather blamed herself for her spiritual defectiveness and was overly self-critical.

Rebecca was a strong believer in her God and in her religious beliefs, but she also had an intense, negative, and private sense of guilt and shame, some of it originating in the sexual abuse. She felt guilty all the time even though she did not believe she was committing any horrible sins, but she was constantly afraid that she might sin or do something terribly wrong. She felt bad about herself for her painful thoughts, indecisiveness, anxiety, and feelings of dread, and had an overall sense of powerlessness to make things better for the people she loved in her life, including her husband. She believed she was the cause of pain and unhappiness in other people's lives. She had lost confidence in her prayers and in her ability to receive answers to them.

In discussing her marriage, Rebecca indicated that she had had a difficult time deciding whether to marry her husband. In fact, she had so much anxiety about making the wrong choice that it created a great deal of confusion, turmoil, and conflict between them during their engagement. After she was married, she began to have intrusive thoughts of having secret affairs with other men or, even worse, murdering her husband in the night while he was sleeping. Rebecca was afraid of losing her husband or not being good enough for him, so these intrusive thoughts made no rational sense to her. She interpreted them to mean that, deep down, she must be a bad person to think and feel this way.

As the assessment proceeded, it was determined that Rebecca had been experiencing obsessive–compulsive disorder (OCD) since she was a child. She had experienced painful intrusive thoughts for as long as she could remember. As these anxiety-provoking thoughts were disclosed and discussed, it became clear that they were always tied to the possibility of her doing something horribly wrong, evil, or hurtful to others or doing disgusting things that violated her core spiritual values and personal code of conduct. She had developed a variety of rituals to combat the intrusive thoughts and to ease the anxiety. These included repeating prayers or phrases, self-castigation, seeking divine forgiveness, excessive scripture reading, compulsive serving of other people, perfectionism in detailed tasks, and distraction through books or movies, studying, and school performance. Because Rebecca's intrusive thoughts often had spiritual and religious implications, she always felt at risk of losing God's approval and love, of being evil in her heart or at her core, and of being capable of giving in to her dark inner impulses, of going to hell and being lost forever. These inner fears had compounded the traumatic experiences of her early life and led to ongoing stress and anxiety.

In using spiritual assessment as a bridge to healing interventions, the psychotherapist pointed out to Rebecca the strength of her determination and will power. Despite her near constant anxiety and fears of acting out her intrusive thoughts, the truth was that she had never acted on them. His affirming feedback caught Rebecca off guard because she had never considered this fact. After a few moments, she shed tears of relief. She felt a sense of self-validation in her own refusal to give in to the painful and intrusive thoughts: It was meaningful to know that she had been successful regarding what she feared the most. In one sense, she saw that she had won the battle. This early discussion laid a therapeutic framework for her to start working on the negative spiritual effects of the OCD-based beliefs and to develop better tactics and strategies for dealing with her anxiety.

Rebecca started on medication that helped decrease the OCD ruminations and her overall anxiety level. Other issues that she worked on with her therapist included (a) addressing and engaging in emotional healing from the childhood sexual abuse (and especially the fact that it had been committed by a cousin); (b) understanding her OCD, panic attacks, and anxiety; (c) developing positive coping strategies and response patterns to her fears, worries, intrusive thoughts, and anxieties; (d) working on the pain of her relationship with her mother and resolving some issues directly with her mother; (e) improving emotional and relationship boundaries and marital communication; and (f) replacing self-contempt and self-criticism with kindness, compassion, and self-care. Regarding Rebecca's spiritual issues, they worked on (a) separating who she is, her personal and spiritual identity, from the OCD and its ramifications on her childhood or adolescent sense of self; (b) understanding the difference between real and false guilt in spiritual matters to help her depersonalize false guilt and to recognize real guilt as based on actually doing something wrong; (c) discerning spiritual truths from OCD-based beliefs and feelings and recognizing the internal difference between spiritual and emotional experiences so she could trust and act on her spiritual impression; (d) learning to listen to her heart as a spiritual connection to love from God, family, and friends; and (e) creating a sense of choice and balance in her personal spiritual life and practices and eliminating the use of spiritual practices as a coping strategy for anxiety or obsessive rituals. These interventions are grounded theoretically in a theistic spiritual framework for psychotherapy (Berrett, Hardman, & Richards, 2010; Richards & Bergin, 2005; Richards et al., 2007).

One example of a spiritual-based intervention that resulted from the information gathered during the assessment had to do with her relationships with her mother and God. Rebecca felt that all the things that she had truly needed from her mother—love, empathy, kindness, encouragement, interest, and acknowledgment—had not been given to her. She felt alone and uncared for by her mother. The therapist asked her to write a letter to her mother (not to be mailed) that detailed her feelings about this key relationship. She read her letter in a session, and she was able to be emotionally honest and shed many tears when describing her childhood sense of being alone and abandoned by her mother. There was a cathartic release of emotions, including anger, in the reading of this letter aloud.

At the end of this session, the psychotherapist suggested that Rebecca go home and pray for God's help in filling in between the lines of her double-spaced letter. In the next session, Rebecca said that praying about the letter to her mother had helped her to feel less alone and less guilty about her anger toward her mother. Thus, the therapist asked her to go back through the letter and in the space below each line that detailed painful life experience to write, "I was not alone in this pain because God was with me and felt love and compassion for me in these painful feelings and experiences." He then asked her to write down any other spiritual thoughts or impressions that came to her and to add them to the between-the-lines messages. In the next session, Rebecca reported that she had completed the assignment and that it had produced in her a powerful sense of God's love and compassion. She now had a real personal and spiritual sense that God knew and understood what she had gone through as a child and that God had loved and cared for her throughout it all. The messages written between the lines were touching and powerful reminders to Rebecca of her importance to God.

REFERENCES

American Psychological Association (2009). *APA Presidential Task Force on post-traumatic stress disorder and trauma in children and adolescents*. Washington, DC: Author.

Bernstein, E. M., & Putnam, F. W. (1986). Development, reliability, and validity of a dissociation scale. *Journal of Nervous and Mental Disease, 174,* 727–735. doi:10.1097/00005053-198612000-00004

Berrett, M. E., Hardman, R. K., & Richards, P. S. (2010). The role of spirituality in eating disorder treatment and recovery. In M. Maine, D. Bunnell, & B. McGilley (Eds.), *Special issues in the treatment of eating disorders: Bridging the gaps* (pp. 367–385). Maryland Heights, MO: Elsevier. doi:10.1016/B978-0-12-375668-8.10022-1

Blake, D. D., Weathers, F. W., Nagy, L. M., Kaloupek, D. G., Gusman, F. D., Charney, D. S., & Keane, T. M. (1995). The development of a clinician administered PTSD scale. *Journal of Traumatic Stress, 8,* 75–90. doi:10.1002/jts.2490080106

Briere, J. (1995). *Trauma Symptom Inventory*. Odessa, FL: Psychological Assessment Resources.

Briere, J. (2004). *Psychological assessment of adult posttraumatic states: Phenomenology, diagnosis, and measurement* (2nd ed.). Washington, DC: American Psychological Association. doi:10.1037/10809-000

Butcher, J. N., Dahlstrom, W. G., Graham, J. R., Tellegen, A., & Kaemmer, B. (1989). Minnesota Multiphasic Personality Inventory *(MMPI–2)*. *Manual for administration and scoring*. Minneapolis: University of Minnesota Press.

Carlson, E. B. (1997). *Trauma assessments: A clinician's guide*. New York, NY: Guilford Press.

Chamberlain, R. B., Richards, P. S., & Scharman, J. S. (1996). Using spiritual perspectives and interventions in psychotherapy: A qualitative study of experienced AMCAP therapists. *Association of Mormon Counselors and Psychotherapists Journal, 22,* 29–74.

Courtois, C. A., & Ford, J. D. (2013). *Treatment of complex trauma: A sequenced, relationship-base approach*. New York, NY: Guilford Press.

Enright, R. D., & Fitzgibbons, R. P. (2000). *Helping clients forgive: An empirical guide for resolving anger and restoring hope.* Washington, DC: American Psychological Association. doi:10.1037/10381-000

Gobin, R. L., & Freyd, J. J. (2013). The impact of betrayal trauma on the tendency to trust. *Psychological Trauma: Theory, Research, Practice, and Policy.* doi.org/10.1037/a0032452

Gorsuch, R. L. (1984). Measurement: The boon and bane of investigating religion. *American Psychologist, 39,* 228–236. doi:10.1037/0003-066X.39.3.228

Hill, P. C., & Hood, R. W. (1999). *Measures of religiosity.* Birmingham, AL: Religious Education Press.

Lawrence, R. T. (1991). The God Image Inventory: The development, validation and standardization of a psychometric instrument for research, pastoral and clinical use in measuring the image of God. *Dissertation Abstracts International: Section A. The Humanities and Social Sciences, 52*(3), 952.

Millon, T. (1994). *Millon Clinical Multiaxial Inventory—III: Manual for the MCMI–III.* Minneapolis, MN: National Computer Systems.

Moriarty, G., & Hoffman, L. (Eds.). (2007). *God image handbook for spiritual counseling and psychotherapy: Research, theory, and practice.* New York, NY: Haworth Press.

O'Grady, K., & Richards, P. S. (2008). Theistic psychotherapy and the God image. *Journal of Spirituality in Mental Health, 9,* 183–209. doi:10.1300/J515v09n03_09

O'Grady, K. A., & Richards, P. S. (2010). The role of inspiration in the helping professions. *Psychology of Religion and Spirituality, 2,* 57–66. doi:10.1037/a0018551

Paloutzian, R. F., & Ellison, C. W. (1991). *Manual for the Spiritual Well-being Scale.* Nyack, NY: Life Advance.

Pargament, K. I., Kennell, J., Hathaway, W., Grenvengoed, N., Newman, J., & Jones, W. (1988). Religion and the problem-solving process: Three styles of coping. *Journal for the Scientific Study of Religion, 27,* 90–104. doi:10.2307/1387404

Richards, P. S., & Bergin, A. E. (Eds.). (2000). *Handbook of psychotherapy and religious diversity.* Washington, DC: American Psychological Association. doi:10.1037/10347-000

Richards, P. S., & Bergin, A. E. (2005). *A spiritual strategy for counseling and psychotherapy* (2nd ed.). Washington, DC: American Psychological Association. doi:10.1037/11214-000

Richards, P. S., Hardman, R. K., & Berrett, M. E. (2007). *Spiritual approaches in the treatment of women with eating disorders.* Washington, DC: American Psychological Association. doi:10.1037/11489-000

Richards, P. S., Smith, T. B., Schowalter, M., Richard, M., Berrett, M. E., & Hardman, R. K. (2005). Development and validation of the Theistic Spiritual Outcome Survey. *Psychotherapy Research, 15,* 457–469. doi:10.1080/10503300500091405

Seirmarco, G., Neria, Y., Insel, B., Kiper, D., Doruk, A., Gross, R., & Litz, B. (2012). Religiosity and mental health: Changes in religious beliefs, complicated grief, posttraumatic stress disorder, and major depression following the September 11, 2001, attacks. *Psychology of Religion and Spirituality, 4*(1), 10–18. doi:10.1037/a0023479

West, W. (2000). *Psychotherapy and spirituality: Crossing the line between therapy and religion.* Thousand Oaks, CA: Sage. doi:10.4135/9781446218488.n7

Wilson, J. P., & Keane, T. M. (Eds.). (2004). *Assessing psychological trauma and PTSD* (2nd ed). New York, NY: Guilford Press.

Worthington, E. L. Jr. (1998). *Dimensions of forgiveness: Psychological research and theological perspectives.* Philadelphia, PA: Templeton Foundation Press.

Worthington, E. L. Jr., Kurusu, T. A., McCullough, M. E., & Sanders, S. J. (1996). Empirical research on religion and psychotherapeutic processes and outcomes: A ten-year review and research prospectus. *Psychological Bulletin, 119*, 448–487. doi:10.1037/0033-2909.119.3.448

Worthington, E. L. Jr., Wade, N. E., Hight, T. L., Ripley, J. S., McCullough, M. E., Berry, J. W., . . . O'Connor, L. (2003). The Religious Commitment Inventory—10: Development, refinement, and validation of a brief scale for research and counseling. *Journal of Counseling Psychology, 50*, 84–96. doi:10.1037/0022-0167.50.1.84

5

RELIGION, SPIRITUALITY, AND THE WORKING ALLIANCE WITH TRAUMA SURVIVORS

E. GRACE VERBECK, MELINE A. ARZOUMANIAN, JAN E. ESTRELLADO, JILLIAN DELORME, KRISTEN DAHLIN, EMILY HENNRICH, HEATHER E. RODRIGUEZ, JESSICA M. STEVENS, AND CONSTANCE DALENBERG

Psychotherapists are trained to take a nonjudgmental stance and be aware of their biases. This ideal, never fully realized, might be particularly challenging to fulfill in the area of religion, a facet of life in which strong and central beliefs are common. Absent graduate-level training and discussion, however, religion is an area in which even seasoned psychotherapists often find themselves unprepared or perplexed.

This chapter explores religious or spiritual beliefs as a central part of the clinical picture, how therapists can discuss such beliefs with clients, and related interventions in the context of the treatment of trauma. Our exploration of the clinical literature shows that after trauma, clients often attempt to use their spiritual or religious knowledge to try to make meaning out of their experience. The conclusions they reach in these circumstances can profoundly affect mood and decisions about future action. Likewise, psychotherapists sometimes struggle with their own reactions to clients' religious interpretation of an event; they may also struggle to use interventions tailored to

http://dx.doi.org/10.1037/14500-006

Spiritually Oriented Psychotherapy for Trauma, D. F. Walker, C. A. Courtois, and J. D. Aten (Editors)

their client's beliefs. Religious issues are difficult to negotiate in trauma treatment, especially when clinicians are expected to be adept enough to juggle countertransference. Using both research and case vignettes to illustrate our professional experience, we discuss approaches to the more common choice points in the therapy working alliance, such as interventions and disclosure of beliefs.

COUNTERTRANSFERENCE TO RELIGIOUS MATERIAL

Religious and spiritual issues are among the most contentious and most meaningful areas for human discussion. Therefore, religion and topics relevant to religion as foci for attention in psychotherapy are to be expected. Among the great questions of the client's life, one would predict that clinician and client would struggle with religious and spiritual dilemmas in the safety of the therapeutic hour: How do I use my spiritual beliefs to comfort myself, address my issues regarding death or justice, or face my future? Why did God allow the struggles that my loved ones or I face?

Surprisingly, many authors have reported that religious and spiritual issues are in fact avoided in psychotherapy (Frazier & Hansen, 2009; Hawkins & Bullock, 1995; Sloan, Bagiella, & Powell, 2001). In a recent study by Frazier and Hansen (2009), 30% or less of professionals reported discussion of religion in their clinical sessions. Further, surveys of directors of American Psychological Association (APA)–accredited programs and internships have found that few programs systematically address religion and spirituality (Russell & Yarhouse, 2006). Eighty-three percent of clinical psychologists recalled that spiritual issues were never or rarely presented in their supervision and training (Shafranske & Malony, 1990). This is despite the fact that 32% of clients reported some distress and 19% reported significant distress that they feel stems directly from religious concerns (Johnson & Hayes, 2003).

The failure to address religious issues in psychotherapy could arise from a number of sources. First, psychotherapists appear to be less religious or find religion to be less important in their daily lives than is typical for their community of clients (Cross & Khan, 1983; Delaney, Miller, & Bisonó, 2007; Hawkins & Bullock, 1995; Plante, 2007). Second, many psychotherapists report that they are poorly trained in dialogue containing religious content, perhaps engendering concern about competence to deal with religious issues (Saunders, Miller, & Bright, 2010). Third, the psychotherapists may struggle with ethical issues, such as beliefs that religious discussion is outside the appropriate role of the psychotherapist (Rosenfeld, 2010) or legal and moral concerns regarding influencing religious behavior (Rosenfeld, 2010), or they may wish to avoid disclosing therapist-held religious beliefs or lack thereof (Gregory, Pomerantz, Pettibone, & Segrist, 2008). Fourth, the psychotherapist might simply be emotionally avoidant of content that may force personal disclosure or discussion of private and emotionally difficult issues (Dalenberg, 2000). Each of these possibilities might result in countertransference dilemmas for the psychotherapist.

Early writings on countertransference generally suggested that the psychotherapist should simply suppress or "overcome" his or her own personal resistances (Freud, 1910/1988), treating countertransference-laden material like any other material. Putting aside the question of whether such an ideal was ever possible, we now see that interventions with spiritual content may raise special challenges for the clinician. For instance, the presence of religious differences or even the general raising of religious issues may lead both psychotherapist and client to feel a judgmental quality to the psychotherapy (Gonsiorek, Richards, Pargament, & McMinn, 2009; Knox, Catlin, Casper, & Schlosser, 2005; Martinez, Smith, & Barlow, 2007). In one example, Martinez et al. (2007) found that one in four clients experienced the religious intervention chosen by the psychotherapist to be ineffective, objectionable, or condescending.

Although psychotherapists are typically hesitant to bring up issues of spirituality and religion, clients still report a desire for at least a discussion of spiritual concerns and often rate treatment satisfaction higher when such discussion does take place (Rosmarin, Pargament, Pirutinsky, & Mahoney, 2010; Williams, Meltzer, Arora, Chung, & Curlin, 2011). For example, out of 3,141 inpatient clients, 41% reported welcoming a discussion about religious and spiritual concerns while they were hospitalized (Williams et al., 2011). In a similar study, 135 Jewish individuals with elevated stress and worry were randomly assigned to one of three groups: spiritually integrated treatment, progressive muscle relaxation, or wait-list control. The participants who received the spiritual component reported the greatest improvements in reducing stress and worry, including greater reports of tolerating uncertainty, compared with the other treatment groups (Rosmarin et al., 2010). Therefore, addressing such concerns in psychotherapy may be important to both treatment outcomes and client satisfaction, especially for clients with anxiety-related treatment goals.

The important predictors of client treatment satisfaction with the integration of religious and spiritual content have not been studied extensively. Also largely unknown is the degree to which dissatisfied feelings of clients are due to content choice, as opposed to inelegant delivery on the part of the psychotherapist. In developing strategies to address content that has such emotional resonance for clients and psychotherapists, literature on countertransference is clearly relevant.

THE VIGNETTES

To aid in discussion and illustrate many of the points from the literature in our chapter, we created three clinical vignettes that center on counter-transference to religious material in the treatment of traumatized clients. The vignettes are based in part on professional experience of the psychotherapist authors. The vignettes represent amalgamated case studies, and content has been altered to protect client confidentiality.

The Religious Client and the Doubting Psychotherapist

Ben is a 25-year-old man who reports social phobia and fear of authority, which is interfering with his job success. Ben was raised Roman Catholic and as a child he served as an altar boy. As a part of his altar boy responsibilities, he began traveling for weddings and baptisms with his priest. Ben reports sexual abuse by the priest that began at age 9 and lasted until the age of 13. He believes that his trauma has affected his ability to connect with God and to participate fully in the Catholicism to which he is still devoted, but with conflict. Ben has several issues that he wishes to discuss that are related to this topic. First, he is torn regarding the religious and moral ramifications of forgiving his perpetrator. Second, he feels great shame about being abused. Did he play some role in allowing it to happen or allowing it to continue for as long as it did? He wonders whether this is a punishment for bad behavior at home as a child, which he believes led to his parents' divorce.

Ben's psychotherapist, a trauma specialist, is not religious. He has been involved in the reporting and prosecution of clergy perpetrators. Partly due to this experience, and especially because the perpetrator is still serving the church, the psychotherapist believes that Ben should press charges to protect other victims. In the most recent session, Ben asked his psychotherapist to pray with him for strength in overcoming his grief and shame. The psychotherapist doubts that praying with Ben will have the positive benefits of decreasing shame and is uncomfortable with the perceived lack of profession-alism involved in praying with a client. Further, the psychotherapist disagrees with Ben's wholly positive view of forgiveness. Ben hopes that by forgiving his perpetrator he will be able to again engage in church activities and be less dis-trusting of authority figures. The psychotherapist, in partial contrast, believes that any such forgiveness will play into the role of avoidance in maintaining Ben's symptoms. Instead, the psychotherapist wishes to continue to lead the discussion toward processing Ben's trauma memories and confronting those who are personally and systemically responsible for his sexual abuse.

Although the treatment approach of the psychotherapist is empiri-cally informed, Ben might feel dismissed or invalidated by the therapeutic approach. However, he may go along with the psychotherapist to be a "good" client. Even with the best intentions and empirical support, the psychotherapist may indirectly reinforce Ben's avoidance of interpersonal conflict and feelings of helplessness with those whom he perceives to be in authority.

The Doubting Client and the Religious Psychotherapist

Maly is an 18-year-old college freshman engaging in risky sexual behavior with multiple partners. This behavior began after a date rape that occurred when she was 16 years old. Maly's parents, who are Theravadan Buddhists, believe that Maly is engaging in wrongful gratification of her senses and view her sexual conduct as a mark of moral degeneration. Because of their mistrust in Western views of sexuality, they have insisted that Maly seek psychotherapy and have chosen a Buddhist psychotherapist who shares their beliefs. Although they are not opposed to premarital sex, they interpret Western views of sexual equality as condoning promiscuity and encouraging irresponsibility with one's body. Not wanting to disappoint her parents, Maly has agreed to attend psychotherapy. However, she is resentful that she did not have a say in the choosing of a psychotherapist. Although she is willing to discuss the rape, Maly does not wish to talk about her ongoing sexual activities with the psychotherapist, stating that the psychotherapist's concerns are religious in nature and irrelevant to her psychotherapy. Maly wants to be respectful of her parents, but she does not ascribe to Buddhism.

Maly revealed in psychotherapy that she is considering leaving her religion. The psychotherapist is bothered by this and believes Maly is betraying her family and cultural traditions. He feels compelled to point out not only what this means in practical terms—that Maly is rejecting her social support network—but also in moral terms. The psychotherapist views Maly's sexual behavior as a symptom of being disconnected with her culture of origin, including Buddhism and her family.

Inarguably, assessing the level of acculturation of any immigrant client is extremely relevant to effectively conceptualizing factors that maintain symptoms and problematic behaviors. The psychotherapist may concentrate on Maly's religious doubt as a symptom of her trauma, rather than recognizing the complex and personal nature of the decision making that Maly is undertaking. Reevaluation of religious affiliation is not uncommon in adolescence and early adulthood, with or without the stimulus of a traumatic experience. Maly's status as a young adult who is developing her own religious and spiritual preferences deserves respect, regardless of whether she also subscribes to a Western cultural view of independence. With the knowledge that trauma can in fact undermine developmentally appropriate attachment and connection, just as the psychotherapist and Maly's family fear, respect for Maly's stage of life must be delicately balanced.

The Religious Psychotherapist–Client Dyad

Lisa, a 40-year-old married African American woman, grew up in an abusive family and has been in a battering marriage for several years. She recalls several early childhood memories of her father beating her mother while she was present. Although her mother eventually divorced her father, Lisa does not consider divorce an option for her. She believes she is to blame not only for the abuse her mother experienced but also for her own current abuse. She is deeply religious and has chosen from a clinic associated with her church a counselor who also ascribes to conservative Christian values. Although both Lisa and her psychotherapist are strongly against violence, they believe that saving the marriage and forgiving the battering spouse are more important than protecting Lisa's safety.

The shared value placed on saving distressed marriages may lead both Lisa and her psychotherapist to underestimate the physical and psychological danger for Lisa. The choice of divorce clearly should be a client decision, but by not including a discussion of divorce among Lisa's list of options, the therapist may be failing to consider the client's safety. In cases like this, where religious values are shared (either in the case where both or neither individual in the dyad are part of a specific religious community), other client options (e.g., temporary shelters, restraining orders) may not be explored. Lisa might dismiss even fleeting consideration of these options because of perceived psychotherapist disapproval.

MANAGING COUNTERTRANSFERENCE IN THE WORKING ALLIANCE

In early writings regarding the psychotherapist's feelings toward his or her analytic clients, Freud (1910/1988) wrote that he was "almost inclined to insist that he [the psychotherapist] shall recognize this counter-transference in himself and overcome it" (p. 145). Countertransference was an experience to be discussed between psychotherapists and consisted of conflict-laden transferences to the clients that were not part of the "real" relationship (cf. Dalenberg, 2000; McGuire, 1974). According to this approach, such experiences were not to be admitted to clients. Feelings toward clients were dichotomized into real or countertransferential on the basis of whether they were objective or subjective, conflict-dependent or conflict-independent. However, as noted by Dalenberg (2000),

The problem with most of these dichotomies is that almost all reactions of the psychotherapist contain both objective and subjective features, both reactions that are dependent on the patient and reactions independent on him or her, both realistic reactions and fantastic/magical/conflict-ridden beliefs, wishes and emotions. (p. 8)

Thus, more modern definitions of countertransference are "totalistic" as in Bouchard, Normandin, and Seguin's (1995) definition of countertransference as "the entirety of the analyst's emotional reactions to the patient within the treatment situation" (p. 719).

Presentation of psychotherapist neutrality as ideal or arguments that countertransference and the psychotherapist's attitude toward the client is irrelevant to psychotherapies that are more behavioral and less analytic in foundation (e.g., cognitive–behavioral therapy) are common. Such approaches have yielded a large body of research demonstrating the importance of psychotherapist variables in client outcomes (Krause & Lutz, 2009; Norcross & Lambert, 2011; Ricks, 1974). In sufficiently large samples of groups of clients with different psychotherapists, research routinely finds "supershrinks" and "pseudoshrinks" (Okiishi, Lambert, Nielsen, & Ogles, 2003)—psychotherapists with reliably higher or lower client improvement results. In 2001, a task force from APA Division 29 (Psychotherapy) presented guidelines for "empirically supported therapy relationships" (Norcross, 2001), which are parallel to the press for greater use of the empirically supported therapeutic strategies that are widespread in the trauma literature (Ponniah & Hollon, 2009; Sigel & Silovsky, 2011).

In our view, statements that psychotherapists should monitor or eradicate countertransference often fail to recognize the depth of the sources of countertransference and the likelihood of harmful impact on the client and/or the client–psychotherapist relationship if countertransference is ignored rather than managed well. Gelso, Fassinger, Gomez, and Latts (1995), for instance, reported that counselors' undisclosed homophobia levels are directly related to avoidance behavior in lesbian clients. Avoidance may be problematic given that such behaviors negatively predict clinical outcome (Henry, Schacht, & Strupp, 1986). Similarly, Hayes, Yeh, and Eisenberg (2007) found that the degree to which psychotherapists missed a deceased loved one was inversely related to client perceptions of psychotherapist empathy.

Thus, totalistic definitions suggest that the strong feelings and strong beliefs that are common in religious discussions might produce countertransference dilemmas for the psychotherapist. So the question is not if but rather how or when Ben's doubting psychotherapist or Maly's religious psychotherapist should raise the issues central to their concerns. Should the psychotherapist handle these concerns internally? In the sections that follow, we first discuss the reasons that religious concerns might surface in trauma treatment and then we discuss the if, when, and how questions of counter-transference disclosure and countertransference management.

Why Might Religious Issues Arise in Trauma Treatment?

There are a number of reasons why religious issues might surface more commonly in trauma treatment than in other types of treatment. First, trauma might directly affect religious feelings. Thus, change in religious attitudes may be a trauma symptom (Andrews, Brewin, Rose, & Kirk, 2000; Seirmarco et al., 2012; Walker, Reid, O'Neill, & Brown, 2009). Second, religious justifications are sometimes given for behaviors that many psychotherapists and laypersons alike would see as abusive (Greven, 1990; Rosenfeld, 2010). This is particularly true in the case when clergy or others in authority in the congregation and/or highly religious parents perpetrate the abuse (Bottoms, Nielsen, Murray, & Filipas, 2004; Horst, 1998). Third, religion and spirituality may be sources of solace (Wong-McDonald & Gorsuch, 2004) or exacerbating factors in treatment of posttraumatic stress (Wortmann, Park, & Edmondson, 2011).

Many clients who have experienced trauma report changes in religious beliefs. In fact, the Catholic church has reported a significant drop in church attendance and applications to the priesthood since the time of the recent scandals (Gonzales, 2008; O'Doherty, 2008). Like Ben in the first vignette, a significant number of adults who met criteria for posttraumatic stress disorder (PTSD) reported becoming less religious after a trauma (Falsetti, Resick, & Davis, 2003). Falsetti et al. (2003) concluded that changes in religious feeling (positive or negative) might be part of the syndrome of PTSD, noting that this shift occurred only in the context of other trauma-related symptoms. Over half of the participants who were studied by Falsetti et al. reported using religious beliefs to cope with the traumatic event.

Attempts to use religion and spirituality to cope after a trauma may have a positive or negative effect on the mental health of survivors. Trauma might violate the individual's worldview that God will protect the faithful, that God is benevolent, or that the world is relatively fair (Gall, Basque, Damasceno-Scott, & Vardy, 2007; Janoff-Bulman, 1992; Walker et al., 2009). Those who have been abused tend to adopt negative views about religion and God, experiencing God as more punitive, unavailable, and harsh (Pritt, 1998; Reinert & Edwards, 2009). Clients who have experienced trauma might lose faith altogether or might change their concept of God to incorporate the traumatic events. For instance, a client of one of the authors came to believe that a car crash that killed her two youngest children was a sign from God indicating a calling for her to become an activist for traffic safety (e.g., child seat belts). Her family, however, was resentful of her new view of God and disagreed that the death of her children was divinely purposed. To them, her idea that God directed the deliberate sacrifice of one individual for the sake of another implied lower relative worth to the one lost compared with the one saved.

Religious clients might also attribute abusive experiences perpetrated by religious personnel to the church's belief system and practices. Similarly, religion is sometimes used to justify activities that would be labeled by most individuals as abusive. For example, parents may justify harsh physical punishment as a use of "crush and love discipline," breaking the will of a difficult child to help the child submit to a loving God (Rosenfeld, 2010). Some religious authorities endorse physical punishment as a strategy for instilling values and inducing fear to produce obedience to authority (Greven, 1990). Psychotic or obsessive disorders in a parent may lead them to take religious activities intended to facilitate a positive relationship with God and make them abusive, turning them into obsessive and painful rituals.

Finally, independent of the source of the trauma, religious beliefs and religious institutions can be powerful sources of coping and support for the traumatized survivor. Some Muslims, who were victims of hate crimes after 9/11, reported an increase in their religious practices in an effort to balance discriminatory actions by others (Abu-Raiya, Pargament, & Mahoney, 2011; Abu-Ras & Abu-Bader, 2008; Abu-Ras & Suarez, 2009). In a related vein, Ano and Vasconcelles's (2005) meta-analysis showed that religious coping (e.g., prayer) was significantly related to better adjustment to stress. In addition, Martinez et al. (2007) noted several helpful religious interventions, including referencing scriptural passages, teaching spiritual concepts, encouraging forgiveness, involving religious community resources, and conducting assessment of client spirituality. Religion and spiritual intervention may be helpful or harmful, depending on the religiousness of the client (Oren & Possick, 2009) and the skill of the clinician (Martinez et al., 2007).

Deciding to Include Religious Content in Trauma Psychotherapy

Depending on the psychotherapeutic orientation, content discussed in a session may be either left up to the client or directed by the psychotherapist. Therapeutic orientation or countertransference might influence how much religion affects the working alliance between the client and psychotherapist and the extent to which religious and spiritual beliefs are within the domain of psychotherapy. Common examples of such situations include when the psychotherapist does not wish to engage in religious discussion although the client continues to prioritize the topic (perhaps true in Ben's case), when shared beliefs of both the psychotherapist and client become the focus of treatment (perhaps true in Lisa's case), and when the client disagrees with the psychotherapist who sees the client's religious issues as relevant to the symptom picture (perhaps true in Maly's case). Negotiation of the content of psychotherapy might be more complicated in trauma treatment due to client sensitivity to authority and the psychotherapist's wish to avoid imposing viewpoints on an individual who had a history of subjugation.

Rosenfeld (2010) discussed the Joint Commission on the Accreditation of Healthcare Organization's (2008) recommendation for the inclusion of religious and spiritual beliefs and practices in assessment for treatment, implying that the psychotherapist might raise religious and spiritual issues in any psychotherapy rather than relying solely on client request or direction. In such situations, psychotherapists might consider lessons learned in racially divergent psychotherapy dyads, in which Black clients of White psychotherapists reported valuing "talking about talking about" race (Dalenberg, 2000; Sue & Sue, 2008). Clients might believe that psychotherapists only raise religious topics in psychotherapy when religion is seen as a symptom or when religious beliefs are being challenged as inappropriate, pathological, or harmful. Similarly, psychotherapists might fear such negative reactions by the client and withhold necessary discussion of religiously relevant topics. A preliminary discussion by the psychotherapist may dispel some of the discomfort of both psychotherapist and client in their engagement of this material. Although most psychotherapists report being open to having these discussions when initiated by a client, a religious client may be hesitant to initiate these conversations (Cragun & Friedlander, 2012). Even in the event that a client declines to discuss religious and/or spiritual beliefs, the psychotherapist has at least demonstrated that such material is "safe" and the psychotherapist is open to its inclusion. Research seems to suggest that simply adding questions about religion and spirituality to an intake session may strengthen the therapeutic alliance (Shumway & Waldo, 2012).

Creating a sense of safety is vital in trauma treatment. Dalenberg's (2000) Trauma Research Institute (TRI) study participants repeatedly reported negative reactions to any unexplained perceived change in psychotherapist behavior (e.g., the psychotherapist reacting differently over time to the same traumatic material). Although many clients would find unpredictable responses from a psychotherapist upsetting, Dalenberg noted that clients with a trauma history often experience these interactions as more frightening. Therefore, discussions about personal spiritual beliefs may be experienced as threatening by traumatized clients, especially if the client finds this to be out of character for the psychotherapist because spiritual or religious issues were not mentioned during informed consent and/or in previous sessions. In addition, research with TRI participants has shown that this kind of "therapeutic trauma" is more likely to be resolved when the psychotherapist discloses his or her countertransference to the processing of a client's traumatic material, acknowledging, for instance, the difficult task the therapeutic dyad is facing and the relevance of the spiritual or religious discussion.

When religion is part of the trauma narrative, as in Ben's case, discussions about religion and spirituality are important components of effective trauma treatment. Both Ben and his psychotherapist recognized the religious context in which his victimization occurred. Yet, they saw different places for religion and spirituality in the course of psychotherapy: Ben wanted to pray, but the psychotherapist wanted Ben to take legal action. Although both of these interventions aim to empower Ben and reduce his shame, the therapeutic process for each differs. Treatment satisfaction and effectiveness could be compromised by not addressing the discrepancy between Ben's expectations and the psychotherapist's approach. If the psychotherapist discloses her countertransference regarding Ben's request for her to pray with him, she may assist Ben in overcoming his anxiety during conversations with authority. The psychotherapist might start this conversation by saying,

> I think that we might have different ideas about where religion fits into our work. When I bring up the idea of taking legal action as a way to feel empowered, you are quick to change the subject. I respect your belief in God and see your wanting to pray as a great way to help cope with some of those negative emotions that you often find overwhelming. I feel honored that you would like me to engage in that process with you. I also feel that your changing the subject when I bring up taking legal action is contrary to your goal of being more assertive in situations where conflict is a possibility. I would be willing to pray with you, but I am not sure what to say and would not want to offend you. Will you show me how you would like me to pray? Also, would you be willing to discuss with me what comes up from you at the thought of taking legal action? I want this to be a safe place for you, and I want to be transparent with you regarding what I think will be helpful in reaching your goals in therapy.

Here the psychotherapist has gently invited the client to discuss how religion or spirituality might be incorporated to increase treatment satisfaction. By disclosing countertransference to the client's requests and observed avoidance in psychotherapy, the psychotherapist has modeled effective communication in situations that the client fears. In addition, the psychotherapist has provided more evidence for the safety of the psychotherapeutic atmosphere by being willing to engage in the client's spirituality despite feeling uncomfortable and unsure.

Disclosure of Psychotherapists' Religious Beliefs

There are many arguments for and against psychotherapist self-disclosure, some of which depend on the therapeutic orientation of the writer (Goldfried,

Burckell, & Eubanks-Carter, 2003). Despite cautions regarding psychotherapist overuse of or indiscriminate self-disclosure, approximately 90% of psychotherapists report using self-disclosure in psychotherapy (Henretty & Levitt, 2010). Although both positive and negative effects have been found after a psychotherapist discloses personally relevant content to a client, these effects certainly depend on the content and manner of disclosure (Yeh & Hayes, 2011) and whether it is done in the interest of the client or of the psychotherapist. Overdisclosure can signify an unrecognized or unmanaged countertransference response to the client.

Denney, Aten, and Gingrich (2008) described spiritual self-disclosures as happening on a continuum of implicit (e.g., sharing a quote) to explicit (e.g., sharing a personal experience) disclosure. As with any intervention, Denney and colleagues strongly suggested giving informed consent about the possibility that the psychotherapists will use spiritual self-disclosure as an intervention. In addition, they suggested assessing compatibility with treatment goals and the impact on therapeutic alliance before any such disclosure is made. Other authors who have discussed the integration of psychotherapy and religious issues have also suggested disclosure of religious orientation in the informed consent (McMinn, Ruiz, Marx, Wright, & Gilbert, 2006). McMinn et al. (2006) suggested specific wording such as

> My approach to psychotherapy is shaped by my Christian worldview. Though I have no expectation that you share my beliefs, you have a right to know them. Christianity teaches that we are to be in relationship to God and one another, but because of the brokenness of our world our frustrated longings for relationship often result in various problems. In this sense psychological problems—like all problems in our world—ultimately stem from our human brokenness. (p. 30)

Including religious affiliation in informed consent, especially when such beliefs inform choice of therapeutic technique, may be acceptable or even preferable for clients who purposely seek a psychotherapist who ascribes to a similar religion. There is evidence that providing this information in the informed consent strengthens a client's anticipated working alliance (Shumway & Waldo, 2012). However, the psychotherapist should consider the possibility that a statement of religious doctrine ("Christianity teaches that _____") rather than statements of personal beliefs ("I believe that _____") could have quite a different effect on the client. A client reading such a statement might feel criticized or guilty regarding his or her own relationship to God, attributing all symptoms to shortcomings in personal religious commitment. McMinn et al. (2006) were writing from a self-identified Christian psychotherapist perspective. But even within such subgroups, vast differences in the definition and practice of Christianity exist.

An informative but less detailed and more neutral alternative to the statement quoted previously might be:

> My psychotherapy approach is informed by my Christian heritage and background. I believe that relationship with God may or may not be one important topic for discussion in our work. I want you to feel free to use your religious beliefs and learning, whatever they may be, as a source of strength. I am open to any discussion of the ways you believe that these values have also created dilemmas for you as you think about your own past.

Alternatively, a statement that is less specific to a religious orientation might be:

> In psychotherapy I strive to be sensitive to and appreciative of multicultural and diversity issues, such as an individual's cultural heritage and values. Regardless of whether or not we share the same worldview and ascribe to the same belief system, I want to understand how you see the world. Your spiritual and religious beliefs may or may not be one important topic for discussion in our work. I want you to feel free to use your religious beliefs and learning, whatever they may be, as a source of strength. I also am open to any discussion of the ways you believe that these values have created dilemmas for you as you think about your own past.

Empirical work has been conducted on the effect of religious disclosure on the client's decision to see a psychotherapist (Gregory et al., 2008). Gregory et al. (2008) found that a Christian, Jewish, and Muslim affiliation was seen more positively than disclosure of atheism. An examination of the methods, however, shows that the subjects of Gregory et al. were reacting to vignettes such as the following: "I am a licensed psychologist who is [atheist/Christian/Islamic/Jewish/no religious information provided]. I have successfully treated numerous clients over my years of practicing."

Perhaps introducing oneself as a "licensed psychologist who is atheist" can place more focus on this aspect of one's identity than is typical in psychotherapy. Therefore, the results might be due to the artificial nature of this disclosure. Although clients generally view disclosure positively, the nature of the disclosure should be in the service of the client's needs (Rachman, 1998; Rachman & Mattick, 2012; Tsai, Plummer, Kanter, Newring, & Kohlenberg, 2010). Religious clients might wish to have a discussion about the religious background of the psychotherapist, particularly because religion is intertwined with culture and may be an important part of understanding the values and goals of the client. Therefore, initiating or opening the door to religious discussion without forcing the client through that door is important.

There may be times when the client does not raise the issue but the psychotherapist perceives that religion is a prominent factor in the aftermath of the client's trauma. Kane, Cheston, and Greer (1993) examined incest survivors' religious participation and found that 61% left their faith communities. Walker et al. (2009) reviewed 34 studies pertaining to the relationship between child abuse and religion or spirituality (with 19,090 participants) and found that the majority of these studies indicated either a decline ($n = 14$) or a combination of growth and decline in religiousness or spirituality after trauma ($n = 12$). The results provided some preliminary support for the conclusion that religion or spirituality may moderate the relationship between child abuse and associated psychopathology (i.e., PTSD and other Axis I disorders).

In some cases, changes in religious behavior after trauma may reflect the avoidance symptoms of PTSD rather than an actual decline in religiosity. Traumatized clients may be avoiding the social situations common to religious practices, avoiding reminders of the moral conflicts, or avoiding a religious ceremony because of the sense of shame and "sin" that is common to trauma experience (Andrews et al., 2000). In such circumstances, psychotherapists in turn might avoid discussion of a trauma symptom that might be quite disturbing to the client because of fear of interfering with free religious choice of the trauma survivor. Each of the individuals discussed in the earlier vignettes did struggle with issues related to attendance of services for many reasons (e.g., avoidance of discussion of sin, avoidance of social interaction, fear of pressure toward forgiveness before the client was ready), and the psychotherapists involved did struggle with their concern about supporting or undermining these choices.

Returning to the concept of "talking about talking about," the psychotherapist might acknowledge to the client the concerns both might hold regarding religious discussion:

> Religion is a personal topic that is sometimes hard to talk about, especially when beliefs are held with strong conviction and come from faith and tradition. Discussions can turn into arguments when people try to convince each other of the truth of their point of view. Here we want to be able to talk about religious issues without feeling the need to convince each other. What are your thoughts?

Both Ben's psychotherapist and Maly's psychotherapists in the vignettes have fundamental religious differences from those of their clients that may affect the psychotherapy. Both psychotherapists might be concerned that their clients are confusing religious and psychological issues, perhaps avoiding one topic by emphasizing the other. From a countertransference perspective, the psychotherapist may be embedded in his or her own religious training or belief in a way that sidetracks discussion of the client's psychological issues and needs. For example, Ben's psychotherapist may feel anger and protectiveness regarding Ben's disclosure of betrayal by the priest and by the church hierarchy and fail to recognize the complexity of rejection of a sustaining faith after a trauma. Maly's psychotherapist is preoccupied with the contradiction of Maly's behavior with the psychotherapist's beliefs, to the detriment of a focus on the contradiction between her own behaviors and her own beliefs. Maly should be the major architect in her own values system and given the opportunity to explore her behavior in the context of the past trauma and the faith tradition of her upbringing.

Differences in levels of commitment to religious institutions between psychotherapist and client might lead to a difference in hierarchies of proposed interventions during the course of treatment. Open discussion of these topics between Ben and his psychotherapist might allow the two individuals to disentangle varying psychological motives for behavior in the wake of trauma. A subtle shifting of the focus from the client's value system to the psychotherapist's value system can limit the development of a collaborative relationship, hinder the client's self-discovery, and in the process, may impair the client's sense of power. The countertransference issues might be the most powerful when psychotherapist and client share the religious belief such that impact of belief on behavior choice becomes invisible.

At times, clients appear to be using religious beliefs as a justification for abusive behavior, either their own behavior or acts of abusive behavior that they have experienced. Giesbrecht and Sevcik (2000) gave the example of an individual who believed that she deserved her spousal abuse because she saw herself as spiritually inadequate. Rosenfeld (2010) also mentioned that individuals may reject medical and psychological treatment because of unique religious beliefs; for example, the mother of a psychotic adolescent was told by her religious leader to withhold psychotropic medications because her son's mental health problems were due to the "devil." Many accounts from those who endured abuse by religious leaders note the use of religious imagery or arguments to coerce or justify the abusive actions (Novšak, Mandelj, & Simonič, 2012). For example, several profiles listed on the Survivors Network of Those Abused by Priests (http://www.snapnetwork.org) describe religious leaders as discussing sexual intercourse to become closer to God through the priest or religious leader, presenting abuse as God's will, and/or warning that God would punish disclosure.

There appears to be little ethical weight to the argument that such clients should be left on their own to resolve such issues in an effort to "protect their religious freedom." As in any other issue of values, the psychotherapist need not make pronouncements about the truth of the religious belief but rather engage the client in an exploration of that belief. For example, the religious beliefs shared by Lisa and her psychotherapist about the sanctity of marriage might lead Lisa to minimize and/or dismiss the extent of the spousal abuse she is experiencing out of fear that her psychotherapist would judge her as not being a "good Christian wife." Failure to explore this religious belief could lead Lisa to see any emphasis on God's compassion and forgiveness made by her psychotherapist as evidence that she is to blame for the abuse, that is, that if she showed her husband enough compassion, the abuse would end. Even the most dogmatic of religious structures can become more nuanced with time and examination. The psychotherapist, however, must become more comfortable in allowing such examination to take place in the therapeutic hour.

Religious Interventions and Religious Behaviors

As we move from religious discussion to religious action, the controversies and concerns become more salient. The most common religious intervention discussed in the literature is the use of prayer (such as in Ben's case discussed earlier). Weld and Eriksen (2007) and Walker, Worthington, Gartner, Gorsuch, and Hanshew (2011) reported that Christian clients have strong expectations for prayer to be included in counseling, that psychotherapists would introduce the subject of prayer, and that psychotherapists would pray for them outside of session. However, Wade, Worthington, and Vogel (2007) found that only 11% of counselors in agencies without religious affiliation believe that praying with or for a client was appropriate. As in other boundary areas, much is written about the ethics of refusal to engage in certain actions, such as accepting gifts and prayer in session (Barnett & Johnson, 2011; Hathaway, 2013). Yet, little is written about benign methods of articulating this refusal. Absent any context, the statement "I prefer not to pray with you or for you" would arguably be invalidating and a potentially harmful. We do not argue that psychotherapists must agree to clients' religious requests. However, we endorse the point of view that the client has a right to an understanding of the psychotherapist's reasoning. For example, a psychotherapist who prefers not to pray with a client might state,

> There is nothing more personal than an individual's relationship with their God. I want to be able to talk with you about what you believe and how that affects your life. I do not want to impose my religious beliefs on you in some accidental way. Perhaps you could pray on behalf of both of us and I would be honored to be here with you during your prayer.

In one case treated by one of the coauthors, a client who was himself a minister disclosed that his loss of ability to pray was one of his central posttraumatic losses. In this instance, the therapist suggested that the client write out a prayer that he would like to be able to offer with conviction and bring this prayer to session to read and discuss. The following three sessions were devoted to this prayer, providing one of the most meaningful and emotionally complex topics for discussion that had occurred within the therapy. At varying times within the session, client and psychotherapist had the feeling of praying together, whereas at other times they were analyzing the needs, wishes, and beliefs at the center of the prayer. In this example, as in others, prayer can be psychotherapeutic intervention.

The strongest countertransference and transference reactions elicited by religious or spiritually related directives by the psychotherapist may be therapeutically relevant to a given situation. Clinicians interviewed in Frazier and Hansen (2009) felt that affirmative religious behaviors such as encouragement to memorize scripture or blessings by the psychotherapist were inappropriate. One of the authors of this chapter had an experience in which her own psychotherapist encouraged meditation on scripture, emphasizing a particular view of God (e.g., God as compassionate). Although the author and the psychotherapist shared a similar faith, the author felt that the intervention was too directive and would have preferred more space to come to her own decisions. In the author's case the intervention also raised an important topic for therapeutic discussion. However, she noted that the psychotherapist had not been aware of the potential negative impact of the intervention and might not have raised the issue for further discussion had the author not chosen to address it herself. Shared religious values or the client's disclosure of positive feelings of religion and spirituality should not be taken as implicit consent for religious interventions.

A contrasting example was offered by a coauthor who specialized in dialectical behavior therapy (DBT). Here, a conservative Christian family was concerned that various DBT interventions were inconsistent with their fundamental Christian beliefs. The author was able to provide the family with resources from Remuda Ranch, one of the nation's leading Christian treatment facilities for eating disorders that offered biblical support for the use of DBT skills. For example, to support the skill of mindfulness, the psychotherapist cited Proverbs 16:23 (English Standard Version): "From a wise mind comes careful and persuasive speech."

Religious Symbols and Religious Holidays

The time-honored values of neutrality in psychotherapy can be used to question any behavioral disclosure of the psychotherapist's religious beliefs or values, such as cancelling sessions on certain holidays but not others, or wearing religious jewelry, such as a cross or the Star of David. In an informal survey of 24 supervisors of interns (conducted by the authors) no psychologist required an intern to see clients on a religious holiday important to them, but many indicated they would ask the intern to make the scheduling changes surreptitiously without disclosing the reason to the client. Although we certainly respect differences in therapeutic modalities, we note two difficulties with this option.

First, there is a therapeutic distinction between psychotherapist nondisclosure as an ongoing part of the psychotherapy process, which is typical of almost all therapies, and therapeutic nondisclosure in specific unusual situations. For instance, the fact that a session might include solely client-related material in a given hour and/or that the psychotherapist might not contribute any personal anecdotes is in keeping with virtually all modalities. However, if the psychotherapist enters the room with clear physical injuries or if the psychotherapist suddenly cancels a week of sessions, a traumatized client may be captured by concerns and fantasies that could undermine the work of psychotherapy. In reanalysis of Dalenberg's (2000) sample of 84 clients who had been in psychotherapy for trauma, more than 25% stated that they had asked their psychotherapist a question regarding personal information, such as an explanation for a cancellation or demographic information about family. Approximately 63% ($n = 313$) of the requests made received an answer, and less than 9% ($n = 17$) believed that the psychotherapist disclosure had a negative impact on psychotherapy. Further, of the requests that were refused ($n = 123$), 40% were identified to have had a negative impact (pp. 233–234). These results fit with a general positive literature on the impact of psychotherapist self-disclosure.

If nondisclosure is due to the psychotherapist's orientation, he or she might consider the importance of a specific discussion of this issue with the client. Dalenberg's (2000) countertransference data suggest that, from the client's perspective, such conversations are rare. However, if nondisclosure appears to be a value to the psychotherapist, it is reasonable and even likely that the client (absent a discussion) will believe that information that they hear or infer about the psychotherapist is off-limits for discussion. Religious affiliation can be inferred from holiday preference or from other sources. Also, an important note is that clients often report that they did not reveal in psychotherapy negative feelings toward information (e.g., religious affiliation) discovered or inferred about the psychotherapist.

The issue of symbols of religious affiliation in the office decor or in the jewelry or clothing of the psychotherapist is more complicated. If the office is part of a religious organization, then specific religious symbols in the decor may be expected and even welcomed by the client. However, if the client enters treatment without the expectation of having a psychotherapist with a specific religious affiliation, the client might see the religious symbol as an endorsement of a specific belief system. We take the position that office decor should be as inclusive as possible for the population that the psychotherapist intends to see and should not include religiously specific symbols any more than it should include posters supporting a particular political candidate.

Personal jewelry or clothing, however, might be encouraged or even mandated by the psychotherapist's own spiritual or cultural beliefs. Therefore, although forbidding the psychotherapist from wearing such symbols would be problematic, the psychotherapist should recognize that his or her choices regarding physical presentation might have an impact on the client. This impact could be positive or negative and may not be raised as an issue for the client without psychotherapist intervention. The psychotherapist who wears or displays religious symbols has a special responsibility to monitor clients' personal reactions and should discuss these issues.

For example, one of the authors of this chapter was a part of a psychotherapy consultation group in which one of the psychotherapist members was a Muslim woman who wore a hijab in the form of a headscarf. An issue that was raised was how to address a client wanting to transfer to another therapist because of "differing beliefs." This feedback was perplexing because the psychotherapist had never discussed her beliefs with this client. The psychotherapist was hesitant to introduce religious and cultural beliefs with clients because she feared that she might come across as defensive, and she did not want to assume that every client would have a negative reaction. Another author, who at times wears a Star of David, has had a number of experiences with clients of German heritage who feared some judgment by the therapist. These fears almost inevitably were undisclosed until the therapist brought up the issue of reactions to the necklace. Another client, a woman who responded to her traumatic childhood by quickly agreeing with any authority figure, falsely reported her religion (stating that like the therapist, she was Jewish) for many months. Again, disclosure only occurred after the religion of the therapist became a legitimate topic of discussion.

Although client responses to the religious and cultural symbols of a psychotherapist range greatly, the trauma psychotherapist is often keen to discern even the subtle form of client avoidance. The psychotherapist introducing the idea that the client's curiosity is "safe" for discussion may provide new learning opportunities that are especially applicable for the trauma client. When a client's fear is not reinforced (e.g., rejection from the psychotherapist), these discussions may serve as a relevant in vivo example to reference when providing psychoeducation and/or preparing the client for other therapeutic exposures.

REFERENCES

Abu-Raiya, H., Pargament, K. I., & Mahoney, A. (2011). Examining coping methods with stressful interpersonal events experienced by Muslims living in the United States following the 9/11 attacks. *Psychology of Religion and Spirituality, 3,* 1–14. doi:10.1037/a0020034

Abu-Ras, W., & Abu-Bader, S. (2008). The impact of 9/11 on the Arab-American well-being. *The Journal of Muslim Mental Health, 3,* 219–242. doi:10.1080/15564900802487634

Abu-Ras, W. M., & Suarez, Z. E. (2009). Muslim men and women's perception of discrimination, hate crimes, and PTSD symptoms post 9/11. *Traumatology, 15,* 48–63. doi:10.1177/1534765609342281

Andrews, B., Brewin, C. R., Rose, S., & Kirk, M. (2000). Predicting PTSD symptoms in victims of violent crime: The role of shame, anger, and childhood abuse. *Journal of Abnormal Psychology, 109,* 69–73. doi:10.1037/0021-843X.109.1.69

Ano, G. G., & Vasconcelles, E. B. (2005). Religious coping and psychological adjustment to stress: A meta-analysis. *Journal of Clinical Psychology, 61,* 461–480. doi:10.1002/jclp.20049

Barnett, J. E., & Johnson, W. B. (2011). Integrating spirituality and religion into psychotherapy: Persistent dilemmas, ethical issues, and a proposed decision-making process. *Ethics & Behavior, 21,* 147–164. doi:10.1080/10508422.2011.551471

Bottoms, B. L., Nielsen, M., Murray, R., & Filipas, H. (2004). Religion-related child physical abuse: Characteristics and psychological outcomes. *Journal of Aggression, Maltreatment & Trauma, 8,* 87–114. doi:10.1300/J146v08n01_04

Bouchard, M. A., Normandin, L., & Seguin, M. H. (1995). Countertransference as instrument and obstacle: A comprehensive and descriptive framework. *The Psychoanalytic Quarterly, 64,* 717–745.

Cragun, C. L., & Friedlander, M. L. (2012). Experiences of Christian clients in secular psychotherapy: A mixed-methods investigation. *Journal of Counseling Psychology.* doi:10.1037/a0028283

Cross, D. G., & Khan, J. A. (1983). The values of three practitioner groups: Religious and moral aspects. *Counseling and Values, 28,* 13–19. doi:10.1002/j.2161-007X.1983.tb01143.x

Dalenberg, C. J. (2000). *Countertransference and the treatment of trauma.* Washington, DC: American Psychological Association. doi:10.1037/10380-000

Delaney, H. D., Miller, W. R., & Bisonó, A. M. (2007). Religiosity and spirituality among psychologists: A survey of clinician members of the American Psychological Association. *Professional Psychology: Research and Practice, 38,* 538–546. doi:10.1037/0735-7028.38.5.538

Denney, R. M., Aten, J. D., & Gingrich, F. C. (2008). Using spiritual self-disclosure in psychotherapy. *Journal of Psychology and Theology, 36,* 294–302.

Falsetti, S. A., Resick, P. A., & Davis, J. L. (2003). Changes in religious beliefs following trauma. *Journal of Traumatic Stress, 16,* 391–398. doi:10.1023/A:1024422220163

Frazier, R. E., & Hansen, N. D. (2009). Religious/spiritual psychotherapy behaviors: Do we do what we believe to be important? *Professional Psychology: Research and Practice, 40,* 81–87. doi:10.1037/a0011671

Freud, S. (1988). The future prospects of psychoanalytic therapy. In B. Wolstein (Ed.), *Essential papers on countertransference* (pp. 16–24). New York, NY: New York University Press. (Original work published 1910)

Gall, T., Basque, V., Damasceno-Scott, M., & Vardy, G. (2007). Spirituality and the current adjustment of adult survivors of childhood sexual abuse. *Journal for the Scientific Study of Religion, 46,* 101–117. doi:10.1111/j.1468-5906.2007.00343.x

Gelso, C. J., Fassinger, R. E., Gomez, M. J., & Latts, M. G. (1995). Countertransference reactions to lesbian clients: The role of homophobia, counselor gender, and countertransference management. *Journal of Counseling Psychology, 42,* 356–364. doi:10.1037/0022-0167.42.3.356

Giesbrecht, N., & Sevcik, I. (2000). The process of recovery and rebuilding among abused women in the conservative evangelical subculture. *Journal of Family Violence, 15,* 229–248. doi:10.1023/A:1007549401830

Goldfried, M. R., Burckell, L. A., & Eubanks-Carter, C. (2003). Therapist self-disclosure in cognitive–behavior therapy. *Journal of Clinical Psychology, 59,* 555–568. doi:10.1002/jclp.10159

Gonsiorek, J. C., Richards, P. S., Pargament, K. I., & McMinn, M. R. (2009). Ethical challenges and opportunities at the edge: Incorporating spirituality and religion into psychotherapy. *Professional Psychology: Research and Practice, 40,* 385–395. doi:10.1037/a0016488

Gonzales, D. (2008, April 15). Facing decline, an effort to market the priesthood. *The New York Times.* Retrieved from http://www.nytimes.com/2008/04/15/us/nationalspecial2/15seminarians.html?pagewanted=all&_r=0

Gregory, C., II, Pomerantz, A. M., Pettibone, J. C., & Segrist, D. J. (2008). The effect of psychologists' disclosure of personal religious background on prospective clients. *Mental Health, Religion & Culture, 11,* 369–373. doi:10.1080/13674670701438739

Greven, P. (1990). *Spare the child: The religious roots of punishment and the psychological impact of physical abuse.* New York, NY: Knopf.

Hathaway, W. L. (2013). Ethics, religious issues, and clinical child psychology. In D. F. Walker & W. L. Hathaway (Eds.), *Spiritual interventions in child and adolescent psychotherapy* (pp. 17–39). Washington, DC: American Psychological Association. doi:10.1037/13947-002

Hawkins, I. A., & Bullock, S. L. (1995). Informed consent and religious values: A neglected area of diversity. *Psychotherapy: Theory, Research, Practice, Training, 32,* 293–300. doi:10.1037/0033-3204.32.2.293

Hayes, J. A., Yeh, Y.-J., & Eisenberg, A. (2007). Good grief and not-so-good grief: Countertransference in bereavement therapy. *Journal of Clinical Psychology, 63,* 345–355. doi:10.1002/jclp.20353

Henretty, J. R., & Levitt, H. M. (2010). The role of therapist self-disclosure in psychotherapy: A qualitative review. *Clinical Psychology Review, 30,* 63–77. doi:10.1016/j.cpr.2009.09.004

Henry, W. P., Schacht, T. E., & Strupp, H. H. (1986). Structural analysis of social behavior: Application to a study of interpersonal process in differential psychotherapeutic outcome. *Journal of Consulting and Clinical Psychology, 54,* 27–31. doi:10.1037/0022-006X.54.1.27

Horst, E. (1998). *Recovering the lost self: Shame healing for victims of clergy sexual abuse.* Collegeville, MN: The Liturgical Press.

Janoff-Bulman, R. (1992). *Shattered assumptions: Towards a new psychology of trauma.* New York, NY: Free Press.

Johnson, C. V., & Hayes, J. A. (2003). Troubled Spirits: Prevalence and predictors of religious and spiritual concerns among university students and counseling center clients. *Journal of Counseling Psychology, 50*, 409–419. doi:10.1037/0022-0167.50.4.409

Joint Commission on the Accreditation of Healthcare Organizations. (2008). *Spiritual assessment*. Retrieved from http://www.jointcommission.org/mobile/standards_information/jcfaqdetails.aspx?StandardsFAQId=290&StandardsFAQChapterId=29

Kane, D., Cheston, S. E., & Greer, J. (1993). Perceptions of God by survivors of childhood sexual abuse: An exploratory study in an underresearched area. *Journal of Psychology and Theology, 21*, 228–237.

Knox, S., Catlin, L., Casper, M., & Schlosser, L. Z. (2005). Addressing religion and spirituality in psychotherapy: Clients' perspectives. *Psychotherapy Research, 15*, 287–303. doi:10.1080/10503300500090894

Krause, M. S., & Lutz, W. (2009). Process transforms inputs to determine outcomes: Therapists are responsible for managing process. *Clinical Psychology: Science and Practice, 16*, 73–81. doi:10.1111/j.1468-2850.2009.01146.x

Martinez, J. S., Smith, T. B., & Barlow, S. H. (2007). Spiritual interventions in psychotherapy: Evaluations by highly religious clients. *Journal of Clinical Psychology, 63*, 943–960. doi:10.1002/jclp.20399

McGuire, W. (Ed.). (1974). *The Freud/Jung letters*. London, England: Hogarth Press and Routledge & Kegan Paul.

McMinn, M. R., Ruiz, J. N., Marx, D., Wright, J. B., & Gilbert, N. B. (2006). Professional psychology and the doctrines of sin and grace: Christian leaders' perspectives. *Professional Psychology: Research and Practice, 37*, 295–302. doi:10.1037/0735-7028.37.3.295

Norcross, J. C. (2001). Purposes, processes and products of the task force on empirically supported therapy relationships. *Psychotherapy: Theory, Research, Practice, Training, 38*, 345–356. doi:10.1037/0033-3204.38.4.345

Norcross, J. C., & Lambert, M. J. (2011). Psychotherapy relationships that work II. *Psychotherapy, 48*, 4–8. doi:10.1037/a0022180

Novšak, R., Mandelj, T., & Simonič, B. (2012). Therapeutic implications of religious-related emotional abuse. *Journal of Aggression, Maltreatment & Trauma, 21*, 31–44. doi:10.1080/10926771.2011.627914

O'Doherty, M. (2008). *Empty pulpits: Ireland's retreat from religion*. Dublin, Ireland: Gill and Macmillan.

Okiishi, J., Lambert, M. J., Nielsen, S. L., & Ogles, B. M. (2003). Waiting for supershrink: An empirical analysis of therapist effects. *Clinical Psychology & Psychotherapy, 10*, 361–373. doi:10.1002/cpp.383

Oren, L., & Possick, C. (2009). Religiosity and posttraumatic stress following forced relocation. *Journal of Loss and Trauma, 14*, 144–160. doi:10.1080/15325020902724586

6

SPIRITUALITY AND MAKING MEANING: IMPLICATIONS FOR THERAPY WITH TRAUMA SURVIVORS

JEANNE M. SLATTERY AND CRYSTAL L. PARK

As three recent and divergent memoirs from members of the same family suggest (i.e., Burroughs, 2002; J. E. Robison, 2007; M. Robison, 2011), the world is not a static and objective place where truth is easily known and recognized. Instead, people may hold very different views of their world than do close family and friends. People's systems of meaning help them interpret and label experiences (e.g., good/bad, fair/unfair, dangerous/desirable), which then creates the emotional and behavioral impact of these experiences as well as later encounters (Park, Edmondson, & Mills, 2010). Meaning systems also guide people's choices of cognitive and behavioral goals (Lazarus & Folkman, 1984; Park, 2005).

Trauma, by definition, is an event so discrepant from a person's meaning system that it alters or damages that person's meaning system (and sometimes those of their family and friends; Janoff-Bulman, 1992). This discrepancy among beliefs, values, goals, and perceptions of events often causes distress and motivates both positive and negative changes (Slattery & Park, 2012a). This definition of trauma applies to all types of trauma.

http://dx.doi.org/10.1037/14500-007
Spiritually Oriented Psychotherapy for Trauma, D. F. Walker, C. A. Courtois, and J. D. Aten (Editors)

Although most writers have focused on the ways that trauma damages or even "shatters" meaning (e.g., Janoff-Bulman, 1992), focusing on meaning and creating an adaptive and growth-promoting sense of meaning can be part of healing from trauma. In this chapter, we outline the meaning-making framework and meaning response styles of people exposed to trauma, then describe and apply the meaning-making framework to spiritually oriented psychotherapy with people exposed to trauma.

MEANING SYSTEMS

The meaning-making model has its roots in both cognitive and existential perspectives, yet is broader than either approach. Meaning comprises not only beliefs but also identity, values, goals, and sense of purpose (Park, 2010; Park & Folkman, 1997). Although existentialists tend to focus on more ultimate meanings (e.g., death, freedom, intimacy, meaninglessness; Yalom, 1980), our perspective also includes more mundane meanings guiding day-to-day behaviors, such as parenting, relating to others, work, and leisure pursuits. Our perspective further differs from those of other approaches in that we more explicitly examine spiritual meanings. For many people, spirituality is the foundation of their meaning system—underpinning their beliefs, identity, goals, and values; providing a sense of purpose; and serving as a primary lens through which they perceive and interpret their world (McIntosh, 1995; Ozorak, 2005).

The meaning-making approach further assumes that people's behavior, problems, and attempted solutions are understandable once their unique meanings (global meaning and appraised meaning) and context are understood (Evans, 1993). This assumption is important because individual appraisals of meaning might help explain why some people and not others develop posttraumatic stress disorder (PTSD; e.g., Bonanno, Moskowitz, Papa, & Folkman, 2005; Rothbaum, Foa, Riggs, Murdock, & Walsh, 1992). Further, as many trauma survivors often seem "crazy" both to themselves and to others, searching for the meanings they hold and helping shift these meanings to more adaptive ones can help them become more understandable to themselves and others and substantially contribute to the healing process.

Meaning systems provide the general framework through which individuals structure their lives (*global meaning*), guiding their appraisals of specific encounters with their environment (*appraised meaning*). Global meaning is central in determining patterns of behavior, thought, and emotion both during everyday life and following trauma (Park, 2005; Silberman, 2005). Its three aspects—beliefs, goals, and sense of meaning and purpose—are further described later (Park & Folkman, 1997), along with some ways that religiousness and spirituality influence them. We return to this framework throughout the chapter.

Global beliefs are widely encompassing assumptions about the world. These beliefs include, for example, beliefs about the benevolence and fairness of the world, personal control, luck, and vulnerability (Janoff-Bulman, 1992; Koltko-Rivera, 2004). Differences in global beliefs can be attributed to individual histories and to cultural, religious, and spiritual factors. Global goals can be secular or spiritual in form, but even more secular goals, such as parenting well, can be influenced by a person's religiousness or spirituality (e.g., a child's sinful nature must be controlled, children are gifts from God) and can contribute to a sense of meaning stemming from believing that one is following a satisfying spiritual path (Baumeister, 1991; Emmons, 2005; McGregor & Little, 1998). Global meaning also has an emotional aspect, which refers to the extent to which people experience a sense of meaning, purpose in life, or connection to something greater than themselves (Klinger, 1977; Peterson, Park, & Seligman, 2005; Reker & Wong, 1988).

Global meaning influences appraised meanings of everyday events, concrete day-to-day goals, and general sense of well-being and life satisfaction (e.g., Emmons, 1999). Many events are simply assimilated into global meaning, requiring little perceptual distortion or cognitive reworking. However, some events, including trauma, require accommodation to make sense of them, given that they are highly discrepant from global meaning (Janoff-Bulman, 1992).

A MEANING-MAKING MODEL OF TRAUMA

Many models of traumatic stress focus on the role of belief violations as a causal factor of trauma symptoms (e.g., Foa & Rothbaum, 1998; Janoff-Bulman, 1992). In their review of the literature, Park, Mills, and Edmondson (2012) concluded that people diagnosed with PTSD have difficulty consolidating trauma into their current meaning system, causing oscillations between avoidance and intrusions. In a related vein, Janoff-Bulman (1992) observed that trauma often shatters previously held assumptions that the world is just, benevolent, and predictable and that the individual is competent and worthy. She concluded that PTSD symptoms stem from these violations. In addition, Foa and Rothbaum (1998) observed that people with rigid pretrauma belief systems are more vulnerable to trauma than those holding more flexible belief systems. People with rigid negative pretrauma beliefs are more likely to have those beliefs confirmed by trauma than people with more flexible belief systems, whereas those with rigid positive pretrauma beliefs are more likely to have difficulty understanding trauma using their previous worldview. Either way, people with rigid pretrauma beliefs are likely to experience the kinds of pervasive threat and feelings of personal unworthiness generally observed in people diagnosed with PTSD. Finally, Davis and Asliturk (2011) extended these ideas further, observing that people who are resilient are also realistic and recognize that adversity happens; nonetheless, they also use proactive coping and accept whatever happens.

People's sense of meaning is influenced by their tendency to pay attention to negatively valenced encounters. This tendency serves to protect them from danger, although it makes them more anxious and afraid in the process (Anderson, Siegel, & Barrett, 2011). Further, those people who have overgeneral autobiographical memories—tending to ruminate in an overly general manner about how unsafe the world is or how vulnerable or guilty they are, rather than perceiving events in specific and nuanced manners—are much more likely to develop PTSD (Bryant, Sutherland, & Guthrie, 2007; Sutherland & Bryant, 2005). Their meaning systems fail to promote a strategy for looking at the world that helps them be resilient in the face of adversity.

The previously described explanations of trauma have focused on cognitions and beliefs, and although the meaning-making model recognizes the importance of beliefs, it also considers the goals structuring and guiding a person's life (Park et al., 2012). For many people, trauma shapes how people see themselves and their future. When asked to identify their goals, for example, trauma survivors with PTSD reported more trauma-related, negatively valenced "defining memories" than control participants or trauma survivors without PTSD (Sutherland & Bryant, 2005). Trauma survivors with PTSD were more likely to identify trauma-related goals as their major personal goals. Discrepancies between current and pretrauma beliefs and goals (e.g., "this cannot happen") can be profoundly distressing, even when no belief violation occurs (Park, 2008, 2010; Park et al., 2012).

Discrepancies Between Appraised and Global Meanings

Laboratory-based experimental research has demonstrated that when people experience discrepancies among their beliefs, behaviors, and goals, they feel distressed and are motivated to reduce the discrepancy (e.g., Heine, Proulx, & Vohs, 2006; Plaks, Grant, & Dweck, 2005). However, consistency between appraised and global meanings creates a sense of peace and harmony. People whose behavior is more congruent with their expressed goals in terms of effort, time, and money are psychologically better off than those who are less closely aligned (e.g., Mahoney et al., 2005; Sheldon & Elliot, 1999). People are motivated to create consistency, and may do so by avoiding discrepant information, distorting it, assimilating it into current meaning systems, or changing global meaning systems to accommodate it.

People experience discrepancies when they interpret situations as violating their global beliefs (e.g., that God is good, omniscient, and omnipotent yet allowed her to be raped) or goals (e.g., wanting to be in an intimate relationship

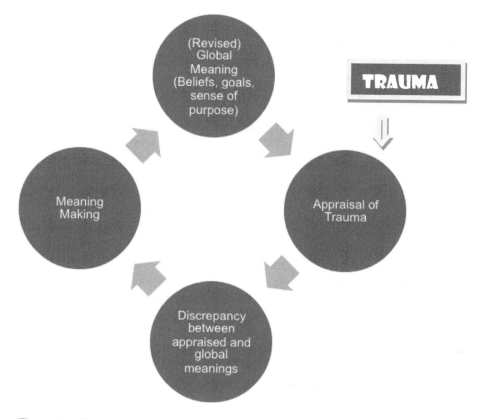

Figure 6.1. The role of trauma in the meaning-making model.

but feeling dirty, unsafe, and undeserving of such a relationship). Discrepancies can also arise when global beliefs or goals are in conflict with one another (e.g., wanting to seek justice but also wanting to put a traumatic event in the past; Baumeister, 1991; Emmons, 2005; Park, 2005).

Discrepancies from global meaning create distress, but that distress also recursively initiates an additional process of *meaning making* (Park, 2010; Park, Edmondson, Fenster, & Blank, 2008; Park et al., 2010), which can lead to changes in appraisals of the trauma (e.g., coming to see it as less damaging or perhaps even fortuitous), changes in global meaning (e.g., viewing God and oneself differently), and stress-related growth (e.g., experiencing increased appreciation for life, stronger connections with family and friends, or greater awareness of one's strengths). This model is summarized in Figure 6.1. The meaning-making process helps people reduce their sense of discrepancy between appraised and global meanings and restore a sense of the world as meaningful and their lives as worthwhile and having purpose.

When successful, the meaning-making process is related to better adjustment to stressful events (for reviews, see Collie & Long, 2005; Gillies & Neimeyer, 2006; Lee, Cohen, Edgar, Laizner, & Gagnon, 2004; Park, 2010; Skaggs & Barron, 2006).

As suggested earlier, people's appraised meanings can be complex and characterized by unstable dialectics. For example, throughout the diagnosis and treatment of cancer, people often experience pervasive sadness, physical loss, and anxiety alongside feelings of gratitude, connection, and personal growth (Zebrack & Cella, 2005). Similarly, following a trauma, people appear to attempt to reconcile their previous beliefs with their discrepant experience of trauma (e.g., betrayal, shame, problems with trust; Gray, Maguen, & Litz, 2007). In fact, posttraumatic symptoms may reflect vacillations between an awareness of a discrepancy between what they believe and what they have perceived, along with a desire to avoid these perceived discrepancies (Gray et al., 2007; Horowitz, 1986; Park et al., 2012; Steger & Park, 2012). These dialectics in meaning can be uncomfortable; people often compensate by simplifying their experience and focusing on only one pole at a time (e.g., the fears and anxieties or the feelings of growth); yet, the very act of simplifying experience and choosing one pole over the other puts the person at greater risk of developing posttraumatic stress symptoms.

Processes of Meaning Making

As already noted, when people experience something that does not fit into their meaning system, they may respond in one of several ways. They may avoid, distort, ruminate, problem solve, attempt to assimilate the information into the current meaning system, or make modifications to global meaning to accommodate discrepant information. Coping strategies have different consequences for well-being, self-concept, self-efficacy, and self-esteem, and may put people at differential risk of depression, anxiety, or posttraumatic stress symptoms (cf. Hardin, Weigold, Robitschek, & Nixon, 2007).

Meaning making refers to attempts to resolve violations of global meaning by reaching a more acceptable appraisal of a distressing event or changing one's global meaning to accommodate it (Steger & Park, 2012). Through the process of meaning making, people come to see or understand the event, their world, or themselves differently and reform their beliefs and goals to regain consistency among them. Meaning-making processes can include both automatic processes (including intrusive thoughts and dreams) and more effortful and deliberate attempts at making meaning (Park, 2010). When meaning making is successful, it can result in improved well-being as well as perceptions of posttraumatic growth or positive life changes (e.g., stronger relationships, changed sense of identity, greater self-confidence and coping abilities, increased spirituality and appreciation for life), a deepened sense of meaning and purpose, and restored core beliefs (e.g., control, a just world; Park, 2010; Park et al., 2008; Park & Folkman, 1997). The process of making meaning, however, can be difficult and is initially associated with a drop in functioning and greater distress, more perceptions of violations of global meaning, and more intrusions and rumination (cf. Park et al., 2012).

The literature regarding the usefulness of meaning making has been mixed; some researchers have reported increased distress and symptoms associated with meaning making following adverse events, whereas others have reported that meaning making is related to improved adjustment (for a review, see Park, 2010). Park and her colleagues (2008) hypothesized that these differences were attributable to differences in when and how adjustment is assessed in the meaning-making process, and proposed that distress actually mobilizes a search for meaning as well as leads to meaning. Therefore, Park (2010; Park et al., 2008) distinguished between the meaning-making process (the search for meaning) and meaning made (the products of a search for meaning), the latter of which is associated with more positive outcomes.

The meaning-making process could leave a person with either positive or negative meanings (cf. Park, 2010), but in terms of therapeutic interventions, meaning making should leave clients with a more optimistic and hopeful sense of self and their world (redemptive stories), rather than as damaged or broken, living in a dangerous world (contamination stories; McAdams, Reynolds, Lewis, Patton, & Bowman, 2001). In fact, consistent with our discussion of meaning made, McAdams and his colleagues (2001) reported that people who told redemptive stories (describing surviving and thriving following adversity) reported higher levels of life satisfaction, self-esteem, and coherence, as well as lower levels of depression, than people telling contamination stories (describing having been crushed by adversity).

SPIRITUAL ASPECTS OF MEANING AFFECTED BY TRAUMA

Trauma clearly affects many people's physical, spiritual, and psychological well-being, interfering with their ability to connect with something larger than themselves, whether it be God, the Divine, some ultimate reality, or the transcendent (Hill & Pargament, 2008). This disconnect can "produce a pervasive state of dispiritedness among [trauma] survivors" (Everly & Lating, 2004, p. 48). Trauma can "violate [people's] faith in a natural or divine order and cast [them] into a state of existential crisis" where they lose faith in an all-powerful and good God, recognize that their world is anything but safe and well-ordered, and begin to believe that they are bad and deserving of bad outcomes (Herman, 1992, p. 51).

This dispiritedness also seems to come from a failure to find meaning and a larger sense of purpose that, paraphrasing Nietzsche, provides the ultimate why and allows us to bear "almost any how" (Nietzsche, 1895/2012, p. 10). In that vein, Frankl (1959/2006) concluded "one had to give [prisoners at Auschwitz] a why—an aim—for their lives, in order to strengthen them to bear the terrible how of their existence" (p. 76). Faith and spirituality provide this greater sense of purpose for many people, shaping their view of the world, making suffering understandable and bearable, while providing a sense of coherence, commitment, hopefulness, meaning, purpose, and trust that allow them to make it through difficult times (Everly & Lating, 2004; Park et al., 2012). In the Judeo–Christian tradition, the Biblical figure of Job, for example, did not understand the unnatural losses that he received, yet his faith allowed him to survive these losses: "The LORD gave, and the LORD hath taken away; blessed be the name of the LORD" (King James Version, Job, 1:21). For many people, however, trauma shatters this sense of meaning and coherence, and instead they experience confusion, anger, bitterness, hopelessness, and disillusionment (Herman, 1992).

For many people, spiritual and more secular issues are intrinsically linked. When religion and spirituality inform people's global meaning, their understanding of God (e.g., loving and benevolent or wrathful) becomes connected to their self-concept (e.g., chosen by God or unworthy), this world (e.g., one step on a journey or illusory), and the next (e.g., heaven, reincarnation, nothing following this life; Park et al., 2012; Slattery & Park, 2012b). This connection between spiritual and psychological processes can be seen in Marsha Linehan's description of her spontaneous spiritual healing when she was "a desperate 20-year-old whom doctors gave little chance of surviving outside the hospital" (Carey, 2011, para. 33):

> "One night I was kneeling in there, looking up at the cross, and the whole place became gold—and suddenly I felt something coming toward me," she said. "It was this shimmering experience, and I just ran back to my room and said, 'I love myself.' It was the first time I remember talking to myself in the first person. I felt transformed."
>
> The high lasted about a year, before the feelings of devastation returned in the wake of a romance that ended. But something was different. She could now weather her emotional storms without cutting or harming herself. (Carey, 2011, para. 35–36)

As Linehan experienced spiritual healing, her self-concept also changed, allowing her to accept and love herself, as well as to begin to cope well with difficult life experiences.

Spiritual connections do not inherently "protect" or "cure" people. Instead, for both religious and spiritual people—and those who are not—there appears to be a meaning-making process, which as described earlier, is initially associated with increased symptoms; nonetheless, with time, religiousness and spirituality appear to be helpful to the meaning-making process and are related to improved functioning (Park et al., 2012).

In sum, people's appraised meanings determine how they understand and bear the trials and sorrows of the human condition. Their religious and spiritual views, as part of their global meaning, may inform their understanding of trauma and direct their responses. As we discuss further later, psychotherapists can work with their clients in such a way as to close discrepancies, develop more positive senses of meaning, and promote psychological and spiritual healing.

CLINICAL IMPLICATIONS OF THE MEANING-MAKING MODEL

Although many people experience depression, anxiety, or posttraumatic stress symptoms following a trauma, PTSD is not an inevitable or even a normative response to trauma (e.g., Bonanno et al., 2005; Rothbaum et al., 1992; Steger & Park, 2012). Whether a trauma survivor develops PTSD seems to be at least in part related to perceived discrepancies between global meaning and appraised meaning, as well as how clients approach resolving these discrepancies. People who cope with these discrepancies in negative ways, including nonproductive rumination, are at greater risk (e.g., Raes et al., 2006). Further, people who maintain overly rigid beliefs about self, others, and the world at large are also at increased risk (Foa & Rothbaum, 1998), as are those holding overgeneral memories for events (Bryant et al., 2007; Raes et al., 2006; Sutherland & Bryant, 2005).

Initial assessments of clients, particularly those with a history of trauma, should consider the following sorts of questions:

- How does the client think about the trauma, self, world, and spiritual and religious concerns? Does trauma contaminate worldview—and to what degree (more specific or global)?
- To what degree does the client see coherence in the self or world? To what degree does the trauma cause a discrepancy between global and appraised meanings? In what ways?
- What dialectics in meaning does the client vacillate between? Does the client believe that only one arm of the dialectic should be experienced? If so, which one?
- How do clients handle the discrepancy (avoidance, rumination, maladaptive coping, problem solving, meaning making)? Are their appraisals rigid and inflexible? To what degree do they exclude some perspectives of the trauma, self, others, and the world? What consequences are associated with their choices?

- Temporally distant trauma may be associated with layers of appraised meaning added during developmental stages and milestones. How have beliefs about trauma, self, others, and the world changed across time?
- In what ways do secular issues connect with godly ones and vice versa (e.g., questioning the nature of God may also raise questions about other people)? If the client has become disconnected from religious and spiritual supports, are there also more pervasive feelings of alienation and feelings of being unprotected (Wilson & Moran, 1998)? These feelings may also arise in the therapy room.
- Clients may have a range of beliefs and feelings (e.g., anger, bitterness, alienation) that are directed at God or a higher power, which they see as irrational or attempt to dismiss (Wilson & Moran, 1998). Again, these concerns may show up in the therapy room, where clients may expect their therapist to confirm their fears that they are alone, evil, dirty, guilty, and/or unforgiveable.
- How are current perceptions of trauma affected by and affecting interpretations of other events (Park et al., 2010)? Assessing the broader context (e.g., previous trauma, loss, oppression) can help psychotherapists recognize their clients' global and situational beliefs and identify places to intervene (Park & Slattery, 2009; Slattery & Park, 2011).
- Although their symptoms may not necessarily make sense to clients, consider that symptoms may make sense from their meaning system. Assuming meaningfulness may help clients develop a sense of coherence and meaningfulness.

In the course of treatment, psychotherapists must help clients (a) develop more flexible ways of thinking about trauma and related stimuli, (b) problem solve and use problem solving and other ways of healthy coping in response to changeable aspects of trauma-related stressors, and (c) reframe and make more adaptive meanings of unchangeable events. Nonetheless, although functioning tends to improve once a positive, self-affirming meaning is made, both clients and therapists should be aware that there is often first a drop in functioning and greater distress during the meaning-making process (Park et al., 2012).

People with a history of trauma may hold global or appraised meanings that are extreme, rigid, demanding, and pessimistic in tone. Therapists can help clients develop more flexible and complex ways of thinking about the trauma, self, others, and the world. They might ask, for example, "Can the actions of one person or group really stand in for those of everyone?" "Is it likely that this other person's views of you are a perfect and infallible perspective?" "Is it really the case that you're safe nowhere?" Challenging extreme and unrealistic views is one step toward closing discrepancies between global and appraised meanings. Although one person or group may have done something terrible, not everyone is terrible.

People with a history of trauma often have difficulty handling distress, which may reflect their difficulties in making sense of past traumas and finding a satisfying sense of meaning in the world. The dialectical approaches of dialectical behavior therapy and mindfulness-based cognitive therapy can be helpful with such clients by encouraging open and nonjudgmental contact with both pleasant or unpleasant life experiences, cognitions, and emotional reactions. Psychotherapists can help clients respond to distress more nonjudgmentally and to stressors without being becoming confused or disoriented or responding in ways that increase their distress.

Psychotherapists can also help clients close discrepancies and make meaning in other ways. Meaning making is often a normal part of psychotherapy. Psychotherapists offer clients reframes and interpretations, challenge them to perceive difficult events from different perspectives, and wonder whether anything positive resulted. With clients, they may consider why traumatic events might have occurred, identify heretofore unrecognized strengths, and develop new skills (that might lead clients to develop new ways of seeing themselves and the trauma). Psychotherapists can help clients draw distinctions between past events and current people and situations to draw more health-promoting meanings (see Figure 6.1). In each of these examples, however, psychotherapists encouraging meaning making may focus on more existential issues than are typically focused on in treatment. In doing so, they help clients achieve some satisfying resolution in how they approach the trauma, themselves, others, the world, and spiritual issues, rather than continuing to ruminate or cycle through avoidance and repetition or rumination.

Of course, the meaning-making model does not preclude other sorts of coping responses to trauma, including problem solving, venting, distraction, and humor. In fact, problem solving changeable aspects of a situation may be more adaptive than solely attempting to make meaning. To illustrate the use of a religion or meaning systems approach to conceptualize a case, we present the following case study, highlighting unique aspects of this approach with survivors of trauma.

An Example

Kenn[1] (age 42) was seen episodically in therapy over a period of 15 years for symptoms of panic, serious depression, and severe paranoia (at one point he believed that there were video cameras watching him). Initially, treatment

---

[1]This case study is a composite of the stories of several clients seen by Jeanne Slattery; identifying information has been changed and a pseudonym was used. Clients gave permission to use case material.

focused on stabilizing him, dealing with current stressors (e.g., significant communication problems in his marriage, feeling targeted at work, negotiating dating) and reducing symptoms.

Kenn was the oldest of four children in a devout upper-middle-class Catholic family. When he initially described his childhood, he said it was "good" and that he was "lucky." Only later did he report a confusing and emotionally abusive family environment. His mother, for example, left his younger siblings in his care for long periods when he was as young as 5 years old. On a number of occasions, his mother threatened to run away from home—and had Kenn's preschool-age siblings help pack her suitcase. When he was about 3 or 4, Kenn was allowed to wear his new sneakers outside in the woods shortly after a rain, and he came home with his shoes muddy. His mother yelled at him and beat him. He remembered his mother frequently and relentlessly criticizing and railing at him at the dinner table, calling him names, and leaving him in tears. Even as an adult, phone conversations with his mother would leave him anxious and upset because he would perceive her attacking his wife and adult children and, by extension, Kenn himself. Annual visits to or from his mother left him feeling panicky and guilty, with a knot in his stomach for months beforehand and afterward. During these periods, he had increased difficulties at work and with his family (e.g., difficulties concentrating, irritability, resentment toward coworkers, communication problems).

Although his family of origin was chaotic and emotionally abusive, Kenn reported they looked good to others—the children were clean and nicely dressed and sat quietly in church. His mother was very involved with the church, being part of the altar committee and teaching Sunday school. His family frequently had nuns, priests, and deacons in and out of the home; the nuns who lived down the street took care of the children after his youngest brother was born. He believed that his mother attributed problems to him alone, rather than to her own unhappiness or alcohol abuse (which Kenn had been unable to identify as a child).

This appraisal that problems were his alone was reinforced by the nuns, priests, and deacons who visited their home and who, despite hearing his mother's frequent railing at the children, sometimes commented on what a close family they were and how lucky the children were to have her as a mother. He believed these adults, despite at some level believing that his mother's behavior—and his father's willingness to overlook it—was wrong; God's authority seemed to underlie their observations. He perceived his early catechism lessons as indicating that right and wrong were clear and easily identified; he continued to believe this long after such ways of thinking were no longer age-typical for someone as bright and thoughtful as he was. This way of thinking further reinforced his conclusions that he was wrong, bad, and a disappointment.

Kenn seemed to endow God and His representatives with an authority and clarity of vision that undermined his ability to trust his own perceptions, especially of authority figures. As a result, he mistrusted his perceptions of others, their behavior, and his emotions. He often felt unsafe and attacked, while simultaneously overlooking and excusing behavior that most people would have clearly found wrong (e.g., abusive behavior in his adult relationships). This may have contributed to difficulties in a prior job, in which he perceived what may have been normal feedback and directions as attacks, and also to the demise of his first two marriages, in which he failed to erect healthy boundaries and accepted abusive behavior.

Early in treatment, Kenn had difficulty attributing problems to his mother, being surprised by the suggestion that she seemed to have a significant history of abusing alcohol, and appeared to have narcissistic and histrionic personality traits. These reframes of his mother's behavior were welcomed but were also threatening, and he left that course of treatment prematurely (he was doing much better than when he entered treatment). During the most recent stage of treatment, Kenn had difficulty identifying anything good about his mother and had difficulty remembering any positive memories of their time together. He attributed problems solely to her, dodged her phone calls, and identified reasons to avoid visiting her. Unfortunately, these responses left him feeling helpless and out of control and compromised his ability to have a positive, anxiety- and guilt-free relationship with his mother. Further, Kenn's mother was aging and physically fragile; he wanted to find some way of ending their earthly relationship on a more positive note.

During this period, Kenn's views of his mother vacillated, leaving him frequently anxious and confused. On the one hand, he held negative views of his mother and her behavior, which he perceived as wrong and which served as a model of what he did not want to be as a person or as a father, yet on the other hand he also accepted God's appraisal (as received through the priests, nuns, and deacons) that their family was close and that he was lucky to have had her as a parent. He was able to identify his mother as narcissistic and her drinking as out of control, yet he could not reconcile these appraisals with other pictures of her (e.g., all her children neatly dressed in church; she being a devout and active Catholic).

Kenn had many cognitive and interpersonal strengths and was currently successful at his job and marriage, suggesting that some positive things came from this abusive period, yet he tended to overlook these strengths unless they were specifically identified. When he was given any sort of negative feedback, he tended to collapse or become defensive—negative feedback reinforced negative self-perceptions and contradicted any tentatively accepted strengths. We began to draw distinctions between his mother's judgmental and critical responses of him and others' responses to him.

Kenn was anxiously attached to his parents and unable to accept a totally negative view of his mother. We explored who his mother was and put her in a context of time and place (genteel, upper-middle-class Boston in the 1970s) to identify what she had done well and why she might have behaved in unacceptable ways. We began to see her as deeply flawed but also as having some real strengths.

This reframe of Kenn's mother's behavior as "deeply flawed" was useful on a number of grounds. First, it allowed him to hold his mother accountable but also to see her as a real person and reconcile opposing dialectics in his view of her (good/bad, loving/abusive). He came to believe that she—and he—had made mistakes, could be held accountable for these mistakes, but that she also was a good person in other ways. Second, and perhaps more important, he was able to see her as deeply flawed but that, like a diamond (his best friend worked for a diamond wholesaler), those flaws might be unperceived by all but a highly trained observer; instead, most people would see the diamond's brilliance. This reframe allowed Kenn to reconcile his view of his mother with that held by their religious visitors ("They hadn't known, were human and not omniscient, and were themselves the product of their time and religion, which was often harsh"). Finally, we discussed Kenn's work to add another dimension to his perception of his mother and himself. He worked in a homeless shelter and appeared to be compassionate even with some of the very difficult visitors to the shelter. Together, we explored what allowed him to be successful in his work, where he was able to hold people responsible but also acknowledge their limitations, given their own deeply flawed natures. As a result, he began to perceive himself differently and to transfer skills that were successfully used in other parts of his life to his relationship with his mother.

While driving one day, Kenn listened to a radio show on which they talked about forgiving the killers of several local police officers. He almost had an accident and had to pull off the road when one caller suggested that forgiving the killer did not mean that the killer was blameless but that forgiveness could allow the families to separate themselves from the trauma and heal. He began to frame his work in therapy using these ideas: He was not trying to hold his mother blameless or forgive her for her sake, but for his own. He was not excusing her behavior, but he needed to accept the depth of the injury that he had incurred.

Analysis

Kenn entered treatment experiencing significant distress, guilt, and confusion surrounding his relationship with his mother, particularly their visits and phone calls. Although Kenn was bright, capable, and accomplished at work, when thinking about his mother and family of origin issues, he tended to hold rigid, dichotomous beliefs. His childhood memories tended to be overgeneral, initially deleting negative events and later in treatment deleting more positive ones.

His distress, guilt, and confusion seemed to reflect discrepancies between global and appraised beliefs as well as goals. People told him that he was "so lucky" to have his mother as a parent. He did not feel lucky, yet believed their attribution. If he was lucky, then they—and by extension God—must have believed that he deserved the abuse he experienced. As a result of these ruminative processes, he had difficulty accurately judging the intentions of authority figures and believing that he deserved to be treated well (although he also wanted to feel safe and accepted and to be treated well). These concerns seemed to bleed across settings and may have been contributing factors in problems with an earlier marriage and job.

Because Kenn (and family friends, religious visitors, and God) put his mother on a pedestal, he perceived her "crimes" as especially serious. Talking about his mother as "deeply flawed" allowed Kenn to begin to hold both positive and negative aspects of his mother simultaneously. Further, his own reframe (that she was flawed in the same ways that diamonds are) allowed him to understand why religious visitors to their home had overlooked and apparently endorsed abusive behavior (untrained observers would have difficulty identifying a diamond's flaws). These discussions humanized his mother (and his perceptions of himself); made it possible for him to recognize and use the critical thinking skills, compassion, and empathy that he already used effectively with his consumers; closed the discrepancies he had experienced; and caused him to accept his mother's limitations, while still working for the best possible relationship he could have with her. These new meanings decreased the amount of distress that he felt in and out of therapy and allowed him to call and visit his parents with less guilt and anxiety.

A Caveat

Potentially traumatic events do not inevitably shatter a person's sense of meaning (Bonanno et al., 2005; Steger & Park, 2012). Some people may experience a sense of loss or grief, yet perceive that loss as a normal part of life. They may still be deemed healthy by both friends and clinicians (Bonanno et al., 2005). Relatively resilient people such as these, who have only minor adjustment problems following potentially traumatic events, are unlikely to present for psychotherapy to help resolve them.

Even people who do experience a great violation of their sense of global meaning may respond to that violation in a variety of different ways. Bonanno, Pat-Horenczyk, and Noll (2011) identified two pathways, each independently associated with good adjustment following trauma: a *trauma focus* (emphasizing processing the trauma) and a *forward focus* (emphasizing moving past the trauma). Each pathway decreases the impact of trauma exposure (in terms of posttraumatic symptoms), although each is composed of different meaning-making strategies. The trauma focus makes meaning by facing "the grim reality head on," whereas the forward focus uses other meaning-making approaches, including "look[ing] for a silver lining," remembering that "things will get better," and maintaining a schedule that is "as constant as possible" (Bonanno et al., 2011, p. 120). Nonetheless, people who are flexible in their coping style, using both approaches to significant degrees, report the fewest posttraumatic stress symptoms.

Meaning making takes many different forms in addition to reexperiencing, including many other cognitive and emotional processes (Steger & Park, 2012). Therapists have to identify which meaning-making approaches specific clients will best respond to, as well as encourage them to become more flexible in their meaning-making processes. As change tends to be more rapid when focusing on symptoms, current situations, and events in conscious awareness than when focusing on historical events (Prochaska & Norcross, 2009), when possible and indicated by client diagnosis, stage of change, interests, and dynamics, therapists might begin with interventions emphasizing forward-focused coping and later emphasize cognitive and emotional reexperiencing, as appropriate.

REFERENCES

Anderson, E., Siegel, E. H., & Barrett, L. F. (2011). What you feel influences what you see: The role of affective feelings in resolving binocular rivalry. *Journal of Experimental Social Psychology, 47*, 856–860. doi:10.1016/j.jesp.2011.02.009

Baumeister, R. F. (1991). *Meanings of life.* New York, NY: Guilford Press.

Bonanno, G. A., Moskowitz, J. T., Papa, A., & Folkman, S. (2005). Resilience to loss in bereaved spouses, bereaved parents, and bereaved gay men. *Journal of Personality and Social Psychology, 88*, 827–843. doi:10.1037/0022-3514.88.5.827

Bonanno, G. A., Pat-Horenczyk, R., & Noll, J. (2011). Coping flexibility and trauma: The Perceived Ability to Cope With Trauma (PACT) scale. *Psychological Trauma: Theory, Research, Practice, and Policy, 3*, 117–129. doi:10.1037/a0020921

Bryant, R. A., Sutherland, K., & Guthrie, R. M. (2007). Impaired specific autobiographical memory as a risk factor for posttraumatic stress after trauma. *Journal of Abnormal Psychology, 116*, 837–841. doi:10.1037/0021-843X.116.4.837

Burroughs, A. (2002). *Running with scissors.* New York, NY: Picador.

Carey, B. (2011, June 23). Expert on mental illness reveals her own fight. *The New York Times.* Retrieved from http://www.nytimes.com/2011/06/23/health/23lives.html?pagewanted=1&_r=4&hp

Collie, K., & Long, B. C. (2005). Considering "meaning" in the context of breast cancer. *Journal of Health Psychology, 10,* 843–853. doi:10.1177/1359105305057318

Davis, C. G., & Asliturk, E. (2011). Toward a positive psychology of coping with anticipated events. *Canadian Psychology/Psychologie Canadienne, 52,* 101–110.

Emmons, R. A. (1999). *The psychology of ultimate concerns.* New York, NY: Guilford Press.

Emmons, R. A. (2005). Emotion and religion. In R. F. Paloutzian & C. L. Park (Eds.), *Handbook of the psychology of religion and spirituality* (pp. 235–252). New York, NY: Guilford Press.

Evans, I. M. (1993). Constructional perspectives in clinical assessment. *Psychological Assessment, 5,* 264–272. doi:10.1037/1040-3590.5.3.264

Everly, G. S., & Lating, J. M. (2004). *Personality-guided therapy for posttraumatic stress disorder.* Washington, DC: American Psychological Association. doi:10.1037/10649-000

Foa, E. B., & Rothbaum, B. O. (1998). *Treating the trauma of rape: Cognitive–behavioral therapy for PTSD.* New York, NY: Guilford Press.

Frankl, V. E. (1959/2006). *Man's search for meaning.* Boston, MA: Beacon Press.

Gillies, J., & Neimeyer, R. A. (2006). Loss, grief, and the search for significance: Toward a model of meaning reconstruction in bereavement. *Journal of Constructivist Psychology, 19,* 31–65. doi:10.1080/10720530500311182

Gray, M. J., Maguen, S., & Litz, B. T. (2007). Schema constructs and cognitive models of posttraumatic stress disorder. In L. P. Riso, P. L. du Toit, D. J. Stein, & J. E. Young (Eds.), *Cognitive schemas and core beliefs in psychological problems: A scientist–practitioner guide* (pp. 59–92). Washington, DC: American Psychological Association. doi:10.1037/11561-004

Hardin, E. E., Weigold, I. K., Robitschek, C., & Nixon, A. E. (2007). Self-discrepancy and distress: The role of personal growth initiative. *Journal of Counseling Psychology, 54,* 86–92. doi:10.1037/0022-0167.54.1.86

Heine, S. J., Proulx, T., & Vohs, K. D. (2006). The meaning maintenance model: On the coherence of social motivations. *Personality and Social Psychology Review, 10,* 88–110. doi:10.1207/s15327957pspr1002_1

Herman, J. (1992). *Trauma and recovery: The aftermath of violence—From domestic abuse to political terror.* New York, NY: Basic Books.

Hill, P. C., & Pargament, K. I. (2008). Advances in the conceptualization and measurement of religion and spirituality: Implications for physical and mental health research. *Psychology of Religion and Spirituality, S*(1), 3–17. doi:10.1037/1941-1022.S.1.3

Horowitz, M. (1986). *Stress response syndromes* (2nd ed.). New York, NY: Jason Aronson.

Janoff-Bulman, R. (1992). *Shattered assumptions.* New York, NY: Free Press.

Klinger, E. (1977). *Meaning and void: Inner experience and the incentives in people's lives.* Minneapolis: University of Minnesota Press.

Koltko-Rivera, M. E. (2004). The psychology of worldviews. *Review of General Psychology, 8*, 3–58. doi:10.1037/1089-2680.8.1.3

Lazarus, R. S., & Folkman, S. (1984). *Stress, appraisal, and coping.* New York, NY: Springer.

Lee, V., Cohen, S. R., Edgar, L., Laizner, A. M., & Gagnon, A. J. (2004). Clarifying "meaning" in the context of cancer research: A systematic literature review. *Palliative & Supportive Care, 2*, 291–303. doi:10.1017/S1478951504040386

Mahoney, A., Pargament, K. I., Cole, B., Jewell, T., Magyar, G. M., Tarakeshwar, N., Murray-Swank, S. A., & Phillips, R. (2005). A higher purpose: The sanctification of strivings in a community sample. *International Journal for the Psychology of Religion, 15*, 239–262. doi:10.1207/s15327582ijpr1503_4

McAdams, D. P., Reynolds, J., Lewis, M., Patton, A. H., & Bowman, P. J. (2001). When bad things turn good and good things turn bad: Sequences of redemption and contamination in life narrative and their relation to psychosocial adaptation in midlife adults and in students. *Personality and Social Psychology Bulletin, 27*, 474–485. doi:10.1177/0146167201274008

McGregor, I., & Little, B. R. (1998). Personal projects, happiness, and meaning: On doing well and being yourself. *Journal of Personality and Social Psychology, 74*, 494–512. doi:10.1037/0022-3514.74.2.494

McIntosh, D. N. (1995). Religion-as-schema, with implications for the relation between religion and coping. *International Journal for the Psychology of Religion, 5*, 1–16. doi:10.1207/s15327582ijpr0501_1

Nietzsche, F. (2012). *Twilight of the idols* (W. Kaufmann & R. J. Hollingdale, Trans.). Calgary, Canada: Theophania. (Original work published 1895)

Ozorak, E. W. (2005). Emotion and religion. In R. F. Paloutzian & C. L. Park (Eds.), *Handbook of the psychology of religion and spirituality* (pp. 216–234). New York, NY: Guilford Press.

Park, C. L. (2005). Religion as a meaning-making framework in coping with life stress. *Journal of Social Issues, 61*, 707–729. doi:10.1111/j.1540-4560.2005.00428.x

Park, C. L. (2008). Testing the meaning making model of coping with loss. *Journal of Social and Clinical Psychology, 27*, 970–994. doi:10.1521/jscp.2008.27.9.970

Park, C. L. (2010). Making sense of the meaning literature: An integrative review of meaning making and its effects on adjustment to stressful life events. *Psychological Bulletin, 136*, 257–301. doi:10.1037/a0018301

Park, C. L., Edmondson, D., Fenster, J. R., & Blank, T. O. (2008). Meaning making and psychological adjustment following cancer: The mediating roles of growth, life meaning, and restored just-world beliefs. *Journal of Consulting and Clinical Psychology, 76*, 863–875. doi:10.1037/a0013348

Park, C. L., Edmondson, D., & Mills, M. A. (2010). Religious worldviews and stressful encounters: Reciprocal influence from a meaning-making perspective. In T. Miller (Ed.), *Handbook of stressful transitions across the lifespan* (pp. 485–501). New York, NY: Springer. doi:10.1007/978-1-4419-0748-6_25

Park, C. L., & Folkman, S. (1997). Meaning in the context of stress and coping. *Review of General Psychology, 1*, 115–144. doi:10.1037/1089-2680.1.2.115

Park, C. L., Mills, M. A., & Edmondson, D. (2012). PTSD as meaning violation: Testing a cognitive worldview perspective. *Psychological Trauma: Theory, Research, Practice, and Policy, 4*, 66–73. doi:10.1037/a0018792

Park, C. L., & Slattery, J. M. (2009). Including spirituality in case conceptualizations: A meaning system approach. In J. Aten & M. Leach (Eds.), *Spirituality and the therapeutic practice: A comprehensive resource from intake to termination* (pp. 121–142). Washington, DC: American Psychological Association. doi:10.1037/11853-006

Peterson, C., Park, N., & Seligman, M. E. P. (2005). Orientations to happiness and life satisfaction: The full life versus the empty life. *Journal of Happiness Studies, 6*, 25–41. doi:10.1007/s10902-004-1278-z

Plaks, J. E., Grant, H., & Dweck, C. S. (2005). Violations of implicit theories and the sense of prediction and control: Implications for motivated person perception. *Journal of Personality and Social Psychology, 88*, 245–262. doi:10.1037/0022-3514.88.2.245

Prochaska, J. O., & Norcross, J. C. (2009). *Systems of psychotherapy: A transtheoretical analysis* (7th ed.). Belmont, CA: Brooks/Cole.

Raes, F., Hermans, D., Williams, J. M. G., Beyers, W., Eelen, P., & Brunfaut, E. (2006). Reduced autobiographical memory specificity and rumination in predicting the course of depression. *Journal of Abnormal Psychology, 115*, 699–704. doi:10.1037/0021-843X.115.4.699

Reker, G. T., & Wong, P. T. P. (1988). Aging as an individual process: Toward a theory of personal meaning. In J. E. Birren & V. L. Bengston (Eds.), *Emergent theories of aging* (pp. 214–246). New York, NY: Springer.

Robison, J. E. (2007). *Look me in the eye: My life with Asperger's.* New York, NY: Three Rivers Press.

Robison, M. (2011). *The long journey home: A memoir.* New York, NY: Random House.

Rothbaum, B. O., Foa, E. B., Riggs, D. S., Murdock, T., & Walsh, W. (1992). A prospective examination of post-traumatic stress disorder in rape victims. *Journal of Traumatic Stress, 5*, 455–475. doi:10.1002/jts.2490050309

Sheldon, K. M., & Elliot, A. J. (1999). Goal striving, need satisfaction, and longitudinal well-being: The self-concordance model. *Journal of Personality and Social Psychology, 76*, 482–497. doi:10.1037/0022-3514.76.3.482

Silberman, I. (2005). Religion as a meaning system: Implications for the new millennium. *Journal of Social Issues, 61*, 641–663. doi:10.1111/j.1540-4560.2005.00425.x

Skaggs, B. G., & Barron, C. R. (2006). Searching for meaning in negative events: Concept analysis. *Journal of Advanced Nursing, 53*, 559–570. doi:10.1111/j.1365-2648.2006.03761.x

Slattery, J. M., & Park, C. L. (2011). *Empathic counseling: Meaning, context, ethics, and skill.* Pacific Grove, CA: Brooks/Cole.

Slattery, J. M., & Park, C. L. (2012a). Clinical approaches to discrepancies in meaning: Conceptualization, assessment, and treatment. In P. T. P. Wong (Ed.), *Human quest for meaning* (2nd ed., pp. 493–516). New York, NY: Routledge.

Slattery, J. M., & Park, C. L. (2012b). Religious and spiritual beliefs in psychotherapy: A meaning perspective. In J. Aten, K. O'Grady, & E. V. Worthington (Eds.), *The psychology of religion and spirituality for clinicians: Using research in your practice* (pp. 189–215). New York, NY: Routledge.

Steger, M. F., & Park, C. L. (2012). The creation of meaning following trauma: Meaning making and trajectories of distress and recovery. In R. A. McMackin, E. Newman, J. M. Fogler, & T. M. Keane (Eds.), *Trauma therapy in context: The science and craft of evidence-based practice* (pp. 171–191). Washington, DC: American Psychological Association. doi:10.1037/13746-008

Sutherland, K., & Bryant, R. A. (2005). Self-defining memories in post-traumatic stress disorder. *British Journal of Clinical Psychology, 44*, 591–598. doi:10.1348/014466505X64081

Wilson, J. P., & Moran, T. A. (1998). Psychological trauma: Posttraumatic stress disorder and spirituality. *Journal of Psychology and Theology, 26*, 168–178.

Yalom, I. D. (1980). *Existential psychotherapy*. New York, NY: Basic Books.

Zebrack, B., & Cella, D. (2005). Evaluating quality of life in cancer survivors. In J. Lipscomb, C. C. Gotay, & C. Snyder (Eds.), *Outcomes assessment in cancer: Measures, methods, and applications* (pp. 241–263). New York, NY: Cambridge University Press.

7

UNDERSTANDING AND RESPONDING TO CHANGES IN SPIRITUALITY AND RELIGION AFTER TRAUMATIC EVENTS

DONALD F. WALKER, KERRY L. McGREGOR, DAVID QUAGLIANA, RACHEL L. STEPHENS, AND KATLIN R. KNODEL

Yea, though I walk through the valley of the shadow of death, I will fear no evil, for thou art with me.

—Psalm 23:1

Do not be overcome by evil, but overcome evil with good.

—Romans 12:1

If you remain patient in adversity and conscious of Him—this, behold, is something to set one's heart upon.

—Surah Ali-'Imran, 3:186

As these quotations from the Hebrew scripture, Christian New Testament, and Qur'an demonstrate, the majority of world religious traditions urge their followers to have courage and to persevere in the midst of evil and adversity. For both child and adult survivors of personal traumas such as childhood abuse or intimate partner violence, these spiritual admonitions are easier said than done. Such traumas are damaging not only physically and damaging but also, typically, spiritually. As a result, as we have noted elsewhere, people often respond in myriad ways after traumatic events involving abuse (see Walker, Reid, O'Neill, & Brown, 2009, for a review). Some individuals turn to God or a higher power and draw on their spiritual and religious faith for help in dealing with the experience. Other people turn away from God or their higher power, angry or hurt that God allowed

http://dx.doi.org/10.1037/14500-008

the trauma to occur. Still others live a spiritual life somewhere in between, unsure of what to make of the experience.

In this chapter, we discuss psychotherapeutic ways of responding to child abuse survivors' changes in faith after trauma. We begin by highlighting research that relates various forms of traumas to spiritual outcomes after experiencing them. We organize the review according to (a) individuals who use their spirituality to cope with and make meaning of their faith, (b) damage to specific aspects of faith, and (c) simultaneous increases and damage to different aspects of faith. After reviewing the literature regarding faith and trauma, we then provide a series of clinical recommendations for responding in psychotherapy to changes in faith after traumatic events. We conclude with a series of case studies demonstrating psychotherapeutic responses to changes in faith among trauma survivors.

LINKS BETWEEN TRAUMA AND DAMAGE TO SPIRITUALITY AND RELIGIOUS INVOLVEMENT

In this section, we review damage to faith stemming from various traumatic experiences. We focus on damage to spirituality and religion from childhood abuse, intimate partner violence, combat, and natural disasters. We also discuss, where literature is available, the moderating effects of specific aspects of traumatic events on faith.

Distant Relationship to God or Negative God Image

Across various forms of traumatic experiences and different ages of survivors, damage to one's relationship to God has repeatedly been found to be a primary outcome after traumatic events. For example, multiple studies have found that adult survivors of child abuse have more distant relationships with God and difficulty trusting God than individuals who have not experienced child abuse (Kennedy & Drebing, 2002; Rossetti, 1995). Furthermore, those survivors report viewing God as more distant, punitive, angry, and unloving than do nonabused individuals (Hall, 1995; Kane, Cheston, & Greer, 1993; Lawson, Drebing, Berg, Vincellette, & Penk, 1998; Pritt, 1998).

Effects of Sexual Abuse

Multiple studies have found that sexual abuse, in particular, is damaging to one's relationship to God. Clergy-related sexual abuse is particularly damaging (see Chapter 8, this volume, for a more complete review). For example, Rossetti (1995) compared three groups of adult Roman Catholics in the United States. These groups included adult Catholics who had not been victims of childhood sexual abuse ($n = 1,376$), adults who had been sexually abused as children but not by a priest ($n = 307$), and adults who were sexually abused by priests as children ($n = 40$). Both groups of adult survivors of childhood sexual abuse reported more difficulty trusting the priesthood, organized religion, and God specifically than did nonabused adults. However, those adults who had been sexually abused by priests as children described experiencing greater difficulty in these areas than either of the other two groups of adults.

There is some evidence across studies that incest committed by one's father or a close family member is particularly damaging to one's relationship to God and other aspects of one's personal spirituality compared with other forms of child abuse. In an early study, Kane et al. (1993) studied the effects of incest by a father figure on 33 adult women incest survivors' perceptions of God. Kane et al. broadly defined a father figure as a biological or adoptive father, biological or adoptive grandfather, a stepfather, or a long-term live-in boyfriend of the survivor's mother. They found that, in comparison with a control group of 33 adult women who had not been abused as children, survivors of childhood incest were more likely to report that God had negative or ambivalent feelings toward them. In addition, they also found that 61% of the incest survivors had left the organized religious denominations of their fathers.

Effects of Anger Toward God on Outcomes After Other Traumas

Trauma survivors report anger toward God after traumatic events other than childhood abuse. Spiritual struggles involving anger toward God have repeatedly been associated with poorer mental health outcomes for other trauma survivors. For example, Edmondson, Park, Chaudior, and Wortmann (2008) found that spiritual struggles reflecting a ruptured relationship with God were associated with depression among 98 terminally ill patients diagnosed with congestive heart failure. Park, Wortmann, and Edmondson (2010) observed higher levels of depression and longer hospital stays among patients diagnosed with congestive heart failure who also experienced spiritual struggles in their relationship with God. More recently, Exline, Park, Smyth, and Carey (2011) found that anger toward God was associated with poorer outcomes after being diagnosed with cancer.

Decreasing Religious Involvement

In addition to childhood abuse, other traumatic experiences have also been implicated in individuals' movement away from organized religion.

As might be expected, some studies have found that survivors of intimate partner violence (IPV) become disillusioned with organized religion (see Stephens & Walker, in press, for a review). For example, Potter (2007) interviewed 40 African American female survivors of IPV, 36 of whom were Christian, one Muslim, and three with no religious affiliation. Of the 40 women, seven of the Christian women sought out a Christian clergy member for assistance in dealing with IPV in their personal relationships. Each of these seven participants considered the consultation unhelpful; all were advised, among other things, to remain in the abusive relationship. Potter found that such experiences often resulted in IPV survivors' disillusionment with organized religion. Studies with primarily Muslim Arab American IPV survivors have found similar results (Kulwicki, Aswad, Carmona, & Ballout, 2010).

LINKS BETWEEN TRAUMA AND FAITH AS A PROTECTIVE FACTOR

In this section, we review studies that have found increases in spirituality and religiousness after trauma. We focus on those studies that also describe ways in which spirituality and religiousness serve as protective factors for the development of mental health symptoms after trauma.

Empowering Relationship With God

In the previous section, we noted that one's relationship with God is often severely damaged following traumatic events. Although this is true, when trauma survivors are able to maintain a relationship with God after traumatic events, this relationship appears to insulate them from the development of mental health symptoms. This finding has been repeated in various studies across different forms of traumatic events. For example, Gall, Basque, Damasceno-Scott, and Vardy (2007) examined links between childhood physical and sexual abuse, God image, and depression and anxiety in a sample of 101 adult men and women. They failed to find a correlation between the age of onset of abuse, duration of abuse, or number of perpetrators and damage to one's relationship with God. However, they found that participants who viewed God as benevolent experienced less overall depression or anxiety.

Multiple studies have found that among female survivors of IPV their relationship with God was a protective factor both in leaving their abusive relationship and in preventing the development of mental health symptoms. In one study, Gillum, Sullivan, and Bybee (2006) interviewed 151 female survivors of IPV. The majority reported that their relationship with God was a source of strength in dealing with the IPV. In addition, greater religious involvement was associated with overall better mental health and decreased depression in the sample of women.

In a more recent study, Wang, Horne, Levitt, and Klesges (2009) surveyed 749 Christian women from the Southeast region of the United States who had experienced IPV. Among a subset of 200 women who reported that they had successfully left an abusive relationship, the most frequently reported factor ($n = 55$) in helping them to leave was their personal relationship with God. In a related vein, Ting (2010) obtained similar results in a sample of 15 African American immigrant survivors of IPV. Ting found that praying to God and believing in divine will were important coping strategies for the abuse survivors in dealing with the abuse while it was occurring.

Positive Impact of Religious Involvement

Although many people are less active religiously after traumatic events, organized religion appears to insulate against debilitating mental health effects for those who maintain their corporate religious practice. Some of the results of research in this area have been striking. For example, Elliott (1994) surveyed 918 adult women who were survivors of childhood sexual abuse. In the sample, Elliott compared women raised by atheistic or agnostic parents with women raised by conservative Christian parents and women raised by conservative parents of other faiths. Elliott found that, regardless of specific religious affiliation, women who engaged in organized religion experienced significantly fewer posttraumatic symptoms than participants who were not actively involved in organized religion. This was true regardless of the specific denomination the participants belonged to.

Doxey, Jensen, and Jensen (1997) surveyed 653 adult women who had been sexually abused as children in comparison with a larger sample of nonabused women. Surprisingly, Doxey et al. found that women who were abused self-reported having better mental health than nonabused women, if they were religiously active. Furthermore, among victims of childhood sexual abuse, participants reporting higher levels of religiousness were less depressed than participants indicating moderate or low religiousness. Organized religion also appears to insulate against negative mental health symptoms after other forms of trauma. For example, McIntosh, Poulin, Silver, and Holman (2011) surveyed 890 men and women in a national sample after the September 11, 2001, attacks. They found that greater participation in organized religion was associated with higher positive affect and fewer intrusive recollections of 9/11.

TRAUMA AND SIMULTANEOUS GROWTH AND DECLINE IN SPIRITUALITY AND RELIGIOUSNESS

It is a confusing and somewhat paradoxical experience that trauma survivors might notice an increase in some aspects of their spirituality and religiousness while simultaneously having a decrease in other parts of their personal faith. Across forms of trauma, when survivors undergo this type of ambivalence, they often feel a pull toward making meaning of and coping with the event using their spirituality outside of the context of organized religion.

This dynamic has repeatedly been observed in research with adult survivors of childhood abuse. For example, Ryan (1998) interviewed 50 adult female survivors of childhood abuse. Close to half of the sample indicated that they had no current religious affiliation. Similarly, 75% of women who were raised in an organized religion indicated that they had left their childhood religious tradition. In terms of spiritual outcomes, over half of the participants stated that they questioned a God that could allow the abuse to occur. However, paradoxically, 64% of the sample also indicated that their spirituality was stronger after the abuse. Furthermore, 31% of the respondents (almost a third) specifically stated that God had been an agent for their survival and healing.

In a more recent study, Grossman, Sorsoli, and Kia-Keating (2006) interviewed 16 adult men from varying ethnic backgrounds about the manner in which they created meaning from their childhood sexual abuse experiences. Half of the male participants reported that their spiritual beliefs aided in their recovery. However, only two of the men were actively involved in an organized religious community. Furthermore, Grossman et al. found that several of the men specifically mentioned that their spirituality developed through 12-step programs such as Alcoholics Anonymous. Although the sample is small, the results support the notion that most participants who turned to spirituality to make meaning of abuse did so outside of the context of organized religion. Participants who did turn to religion were those who were uninvolved with organized religion as children.

Similar findings have been observed among survivors of IPV. For example, Senter and Caldwell (2002) interviewed nine adult women who successfully left an abusive partner about the role of spirituality in leaving their partner. Participants reported mixed feelings about spirituality, particularly their relationship with God. One participant indicated that God was a source of support in her decision to leave the abusive relationship. Three other women reported feeling angry with God, particularly for failing to answer prayers related to the abuse. All the women stated that they had remained involved in organized religious activities while they were being abused, though the level of involvement varied among participants. All the women also reported having a stronger relationship with God after the abuse was over. Several participants reported feelings of gratitude to God for helping them through the abuse.

In a related study, Schneider and Feltey (2009) interviewed 12 women who had been victims of IPV and subsequently killed their abusive partners and were currently incarcerated. Many of the participants reported being at extreme ends of a continuum with respect to religious upbringing. For example, the majority of participants stated that they had either no religious upbringing whatsoever or a strict fundamentalist religious one. Both sets of women (those raised without religious involvement and those raised in organized religion) continued their religious involvement into adulthood. Women who actively participated in organized religion and survived IPV reported disappointment over the lack of support they received from their faith communities when they attempted to receive faith-based social support in their congregations. However, several women reported specifically turning to God (not their religious congregation) for support to either endure the abuse and/or to leave their abuser. One participant acknowledged feeling angry with God for allowing the abuse to occur.

The experience of simultaneous spiritual and religious growth and decline after traumatic events is not limited to survivors of abusive experiences alone. For instance, Park, Edmondson, Hale-Smith, and Blank (2009) studied 167 cancer survivors and found that religious attendance was unrelated to health behaviors after cancer treatment. However, Park et al. also found that daily spiritual experiences were associated with increased health behaviors. Similar findings have occurred with survivors of natural disasters (see Chapter 9, this volume, for a discussion).

CLINICAL RECOMMENDATIONS TO ADDRESS CHANGES IN FAITH IN THERAPY

In this section, we review psychotherapy recommendations to assist clinicians in responding to client changes in spirituality and religiousness. We begin by discussing respect for client spirituality and religiousness. We then describe best practice assessment for changes in faith. We conclude by describing ways to assist clients in maintaining a connection to their preabuse faith, where applicable.

Respect for Clients' Spirituality and Religiousness

The ethical mandate for psychologists to respect and therapeutically address clients' spirituality and religiousness in treatment is particularly complicated in trauma cases (Walker et al., 2009). Changes often occur in multiple dimensions of one's faith simultaneously. Because this is the case, we believe that it is important for psychotherapists to carefully evaluate what it means for clients to have their faith respected in such situations. From our literature review, we think it likely that clients recovering from abuse will experience mixed feelings about their spirituality and religiousness. As a result, we have repeatedly urged psychotherapists to begin treatment with an open but somewhat neutral stance with respect to religion and spirituality as it relates to recovery from childhood physical and sexual abuse. What would an open but therapeutically neutral stance look like? We suggest that this involves respecting clients' views and any analysis they may share regarding their spirituality and religion when they initially present for treatment, while simultaneously recognizing that their feelings toward their faith may change over the course of psychotherapy.

Trauma psychologists should be aware of potential initial value differences with regard to religion and spirituality and thoughtfully consider the impact of these potential differences on the treatment process (Walker et al., 2009). In our previous research, we observed that psychotherapists participate in organized religion to a lesser extent than that does the American public, although they often engage in a personal spirituality absent of organized religion (see Delaney, Miller, & Bisono, 2007; Walker, Gorsuch, & Tan, 2004).

In our earlier work, we encouraged psychotherapists to consider whether they might experience an unconscious tendency to encourage clients to move away from organized religion and related resources for recovery in favor of spiritual resources for recovery outside that context (Walker et al., 2009). When working with trauma clients who are experiencing significant changes in their spiritual and religious faith, psychotherapists should consider their own countertransference as well as the potential impact of their own approach to spirituality and religion on their therapeutic trauma work.

Assessments Over the Course of Therapy

Given that people typically experience changes to their faith over time, psychotherapists should carefully assess the role of client spirituality and religiousness at intake and then reevaluate client personal faith over the course of psychotherapy. We have found Richards and Bergin's (2005) Level 1–Level 2 assessment of client religiousness to be a helpful model in this regard (see Chapter 4, this volume, for a complete review and description of the model applied to trauma psychotherapy). Given that damage frequently occurs to (a) one's relationship to God or a higher power and (b) to one's participation in organized religion, we encourage psychotherapists to make sure to assess these areas. Assessment should include consideration of clients' past and current relationships with God and participation in organized religion, as well as clients' perceptions of their own changes in these areas following traumatic events. Assessment of client personal faith need not be limited to these areas (see Chapter 4, this volume, for further discussion).

Maintaining Connection to Preexisting Spirituality and Religiousness

Although we urge caution and respect for clients' spiritual struggles related to the traumas they are presenting with, research regarding spirituality and various forms of trauma has repeatedly found that people who have maintained some connection to their preexisting faith structures experience better mental health outcomes than those who do not. As a result, we recommend that, when appropriate, psychotherapists encourage clients to maintain some connection to their preexisting faith in ways that clients find congruent with their current spiritual and religious functioning. The balance between respect for the client's current faith system and encouragement to maintain a connection to their previous faith system is a delicate one. We still recommend beginning psychotherapy with an open but neutral stance toward client religious and spiritual beliefs after trauma. Furthermore, we are not advocating telling clients what spiritual or religious beliefs to maintain. However, after developing a strong working alliance with clients, we do believe that those who are struggling with their spiritual functioning should be encouraged to consider what aspects of their previous faith they still adhere to. They should also be informed that, everything else being equal, other trauma survivors who are able to maintain some connection to their preexisting religious and spiritual faith and who have been able to resolve spiritual struggles related to their faith typically experience better mental health and spiritual outcomes after trauma. In particular, psychotherapists should encourage clients to consider the kinds of personal spiritual connections to God or a higher power and religious attendance or other participation in organized religion they currently feel comfortable continuing at their current point in treatment. We believe that encouragement to maintain faith will be most effective after a strong working alliance has been developed (see Chapter 5, this volume, for further discussion).

Spiritual Struggles Related to God Image

Damage to one's image of God and one's relationship to God is a frequent spiritual sequela of trauma, particularly after abuse. Survivors of trauma may project onto God various images, including an image of God that is distant, unloving, or harsh. As a result, psychotherapists should explicitly assess clients' God images and, if necessary, consider consulting with religious resources or clergy members to better understand denominational images of God from clients' particular traditions. As our case studies illustrate, psychotherapists may incorporate religious texts (e.g., the Torah or the Bible) that provide alternative images of God and explore these images with clients.

In resolving spiritual struggles related to God image, many trauma clients may need to openly talk to God about the conflicting feelings that they may have toward God after traumatic events. We encourage psychotherapists to assist clients in having this dialogue with their personal God. In doing so, psychotherapists may find it helpful to initially begin with a stance in which they consider their primarily role to be that of bearing witness to clients' struggles related to their traumatic experience, then later in treatment expanding clients' interpretations of their spiritual struggles and even offering alternative explanations of their understanding of events. For example, in working with Christian child clients, one of us (DFW) has provided the following explanation for why God allows abuse to occur to clients who have asked about it in therapy, after allowing clients to come to their own conclusions about this first and modifying the explanation as necessary depending on clients' ages:

> First of all, no one can tell you exactly why your abuse happened. Anyone who pretends to know that doesn't really know. I don't know why it happened either, and I won't try to tell you why it happened. This is something you're going to be working out in your relationship with God your entire life. However, I do have a way of thinking about your abuse that I think could be helpful to you. When I think about why God allows abuse to happen, I think of two things. First, my own personal belief is that, in order to be a loving God, God set up the world so that people could make their own choices. I think God believed that forcing people to do things, including following Him, wasn't loving on His part. Because God set up the world to allow people to choose, to do evil things or good things, some people choose to do evil things, and the person who abused you chose to do an evil thing. When they did that, that was their choice, not God's. I don't personally believe that God meant for or wanted your abuse to happen. When I think about your abuse, I think about the fact that Jesus knew what your abuse was like. Before He died, Jesus was taken by the Roman soldiers, and He was beaten, spit on, and made fun of. Then He was crucified. He did not specifically want it to happen, but He knows what your abuse was like.

This explanation for how God thinks about abuse is clearly my (DFW's) own, and obviously considered through an evangelical Christian religious lens. I do not and would not attempt to force this explanation on anyone, including Christian clients. If I offer this explanation in trauma psychotherapy, I only do so after exploring what clients believe about God and the way in which God was involved in their abuse. In those situations in which I choose to offer this explanation, I am always careful to couch the explanation as my own belief and to make it clear that I am not trying to force clients to accept my personal beliefs. It is offered as a potentially helpful alternative for clients to consider in addition to their own explanations for why God allows abuse to occur. I find this most helpful for clients who are "stuck" in chronic anger toward God.

CASE STUDIES THAT ILLUSTRATE DEALING WITH DAMAGE TO FAITH

Throughout the chapter, cases have been deidentified in one of two ways. First, in some instances, amalgamated cases involving aspects of real cases with two or three clients are presented. In these instances, the core presenting problem is real, but aspects of gender, age, and ethnicity have been combined across two or three actual cases to deidentify any single client that the author describing the case study had seen. Second, in other case studies, two to three client variables (e.g., race or ethnicity, gender, age) have been altered for a single client for whom the case is based on.

Rachel: Responding to Spiritual Damage After Abuse

Rachel was a 9-year-old Caucasian girl who presented for outpatient spiritually oriented trauma-focused cognitive behavior therapy (SO–TF–CBT; Walker et al., 2010) with Kerry McGregor. Rachel's mother sought mental health services shortly after it was revealed that Rachel had been sexually abused by a 15-year-old neighbor who had been a close friend of the family. A younger sibling reported the abuse after witnessing it, and Rachel refused to talk to her mother or anyone else about the incidents. Before learning of the abuse, Rachel's mother had noticed several symptoms of anxiety and depression, including developmentally inappropriate separation anxiety, school refusal, blunted affect, excessive crying, and general emotional lability. She also indicated that Rachel, who had always been a soft-spoken, gentle child, appeared to get angry frequently for no reason.

Rachel and her family endorsed a strong Christian faith, and her parents indicated that they attended church multiple times a week. Before the abuse, Rachel had enjoyed church, but her family had observed a decline in her enthusiasm. After learning of Rachel's abuse, her parents struggled with issues of faith and reported feelings of guilt and anger. When asked at intake about her faith, Rachel reported that nothing had changed. However, when given a pretreatment measure for SO–TF–CBT, she endorsed attending church less (she asked to stay home, and her parents permitted her to do so), praying infrequently, and denied currently reading the Bible. These response patterns were in direct contrast to her answers about her functioning preabuse, which stated that she prayed, attended church, and read the Bible frequently (to explore the stories she initially learned in church school). When asked about this contrast, Rachel indicated that everything was fine and refused to talk further.

As per the SO–TF–CBT protocol, therapy began with psychoeducation of both Rachel and her parents. In addition to explaining Rachel's diagnosis of posttraumatic stress disorder and providing symptom management strategies, McGregor also normalized the spiritual struggles that all three individuals were experiencing. Rachel admitted that she identified with what the therapist was saying and seemed relieved that other kids had experienced the same spiritual difficulties that she was currently dealing with. Rachel's parents were also encouraged to involve their church in the therapy process and to process their spiritual concerns with a pastor. McGregor indicated that she would be willing to work conjointly with the church if needed.

The next four sessions were spent working with Rachel individually and covered relaxation training, affective expression and modulation, and cognitive coping. When relaxation was first introduced to Rachel, she was asked whether she would like to incorporate prayer into her relaxation, but she was not currently praying at that time and felt uncomfortable doing so. As a result, McGregor continued using the secular treatment modules in TF–CBT until she reached the trauma narrative.

When it was time to do the trauma narrative, Rachel was nervous. At the beginning of therapy, she had been told that she would not have to do the narrative until the middle of counseling. After each session, she was reminded of how many sessions remained, so that she could mentally prepare. The first day of the trauma narrative, Rachel only briefly outlined the events she had experienced. Over the next few sessions, she outlined the details and was able to share with McGregor the specific details of the sexual abuse. Rachel chose to make a book about her experiences. Rachel and the therapist first wrote about the facts of the abuse, then added in what she was thinking while the events were happening, and ended with her feelings and thoughts about God. In particular, Rachel felt that God was upset about her abuse but was also angry at her; she feared the abuse had been her fault and that God would not forgive her. Together, the therapist and Rachel examined the validity of these thoughts and feelings using Rachel's faith history and her knowledge of God. After some time, Rachel stated that she felt that God was not mad at her and that the events were not her fault. In fact, she felt that God was sad for her and upset that she was hurting. When McGregor asked whether she would like to pray to God in session, she declined, but did pray at home later that night. The next week, Rachel was happy that she had been able to communicate with God once again and indicated that she had prayed every night that week.

When it was time for the parent–child sessions, McGregor first met with Rachel's parents to discuss the trauma narrative in advance. This step was especially important given the parents' feelings of guilt regarding the abuse.

Reviewing the trauma narrative in advance also helped limit any excessive emotional displays during the session. On the day of the conjoint session, Rachel asked the therapist to read the trauma narrative. Afterward, she asked a list of prepared questions to her parents, including whether they still loved her and whether they thought the abuse was her fault. After her questions were answered, she was able to share with her parents what she thought about God's opinion about her abuse. The session was powerful because it was the first time that Rachel had directly told her parents about what she had experienced.

When given assessment posttreatment, Rachel appeared to be functioning normally. Her anxiety and depression symptoms had abated, and she was reporting few to none of the bad dreams and flashbacks she had experienced prior to therapy. Rachel was once again attending church regularly, praying every night, and reading the Bible frequently. She no longer felt that God was angry with her and instead felt that He loved her and was upset by what happened to her. Her parents had consulted with their pastor and were currently feeling less guilty.

This case illustrates the need for sensitivity in responding to spiritual damage after abuse. In Rachel's case, she needed to process her abuse to some degree before she could address the changes in her personal faith. Had her psychotherapist attempted to artificially force inclusion of spiritual interventions early in treatment, the working alliance would have been severely disrupted and treatment would have likely been unsuccessful.

Brittany: Psychodynamic Reparenting and Transferential Healing

Brittany was a 20-year-old, single, White female who presented to therapy with Dr. David Quagliana to address the negative effects of sexual abuse at the hands of her uncle that had occurred for approximately seven years, from the time she was 5 years old. Brittany denied an abuse history for her two male siblings. At the time that she was seen for treatment, she was living on a Christian college campus 10 hours away from home. In addition to her childhood sexual abuse, Brittany also reported unwanted sexual experiences with a former boyfriend in high school. When she began treatment, Brittany expressed concerns about problems with interpersonal relationships, especially fear of adult men, avoidance of intimate connection in romantic relationships, and emotional volatility (especially anger) in a broad range of relationships.

Brittany endorsed a Christian religious faith system present throughout her childhood and important to her personal identity and life functioning at the time of therapy. During psychotherapy, she frequently emphasized the importance of being a "good" person, both in terms of overt moral behavior as well as a high value placed on "Type A" traits such as organization, academic motivation, and high achievement. Brittany saw these traits as spiritual imperatives and often expressed strong anger toward others who did not exemplify similar traits, especially in others' romantic relationships or when others failed to empathically understand and provide care for Brittany. Brittany presented with damage to her spiritual and religious functioning; she experienced spiritual struggle in trying to live out a moral life in her own religious tradition, as well as anger toward God that she struggled to allow herself to express.

In treating Brittany, Quagliana primarily used psychodynamic interventions, with specific integration of spiritually oriented interventions throughout the course of therapy. The therapeutic relationship therefore became an essential means of identifying and processing Brittany's dynamics in her relationships with adult males, God and her religious faith, and interpersonal relationships in general. Brittany found it easy to vent her current interpersonal frustrations to Quagliana throughout therapy and to discuss the role of her religious beliefs in the high moral expectations she placed on herself and others. However, she was initially fearful of discussing her trauma experience and her anger at God. Brittany also openly and frequently lashed out at Quagliana in anger when she felt misunderstood, uncared about, or hurt by him in therapeutic interactions, responding by "punishing" him by shutting down her unguarded presentation and glaring angrily in silence at him.

Consistent with our clinical recommendations, Quagliana responded with an open but therapeutically neutral stance regarding Brittany's spiritual struggles. In addition, he used Brittany's reluctant willingness to listen to his attempts at understanding and reengagement as opportunities to "reparent" her, aware that this would not only bring insight and healing regarding her relationship with parents and friends but also with God as well. These demonstrations of unconditional love, interpretations of projection, willingness to apologize for imperfections and their resultant hurt, and bids for relational repair were essential for repairing negative beliefs about self and others. This dynamic allowed Brittany to be more open about the faith questions, doubts, and emotions. Specifically, she wrestled with *theodicy*, or her experienced contradiction between her faith's depiction of a loving and powerful God and the harmful experiences she had undergone throughout life, both in her sexual trauma experiences and her perceived chronic interpersonal neglect from parents and Christian friends.

Brittany was able to move from anger to grieving and acceptance through exploration of Biblical texts and theological ideas in therapy. Quagliana found that Brittany was initially encouraged to more openly express her anger at God and Christians by exploring Biblical texts related to God's provision of care and protection that contradicted her own hurtful experiences, such as Lament Psalms (Psalm 3, Psalm 18) and other expressions of disillusionment after experiencing perceived injustice or neglect from God by "holy" or "good"

Biblical characters, such as Old Testament prophets and the apostle Paul; this empowered Brittany to realize that "good Christians" experience suffering and are permitted to express their emotional reactions to God, even negative ones (e.g., 1 Kings 19, Ecclesiastes, Job, 2 Corinthians 12, James 1). These latter texts also served to help Brittany transition from anger and splitting to a mournful acceptance that God might still love and provide for her despite her suffering. Theological writings, such as Wolterstorff's (1987) *Lament for a Son*, and Quagliana's disclosure of personal experiences and the resultant theological processing further enabled Brittany to experience God as emotional. Specifically, these experiences helped her see that God empathically and emotionally suffered along with Brittany when human fallenness caused her to suffer. In Brittany's object relations, God moved from an object of anger to a comforting presence in Brittany's experience of suffering.

Meanwhile, processing of the therapeutic relationship revealed Brittany's growing romantic attraction to Quagliana as splitting resolved and he became the representation of hope for both Brittany's healing and her acceptance of imperfect relationships with "good enough" (or safe enough) others. Although expression and maintenance of appropriate boundaries created safety from therapeutic boundary violations or feared reexperience of sexual trauma, the attraction and related safety in the therapeutic relationship were used to grow Brittany's capacity for intimacy (romantic and otherwise) with others.

Throughout therapy, Quagliana was explicit in labeling his theoretical integration of faith and psychodynamic theory regarding the role of his relationship with Brittany in her psychological and spiritual healing. The concept of psychodynamic reparenting and transferential healing took on spiritual overtones as Quagliana discussed Nouwen's (1994) parallel between the father figure in the Prodigal Son parable and his role in providing one-directional caring relationships for others.

At the conclusion of 1.5 years of therapy, significant progress had been made while Brittany identified a need for additional levels of processing her current relationship with her uncle in light of her abuse history. She had gained insight into the role of anger in expressing hurt and creating safety and control through proactively creating distance or rejection in relationships. Having healed many aspects of this hurt and grown in her understanding and successful engagement in forgiveness and grace toward others, she was able to reduce her destructive relational anger and engage more effectively and intimately in relationships. Brittany specifically asked Quagliana whether it would be appropriate to invite him to her wedding when and if it occurred, expressing her grateful belief that she would never have been able to get married if it were not for the healing that resulted from their therapeutic relationship. Quagliana thanked her for this and encouraged her to invite him to her wedding.

Brittany had also sufficiently resolved many of the hurts, doubts, and questions in her Christian faith. She found her faith and relationship with God to be a greater supportive factor in her life and also reduced her control-based application of moralistic standards to herself and others, finding ways to balance pursuit of being "good" with offering gracious acceptance to herself and those with whom she interacted.

Darius: How Increasing Faith Can Be a Protective Factor

Darius, a 10-year-old African American boy was brought for SO–TF–CBT (Walker et al., 2010) with Katlin Knodel by his paternal grandparents. His grandparents were concerned for Darius's well-being because he was exhibiting outbursts of anger, nightmares, depression, and tension. Darius's grandparents reported receiving frequent phone calls from his school because of his acting out behavior. Darius defied his schoolteacher, hit other children, ran down the halls screaming, and refused to complete his work. He lived with his grandparents after his father lost custody because he had physically abused Darius 3 years before he was referred for psychotherapy.

Before beginning psychotherapy, Darius was assessed for both mental health symptoms and spiritual functioning. He was diagnosed with post-traumatic stress disorder. In addition, his grandparents reported that he did not attend church at all with his biological father when he lived with him, because his biological father did not take him. Currently, he attended church, and they engaged him in family devotionals based on the Bible during the week. Darius reportedly enjoyed attending youth groups at church. His grandparents served as children's ministry workers, and Darius had developed a close friendship with one other boy his age in church.

During SO–TF–CBT sessions, Darius expressed feeling angry most of the time. He wanted to stop the outbursts but did not know how. He felt hopeless and believed he could never get better. Guilt, sadness, and the fear of being judged for his abuse caused him to frequently shut down during sessions. Darius often curled into a ball on the floor at the mention of his father or the abuse. In those moments he refused to move, talk, or even look at the therapist.

During the relaxation module, Darius was aided by his psychotherapist in memorizing a verse. This was a natural spiritual intervention for Darius because his youth group frequently had children memorize Bible verses as part of their ministry. In his case, he memorized Joshua 1:9, which states, "Be strong and courageous. Do not be afraid; do not be discouraged, for the LORD your God will be with you wherever you go." During the first cognitive coping and processing module, examples from times when he was at church were used to illustrate the interconnection between thoughts, feelings, and behaviors. When it came time for the trauma narrative, Darius asked his psychotherapist to pray prior to beginning the narrative. Knodel prayed for strength for Darius to complete the narrative and for God to be with both of them while Darius was telling it.

In the second cognitive coping and processing module, Darius decided that God had been with him throughout the abuse and that it made God sad. He determined that God had intervened for him by sending him to live with his grandparents, who provided a loving and nurturing home for him.

At the end of therapy, Knodel asked Darius what symbol he would like to choose to represent his experience and progress in therapy. Darius asked for a cross to help him remember his time in therapy, the progress he made by being brave and telling his story, and that God had stayed with him during the whole process.

Nicole/Nicholas: Damage to Spirituality and Increase in Faith

Nicole was a 21-year-old biracial (Native American and Caucasian with Ukrainian cultural heritage) transgender client who presented for therapy with Dr. David Quagliana in her second year of college at a private Christian university in a conservative area of the United States. At the time of presentation, Nicole, female, had only identified depressive symptoms and disillusionment related to her religion major. She discussed the university's termination of a mentoring female faculty member, resulting in Nicole's subsequent unsuccessful attempts to find fulfillment in pursuit of new majors in exercise science and, later, psychology. Throughout treatment, it became apparent that the rejection of her religion major and of religion itself had far more complex causes. Though often guarded, Nicole revealed significant maternal neglect due to her mother's chronic depression, which often required hospitalization. Nicole had also experienced physical abuse and neglect from caretaking grandparents. At intake she was diagnosed with gender identity disorder and psychotic features, including paranoia and visual hallucinations.

Consistent with our research review, Nicole presented with a decrease in participation in the organized religion of her childhood (Christianity) and an increase in spiritual exploration of an alternative faith tradition (Buddhism). Nicole's faith in Christian religion had been tenuous at the time of her mentor's dismissal, which triggered rejection of religion and endorsement of atheism while exploring Buddhism and other spirituality practices not based on belief in the existence of a deity. Throughout therapy, Nicole was resistant to discussion about her spiritual identity, presuming that Quagliana would be offended and unsupportive (because of her assumptions about his own spirituality) if she discussed what she later revealed as angry beliefs about how "stupid" one must be to believe in God or organized religion.

Understanding the necessity of processing her spiritual identity and hypothesizing its connections to her gender identity questions, mental health difficulties, and traumatic experiences, Quagliana sought safe ways to approach these topics. Quagliana initially encouraged Nicole to verbally process reasons for changing her major, hoping for future opportunities to move from vocational problem solving to broader identity and existential themes. Meanwhile, Quagliana worked to establish safety and trust in the therapeutic relationship, overtly expressing and demonstrating unconditional care for Nicole and capacity to contain and assist with difficult aspects of Nicole's narrative, whether the difficulty stemmed from emotional distress or culturally risky responses to Christian faith. Safety was difficult to demonstrate reactively because Nicole's resistance caused her to take few relational or emotional risks in therapy. Thus, it was necessary for Quagliana to proactively predict and verbally hypothesize about aspects of Nicole's rejection of Christian beliefs and trauma experiences, offering overt acceptance of her perspective. Psychodynamically, this approach addressed past neglect through Quagliana's proactive pursuit of Nicole, as well as addressing past abuse through demonstration of care and safety.

It was also essential to label but demonstrate acceptance of and curiosity about Nicole's resistance. Therapy sessions were often about Nicole's interest in martial arts or frustration with "stupid people" in her classes (her IQ was 156). This built confidence for Nicole in the therapeutic relationship and enabled her to take more risks in discussing the negative emotions and experiences that caused the resistance, usually beginning with expression of anger or frustration. Nicole communicated, "I hate it when people quote scripture," which did not close the door to exploration of spiritual topics but instead empowered articulation and acceptance of Nicole's current spiritual beliefs. This included discussion of theological concepts (especially suffering and theodicy—that is, why a beneficent God permits evil to happen) and Quagliana's intentional demonstration of interest in and client-centered discussion regarding Buddhist principles. Nicole also eventually revealed that she was uncomfortable discussing her trauma, gender issues, and spirituality because of how scary and unacceptable she perceived herself to be. Similarly, accepting but processing this resistance enabled therapeutic exploration of broader self-concept themes including the impact of Nicole's trauma history, maternal mental health issues, and personal mental health issues on spiritual identity and overall functioning.

During the course of treatment, Nicole discussed the "darkness" she believed she possessed and the way in which she feared it would harm anyone she came in contact with. This theme became crucial throughout therapy, representing not psychotic delusions but trauma-influenced self-concept and spirituality. Nicole rejected God because she believed that no loving God would allow a mother to have severe mental health issues that so damaged a child as her own mother's illness had damaged Nicole. Later, similar reactions were communicated regarding Nicole's own mental health issues and the obstacles they created for her perceived success in life. In addition, the way in which the fundamentalist Christian religion of Nicole's childhood family and local community was used to justify physical abuse as moral punishment in her grandparents' house further facilitated rejection of organized religion.

Overt processing of the trauma narrative, or any aspect of her emotional experience in life, was never comfortable for Nicole. Significant family events during the course of therapy, including the death of Nicole's grandfather and her father's loss of employment, created emotional reactions that overwhelmed her guardedness and offered opportunities for overt expression of both childhood content as well as Nicole's interpretations of such content and its impact on her. In the case of her grandfather's death, Nicole reinterpreted her grandfather's punishment as culturally acceptable, denying its abusive nature. In the next session, however, Nicole was able to acknowledge the abusive and impactful nature of her grandfather's behavior, making progress in holding a tension between the need to find peace with the abuse (and abuser) and the necessity of acknowledging and reacting to the abuse. Similarly, financial hardships from the past were emotionally revisited when Nicole's father lost his job, allowing expression of conflict between empathy for her hardworking father and anger over the neglectful and abusive childcare she received in his absence due to work.

The first 3 years of therapy, consisting more of unconditionally supportive care than overt psychological processing, gave Nicole the courage to acknowledge male gender identification and begin hormone therapy for gender reassignment, kept Nicole engaged in therapy through multiple bouts of suicidal depression, allowed her to discover career interests for graduate school and hope for societal impact using her high intelligence and vocational aspirations, and empowered her to explore Buddhist and nontheistic spirituality.

By the fourth year of therapy, Nicholas (having legally changed names from Nicole) found effective stabilizing medications for his mood and psychotic symptoms, became skilled at discerning hallucinations and delusions from reality, and improved his capacity to both develop his own identity and share it with others. He disclosed his gender transition to the family (experiencing healing and loving responses from everyone in his family), more frequently brought emotional and psychological material into therapy sessions, and built meaningful relationships with roommates and a first romantic partner. Nicholas remained aware of the need to understand regional and cultural childhood influences on self-concept, though these issues were rarely explored in therapy.

Detailed trauma narratives were never disclosed or used in Nicholas's treatment, though he became increasingly able to work on improving his current perception of and relationship with various family members involved in his traumatic childhood environments, and he also consistently improved engagement in therapeutic work related to the impact of his complex trauma. Having achieved greater awareness and acceptance of the spiritual, gender, vocational, and mental health aspects of his identity, Nicholas found the impact of his complex trauma partially remediated as well. Acceptance of his own imperfections helped him move from cognitively understanding his mother's neglect of him toward forgiveness of his parents.

REFERENCES

Delaney, H. D., Miller, W. R., & Bisono, A. M. (2007). Religiosity and spirituality among psychologists: A survey of clinician members of the American Psychological Association. *Professional Psychology: Research and Practice, 38,* 538–546. doi:10.1037/0735-7028.38.5.538

Doxey, C., Jensen, L., & Jensen, J. (1997). The influence of religion on victims of childhood sexual abuse. *International Journal for the Psychology of Religion, 7,* 179–186. doi:10.1207/s15327582ijpr0703_6

Edmondson, D., Park, C. L., Chaudior, S. R., & Wortmann, J. H. (2008). Death without God: Religious struggle, death concerns, and depression in the terminally ill. *Psychological Science, 19,* 754–758. doi:10.1111/j.1467-9280.2008.02152.x

Elliott, D. M. (1994). The impact of Christian faith on the prevalence and sequelae of sexual abuse. *Journal of Interpersonal Violence, 9,* 95–108. doi:10.1177/088626094009001006

Exline, J. J., Park, C. L., Smyth, J. M., & Carey, M. P. (2011). Anger toward God: Social cognitive predictors, prevalence, and links with adjustment toward cancer. *Journal of Personality and Social Psychology, 100,* 129–148. doi:10.1037/a0021716

Gall, T. L., Basque, V., Damasceno-Scott, M., & Vardy, G. (2007). Spirituality and the current adjustment of adult survivors of childhood sexual abuse. *Journal for the Scientific Study of Religion, 46,* 101–117. doi:10.1111/j.1468-5906.2007.00343.x

Gillum, T. L., Sullivan, C. M., & Bybee, D. I. (2006). The importance of spirituality in the lives of domestic violence survivors. *Violence Against Women, 12,* 240–250. doi:10.1177/1077801206286224

Grossman, F. K., Sorsoli, L., & Kia-Keating, M. (2006). A gale force wind: Meaning making by male survivors of childhood sexual abuse. *American Journal of Orthopsychiatry, 76,* 434–443. doi:10.1037/0002-9432.76.4.434

Hall, T. (1995). Spiritual effects of childhood sexual abuse in adult Christian women. *Journal of Psychology and Theology, 23,* 129–134.

Kane, D., Cheston, S., & Greer, J. (1993). Perceptions of God by survivors of childhood sexual abuse: An exploratory study in an underresearched area. *Journal of Psychology and Theology, 21,* 228–237.

Kennedy, P., & Drebing, C. E. (2002). Abuse and religious experience: A study of religiously committed evangelical adults. *Mental Health, Religion & Culture, 5,* 225–237. doi:10.1080/13674670110112695

Kulwicki, A., Aswad, B., Carmona, T., & Ballout, S. (2010). Barriers in the utilization of domestic violence services among Arab immigrant women: Perceptions of professionals, service providers & community leaders. *Journal of Family Violence, 25,* 727–735. doi:10.1007/s10896-010-9330-8

Lawson, R., Drebing, C., Berg, G., Vincellette, A., & Penk, W. (1998). The long-term impact of child abuse on religious behavior and spirituality in men. *Child Abuse & Neglect, 22,* 369–380. doi:10.1016/S0145-2134(98)00003-9

McIntosh, D. N., Poulin, M. J., Silver, R. C., & Holman, E. A. (2011). The distinct roles of spirituality and religiosity in physical and mental health after collective trauma: A national longitudinal study of responses to the 9/11 attacks. *Journal of Behavioral Medicine, 34,* 497–507. doi:10.1007/s10865-011-9331-y

Nouwen, H. J. M. (1994). *The return of the prodigal son: A story of homecoming.* New York, NY: Doubleday.

Park, C. L., Edmondson, D., Hale-Smith, A., & Blank, T. O. (2009). Religiousness/spirituality and health behaviors in younger adult cancer survivors: Does faith promote a healthier lifestyle? *Journal of Behavioral Medicine, 32,* 582–591. doi:10.1007/s10865-009-9223-6

Park, C. L., Wortmann, J. H., & Edmondson, D. (2010). Religious struggle as a predictor of subsequent mental and physical well-being in advanced heart failure patients. *Journal of Behavioral Medicine, 34,* 426–432.

Potter, H. (2007). Battered Black women's use of religious services and spirituality for assistance in leaving abusive relationships. *Violence Against Women, 13,* 262–284. doi:10.1177/1077801206297438

Pritt, A. F. (1998). Spiritual correlates of reported sexual abuse among Mormon women. *Journal for the Scientific Study of Religion, 37,* 273–285. doi:10.2307/1387527

Richards, P. S., & Bergin, A. E. (2005). *A spiritual strategy for counseling and psychotherapy* (2nd ed.). Washington, DC: American Psychological Association. doi:10.1037/11214-000

Rossetti, S. J. (1995). The impact of child sexual abuse on attitudes toward God and the Catholic church. *Child Abuse & Neglect, 19,* 1469–1481.

Ryan, P. L. (1998). An exploration of the spirituality of fifty women who survived childhood violence. *Journal of Transpersonal Psychology, 30,* 87–102.

Schneider, R. Z., & Feltey, K. M. (2009). "No matter what has been done wrong can always be redone right": Spirituality in the lives of imprisoned battered women. *Violence Against Women, 15,* 443–459. doi:10.1177/1077801208331244

Senter, K. E., & Caldwell, K. (2002). Spirituality and the maintenance of change: A phenomenological study of women who leave abusive relationships. *Contemporary Family Therapy, 24*, 543–564. doi:10.1023/A:1021269028756

Stephens, R., & Walker, D. F. (in press). White Evangelical and Fundamentalist churches. In A. Johnson (Ed.), *Religion and men's violence and against women*. New York, NY: Springer.

Ting, L. (2010). Out of Africa: Coping strategies of African immigrant women survivors of intimate partner violence. *Health Care for Women International, 31*, 345–364. doi:10.1080/07399330903348741

Walker, D. F., Gorsuch, R. L., & Tan, S. Y. (2004). Therapists' integration of religion and spirituality in counseling: A meta-analysis. *Counseling and Values, 49*, 69–80. doi:10.1002/j.2161-007X.2004.tb00254.x

Walker, D. F., Reese, J. B., Hughes, J. P., & Troskie, M. J. (2010). Addressing religious and spiritual issues in trauma-focused cognitive behavior therapy with children and adolescents. *Professional Psychology: Research and Practice, 41*, 174–180. doi:10.1037/a0017782

Walker, D. F., Reid, H., O'Neill, T., & Brown, L. (2009). Changes in personal religion/spirituality during and after childhood abuse: A review and synthesis. *Psychological Trauma: Theory, Research, Practice, and Policy, 1*, 130–145. doi:10.1037/a0016211

Wang, M. C., Horne, S. G., Levitt, H. M., & Klesges, L. M. (2009). Christian women in IPV relationships: An exploratory study of religious factors. *Journal of Psychology and Christianity, 28*, 224–235.

Wolterstorff, N. (1987). *Lament for a son*. Grand Rapids, MI: Eerdmans.

8

GOD IMAGES IN CLINICAL WORK WITH SEXUAL ABUSE SURVIVORS: A RELATIONAL PSYCHODYNAMIC PARADIGM

MARY GAIL FRAWLEY-O'DEA

So God created mankind in His own image, in the image of God He created them; male and female He created them.

—Genesis 1:27

Men create gods after their own image, not only with regard to their form, but with regard to their mode of life.

—Aristotle

Scripture teaches that God created mankind in His own image. Others, like Aristotle, contend that human beings always have created images of and relationships with the divine that reflect their relevant historical, cultural, political, religious and spiritual, communal, and personal experiences and relationships. To the extent that one's image of God, then, is a relationally and experientially constructed phenomenon, it is organic and can be cast and recast throughout the life cycle (Rizzuto, 1979). Further, an individual's relationship with the divine, like any other, may be accessed to serve growth and psychic health, may exist dynamically as a defense against psychological complexity and mature relatedness, or may be experienced as a self-limiting prison guarded by a judgmental or punishing super-being. When a person has been subject to developmental betrayal trauma (Freyd, 1996), including sexual abuse, and perhaps especially sexual abuse by a member of the clergy, their internalized relationship with the divine can be harnessed to the trauma for the rest of their lives.

http://dx.doi.org/10.1037/14500-009
Spiritually Oriented Psychotherapy for Trauma, D. F. Walker, C. A. Courtois, and J. D. Aten (Editors)
Copyright © 2015 by the American Psychological Association. All rights reserved.

In this chapter, I offer a relational paradigm of an individual's development of a God image, then discuss the potential impact of sexual abuse on the victim–survivor's relationship with the divine. In considering the possible effect of relational psychodynamic trauma psychotherapy (Davies & Frawley, 1994) on the patient's image of and relationship with God, I focus particularly on the role of the therapist as a transformational or transitional figure.

It is important to note that this chapter does not engage the question of God's existence. Rather, the emphasis here is on what can happen to a child's or adolescent's God when he or she is sexually abused and what can happen later to that God during trauma recovery. In addition, although sexual abuse occurs to children of all faiths and of no faith, I focus here on individuals raised in a Christian tradition, the religious and spiritual realm in which I have the most personal and clinical knowledge and experience.

CASE STUDIES: FLORENCE, WALT, AND DENISE

Throughout this chapter, I use Florence, Walt, and Denise to illustrate the points made. These are composites of patients with whom I have worked and, as such, are to some extent archetypal, lacking the paradox, complexity, and nuance inherent in case presentations of actual patients and treatments. At the same time, they do represent three ways in which sexual abuse survivors have presented and used their images of and relationship with God to further or to impede their healing and growth.

Florence spent many afternoons from ages 7 to 10 with her paternal grandfather at his home on the banks of the Hudson River. He was a woodworker, and Flo watched in awe as he turned rough pieces of wood into playful animal sculptures. Gramps also taught Flo about the history and majesty of the Hudson River and the valley around it, and, as they strolled in his garden, he instilled in her a lifelong love of gardening, introducing her to the beauty of English roses, peonies, and lavender. After sharing late afternoon tea and cookies on her favorite garden bench, Gramps often took Flo onto his lap, tongue kissed her, and had her "pet" his penis until he ejaculated and sank back against the bench. He always whispered to her that she was his favorite "flower" and that she could never tell anyone about their "teatime treats" because they would be jealous and never let her see him again. Flo complied.

Flo's family members belonged to a small Episcopalian church surrounded by woods and mountain foothills. Her parents had a strong marriage and thoroughly enjoyed their only child. Flo recounted her bedtime ritual with her mom: After tucking her daughter in, her mom regularly read a book of Flo's choice after which, snuggling together, the two of them recited the familiar prayer, "As I lay me down to sleep, I pray the Lord my soul to keep.

If I should die before I wake, I pray the Lord my soul to take." Kissing Flo goodnight, her mom told her she was loved by God and her whole family and turned on the Winnie-the-Pooh night light before leaving the room. For Flo, God/Mom/Pooh morphed into a merged, divinely laced internalized image that infused her room and psyche with hope, safety, and respite from confusing and somewhat scary times with her otherwise beloved grandfather.

Walter, also an only child, grew up in a strict Southern Baptist home. Every Sunday, parents and son spent most of the day at church where God was presented as a strict, foreboding judge ever alert to sin, itself strictly defined and often related to sex. Despite the denomination's prohibition against drinking, Walt's father was an alcoholic who, in drunken rages, berated both his wife and his son. Walt's mom was a "Goddamned whore bitch," whereas Walt was a "Goddamned shit of a little prick." Walter was sexually abused for 3 years by a Boy Scout troop leader who also had authority at Walt's church. Because his mom worked nights, she dropped Walt off at church early every Wednesday evening for his Boy Scout meeting. There, from ages 11 to 14, he was sexually violated by his troop leader, Mr. P, before the troop meeting began. Mr. P took Walt home after school and always warned him that God would punish him if he ever told anyone about their "special Scout game." Once inside, Walt put himself to bed while his father watched TV and drank. In Walt's childhood world, God/father/Mr. P/sin/sex/judgment were merged in an internalized image of a punitive divine figure who allowed Walt to be tortured then blamed him for it.

Denise, the fourth of six children, was raised in a devout Irish Catholic family. The family attended Mass every Sunday, and Denise was a student at the parish elementary school. As each child was tucked into bed, mom and child recited an Our Father and a Hail Mary. Mom tended to "turn things over to God." If a child was physically or emotionally hurt or betrayed by a friend, he or she was told to "offer it up" to the souls in purgatory to shorten their stay there. Once in heaven, those folks would remember who got them there and return the favor. Jesus, Denise knew, and was reminded often in church, school, and at home, suffered horribly for humankind's sins, so her own earthly suffering could never compare with what the Lord endured for her. The more one suffered, the closer she was to God, and prayerful stoicism was the holiest response to suffering.

In sixth grade, Fr. Kevin, the parish priest, chose Denise to help him with office work after his secretary had left the rectory for the day. Denise and her parents were thrilled that their revered pastor had selected her for a special chore. After a few weeks on the job, during which Fr. Kevin praised Denise's organizational skills and good manners, he began to molest her. The sexual violation began with kisses and caressing of her breasts, but by the end of seventh grade had progressed to cunnilingus, fellatio, and digital penetration of her vagina. The priest assured Denise that God loved her and had chosen her for this special closeness with a priest. Her parents, however, would not understand and would send her away to an orphanage if they knew, so she had to keep it a secret between her, Fr. Kevin, and God. Because Fr. Kevin was also her confessor, she did not have to worry about telling it in confession either. Sometimes after the molestation, Fr. Kevin administered the Eucharist to her, telling her that God wanted to reward her for being such a good girl. Fr. Kevin was transferred to another parish after Denise's seventh grade, and she never saw him again. Her mom was sad that Fr. Kevin was gone, often remembering him as the best priest the parish had ever had.

Denise believed that God had a reason for everything that happened in her life. Even if she could not understand it, God knew why it was important, and if a relationship or experience involved suffering, Denise knew God would reward her later, as He did by allowing her to receive His body and blood after Fr. Kevin hurt her. She was not angry with Fr. Kevin, believing that he did not understand that he hurt her. She forgave him and knew God would too, just as she was sure He would forgive her. Dissociated were Denise's soul-searing sense of betrayal and her fury at Fr. Kevin, as well as the hurt by and rage at her mom and God for not knowing what was happening in that rectory.

Flo, Walt, and Denise, all raised as Christians, had vastly different God images and equally disparate relationships with God, reflecting their unique developmental experiences.

- Although Flo's life was marked by symptoms and relational dysfunctions influenced by her grandfather's violations, she also had a sense of herself as a basically worthwhile person in the eyes of a compassionate God. God, she felt, helped her bear the unbearable reality of her grandfather's abuse.
- Walt, on the other hand, loathed himself as wholly defective and inherently unloveable, "Goddamned" from birth. He acted out in many self-destructive and sometimes life-threatening ways. For Walter, God was an equally loathsome, unforgiving, toxic internalized object, a grotesque divine overseer who Walt feared and hated, yet more unconsciously yearned to appease, please, and be accepted by.
- Denise consciously believed that God loved her and chose her to suffer as way of being closer to him; she was special to him. Denise was in fact an angry woman, but she dissociated the anger and projected it onto others to whom she reacted with self-righteousness and contempt, the latter often a defense against intense envy.

Florence, Walter, and Denise related to three different Gods, imagined and internalized through divergent developmental relationships amidst which they experienced sexually abusive betrayal trauma.

RELATIONAL DEVELOPMENT OF GOD AND GOD IMAGES

A number of writers have described the development of God images as inextricably linked with the child's good-enough relationships with transformational objects, transitional objects or subjects, and transitional experience (Bollas, 1987; LaMothe, 2010a, 2010b; Rizzuto, 1979; Winnicott, 1953). British psychoanalyst Christopher Bollas (1987) looked to the earliest relationship with the mother as the template for transformational processes. At this stage of life, the mother literally transforms the infant's internal and external experiences through her caregiving processes. She is "known" by her child existentially as an enviro-somatic presence whose ministry transforms inner and outer life in profound ways (p. 14). Bollas contended that adults pursue aesthetic moments reminiscent of these primary transformative experiences. Spirituality and religion, along with art, poetry, music, or nature, provide such instances, which are then held in reverence and deemed sacred by the individual. According to Bollas, aesthetic moments are timeless and wordless, experienced more as "a spell which holds self and other in symmetry and solitude" (p. 30); they are often followed by a "sense of profound gratitude" and a desire to reenter the aesthetic moment (p. 31). When the early transformational object has been inadequate or hurtful, or when later life events are so shattering that the individual's ability to surrender to another is rent asunder, that person may seek "negative aesthetic experiences" (p. 17) that recreate the existential somatic and affective aspects of trauma.

Winnicott (1953) conceptualized a somewhat later developmental stage marked by transitional phenomena. These experiences occupy an intermediate psychological space and mode of experiencing to which both external reality, particularly primary caregiving relationships, and inner reality—reflecting the internalization and creative internal elaboration of those external experiences—contribute. Illusion, which combines aspects of both external reality and the child's creative operation on their external relationships and experiences, is the hallmark of transitional phenomena (Winnicott, 1953) and, in the adult, is perpetuated in aesthetic and spiritual experiences. Play is another central concept in Winnicottian theory and, like illusion, characterizes the transitional space between inner and outer space (Winnicott, 1971). Transitional space is where something happens, the something that happens is an illusion, and play is the creative interaction with or operation on the illusion that is happening.

The arts and religion at their best are "highly developed forms of playing" (van Eerden, 2010). Rodin, for example, played with the illusion he created of the Burghers of Calais being led in chains to an anticipated slaughter for which they volunteered in order to save their town and from which their selfless bravery rescued them (Benedek, 2000). There is the external and historical story, there is Rodin's aesthetic illusion of it, and there is the magnificent and moving sculpture that, at least for me, is not confined by bronze, but rather extends into a transitional, deeply spiritual portrayal of divine grace. For me, then, the sculpture is the external reality and my illusion of its meaning (internal reality) results in a transitional experience of meaning (my spiritual experience and its physical, cognitive, and affective elaboration). Play thrives amidst creative freedom and can be stultified by a surfeit of anxiety or excessive demands to comply with rigid external expectations.

Transitional objects such as blankets and teddy bears carry the safety and ongoingness of good-enough caretakers. The presence of transitional phenomena in the child's life, the child's illusions of them as paradoxically and simultaneously real and imaginary, and the child's creative freedom to play with these objects and experiences empower the child to contend with anxiety, crises, and relational disruptions (Last, 1988). God, too, can become a transitional object reflective of the child's relational environment. For example, the child who is awakened by an unfamiliar noise and who soothes herself back to sleep by reassuring herself that God is watching over her, her family, and her home is imaginatively relating to God as a transitional object watching over her as well as her parents do.

LaMothe (2010b) extended Winnicott's (1953) notion of transitional objects by introducing the child's creation of transitional subjects, a developmental progression of relational capability that influences the individual's relationship with the divine. Transitional subjects are created when the child perceives the other first as a person and only secondarily as an object (p. 623)—in other words, when the child can intuit and have faith that he or she is a subject recognized and respected by other subjects. LaMothe (2010b) wrote, "The child . . . loves, trusts, and is loyal to the parent primarily because the parent is a person—a person who evokes obligation precisely because she is a person. The parent's role and function are secondary, though not unimportant" (p. 627). If the relational surround of the child continues to provide trustworthy care and respect, eventually the child will develop a consistent intentionality to construct and respond to themselves and others as subjects to be recognized rather than objects to be used. God also can become a transitional subject:

> A religious believer recognizes and constructs God as a transcendent person . . . and experiences God as recognizing him as a person, which secures absolutely his experience of himself as an-end-in-himself. . . . This may provide him with a deep sense of trust in the face of experiences that are painfully disruptive, impersonal, or even depersonalizing. (p. 628)

Transformational and transitional phenomena usually have been discussed as mediated primarily through the relationship with the mother, perhaps extended to other immediate caretakers such as fathers, grandparents, or nannies. The images these people have of God become part of the beliefs and values narrative internalized by the child over the course of development and therefore contribute to that child's own image of and relationship with God. In addition, however, God often is presented to the child consistently and over years through affiliation with an organized religion, socioreligious traditions and rituals, and through direct and indirect God-talk with friends, coaches, and other influential people in the child's life. As we have seen with Flo, Walt, and Denise, the gods endowed to children by their families, religious leaders, and others can be markedly different.

Many of us believe that God has opinions about us based on our actions or on our inherent substance.

- Flo's God is forgiving, tolerant, protective, dependable. Her God sees her as a subject, respects her courage and willingness to grow, holds her when she suffers, and wants her to thrive. He is deeply sorry that she was mistreated by her grandfather and wants her to heal. She thinks He is happy that she is in treatment and will hold us both as we work together.
- Walt's God is damning, demanding, and always on alert to judge harshly infractions against His rules. His God sees Walt as a worthless loser, an object better never having been born, a sinner who got only what he deserved in life. Walt does not want God anywhere near his therapy and sees part of his healing as getting God out of his life once and for all. At the same time, Walter yearns for the paternal acceptance and mentoring a worthy individual would earn from the divine.
- Denise's God is most responsive to and pleased with her when she is suffering and offering that suffering as a sacrifice to Him and to souls in purgatory. Suffering and sacrifice are the relational threads binding her to a divine who is indifferent to earthly life, always urging her to think ahead to a perfect life with Him after death.

Whereas Bollas's (1987) quest for transformational experience continues throughout life, Winnicott's (1953) transitional objects eventually are discarded as the child's internalization and identification with the caretakers' good-enough caring is solidified, obviating the need for tangible symbolic representation. I argue, however, that adults too continue to use transitional objects and subjects all their lives. George, a middle-aged man, wears his purple and green striped tie to every major business meeting. A transitional object, the tie evokes internal early experiences of confidence, success, and security about his competence and ability to reach a goal. Teresa began spiritual direction soon after her devoutly religious mother passed away. Her spiritual director is warm, bright, and funny, characteristics the woman cherished in her mother. In their work together, the spiritual director becomes a transitional subject for Teresa, a present-day mentor who also is a symbolic evocation of Teresa's experiences with her mom and to the spirituality her mother practiced.

God, of course, is not usually outgrown but rather is available throughout the life cycle to be modified and developed as a transitional object and/or a transitional subject reflecting the individual's internalization and elaboration of their personal, religious, and community relational surround. In addition, the divine can be experienced as an object who can be met in reverential aesthetic moments that are sacred and transformative. I further propose that God can be encountered as a transformative subject in relationship with a believer who has faith that he or she, as coparticipant in the ongoing project of creation, can also provide aesthetic moments of transformation for God, as perhaps happened when Moses persuaded the Lord to spare Israel from destruction (Exodus 32:14).

The soul, when things go well enough, dwells in transitional space where it is created, elaborated, and transformed from infancy through the rest of life through the individual's playful interweaving of relationally mediated personal and community realities and myths and his or her surrender to transformative experiences.[1] Before considering how psychotherapy may be implicated in that process, I consider the potential impact of sexual abuse on an individual's God image and relationship with God.

THE IMPACT OF SEXUAL ABUSE ON A SURVIVOR'S IMAGE OF AND RELATIONSHIP WITH GOD

Since the 1980s, researchers and clinicians have identified a spectrum of psychological (e.g., Davies & Frawley, 1994; Gartner, 1999), physical (e.g., Irish, Kobayashi, & Delahanty, 2010), psychobiological (e.g., van der Kolk, McFarlane, & Weisaeth, 1996), and spiritual (e.g., Pargament, Murray-Swank, & Mahoney, 2008) sequelae associated with childhood or adolescent sexual abuse. Sexual abuse can be so spiritually devastating, in fact, that it is frequently referred to as "soul murder" (Rivera, 2002; Shengold, 1989). In Shengold's (1989) words, "Soul murder [is] the deliberate attempt to eradicate or compromise the separate identity of another person" (p. 2). Soul murder, in turn, suggests that the possibility of an ongoing, creative engagement with God as a transitional subject—a good-enough subject

---

[1]I thank the Rev. Dr. Louis Reed for this conceptualization of *soul* as dwelling in transitional space, a precipitate of creative processes involving transitionality and transformation. Louis also read and reread this work as it evolved and pointed me to Bollas's work, which added an important element to this theoretical section of the chapter.

recognizing and respecting the victim as a good-enough subject—has been killed or at least severely damaged by the concretizing and deadening experience of sexual abuse. To that extent, sexual violation of a child bonds what should be developmentally appropriate and safe erotic fantasies and feelings to a boundary bashing invasion of stultifying reality that renders imaginative play dangerous. Rather, "the victims of soul murder remain in larger part possessed by another, their souls in bondage to someone else" (p. 2).

In soul murder, trauma becomes a god to the victim (Mogenson, 1989). Instead of having access to transitional space within which the individual can play imaginatively with a divine transitional subject and rather than being open to surrender to aesthetic moments, he or she is possessed by the trauma, which becomes an "infinite, all-powerful, and wholly other" (Mogenson, 1989, p. 2) event. Often the "event" is anthropomorphized and is subjectively experienced indeed as possession by a demonic or persecutory self or other representation. It may also appear in dreams or hypnogogic experiences as a terrifying evil presence holding the victim–survivor in a deadly embrace, a perverted analogue to the aesthetic moment. Here, the individual is forced to submit to an existential threat that, like the transformative experience, is wordless and profound but serves disintegration rather than wholeness.

The degree to which a sexual abuse victim's soul, and thus her relationship with the divine, is murdered, critically damaged, or "just" wounded may depend on the rest of the individual's relational surround and the extent to which he or she maintains a capacity to play in transitional space and to be available to transformation. Reinert and Edwards (2009) found that compensatory relational experiences, including secure attachment to parents, do not mediate the sexual abuse survivor's attachment to God, who usually is perceived as "less loving, more controlling, and distant" (p. 31) than the God of nonabused individuals. My clinical experience is different, however, and Florence is a good example.

Flo's attachment to her parents was secure and characterized by respect for her individuality and creative pursuits. Both her parents and, in fact, her grandfather had highly developed aesthetic and religious and spiritual senses. Most of Flo's time with Gramps was literally wonder-full as she watched him create art from pieces of wood and gardens from rocky dirt. When he talked about the Hudson Valley, Flo could see the American Indians walking silently through the woods and imagine the Dutch colonials fishing the banks of the mighty Tappan Zee. At home, she had colonial girl and Native American princess dolls with which she acted out imagined historical events and that were also transitional connections to afternoons with her "good Gramps."

Flo's God was perceived as an immanent presence in her life, a familiar figure who knew her, liked her, felt bad about her trauma, and helped her bear it in secrecy. Flo was certain that her parents would have protected her from Gramps had they known about the abuse, and she was sure that she maintained the secret to not hurt her parents, to whom she related as subjects first. Florence coped with her abuse by creating two Gramps: the creative, loving one who recognized her as a subject and the late afternoon Gramps who objectified her and used her for his own gratification. She seemed to have had an intuitive sense even as a child that, through the sexual abuse, Gramps used her as a fetishized object connecting him to some earlier set of relational experiences. Flo was, in other words, a pawn in Gramps's own negative aesthetic process. She was saddened and hurt by his abuse, but also had compassion for what she imagined were areas of deep inner pain for him. God knew about and saw all of this, but did not orchestrate it, and Flo had faith that He held Gramps, her parents, and her in a compassionate embrace. As she grew, Florence maintained and developed a capacity for creating transitional space and surrendering to transformational objects and subjects that elaborated her intellectual, spiritual, and aesthetic lives. An early childhood teacher, avocational harpist, and avid gardener, Flo could play in ways that enriched her soul in relationship with a pleasing and pleased good-enough God. Flo's faith in the ongoing, divinely inspired process of creation and in her place as a worthy and welcome participant in that process was abundant.

Walter, unlike Flo, did not have a secure attachment to his parents. He was furious at and terrified of his father, yet yearned to be accepted by the man. At the same time, he was angry at and contemptuous of his mother, whom he perceived as weak and voluntarily disempowered by his father. Both, he thought, were hypocrites marching off to church each week while living in a home awash in alcohol and an ever-present aura of impending violence. Walt also thought the rest of his Baptist congregation were hypocrites. He believed that they must have known about his father's alcoholism and about Mr. P's abuse, but turned a blind eye. Consciously, he turned his back on them as he felt they once did on him, eschewing all religion and claiming a hatred for the God that held those people up while abandoning him. Worse, his God blamed Walter and his sinfulness for what happened to him, and Walter hated Him even more for that. Unconsciously, Walt projected his own shame, guilt, and self-loathing onto a persecutory and sadistic God whom he hated but could not escape even by leaving church. Beneath his facade of anger, Walt was a young boy almost literally dying for redemption, peace, and solace from the divine. His capacity to imagine and play with such a transitional God subject, however, had been crushed, and there was no template for safe, much less transformative, surrender to anyone or anything. Instead, Walter was a "traumatized soul devoutly repeat(ing) the events which have proved so transfixing for it, as if trying to recover its capacity to experience and feel" (Mogenson, 1989, p. 11). Hustling, alcohol abuse, gambling, and peep shows constituted Walter's weekly liturgical offerings to the fallen angels tearing at his soul.

CLERGY SEXUAL ABUSE

Sexual abuse of a young person by a clergy person is the most heinous act of soul murder. The clerical perpetrator desecrates the victim's soul, desacralizes what should be sacred spaces, and deforms the image of God through depraved indifference to his victim and to the sacred fiduciary trust conferred on him at ordination. In many Christian denominations, in fact, the priest or minister is presented as the mediator between the individual, the community, and God. Transferentially, the cleric frequently is confused with God. Faith is placed in the cleric, rather than the divine, to "operate as the one who spoke for God, who held grace and forgiveness, knowledge and power, and who was a conduit for salvation" (Ferguson, 2007, p. 191). It is therefore impossible for the victim of clergy sexual abuse to emerge from the experience without a destroyed or perverted image of God. God is even more degraded when the clergy person invokes God as an accessory to soul murder as when Fr. Kevin administered the Eucharist to Denise after abusing her, telling her that God wanted to reward her for being so special. Here, God knows what Fr. Kevin is doing, approves of it, maybe gets off on it, and reverences it with His body and blood, perverting a sacrament in a way likely to be experienced by Denise, if even unconsciously, as a profoundly negative aesthetic moment. Transformation may have occurred but in a soul scorching, spiritually macabre, and stultifying distortion of sacred ritual.

As the worldwide sexual abuse scandal in Roman Catholicism has demonstrated, the sexual abuse of the churches' young historically has almost always been aided and abetted by hierarchs and denominational officials who privileged the safety and security of the perpetrator at the expense of his victims (Frawley-O'Dea, 2007). Even when victims or their families reported abuse, they were met with false promises, threats, or indifference. Their religious environmental surround communicated that God's lambs were expendable sacrifices to be offered up on the altar of clerical power and prestige. For many survivors of clergy abuse and their families, therefore, long reverenced and beloved transitional objects of divinity turned up as accessories to soul murder. In so many cases, the ability to believe in a just, merciful, and trustworthy God was dismantled and/or church became for the victims and their families a charnel house for souls rather than a source of spiritual transformation and transitional play. As Dr. X (Gartner, 2007, p. 98), a survivor of abuse by a Catholic priest, said,

> I felt it was God's representative on earth that opened my eyes to God's failing. I don't believe in God today at all. . . . I grew to hate the smells, sounds, feelings of the Church—the incense, the collars, the robes. My spirituality and ability to believe in a higher power were destroyed.

Dr. X described his hatred of the somatic–affective aspects of his former spiritual home—smells, sounds, feelings, colors. These are the stuff of which transformational aesthetic moments are made, but for Dr. X, all of them were harbingers of profoundly painful negative aesthetic moments.

Denise continues to believe in God and attends a Catholic church. She goes to an early Sunday morning Latin Mass at a conservative church pastored by a priest who frequently preaches about the evils of modern society and has cast the church's sexual abuse scandal as an exaggerated effort by non-Catholics, lapsed Catholics, and spiritually lazy Catholics to discredit the church's teachings. He also scorns victims who sue the church as money-hungry weaklings used by greedy plaintiffs' attorneys to make millions for themselves. If they were really abused, they ought to forgive the priests who sinned and get on with life instead of indulging themselves as eternal victims. Denise agrees. She thinks victims should turn to God in prayer, use their suffering to know how much God loved mankind to have suffered on the cross for us, and trust that He will judge and reward every earthly person in His great wisdom.

Denise's parents were good-enough custodial caretakers. Stoic in coping with daunting financial and child care responsibilities, however, they had little time or energy to encourage their children's transitional play and sometimes stifled it. For example, Denise had an imaginary friend, Louisa, who slept in her room, "read" stories to Denise at bedtime, and sang her lullabies. Louisa was a transitional object for Denise, providing in illusion the somatic and affective care her mom was too overwhelmed to offer, but perhaps did when there were fewer children in the house. When Denise's mom found out about Louisa, however, she told Denise that it was "Devil's play" to have imaginary friends and that Denise should never speak about or to Louisa again. God had assigned Denise her own guardian angel, her mother said, and Denise could pray to her if she needed that support. Denise complied.

Even before Fr. Kevin abused her, Denise's mother had conveyed an image of God as a demanding figure whose love and blessings were contingent on good behavior. Grace was transactional (e.g., five Hail Marys could be traded for some time off one's future purgatorial sentence). Sin, though, even confessed sin, added time, so it was always difficult to figure out one's spiritual balance sheet. Sacrifice and stoic suffering were idealized as royal roads to the divine. Transformation was possible, but only if you worked hard to earn it. Priests were considered to be truly "other Christs" and were accorded the respect and adoration a man perfumed with the scent of heaven deserved. Denise's Catholic school teachers and the priests at church echoed her mother's paradigm of faith.

When Fr. Kevin abused Denise, she had little choice but to force fit those experiences into the blueprints of God, religion, and spirituality with which she had been surrounded all her life. Dissociating somatic and affective experiences of terror, pain, rage, and helplessness, Denise embraced the abuse as a gift from God to a child so special that she was chosen by Him to sacrifice her girlhood innocence and the potential life of her soul by merging with His suffering. Unconsciously, she projected her shame and rage onto others whom she perceived as sinful and in need of salvation, for which she prayed arduously every day. Intensely envious of her siblings, colleagues, and others whom she considered insufficiently responsible, hard-working, or prayerful, she defended against knowing and feeling that envy through self-righteous contempt. God is a trauma (Mogenson, 1989) for Denise, albeit a defensively idealized trauma that she is "better off" having experienced. She submitted to and identified with a demanding, even sadistic, God or perpetrator she exhausted herself in appeasing every day. There was no space in Denise's life for comforting, hopeful transformation or transitional illusion and play. The little girl who played with her imaginary friend, Louisa, was soul murdered.

GOD, RELIGION, AND SPIRITUALITY IN PSYCHODYNAMIC PSYCHOTHERAPY WITH SEXUAL ABUSE SURVIVORS

In recent years, there has been increasing recognition among psycho-dynamic psychotherapists that our patients' spiritual lives and stories, their experiences of religion, and their images of and relationships with God demand inclusion in the therapeutic conversation (e.g., Sorenson, 2004; Spezzano & Gargiulo, 2003). Given the shattering of faith often implicated in betrayal trauma, this may be particularly important for sexual abuse survivors. In addition to encouraging and supporting conversation about God, religion, and spirituality during the therapeutic process, the psychodynamic therapist can use notions of transformational and transitional objects, subjects, and experiences to help survivors to free their bodies, psyches, and souls from bondage to trauma to enable survivors to resurrect their spirits from the deadness inherent in soul murder.

Florence came to treatment because she yearned for a love relationship leading to marriage and perhaps to a child. This was the one area of her life that had not thrived, and she sensed that her romantic and sexual solitudes were connected in some way to Gramps's betrayal of their otherwise deeply loving bond. As depicted earlier, she had a compassionate and sophisticated theory about her grandfather and the abuse. She also had a strong spirituality connected to music, art, and nature, although she had not gone to church in years.

As we explored her life and relationships, it became clear that her attachment to her own explanation and understanding of her sexual traumas was both highly adaptive and somewhat limiting, especially in the area of intimate relationships. Because she was bright, psychologically minded, and had a developed capacity for insight into another's woundedness, Flo had come to terms with her experiences with Gramps without fully feeling the travesty of his betrayal. She had been neither angry with her grandfather nor had she mourned what more her childhood might have been without the abuse. She also gave God and her parents a pass for not protecting her. Although she had a fulfilling career and enriching avocations, she had shut herself off from chances to develop intimate relationships with men, unconsciously fearing that they, like Gramps, would ultimately betray her no matter how compatible with her they seemed to be.

In her therapy, Flo began to recognize, feel, and give voice to her rage at Gramps for desecrating otherwise idyllic afternoons. Although she was quite insightful about the probable psychodynamics leading to his use of her, she fully realized for the first time that she should never have had to figure him out as a child, that his job was to know her, appreciate her as a subject, and care well for her. As her anger rose and then spent itself, she mourned the lost innocence and fractured connection with her grandfather with long-staved-off tears. During this period, she also railed at God, often asking often, "Why?" How could God let a little girl be used like that? Why did God not help Gramps so he would not hurt her? Although she still experienced the presence of divine compassion and warmth in her life, she went through a period of devaluing that as too little, too late, once lamenting that, "It's all well and good for God to offer solace now, but where the hell was He when I was a kid?" At times, she also was scornfully irritated with me. I was compassionate, she said, but on my time only and for a price. After letting her "spend afternoons in (my) office with Gramps," I sent her home where she was alone with the ensuing thoughts, feelings, and reactions.

In some ways, Flo used God and me as transitional objects, using us to express questions she was not yet ready to ask about her parents. She had sufficient faith in our capacity to understand her and to hold her hate without retaliating that she could use us like a child who throws her teddy bear in the corner when she is really angry with her mom. Eventually, Flo was also able to get angry about her parents' failure to see the abuse. Their idealization of Gramps was such that they literally could not imagine him hurting their daughter, and they missed indications that something was awry during Flo's afternoons with him. She mourned that loss of protection.

Like the child who retrieves the teddy bear from the corner, dusts him off, apologizes, and cuddles him to sleep, Flo repaired her relationship with God as a source of grace in her life. She returned eventually to the little Episcopal church in the woods where she occasionally played the harp during services. By then, the church was not a potential trigger for dissociated pain, but could be embraced by the adult Flo as a present-day spiritual resource and as a connection to the loving and aesthetic aspects of her childhood. At the same time, she became more relational in her pursuit of music, art, and nature, joining a local classical music group and taking some classes in

English rose cultivation at a botanical garden. There she met a rose enthusiast and botanist with whom she developed her first serious romance. She left treatment a few months later, but I heard that they married about a year later in that little church in the woods.

Flo was relatively healthy in most areas of life when she came to treatment. Her inability to form and flourish within an intimate relationship with a man was her major source of pain and the area of her life most affected by Gramps's betrayal. Her perception that God and I as transitional objects could "take it," could hold and respond to her rage and mourning without excessive injury, abandonment, or retaliation, allowed her to trust herself and others enough to expand her relational world, in time to include intimacy with a man.

Walt came to treatment after he was discharged from a 90-day alcohol rehab program where he had begun to speak about his sexual abuse and traumatic relationship with his father for the first time. He was emotionally raw, deeply distrustful that anyone could or would want to help him, and besieged by impulses to act out in familiar ways. He knew he needed Alcoholics Anonymous (AA), but was scornful of surrendering to a higher power, an action he consciously considered "weak" and unconsciously found terrifying. He went to meetings grudgingly but refused to find a sponsor for a long time.

The focus of our work for an extended period was to co-construct some ego "scaffolding" that would allow Walt to refrain from acting on impulse and to cope with the flashbacks, terrifying hypnogogic experiences, and memories now flooding his sober body, mind, and spirit. I worked with Walt on techniques to put time between impulse and action, and on deep breathing and grounding strategies to calm himself when he was regressed and overwhelmed. I provided books for him to read on male sexual abuse and suggested he visit MaleSurvivor.org, a website offering multiple resources for men who were sexually abused as kids. We met twice a week with occasional phone check-ins between sessions.

After some months, Walt realized that the scaffolding was helping. His transference to me was as a transformational object, someone in whose care his inner and outer worlds were changing. At one point, he asked whether he could "borrow" a stone from a fountain in my office. He carried the stone in his pocket and rubbed it when he wanted to skip a meeting. The stone was a transitional object to my grounding presence in his life.

Through AA, Walt began to wonder whether a higher power could be accessed that was substantively different, even antithetical, to the God of his childhood. It was an intriguing yet threatening idea to him. I suggested that he look for a sponsor who would give him space to go slowly, even though surrendering to a higher power is the sine qua non of AA. He did find such a sponsor, a male high school teacher, with whom he eventually developed a strong relationship.

In therapy, Walt revealed that he loved Tolkien's *Lord of the Rings* trilogy (2002). He had never read the books but had seen each movie several times. When he described his experience of Galadriel, it seemed like an aesthetic moment, a wordless time of wonder at and yearning for something beautiful, complete but ineffable. He was literally in awe of her, describing her as a powerful but compassionate being, an elf queen who could have taken the ring and become corrupted but chose to refuse that power and to do good instead. When he talked about how kind she was with the hobbits, he sometimes filled up with tears. I wondered with him whether Galadriel could be in his imagination a higher power to whom he could surrender, at least for now. The look on his face indeed defied verbal description as he whispered, "Do you think that would be OK?" When I asked, "OK with whom?", he answered, "The real God?" I quietly responded that I thought the "real God" would be pleased for him to have a source of solace that, for him, was safe yet in some way divine. I did not interpret, but held in mind, that Galadriel was for Walt the divine mother, the courageous mother who confronted evil rather than embrace it and who could know what the hobbits needed to protect them and willingly provide it—the mother he never had.

Much later, Walt began to talk about Gandalf as another iconic figure with hints of the divine. Gandalf too had the opportunity to assume enormous but evil power and, like Galadriel, had the fortitude and moral compass to resist great temptation. Instead, he gathered armies to defeat evil and protected the hobbits for as long as possible. Shyly, Walt wondered whether Gandalf also could be a higher power for him. I saw this as Walt opening up to the possibility of a divine father, a male who was brave, sober, smart, funny, had integrity, and sacrificed for good. Walt had small statues of Galadriel and Gandalf at home, and they became his spiritual touchstones to which he turned in times of despair and doubt. At times, we played with the notion of *Galadalf*, a combined deity-like being encompassing both maternal and paternal love. In the therapy, I functioned, among other ways, as a transformational object whose acceptance of and willingness to enter into his playful relationship with Galadriel and Gandalf helped change his internal life and his external reality, as his cravings for alcohol, promiscuous sex, and gambling receded and as he began to sponsor other men in AA. All this time and in the background, Walt's notion of God was expanding beyond the rejecting fire-and-brimstone deity of his childhood.

Another major aspect of Walter's therapy was coming to terms with his homosexuality and seeing it as acceptable to him and to God. There is not space here to recount the vicissitudes of that part of his journey, but Walt eventually met a man who cherished him and with whom he fell deeply in love. Carl attended a church that welcomed gays and lesbians; Carl and Walt began to worship together there. One day, Walt told me that Gandalf and Galadriel were going to board the ship for the Havens and that he was ready to let them go. He felt he could embrace God directly, at church, in his relationship with Carl, in nature, at AA. The statues of Gandalf and Galadriel would remain on a bookshelf as reminders of a time both precious and painful, but outgrown, much like one of Winnicott's no-longer-needed transitional objects.

Denise came to therapy at the behest of her sisters after their mother died. Denise had been her mother's caregiver, and the sisters worried about what she would now do with the spare time in her life. It was clear that they did not want to incorporate their sister too much into their own lives. Denise reported that to me with some apparent satisfaction, perceiving that they knew she disapproved of much in their lives, including their more casual relationship with Catholicism, and did not want to experience the shame her presence evoked.

In the early days of a brief treatment, Denise shared her story in clipped sentences. When I expressed sadness for what she had experienced, she cut me off, explaining that many people in the world had it much worse than she and that God had been good to her. When I asked her to tell me about the graces in her life, she responded that I probably would not be able to under-stand unless I were a "real" Roman Catholic and lived according to their teachings. She doubted that was true.

For several months, I tried to connect somehow with Denise. We talked about her mother, whom she had served her whole life but for whom she seemed to have little more than a sense of duty. I asked about early memories, I was curious about Louisa the imaginary friend, I talked about how confused she must have been as a little girl when her beloved priest betrayed her. No matter what I said, I was met with religious platitudes about the beauty of suffering, the closeness to God that suffering brought, God's infinite wisdom, God's refusal to put more on your plate than you could handle, and the free-dom won by turning everything over to God. Denise, however, seemed any-thing but free or freeing toward others. I began to empathize with her sisters' desire to keep a distance from Denise as she overtly and covertly devalued me as almost surely insufficiently holy or long-suffering.

Denise peeled off a small slice of Catholic theology—an emphasis on grace through suffering—and fetishized it as the whole. Her God was a one-trick deity whose approval could be attained only through stoic suffering and self-denial. Although she did not act out like Walt, God was trauma for her, an internal persecutory object with whom she identified and emulated in her relationships with others through self-righteousness. Denise's brittle func-tionality depended on her preservation of this perverted religious paradigm. If she allowed herself to attach to and use others, including me, as transforma-tional or transitional objects—if she played as she once did with Louisa—her defenses would be endangered. She unconsciously sensed the power of the potential regression that could ensue and left treatment long before I could become at all a positive possibility for her.

In retrospect, I may have been a bad therapeutic fit for Denise. Raised in an Irish Catholic family myself, I was familiar with—although not subjected to—the kind of self-righteous, suffering-centered Catholicism Denise was attached to. I was indeed a "bad Catholic" in her paradigm, which I am sure she sensed in some way. I also had trouble finding compassion for the adult Denise, although I ached for the long-lost child. Although I could evoke an intellectualized compassion for a soul entrapped in such persecutory religiosity, I could not feel it in my gut, an absence she may also have sensed unconsciously.

Florence and Walter each rediscovered church as their psychotherapy progressed; Denise never left her church. Other survivors, however, if they embrace God, religion, or spirituality at all, may not ever return to formal religion. Instead, they may embrace a God image of the feminine divine or find their spiritual succor in music, art, literature, or nature, Eastern religious traditions, neo-paganism, Native American spirituality, or some combination of these. As their psychotherapists, we honor anything that is not hurtful to them or others and that breathes life into battered and torn souls.

A national study found that therapists working with sexual abuse survivors experienced a deepening of their own spirituality (Brady, Guy, Poelstra, & Brokaw, 1999), even if they also had experienced symptoms of the vicarious traumatization described in the trauma literature (Pearlman & Saakvitne, 1995). I have been working with sexual abuse survivors for almost 30 years. Although I have many moments of despair about the human condition and the capacity of people to enact unspeakable harm against the young, including men of God who defile the sacred they are foresworn to uphold, I have also been privileged to share in the resilience, courage, and determined fight for healing and life played out over decades in my consultation rooms. I feel strongly that at times I am but a transmitter of grace, an awed observer of a patient's wordless aesthetic moments. I have witnessed resurrection from soul murder; it is a grace-full honor that infuses my own soul with hope and inspiration.

REFERENCES

Benedek, N. S. (2000). *Auguste Rodin: The Burghers of Calais*. New York, NY: Metropolitan Museum of Art.

Bollas, C. (1987). *The shadow of the object*. London, England: Free Association Books.

Brady, J. L., Guy, J. D., Poelstra, P. L., & Brokaw, B. F. (1999). Vicarious traumatization, spirituality, and the treatment of sexual abuse survivors: A national survey of women psychotherapists. *Professional Psychology: Research and Practice, 30*, 386–393. doi:10.1037/0735-7028.30.4.386

Davies, J. M., & Frawley, M. G. (1994). *Treating the adult survivor of childhood sexual abuse: A psychoanalytic approach*. New York, NY: Basic Books.

Ferguson, L. J. (2007). A Protestant approach to clergy sexual abuse. In M. G. Frawley-O'Dea and V. Goldner (Eds.), *Predatory priests, silenced victims: The sexual abuse crisis and the Catholic church* (pp. 189–194). Mahwah, NJ: Analytic Press.

Frawley-O'Dea, M. G. (2007). *Perversion of power: Sexual abuse in the Catholic Church*. Nashville, TN: Vanderbilt University Press.

Freyd, J. J. (1996). *Betrayal trauma: The logic of forgetting childhood abuse*. Cambridge, MA: Harvard University Press.

Gartner, R. B. (1999). *Betrayed as boys: Psychodynamic treatment of sexually abused men*. New York, NY: Guilford Press.

Gartner, R. B. (2007). Failed "father," boys betrayed. In M. G. Frawley-O'Dea & V. Goldner (Eds.), *Predatory priests, silenced victims: The sexual abuse crisis and the Catholic church* (pp. 85–100). Mahwah, NJ: Analytic Press.

Irish, L., Kobayashi, M. A., & Delahanty, D. L. (2010). Long-term physical health consequences of childhood sexual abuse: A meta-analytic review. *Journal of Pediatric Psychology, 35*, 450–461. doi:10.1093/jpepsy/jsp118

LaMothe, R. W. (2010a). Heresies of the heart and the problem of the Other: A psychoanalytic and theological perspective. *Pastoral Psychology, 59*, 603–616. doi:10.1007/s11089-010-0275-x

LaMothe, R. W. (2010b). The transition from object faith to personal faith: Transitional subjects. *Pastoral Psychology, 59*, 617–630. doi:10.1007/s11089-010-0276-9

Last, J. M. (1988). Transitional relatedness and psychotherapeutic growth. *Psychotherapy: Theory, Research, Practice, Training, 25*, 185–190. doi:10.1037/h0085332

Mogenson, G. (1989). *God is a trauma*. Dallas, TX: Spring.

Pargament, K. I., Murray-Swank, N. A., & Mahoney, A. (2008). Problem and solution: The spiritual dimension of clergy sexual abuse and its impact on survivors. *Journal of Child Sexual Abuse: Research, Treatment, & Program Innovations for Victims, Survivors, & Offenders, 17*, 397–420. doi:10.1080/10538710802330187

Pearlman, L. A., & Saakvitne, K. W. (1995). *Trauma and the therapist: Countertransference and vicarious traumatization in psychotherapy with incest survivors*. New York, NY: Norton.

Reinert, D. F., & Edwards, C. E. (2009). Attachment theory, childhood mistreatment, and religiosity. *Psychology of Religion and Spirituality, 1*, 25–34. doi:10.1037/a0014894

Rivera, J. (2002, September 25). Keeler letter reveals abuse: Cardinal says 83 priests accused over 7 decades; "spiritual equivalent of murder"; $4.1 million in settlements go to 8 victims in 20 years. *The Baltimore Sun*, p. 1A.

Rizzuto, A.-M. (1979). *The birth of the living God: A psychoanalytic study*. Chicago, IL: Chicago University Press.

Shengold, L. (1989). *Soul murder: The effects of childhood abuse and deprivation*. New Haven, CT: Yale University Press.

Sorenson, R. L. (2004). *Minding spirituality.* Mahwah, NJ: Analytic Press.

Spezzano, C., & Gargiulo, G. J. (Eds.). (2003). *Soul on the couch: Spirituality, religion, and morality in contemporary psychoanalysis.* Mahwah, NJ: Analytic Press.

Tolkien, J. R. R. (2002). *Lord of the Rings trilogy.* New York, NY: HarperCollins.

van der Kolk, B. A., McFarlane, A. C., & Weisaeth, L. (Eds.). (1996). *Traumatic stress: The effects of overwhelming experience on mind, body, and society.* New York, NY: Guilford Press.

van Eerden, M. (2010, September 19). *The creative space of play: D. W. Winnicott.* Retrieved from http://onluminousgrounds.wordpress.com/2010/09/19/the-creative-space-of-play/

Winnicott, D. W. (1953). Transitional objects and transitional phenomena—A study of the first not-me possession. *The International Journal of Psychoanalysis, 34,* 89–97.

Winnicott, D. W. (1971). *Play and reality.* London, England: Tavistock.

9

PROVIDING SPIRITUAL AND EMOTIONAL CARE IN RESPONSE TO DISASTER

JAMIE D. ATEN, KARI A. O'GRADY, GLEN MILSTEIN, DAVID BOAN, MELISSA A. SMIGELSKY, ALICE SCHRUBA, AND ISAAC WEAVER

According to Ronan and Johnston (2005), the number of people who will experience a disaster will double by 2050 from 1 billion to 2 billon people. Since 1985, there has been an almost 400% increase in global natural disasters (Centre for Research on the Epidemiology of Disasters, 2007). Researchers managing the Global Terrorism Database have reported a similar increase in terrorist events over the past decade, with almost 5,000 events annually. Some of the worst disasters, such as Hurricane Katrina, the Haiti earthquake, and the Japan tsunami, occurred in the past decade alone. Disasters are becoming more complex, with primary ones (e.g., earthquake) often triggering secondary disasters (e.g., nuclear meltdown). Research has shown that disasters often leave a significant psychological "footprint" on affected communities (Norris, Friedman, & Watson, 2002). As a result, there is often a surge in disaster survivors seeking mental health services in the wake of catastrophe.

http://dx.doi.org/10.1037/14500-010
Spiritually Oriented Psychotherapy for Trauma, D. F. Walker, C. A. Courtois, and J. D. Aten (Editors)

Many of the issues that emerge for the types of trauma described elsewhere in this text surface for survivors of disaster trauma as well. Clients are likely to experience posttraumatic stress disorder (PTSD) symptoms, feel disoriented, and in cases of community violence disasters, experience a decrease in trust of humanity. As is the case with other types of trauma, disasters affect clients' spirituality such that they have to grapple with issues of God or gods attributions and other areas of spiritual struggle. Likewise, disaster survivors often find healing and recovery from their faith.

Although disaster survivors often need individual clinical treatment, it is important for mental health professionals to be cognizant that disaster trauma is different from many other types of trauma in that it is a collective experience. One of the primary traumas that occur for individuals during a disaster is the loss of the community and the resources in it. The complexity inherent in such trauma requires mental health professionals to be adept at both treating the individual within the context of the community and working to help restore the psychological resources of the community. Chapter 2 of this volume describes the insights of an air force chaplain who argued that healing was most likely to occur by creating a community, particularly a church community that surrounds the survivors and allows them to reclaim their sense of self and place in the world. A goal for clinical intervention for trauma survivors is to activate resilient capacities within the client. An ecological view of disaster trauma asserts that this goal is best obtained through creating social contexts that foster resilience and that healing is most sustainable when it takes place within a community context (Harvey, 2007). From this perspective, mental health professionals may wish to offer consultation to the community as well as leveraging the community as a resource for treating clients postdisaster.

An important avenue for activating individual and community healing is religious organizations. Many disaster survivors—before ever seeking mental health services—turn first to their faith and faith communities (Benedek & Fullerton, 2007). Recent research has shown that religion and spirituality help buffer disaster survivors from negative emotional and physical consequences commonly experienced in the aftermath of a disaster (e.g., depression, trauma, psychosomatic symptoms; Calhoun & Tedeschi, 2006; O'Grady, Orton, Schreiber-Pan, Wismick, in press; O'Grady, Rollison, Hanna, Schreiber-Pan, & Ruiz, 2012). The purpose of this chapter is to provide an overview of current research on the psychology of religion and disasters and to review practice guidelines for professional psychology and spiritual and emotional care in response to disaster.

RELIGIOUS AND SPIRITUAL COMMUNITY RESPONSES ACROSS THREE DISASTER PHASES

Disaster recovery requires a flow of interventions that respond to the changing needs of the persons in a community. This flow can be described across three phases: (a) emergency, (b) early postimpact, and (c) restoration (Young, Ford, Ruzek, Friedman, & Gusman, 1998).

The *emergency phase* is immediately after a disaster, when there is an urgent need to deploy first responders. Survivors must be located and triaged to then provide acute care. Basic needs must be assured to preserve life and property and minimize infrastructure damage. Ideally, the community had made disaster preparations and there is ready information available to first responders who come from outside the community.

Religious affiliation may affect disaster preparedness behavior on both the individual and community levels. Nelson and Dynes (1976) found that predisaster church attendance was positively correlated with emergency helping behavior, such as making monetary donations, and spending time in relief care. Similarly, Powell, Hickson, Self, and Bodon (2001) found that persons with greater church attendance were more prepared for the feared Y2K disaster. During the emergency phase, many religious congregations see it as their role to provide a gathering place for those who require shelter or other basic needs as well as centers for information dissemination. Cain and Barthelemy (2008) found that nearly 87% of churches in the Baton Rouge area post-Katrina reported that they provided assistance to Hurricane Katrina evacuees, primarily in the form of food, financial assistance, and clothing. Pant, Kirsch, Subbarao, Hsieh, and Vu (2008) studied religious leaders and faith-based organizations and found that these organizations responded in earnest and as a result were able to serve a significant number of evacuees.

After the immediate danger has passed, communities find themselves in an *early postimpact phase*. In this phase the first assessments are made as to the breadth and severity of the damage. There is loss of property, loss of life, and disruption of the social roles as well as the social context of one's community. People find their rhythms of personal, family, community, and work life disrupted. Things they built have been destroyed, persons they loved and children they raised may be grievously injured or dead. In place of hope and plans, there is trauma. The adults' developmental role as providers and protectors has lost its context. It is in these early weeks of loss and disruption that people return to their religious congregations in large numbers: "Much like the grounding effect of a lightning rod to a lightning strike, religious institutions offer a 'grounding effect' in the midst of trauma" (Milstein & Manierre, 2010, p. 222; see also Tillich, 1951).

Religion and spirituality foster social support, meaning, connectedness, and purpose in disaster circumstances (Darling, Hill, & McWey, 2004; Guthrie & Stickley, 2008). As mentioned in Chapter 11 of this volume, church attendance is often affected by traumatic life events. For example, when coping with stress, over 70% of Americans reported turning to faith communities for assistance (Weaver, Flannelly, Garbino, Figley, & Flannelly, 2003). Therefore, it is not surprising that there is a pattern of increased involvement with faith communities in the postimpact phase of disaster (Koenig, 2006). With the loss of their normative rhythms, people look to religion to restore a sense of control and stability (Figley, 1989; Spence, Lachlan, & Burke, 2007). Ai, Cascio, Santangelo, and Evans-Campbell (2005) stated that following the 9/11 terrorist attacks, over 60% of New York City residents reported prayer as one of the key coping mechanisms they used. Similarly, Schuster et al. (2001) found that approximately 90% of a national sample of Americans reported using religion as a coping mechanism following the 9/11 terrorist attacks.

Within 5 years, church attendance and other measures of spiritual and religious salience had fallen to the same levels as before the 9/11 terrorist attacks (Barna Group, 2006). Uecker (2008) observed similar increases in religious and spiritual resurgence of young adults, which were also largely short-lived. However, preliminary findings from a longitudinal study of survivors of the 2010 Haitian earthquake found that church attendance doubled for some religious congregations immediately following the earthquake and endured at a 3-year follow-up (O'Grady & O'Grady, 2013).

Whether the increase in church attendance is short-lived or enduring, the fact is that during the postimpact phase people congregate in their religious institutions. Therefore, in this phase—through collaboration with religious leaders—mental health service providers can readily identify locations to conduct community-based assessments and interventions and promote professional mental health care for individuals. In the early weeks after disaster, local clergy and religious congregations are powerful community partners in education and assessment, as well as intervention (Milstein & Manierre, 2010).

The months (and sometimes years) that follow represent the *restoration phase*. Individuals and communities must now determine and create their new normality. After individual congregations respond to their congregants, many communities find forums for multifaith memorials and commemorations. These commemorations are again an opportunity for mental health professionals to provide psychoeducational and referral materials.

SPIRITUALITY AND RELIGION AND POSTTRAUMATIC TRANSFORMATION FOLLOWING DISASTERS

Disasters can create psychological and spiritual transformation in communities and in individuals. Depending on the resources in place in people's lives, the transformation can be toward decline, such as in, but not limited to, PTSD, or toward growth (Calhoun & Tedeschi, 2006; Roberts, 2005). For example, Ochu (2013) studied 407 adult Liberian civil war survivors living in refugee camps. The study indicated that negative religious coping correlated with posttraumatic symptom severity and that forgiveness and positive religious coping linked to posttraumatic growth. Similarly, a study of Haitian earthquake survivors found that those who relied on their spirituality for meaning making and coping evidenced greater resilience during and after the trauma than those who did not do so. Participants attributed their description of posttraumatic growth to positive framing—that there is a sense of a larger purpose or sense of order amidst disaster. Some saw the disaster as a potentially growth-stimulating experience for Haiti (e.g., a chance to rebuild a better country; O'Grady et al., 2012, in press). Jang and LaMendola (2007) studied 607 survivors of a major earthquake in Taiwan and found that survivors' spirituality had a direct link with posttraumatic growth and that the community's collective spiritual narratives about suffering contributed to the psychological growth following the earthquake.

Influence of Religious and Spiritual Appraisal on Reactions to Disaster

Research has demonstrated relationships between religious and spiritual appraisal and disaster reactions. Kroll-Smith and Couch (1987) examined religious attributions and coping in a community in Pennsylvania affected by a 23-year-long mine fire that eventually led to calamity. They found that most participants attributed this technical disaster to human failure rather than to God. Ai et al. (2005) found similar reactions to human-made disasters in their study of survivors of 9/11. However, their data revealed an additional insight into another possible difference in how people respond across disasters: that negative coping was associated with defense or retaliation patterns of reaction to 9/11, in effect creating an ingroup versus outgroup difference based on religious ideology.

Likewise, Pargament et al. (1994) conducted a longitudinal study of the Gulf War crisis in which they learned that negative religious coping was significantly tied to psychological distress. Conversely, survivors of natural disasters, which are sometimes referred to as "acts of God," appear to more readily incorporate spiritual and religious meaning into their interpretation of the disaster as well as their responses and coping mechanisms. For instance, survivors of the Haiti earthquake referenced God as the author of the earthquake and cited prophetic references from the Bible to make sense of the event (O'Grady et al., in press). In addition, Smith, Pargament, Brant, and Oliver (2000) found that positive religious coping strategies had a positive effect on postflood spiritual growth, in addition to leading to the reduction of psychological distress for survivors of a Midwest flood.

Impact of Disasters on the Way Survivors View and Experience the Sacred

The way people view the divine is influenced by a number of factors, including traumatic life experiences. Likewise, certain views of God or the divine affect psychological functioning during and following trauma events, including large-scale disasters (Moriarty & Davis, 2012; O'Grady & Richards, 2007). After 9/11 Briggs, Apple, and Aydlett (2004) found that this tragic event appeared to increase participants' connection with transcendence. O'Grady et al. (2012) found that 80% of earthquake survivors agreed or strongly agreed with the statement "My faith in a God/higher power has grown since the earthquake." In addition, 23% of participants agreed or strongly agreed that they felt more distant from God or a higher power since the earthquake, and 20% indicated that they were less spiritual since the earthquake. People's daily spiritual experiences with God, their perceptions of God's awareness of them, and their sense of "specialness" to God predicted their degree of spiritual transformation above and beyond the amount of loss they experienced in the earthquake.

Aten, Madison, Rice, and Chamberlain (2008) found that Hurricane Katrina survivors often held a multifaceted view of God that existed on a continuum from a loving and caring parental figure to a judging and even punishing figure. Newton and McIntosh (2009) found that Jewish survivors of Hurricane Katrina held more positive and benevolent views of God than did Christian survivors, who were more apt to report feeling as though God was sending punishment. According to the conservation of resources stress theory, "loss is the primary operating mechanism driving stress reactions" (Hobfoll, Freedy, Green, & Solomon, 1996, p. 324). After Hurricane Katrina, Aten et al. (2013) found that increased levels of resource loss were related to a more negative God concept and to viewing God as less in control.

Relationship Between Disaster Survivors' Religion or Spirituality and Well-Being

Religion and spirituality may moderate the impact of disaster on individuals' well-being. Research has suggested that religion and spirituality serve as a buffer for the potential deleterious effects of disaster and/or as a contributor to psychological distress following disasters. Following 9/11, Ai et al. (2005) discovered stronger faith, hope, and spirituality to be inversely correlated with depression and anxiety related to the exposure of direct and indirect 9/11 trauma. Further, researchers found that religious comfort helped to protect participants from negative emotional and physical health outcomes commonly associated with resource loss, and it was also associated with posttraumatic growth. Religious strain, however, was linked to poorer emotional and physical health outcomes following disaster resource loss (Cook, Aten, Moore, Hook, & Davis, 2013). Likewise, Johnson, Aten, Madson, and Bennett (2006) surveyed approximately 600 residents of Mississippi who survived Hurricane Katrina. In this study, individuals who possessed positive religious and spiritual beliefs (e.g., God concept, religious coping strategies, religious support, meaning making) were shown to be less affected by the effects of exposure to hurricanes as well as the degree of resource loss (i.e., material and interpersonal). These individuals also experienced reduced rates of PTSD symptoms, depression, and alcohol use.

Taken as a whole, this body of burgeoning research may indicate that it is not so much how religious or spiritual one is but rather how one uses their faith (e.g., positive religious coping vs. negative religious coping strategies) that appears to have the most significant impact on well-being outcomes. Of course, the reader must be cautious in drawing conclusions because much of this research is correlational in nature. It is equally likely, for example, that there is an underlying mental health or personality factor at work in both faith and response to significant life events.

RECOGNIZING SPIRITUAL AND EMOTIONAL REACTIONS TO DISASTERS

Recovering from a disaster is usually a gradual process. The spiritual and emotional toll that disaster brings can sometimes be even more devastating than the financial strains of damage and loss of home, business, or personal property. A number of variables are involved in the recovery trajectory of disaster survivors. In this section, we describe a trauma recovery model that outlines this trajectory, followed by a more in-depth discussion of some of the common experiences of individuals and communities encountering disasters and their movement through the recovery process, as outlined in the posttraumatic transformation model.

O'Grady et al. (in press) proposed a posttraumatic transformation model describing the psychological processes of individuals and communities following disasters. According to this model, change is activated by a traumatic life event defined as a *cosmology episode* (Weick, 1993). A cosmology episode is a "bracketed cue" (Weick, 1993) that challenges the global cognitive framework of an individual to the extent that the experience is often referred to as a "watershed that divides a life into 'before and after' the event" (Calhoun & Tedeschi, 2006, p. 9). As mentioned in Chapter 12 of this volume, when the global cognitive framework that a person has in place is no longer viable for making sense of her or his current circumstance, the person enters into a state of chaos or upheaval. This unraveling of cognitive structures has been defined as *senselosing* (Orton, 2000). The extreme discomfort of senselosing encourages *sensemaking*, in which global cognitive structures have to be reconsidered, reorganized, and reconciled with the cosmology episode (Park, 2005).

The process of senselosing and sensemaking does not always result in healthy new global cognitive frameworks. Some engage in unhealthy sensemaking processes, such as denial of the cosmology episode or the adoption of a cynical or fearful global view of themselves, others, the world, or a higher power. However, research has indicated that a traumatic event can be an impetus for stress-related growth when healthy sensemaking processes are used (O'Grady et al., in press). The extent to which a traumatic event develops into posttraumatic growth or decline is mediated by a number of cognitive processes, such as causal attributions, reframing, reappraisal, and perceived support from others (Calhoun & Tedeschi, 2006).

Some research has indicated that spiritual and religious cognitive processes, such as causal attribution of a higher power's role, religious coping, gratitude, and perceived experience with or support from a higher power, can play important roles in posttraumatic change processes (Exline, 2009; Mallery, Mallery, & Gorsuch, 2000; O'Grady et al., 2012). Likewise, social support and sense of community seem to be essential to healthy posttraumatic recovery (Harvey, 2007). Church communities can be especially helpful in fostering a positive recovery trajectory because they offer a supportive context for people to work through religious struggles and create shared meaning and purpose. In addition, church communities can provide a venue for outward-focused activities, such as community service projects and grief vigils, that can promote healthy recovery (O'Grady et al., in press).

COMMON SPIRITUAL REACTIONS TO DISASTERS

Religious and spiritual beliefs are part of the overall sense that people create about the world and the way it functions. This sense may foster more constructive and adaptive responses and thus be a source of strength and comfort in a crisis. In these cases, survivors may seek comfort from their beliefs, and their spiritual beliefs may support coping and resilience. At the same time, disasters can also lead to spiritual struggles or "spiritual crisis" as survivors attempt to make meaning of their disaster experience (McBride, 1998). Research has shown that persistent spiritual struggles are linked to more negative emotional and physical health symptoms among disaster survivors. Agrimson and Taft (2009) suggested that disasters can cause impairment in seven constructs of a person's sense of spirituality. The following is a list of those constructs and examples of common struggles, as adapted from Murray-Swank (2012):

- Connectedness—"I feel like God is so far away right now." "Has God abandoned me?"
- Faith and religious belief or value systems, in which beliefs about control and responsibility can be upended—"Did I do something to cause God to punish me?" "Why would God allow this to happen?"
- Meaning and purpose in life—"Why would God let such a bad thing happen?" "I just can't understand." "What do I do with my life now?"
- Self-transcendence—"Why won't God help me overcome the pain I am feeling?"
- Inner peace and harmony—"My life feels chaotic. I thought believing in God was supposed to bring feelings of peace."
- Inner strength and energy—"I do not feel God's support in my life anymore. Does God even care about me?"

Religion and spirituality offer unique psychosocial resources for survivors. Some researchers have suggested that spirituality and religion provide a structure for individual meaning construction and have offered a collective meaning framework for communities following disaster (Newport, Agrawal, & Witters, 2010; O'Grady et al., in press). Koenig (2006) suggested that spirituality and religion have the potential to promote resilience among survivors by providing a positive worldview and meaning and purpose, among other things.

RESOURCES FOR DISASTER SPIRITUAL AND EMOTIONAL CARE

Prior to a disaster, mental health professionals should familiarize themselves and their spiritual community stakeholders with helpful resources, such as *Light Our Way* (National Voluntary Organizations Active in Disaster, 2006), *Religious Responses to Catastrophe* (Koenig, 2006), and *Creating Spiritual and Psychological Resilience: Integrating Care in Disaster Relief Work* (Brenner, Bush, & Moses, 2009). For helpful online resources, mental health professionals may visit Wheaton College's Humanitarian Disaster Institute resource page (http://www.wheaton.edu/HDI/Resources), which has numerous tip sheets, tools, bibliographies, and manuals on disaster spiritual and emotional care available to download.

Mental health professionals interested in providing disaster spiritual and emotional care might consider becoming familiar with, and consider joining, local or national groups providing emotional and spiritual care services. One particular umbrella organization is the National Voluntary Organizations Active in Disaster (NVOAD). It consists of many emergency service organizations that collaborate with communities to orchestrate planning and services throughout the disaster cycle. Members of the American Psychological Association (APA) can find valuable tools and assist with response by joining the organization's Disaster Response Network or by joining one of the many state psychological association networks. Another organization helpful for mental health professionals to get to know is the National Disaster Interfaiths Network, which seeks to connect and equip disaster interfaith organizations across the United States.

Another way mental health professionals can get involved in disaster spiritual and emotional care is to work with and deploy through an established nongovernmental organization such as the Salvation Army or Green Cross. Overall, whenever possible, it is best to respond through preexisting infrastructures or organizations when responding to disasters. "Parachuting in" to a disaster zone is to be discouraged unless one is a part of the community, has direct ties, or is working through an established organization. Otherwise, those that spontaneously help risk draining resources from the community rather than being a resource to the community they are trying to help (Milstein & Manierre, 2010).

ETHICAL GUIDELINES AND PRINCIPLES FOR DISASTER SPIRITUAL AND EMOTIONAL CARE

Before providing disaster spiritual and emotional care, mental health professionals should be aware of their own limitations and the professional guidelines for ethical practice. We encourage mental health professionals to adhere to the ethical guidelines presented in Chapter 3 of this volume. It should be noted, however, that being a competent psychotherapist does not necessarily translate to disaster competency. To help with preparation, mental health professionals may familiarize themselves with the NVOAD points of consensus for disaster spiritual care (which can be downloaded for free from http://www.nvoad.org/library/cat_view/9-points-of-consensus). NVOAD's Emotional and Spiritual Care Committee published this document to inform, encourage, and affirm those who respond to disasters and to encourage standards insuring those affected by disaster receive appropriate and respectful spiritual care services.

APA (2008) has also provided ethical guidelines for circumstances in which the professional practice of psychology interacts with religious thought and action or, alternatively, when the use of religious content is outside the purview of the professional practice of psychology. The guidelines remind mental health professionals that although "contemporary psychology as well as religious and spiritual traditions all address the human condition, they often do so from distinct presuppositions, approaches to knowledge, and social roles and contexts" (APA, 2008, p. 2).

Further, mental health professionals are encouraged to consider the following principles for mental health disaster response:

- Do no harm—be wary of moving ahead with individual interventions that lack adequate planning and awareness of the community context.
- Provide help that is community based—adapt to local interest groups, and build on their strengths.
- Provide help that is sustainable—interventions and programs must have sufficient merit and community participation to engage the community in maintaining them.
- Build on the strengths of the community served—recognize the local culture's strengths, and build on these so there is a sense of local ownership.
- Use local expertise—use local people who will be there for the long-term recovery.
- Address ordinary reactions to extraordinary events—do not address pathology, but focus on normal reactions to abnormal events.
- Offer psychological support—recognize that everyone is affected and serve the entire community, not just an identified portion of the community. (Jacobs, 2007)

According to the National Institute of Mental Health (2002), interventions should be matched to the phase of disaster response (e.g., preparedness, response, recovery). For example, research has shown that psychoeducational and psychosocial support-based approaches (e.g., psychological first aid) are more effective in the emergency and early postimpact phases, whereas traditional psychotherapy approaches (e.g., cognitive behavior therapy [CBT]) appear more effective during the longer restoration phase. Research has shown that poor matching of disaster mental health interventions will not only lead to ineffective treatment but also can actually cause harm (Aten, 2012a). Taken together, the aforementioned recommendations provide mental health professionals with a solid footing for the ethical practice of disaster spiritual and emotional care.

PRACTICING DISASTER SPIRITUAL AND EMOTIONAL CARE

Mental health professionals are in a unique position to help disaster survivors address both mental health and spiritual issues, as well as to collaborate with spiritual communities, in times of disaster. This section begins with some general recommendations for how to (and how not to) respond to disaster spiritual issues.

General Guidelines for How to (and How Not to) Respond to Spiritual Issues in a Disaster

The following is a compilation of recommended strategies for responding to spiritual issues that may surface after a disaster:

- Use reflective listening and active listening techniques when working with survivors.
- Be honest and compassionate, and do not assume you know what survivors will say or believe.
- If you do not feel comfortable discussing spiritual or religious issues, listen quietly and refer survivors to someone who can help them appropriately.
- Do not try to explain or give answers to spiritual questions.
- Do not argue with survivors' beliefs or try to persuade them to believe as you do.
- Let survivors tell you what their religious or spiritual beliefs are. Do not assume anything.
- Help survivors use their spiritual or religious beliefs to cope.
- Survivors may need reassurance that it is "normal" to ask questions about God and/or their religious beliefs.
- Allow expressions of anger toward God or others, and assess that survivors are not a danger to themselves or others.
- Do affirm survivors' search for spiritual or faith-based answers. Do not impose your thoughts or beliefs on them.
- Do affirm the wrongness and/or injustice of what has happened, especially if the trauma was caused by people.
- Encourage survivors to turn to religious or spiritual writings within their culture that bring them comfort and help them in their search for meaning or their search for spiritual answers

- Emphasize that everyone has to find their own answers and way of understanding in traumatic events.

When providing support, you should avoid saying the following phrases. On the surface, these phrases may be meant to comfort the survivors, but they can be misinterpreted.

- "I understand." In most situations we cannot understand unless we have had the same experience.
- "Don't feel bad." The survivor has a right to feel bad and will need time to feel differently.
- "You're strong" or "You'll get through this." Many survivors do not feel strong and question whether they will recover from the loss.
- "Don't cry." It is OK to cry.
- "It's God's will" or "They are in a better place." With a person you do not know, giving religious meaning to an event may insult or anger the person.
- "It could be worse," "At least you still have _____," or "Everything will be OK." It is up to the individual to decide whether things could be worse or whether everything can be OK. (Adapted from Hacker, 1996)

Rather than provide comfort, these types of responses could elicit a strong negative response or distance the survivor from the listener. It is OK to apologize if the survivor reacts negatively to something that was said.

Disaster Spiritual and Emotional Care Interventions

This section builds on the aforementioned general guidelines by providing examples of both micro (person-focused) interventions and macro (community-focused) interventions key to successful disaster spiritual and emotional care in professional psychology. This is not meant to be an exhaustive overview; rather, the following is meant to serve as an introduction of several helpful practices.

Clergy–Mental Health Professional Collaboration

Mental health professionals should take steps to engage key spiritual community stakeholders to build collaborative relationships that can be leveraged in response to disasters. Spiritual leaders, who often act as "gate-keepers" in their respective communities, are more willing to refer members to professionals when they have an established relationship (e.g., Aten, 2004). Therefore, mental health professionals should make a strategic effort to build partnerships with religious leaders in their community prior to disasters so that a relationship is already in place if and when disaster strikes (Evans, Kromm, & Sturgis, 2008; Roberts & Ashley, 2008). This will help ensure greater collaboration in response to disasters. Religious leaders are the experts about their communities, so mental health professionals should use a dialogical rather than didactic approach to collaboration. When meeting with spiritual community stakeholders, mental health professionals should invite the stakeholders to educate them about the specific dynamics of their faith community members and cultural contexts so that the mental health professionals and stakeholders can create a community-specific and culturally sensitive approach to disaster preparedness and response (O'Grady et al., 2012).

Disaster Planning for Faith Communities

Successful disaster response is often tied to level of preparedness. Mental health professionals can help engage faith communities in disaster planning. For example, Aten and Topping (2010) developed an online social networking tool to help faith communities prepare for disaster by partnering with a mental health professional who acts as a facilitator in developing and implementing the preparedness plan. The tool design was initially based on the researchers' own consultation experience helping a local faith community in preparation for Hurricane Gustav (see Figure 9.1). This tool helped strengthen social networks within and between faith communities in preparation for the threatening storm by improving information sharing and gathering, communication, and support between congregational leadership and attendees.

A networking tool can be developed using an online cloud-based service, such as Google Docs or SurveyMonkey, and this can be e-mailed to participants. This allows leaders to share information in real time; it can be accessed once the Internet is brought back online or from evacuation sites with an Internet connection. The tool can also be used to help members of the faith community to communicate with one another, leave messages, check-in to let others know whether they are OK, and share needs and resources. The tool can be used to collect such data as (a) contact information, (b) disaster-related residence plans, (c) special needs, and (d) "host-homes" volunteers (i.e., members who open their residences for others to stay with them for shelter). For more on how to develop and implement this tool, see Aten and Topping (2010).

Psychological First Aid for Community Religious Professionals

Early intervention can moderate the impact of a disaster. The purpose of psychological first aid (PFA) is to provide children, adults, and families with support that decreases their risk factors and increases their resiliency

Hurricane Gustav Preparedness Form

Please fill this out as best as you can. If you change your mind later on, just return to this form and do another one. We will e-mail lists of host homes and bring lists of host homes, etc., on Sunday night.

Name [   ]

Phone Number [   ]

If Hurricane Gustav comes to Hattiesburg/Gulf Coast will you:

    ○ Stay in Hattiesburg

    ○ Leave Hattiesburg to stay elsewhere

If you are leaving town is there a number or address where you could be reached?

[   ]

If you are staying in Hattiesburg would you need or want to stay someplace other than your house?

    ○ I would rather stay with someone else

    ○ I will stay at my house

If you are staying at your house through the hurricane, would you be willing to open your house up for others if they need a place to stay?

    ○ Yes, we could host others

    ○ Our house would not be good for hosting

If you would like to be a host home, please type in your address below.

[   ]

If you are staying in town and have any special needs you would like us to know about please indicate it below.

[   ]

Figure 9.1. Sample online social networking disaster preparedness tool.

to trauma (Vernberg et al., 2008). PFA is an evidence-informed intervention. It is less clinically oriented in nature and primarily focuses on addressing the immediate needs of disaster survivors. PFA consists of nine core actions: (a) contact and engagement, (b) safety and comfort, (c) stabilization, (d) information gathering, (e) current needs and concerns, (f) practical assistance, (g) connection with social supports, (h) information on coping, and (i) linkage with collaborative services (Forbes et al., 2011). PFA has more of a triage focus, with the goal of helping to secure and stabilize disaster survivors. As a result, PFA has been adapted for delivery by a wide range of community professionals.

Of particular relevance to this chapter, PFA has also been contextualized for community religious professionals. In *Psychological First Aid: Field Operations Guide for Community Religious Professionals*, the authors introduce a variation of PFA that addresses religious and spiritual themes, including (a) clarifying religious, spiritual, and existential terminology; (b) how to worship with someone of a different faith; and (c) talking to children and adolescents about their spiritual or religious concerns and involving them in religious activities (Brymer et al., 2006). Mental health professionals could use this resource to train clergy and other religious leaders in this intervention, thereby increasing a community's capacity to provide disaster spiritual and emotional care. Mental health professionals are encouraged to acquire this more spiritually focused resource to enhance their own practice. Mental health professionals will benefit by learning strategies for effectively integrating and addressing religious and spiritual issues in the immediate aftermath of a disaster.

Consultation, Outreach, and Advocacy

Mental health professionals can promote disaster spiritual and emotional care through consultation, outreach, and advocacy efforts. Aten, Topping, Denney, and Hosey (2011) developed a three-tier consultation and outreach model to provide mental health training for clergy and faith communities. In Tier One, mental health professionals provide basic disaster mental health information to local clergy. In Tier Two, mental health professionals and religious leaders pair together to help educate their congregation members. In Tier Three, congregation members reach out to their local communities to provide information on topics such as common reactions and problems, as well as when and where help can be found in the region (Aten et al., 2011).

Similarly, mental health professionals can advocate on behalf of religious and spiritual community causes by applying the best science and information available to address disaster needs and policy. In this role, mental health professionals can work with local faith communities and organizations to identify needs and gaps in services and help them bring those needs to light

(Aten, 2008). For example, after Hurricane Katrina, several faith communities were concerned that local authorities were planning to use relief dollars to expand a local port used for industry rather than fund low-income housing. In this case, several local mental health professionals collaborated with faith communities to help them develop a "voice" and refine their message. Empirical data was provided to faith leaders to help support their arguments and help them influence policy.

Overall, successful consultation, outreach, and advocacy interventions (a) establish relationships with local community and religious leaders, (b) are culturally appropriate, (c) foster bidirectional collaboration, (d) promote a cyclical approach (e.g., implementation, evaluation, refinement), (e) are community contextualized, and (f) help organize resources (Aten, O'Grady, Milstein, Boan, & Schruba, 2014; Milstein, Manierre, & Yali, 2010).

Clinical Services

In addition to preparedness and community-level interventions, mental health professionals may have the opportunity to develop therapeutic relationships with individuals and families affected by disaster. Research has found that in most cases more traditional psychotherapy is better suited for helping disaster survivors in recovery settings (e.g., the first few weeks or months after a disaster). In contrast to support interventions, this set of interventions seeks to explore and understand how survivors' ways of thinking, feeling, and behaving are affecting their adjustment. In many cases, these interventions are more change oriented than support oriented, seeking to help people either change or accept their circumstances. For example, strong evidence exists for the usefulness and effectiveness of CBT to treat disaster survivors. Though not within a disaster context, there is strong support for religious accommodative CBT (Aten, 2012a).

In working with survivors' long-term situations, it is helpful to integrate spiritual and religious themes into treatment. Thus, mental health professionals may find it useful to merge elements from postdisaster CBT and from religious accommodative CBT when religious and existential issues present in the context of psychotherapy (Aten, 2012b). To determine whether such an approach would be beneficial to clients, mental health professionals may do a thorough assessment that includes inquiring about clients' religious and spiritual history and commitments. Other researchers have encouraged the use of pastoral counseling for disaster survivors. For example, Harris et al. (2008) recommended that survivors use pastoral counseling and services when in a disaster; they also called to attention the need for additional strategies and guidance on the use of religious resources before, during, and after a disaster.

REFERENCES

Agrimson, L. B., & Taft, L. B. (2009). Spiritual crisis: A concept analysis. *Journal of Advanced Nursing, 65*, 454–461 doi:10.1111/j.1365-2648.2008.04869.x

Ai, A., Cascio, T., Santangelo, L. K., & Evans-Campbell, T. (2005). Hope, meaning, and growth following the September 11, 2001, terrorist attacks. *Journal of Interpersonal Violence, 20*, 523–548. doi:10.1177/0886260504272896

American Psychological Association. (2008). Resolution on religious, religion-based, and/or religion-derived prejudice. *American Psychologist, 63*, 431–434.

Aten, J. D. (2004). Improving understanding and collaboration between campus ministers and college counseling center personnel. *Journal of College Counseling, 7*, 90–96. doi:10.1002/j.2161-1882.2004.tb00263.x

Aten, J. D. (2008). The church disaster mental health project: www.churchdisaster help.org. *Applied Research in Economic Development, 5*, 56–57.

Aten, J. D. (2012a). Disaster spiritual and emotional care in professional psychology: A Christian integrative approach. *Journal of Psychology and Theology, 40*, 131–135.

Aten, J. D. (2012b). More than research and ruble: How community research can change lives (including yours and your students'). *Journal of Psychology and Christianity, 31*, 314–319.

Aten, J. D., Boan, D. M., Hosey, J. M., Topping, S., Graham, A., & Im, H. (2013). Building capacity for responding to disaster emotional and spiritual needs: A clergy, academic, and mental health partnership model (CAMP). *Psychological Trauma: Theory, Research, Practice, & Policy, 5*, 591–600. doi:10.1037/a0030041

Aten, J. D., Madison, M. B., Rice, A., & Chamberlain, A. K. (2008). Post disaster supervisor strategies for promoting supervisee self-care: Lessons learned from Hurricane Katrina. *Training and Education in Professional Psychology, 2*, 75–82.

Aten, J. D., O'Grady, K. A., Milstein, G., Boan, D., & Schruba, A. (2014). Spiritually oriented disaster psychology. *Spirituality in Clinical Practice, 1*, 20–28. doi:10.1037/scp0000008

Aten, J. D., & Topping, S. (2010). An online social networking disaster preparedness tool for faith communities. *Psychological Trauma: Theory, Research, Practice, and Policy, 2*, 130–134. doi:10.1037/a0019157

Aten, J. D., Topping, S., Denney, R. M., & Hosey, J. M. (2011). Helping African American clergy and churches address minority disaster mental health disparities: Training needs, model, and example. *Psychology of Religion and Spirituality, 3*, 15–23. doi:10.1037/a0020497

Barna Group. (2006). *Five years later: 9/11 attacks show no lasting influence on Americans' faith*. Retrieved from https://www.barna.org/barna-update/culture/148-five-years-later-911-attacks-show-no-lasting-influence-on-americans-faith

Benedek, D. M., & Fullerton, C. S. (2007). Translating five essential elements into programs and practice. *Psychiatry: Interpersonal and Biological Processes, 70*, 345–349. doi:10.1521/psyc.2007.70.4.345

Brenner, G., Bush, D., & Moses, J., (2009). *Creating spiritual and psychological resilience: Integrating care in disaster relief work.* Hoboken, NJ: Taylor & Francis.

Briggs, M. K., Apple, K. J., & Aydlett, A. E. (2004). Spirituality and the events of September 11: A preliminary study. *Counseling and Values, 48,* 174–182. doi:10.1002/j.2161-007X.2004.tb00244.x

Brymer, M., Jacobs, A., Layne, C., Pynoos, R., Ruzek, J., Steinberg, A., . . . Watson, P. (2006). *Psychological first aid field operations guide* (2nd ed.). Los Angeles, CA: National Child Traumatic Stress Network and National Center for PTSD.

Cain, D. S., & Barthelemy, J. (2008). Tangible and spiritual relief after the storm: The religious community responds to Katrina. *Journal of Social Service Research, 34,* 29–42. doi:10.1080/01488370802086005

Calhoun, L. G., & Tedeschi, R. G. (2006). The foundations of post-traumatic growth: An expanded framework. In L. G. Calhoun & R. G. Tedeschi (Eds.), *Handbook of posttraumatic growth: Research and practice* (pp. 1–23). Mahwah, NJ: Penguin.

Centre for Research on the Epidemiology of Disasters. (2007, March). *Disaster data: A balanced perspective.* Retrieved from http://www.em-dat.net/documents/CRED%20CRUNCH%208%20-%20March%2020071.pdf

Cook, S. W., Aten, J. D., Moore, M., Hook, J. N., & Davis, D. E. (2013). Resource loss, religiousness, health, and posttraumatic growth following Hurricane Katrina. *Mental Health, Religion & Culture, 16,* 352–366. doi:10.1080/136746 76.2012.667395

Darling, C. A., Hill, E. W., & McWey, L. M., (2004). Understanding stress and quality of life for clergy and clergy spouses. *Stress & Health, 20,* 261–277. doi:10.1002/smi.1031

Evans, D., Kromm, C., & Sturgis, S. (2008). *Faith in the Gulf: Lessons from the religious response to Hurricane Katrina.* Durham, NC: Institute for Southern Studies, Southern Exposure.

Exline, J. J. (2009). Relationships with God. In H. Reis & S. Sprecher (Eds.), *Encyclopedia of human relationships* (Vol. 1, pp. 767–768). Thousand Oaks, CA: Sage.

Figley, C. R. (1989). *Helping traumatized families.* San Francisco, CA: Jossey-Bass.

Forbes, D., Lewis, V., Varker, T., Phelps, A., O'Donnell, M., Wade, D. J., . . . Creamer, M. (2011). Psychological first aid following trauma: Implementation and evaluation framework for high-risk organizations. *Psychiatry: Interpersonal and Biological Processes, 74,* 224–239. doi:10.1521/psyc.2011.74.3.224

Guthrie, T., & Stickley, T., (2008) Spiritual experiences and mental distress: A clergy perspective. *Mental Health, Religion & Culture, 11,* 387–402. doi:10.1080/13674670701484303

Hacker, C. L. (1996). *Too much, too ugly, too fast! How faith communities can respond in crisis and disasters.* Retrieved from http://www.google.com/url?sa=t&rct=j&q=&esrc=s&source=web&cd=1&ved=0CCkQFjAA&url=http%3A%2F%2Fwww.lssnd.org%2Ffile_download%2F8bfc0ffc-1f66-4473-9e49-53ff143f9346&ei=AiUCU5W7KOW70wXb3oAw&usg=AFQjCNEOmUdKeH4_kbXTJdwQt5WJtsjBZQ&sig2=l_8FAeyH8nvsEnR8ofXN3A&bvm=bv.61535280,d.d2k

Harris, J. I., Erbes, C. R., Engdahl, B. E., Olson, R. H. A., Winskowski, A. M., & McMahill, J. (2008). Christian religious functioning and trauma outcomes. *Journal of Clinical Psychology, 64*, 17–29. doi:10.1002/jclp.20427

Harvey, M. R. (2007). Towards an ecological understanding of resilience in trauma survivors. *Journal of Aggression, Maltreatment & Trauma, 14*, 9–32.

Hobfoll, S., Freedy, J., Green, B., & Solomon, S. (1996). Coping in reaction to extreme stress: The roles of resource loss and resource availability. In M. Zeidner & N. Endler (Eds.), *Handbook of coping: Theory, research, applications* (pp. 342–349). Oxford, England Wiley.

Jacobs, G. A. (2007). The development and maturation of humanitarian psychology. *American Psychologist, 62*, 932–941. doi:10.1037/0003-066X.62.8.932

Jang, L., & LaMendola, W. (2007). Social work in natural disasters: The case of spirituality and post-traumatic growth. *Advances in Social Work, 8*, 305–317.

Johnson, T., Aten, J. D., Madson, M., & Bennett, P. (2006, August). *Alcohol use and meaning in life among survivors of Hurricane Katrina.* Paper presented at the International Conference on Personal Meaning: Addiction, Meaning, & Spirituality, British Columbia, Canada.

Koenig, H. G. (2006). *In the wake of disaster: Religious responses to terrorism and catastrophe.* Philadelphia, PA: Templeton Foundation Press.

Kroll-Smith, J. S., & Couch, S. R. (1987). A chronic technical disaster and the irrelevance of religious meaning: The case of Centralia, Pennsylvania. *Journal for the Scientific Study of Religion, 26*, 25–37. doi:10.2307/1385839

Mallery, P., Mallery, S., & Gorsuch, R. (2000). A preliminary taxonomy of attributions to God. *International Journal for the Psychology of Religion, 10*, 135–156. doi:10.1207/S15327582IJPR1003_01

McBride, J. L. (1998). *Spiritual crisis: Surviving trauma to the soul.* Binghamton, NY: Haworth Press.

Milstein, G., & Manierre, A. (2010). Normative and diagnostic reactions to disaster: Clergy and clinician collaboration to facilitate a continuum of care. In G. H. Brenner, D. H. Bush, & J. Moses (Eds.), *Creating spiritual and psychological resilience: Integrating care in disaster relief work* (pp. 219–226). New York, NY: Routledge.

Milstein, G., Manierre, A., & Yali, A. M. (2010). Psychological care for persons of diverse religions: A collaborative continuum. *Professional Psychology: Research and Practice, 41*, 371–381. doi:10.1037/a0021074

Moriarty, G. L., & Davis, E. B. (2012). Client God images: Theory, research, and clinical practice. In J. D. Aten, K. O'Grady, & E. Worthington, Jr. (Eds.), *The psychology of religion and spirituality for clinicians: Using research in your practice* (pp. 131–160). New York, NY: Routledge.

Murray-Swank, N. A. (2012). Navigating the storm: Helping clients in the midst of spiritual struggles. In J. D. Aten, K. O'Grady, & E. Worthington, Jr. (Eds.), *The psychology of religion and spirituality for clinicians: Using research in your practice* (pp. 217–244). New York, NY: Routledge.

National Institute of Mental Health. (2002). *Mental health and mass violence: Evidence-based early psychological intervention for victims/survivors of mass violence: A workshop to reach consensus on best practices* (NIH Pub. No. 02–5138). Washington, DC: U.S. Government Printing Office.

National Voluntary Organizations Active in Disaster. (2006). *Disaster spiritual care: National Voluntary Organizations Active in Disaster points of consensus.* Arlington, VA: Author.

Nelson, L. D., & Dynes, R. R. (1976). The impact of devotionalism and attendance on ordinary and emergency helping behavior. *Journal for the Scientific Study of Religion, 15,* 47–59. doi:10.2307/1384313

Newport, F., Agrawal, S., & Witters, D. (2010). *Very religious Americans report less depression, worry.* Retrieved from http://www.gallup.com/poll/144980/Religious-Americans-Report-Less-Depression-Worry.aspx

Newton, A. T., & McIntosh, D. N. (2009). Association of general religiousness and specific religious beliefs with coping appraisals in response to Hurricanes Katrina and Rita. *Mental Health, Religion & Culture, 12,* 129–146. doi:10.1080/13674670802380400

Norris, F. H., Friedman, M. J., & Watson, P. J. (2002). 60,000 disaster victims speak: Part II. Summary and implications of the disaster mental health research. *Psychiatry: Interpersonal and Biological Processes, 65,* 240–260. doi:10.1521/psyc.65.3.240.20169

Ochu, A. C. (2013). *Forgiveness and religious coping as predictors of posttraumatic outcomes* (Unpublished doctoral dissertation). Loyola University, Baltimore, MD.

O'Grady, K. A., & O'Grady, S. D. (2013). *Haiti then and now: A longitudinal study of earthquake survivors in Haiti.* Manuscript in preparation.

O'Grady, K. A., Orton, J. D., Schreiber-Pan, H., & Wismick, J. C. (in press). International community trauma and the posttraumatic transformation model. *International Psychology Bulletin.*

O'Grady, K. A., & Richards, P. S. (2007). God image and theistic psychotherapy. *Journal of Spirituality and Mental Health, 9,* 183–209.

O'Grady, K. A., Rollison, D. G., Hanna, T. S., Schreiber-Pan, H., & Ruiz, M. A. (2012). Earthquake in Haiti: Relationship with the sacred in times of trauma. *Journal of Psychology and Theology, 40,* 289–301.

Orton, J. D. (2000). Catastrophes, strategy-losing, and strategy-making. *Academy of Management Learning and Education, 1*(1), 14–37.

Pant, A. T., Kirsch, T. D., Subbarao, I. R., Hsieh, Y.-H., & Vu, A. (2008). Faith-based organizations and sustainable sheltering operations in Mississippi after Hurricane Katrina: Implications for informal network utilization. *Prehospital and Disaster Medicine, 23,* 48–54.

Pargament, K. I., Ishler, K., Dubow, E. F., Stanik, P., Rouiller, R., Crowe, E. P., . . . Royster, B. J. (1994). Methods of religious coping with the Gulf War: Cross sectional and longitudinal analyses. *Journal for the Scientific Study of Religion, 33,* 347–361.

Park, C. L. (2005). Religion and meaning. In R. F. Paloutzian & C. L. Park (Eds.), *Handbook of the psychology of religion and spirituality* (pp. 295–314). New York, NY: Guilford Press.

Powell, L., Hickson, M., Self, W. R., & Bodon, J. (2001). The role of religion and responses to the Y2K macro-crisis. *North American Journal of Psychology, 3,* 295–302.

Roberts, A. R. (Ed.). (2005). *Crisis intervention handbook: Assessment, treatment, and research* (3rd ed.). New York, NY: Oxford University Press.

Roberts, S. B., & Ashley, W. C., Sr. (Eds.). (2008). *Disaster spiritual care: Practical clergy responses to community, regional, and national tragedy.* Woodstock, VT: SkyLight Paths.

Ronan, K. R., & Johnston, D. M. (2005). *Promoting community resilience in disasters: The role of schools, youths, and families.* New York, NY: Springer.

Schuster, M. A., Stein, B. D., Jaycox, L. H., Collins, R. L., Marshall, G. N., Elliott, M. N., . . . Berry, S. H. (2001, November 15). A national survey of stress reactions after the September 11, 2001, terrorist attacks. *The New England Journal of Medicine, 345,* 1507–1512. doi:10.1056/NEJM200111153452024

Smith, B. W., Pargament, K. I., Brant, C., & Oliver, J. M. (2000). Noah revisited: Religious coping by church members and the impact of the 1993 midwest flood. *Journal of Community Psychology, 28,* 168–186. doi:10.1002/(SICI)1520-6629(200003)28:2%3C169::AID-JCOP5%3E3.3.CO;2-9

Spence, P., Lachlan, K., & Burke, J. (2007). Adjusting to uncertainty: Coping strategies among the displaced after Hurricane Katrina. *Social Spectrum: Mid-South Sociological Association, 27,* 653–678.

Tillich, P. (1951). *Systematic theology* (Vol. 1). Chicago, IL: University of Chicago Press.

Uecker, J. E. (2008). Alternative schooling strategies and the religious lives of American adolescents. *Journal for the Scientific Study of Religion, 47,* 563–584. doi:10.1111/j.1468-5906.2008.00427.x

Vernberg, E. M., Steinberg, A. M., Jacobs, A. K., Brymer, M. J., Watson, P. J., Osofsky, J., . . . Ruzek, J. J. (2008). Innovations in disaster mental health: Psychological first aid. *Professional Psychology: Research and Practice, 39,* 381–388.

Weaver, A., Flannelly, L., Garbino, J., Figley, C., & Flannelly, J. (2003). A systematic review of research on religion and spirituality in the Journal of Traumatic Stress: 1990–1999. *Mental Health, Religion & Culture, 6,* 215–228. doi:10.1080/1367467031000088123

Weick, K. E. (1993). The collapse of sensemaking in organizations: The Mann Gulch disaster. *Administrative Science Quarterly, 38,* 628–652. doi:10.2307/2393339

Young, B. H., Ford, J. D., Ruzek, J. I., Friedman, M. J., & Gusman, F. D. (1998). *Disaster mental health services: A guidebook for clinicians and administrators.* Retrieved from http://www.hsdl.org/?view&did=441325

10

ADDRESSING INTIMATE PARTNER VIOLENCE WITHIN A RELIGIOUS CONTEXT

HEIDI M. LEVITT, SHARON G. HORNE, EMILY E. WHEELER, AND MEI-CHUAN WANG

The United States is a religious country, with the majority of Americans reporting a faith affiliation. According to the results of a recent Gallup poll taken in the United States, 82.5% of respondents reported having a religious affiliation, with the largest number identifying their affiliation as Protestant or other Christian religion (52.5%) and the remaining identifying as Catholic (23.6%), Mormon (1.9%), Jewish (1.6%), Muslim (0.5%), other non-Christian religion (2.4%), and atheist, agnostic, or no religion (15%), with 2.5% not responding (Newport, 2011). Although the majority of Americans agree that they are religious, how they define their religiosity or spirituality is less clear. As Zinnbauer and Pargament (2005) described, *spirituality* and *religiosity* have traditionally been interchangeable terms. Currently, religion and spirituality often are conceptualized as opposite poles, with religion as belief based, institutional, and static, and spirituality as personal, emotion based, and dynamic explorations of the transcendent. In this chapter, we use

http://dx.doi.org/10.1037/14500-011
Spiritually Oriented Psychotherapy for Trauma, D. F. Walker, C. A. Courtois, and J. D. Aten (Editors)

their definition of spirituality as an umbrella construct, with religion as the practice of spirituality in a particular context.

Although religion is often a source of healing and comfort, at times its tenets can be applied by religious communities in ways that sometimes support the abuse of women in intimate relationships. This concern may be stronger in faith communities that endorse power imbalances within marriages, especially those that teach that husbands are the leaders in their families, have the ultimate authority, and have the right to impose their wishes by any means, up to and including verbal and physical coercion and violence. Parallel teachings portray wives as subservient and as needing to defer to the wishes of their husbands in all matters. Religion-driven pressure to remain within marriages even when they are abusive and destructive may come from the teachings of the particular religion and its interpretation of the scriptures, from the faith-based beliefs of the family of origin of one or both spouses, from other members of the congregation, and from the clergy. Although there are many religious communities that go to lengths to prevent intimate partner violence (IPV), this chapter focuses on the personal and community interactions and messages that reinforce IPV in faith-based families.

The experience of IPV for individuals in these contexts might be influenced strongly by their religious beliefs and those of their religious communities. In this chapter, we explore the psychological literature on the role of religion and spirituality in the experience of survivors of IPV. We also include case studies that were developed from within a research program carried out in the mid-south region of the United States investigating the interaction of religiosity and domestic violence. Case studies describing ways to address the potentially destructive aspects of religion that perpetuate IPV against women are presented.

INTIMATE PARTNER VIOLENCE AND TRAUMA

IPV is a critical issue not only in terms of survivors' physical safety but also their mental health. A growing body of research has examined trauma resulting from IPV experienced by women survivors. A meta-analysis estimated that between 31.0% and 84.4% of women who had been exposed to IPV met criteria for posttraumatic stress disorder (PTSD), with a weighted mean of 64% (Golding, 1999). Research also has demonstrated a correlation between PTSD symptomatology and IPV (Becker, Stuewig, & McCloskey, 2010) that crosses ethnic and racial groups (Duran et al., 2009; Kelly, 2010; Lilly & Graham-Bermann, 2009). A population-based study found rates of moderate-to-severe PTSD symptoms at 20% for men and 24% for women (Coker, Weston, Creson, Justice, & Blakeney, 2005). Coker et al. (2005)

identified risk factors for PTSD resulting from IPV for both men and women as current experiencing of depressive symptoms, as well as a history of IPV for women and history of childhood abuse for men; protective factors include higher socioeconomic status, being married, and the ending of the abuse.

Previous research also has identified religion and spirituality as a source of resilience and positive coping as well as increased distress and negative coping (Gerber, Boals, & Schuettler, 2011; Harris et al., 2008; Peres, Moreira-Almeida, Nasello, & Koenig, 2007). Although traditionally overlooked in mental health scholarship, more recently the roles of religion and spirituality have been explored as relevant factors in the traumatic stress and coping related to IPV (see Chen & Koenig, 2006, for a review). This work documents the roles of religion and spirituality as sources of resilience for people experiencing trauma.

PREVALENCE OF INTIMATE PARTNER VIOLENCE

Although the importance of developing an understanding of the mechanisms underlying the perpetration and experience of IPV is unquestionable, the extent of IPV is not well known. Acknowledging the difficulty in documenting the prevalence of IPV against women, the World Health Organization (2005) conducted a multicountry study on women's health and domestic violence to produce more reliable data and to guide legal and civil action to eliminate such violence. Data from interviewing more than 24,000 women around the world revealed that the lifetime prevalence rate of physical or sexual violence by an intimate partner ranged from 15% to 71%, with most countries falling between 29% and 62%. IPV appears to be especially underreported in countries where forms of IPV are considered socially or even legally acceptable and victims were either unable or reluctant to report (Hajjar, 2004; Malley-Morrison, 2004).

In 2010, the National Intimate Partner and Sexual Violence Survey (Black et al., 2011) interviewed a total of 9,970 women in the U.S. general population. They found that 35.6% of women in the United States reported having experienced rape, physical violence, and/or stalking by an intimate partner. A third of the women (32.9%) had experienced physical violence of some kind in their lives, and approximately 5.9% reported that these forms of violence happened within the year prior to the survey.

Prevalence rates of IPV within specific religious communities have been investigated, although data are scarce. Religious women may be reluctant to report IPV incidents because of cultural stigma and religious beliefs and pressures that they should put their families' welfare above their own. Lifetime prevalence estimates for particular Christian denominations have ranged from 24% of women (Brinkerhoff, Grandin, & Lupri, 1992) to 28% (Annis & Rice, 2001). Among Jewish women, some data indicate a rate between 15% to 30% for lifetime occurrences (Horsburgh, 2005; Jewish Coalition Against Domestic Abuse, n.d.). The limited data available suggest that 10% to 20% of Muslim women have experienced IPV (Abugideiri, 2005, 2012).

RELIGION AND THE EXPERIENCE OF INTIMATE PARTNER VIOLENCE

Although research on the intersection of religion and IPV is relatively new, albeit growing, the predominant conclusion is that religion can act to both prevent and exacerbate IPV (e.g., Bowland, Biswas, Kyriakakis, & Edmond, 2011; Knickmeyer, Levitt, Horne, & Bayer, 2003; Levitt, Todd-Swanger, & Butler, 2008; McAllister & Roberts-Lewis, 2010; Yick, 2008). For perpetrators, survivors, and community leaders, tensions can exist because religion can serve as both a barrier to ending abuse and a positive resource for coping and support. Understanding both of these functions can aid clinicians in treating IPV within a religious context. It is also important to acknowledge the diversity of beliefs, teachings, and customs that exist between and within different religious groups in different locations, denominations, and congregations.

Christianity

Christianity is the predominant religion in the United States, with an estimated 78.4% of Americans identifying as Christian (The Pew Forum, 2008). It is also the religion that has been subject to the most research on the intersection of IPV and religious factors. Even so, firm conclusions about the role of Christianity or any of its specific faith beliefs or teachings in relationship to IPV are difficult to reach. Some research has found that more conservative beliefs are associated with a higher likelihood of perpetration of IPV (e.g., Brinkerhoff et al., 1992; Ellison, Bartkowski, & Anderson, 1999). Approval of perpetration of IPV (Koch & Ramirez, 2010) also has been associated with conservative Christian beliefs. Wang, Horne, Levitt, and Klesges (2009) conducted a survey of women in a southeastern metropolitan area and found that 50.7% of religious Christian women participants reported some form of sexual assault, physical abuse, stalking, or threat by a current or past intimate partner, and these rates were notably higher than the national average. Those women who were in congregations that did not support divorce were more likely to be victims of abuse. In contrast, Todhunter and Deaton (2010) conducted a national survey of Christian young men and did not find that religion or religious beliefs or practices predicted IPV. Because this last survey was the only one to explore this issue with male respondents, it may be of interest to explore whether religious women respondents report higher incidence of IPV than religious men.

Qualitative inquiries of clergy, victims, and perpetrators have explored the Christian or Christianity-based beliefs and attitudes that may perpetuate IPV. Copel (2008) interviewed women who had sought guidance from leaders of their religious communities about an abusive relationship and found that these discussions contributed to their feelings of devaluation and powerlessness as well as spiritual suffering and loss. Each of Copel's 16 participants felt obliged to endure the abuse rather than leave the relationship after the consultation with their faith leader. In addition to community pressures, religious women's role-based identities may be an internal barrier to leaving abusive relationships (Nason-Clark, 2004). In their analysis of Evangelical women who had experienced IPV, Popescu et al. (2009) identified three major beliefs that served as barriers to leaving abusive relationships: beliefs about sustaining marriage and avoiding divorce, internalized stereotypes about the inability of Christians to perpetrate abuse and have unhappy relationships, and gender roles that assign women a submissive position. Knickmeyer et al. (2003; Knickmeyer, Levitt, & Horne, 2010) described several stages women went through when leaving IPV relationships—participants tended to initially be silenced by systemic social pressures to appear as a good Christian family within their congregations but gradually came to the conclusion that "God hates abuse more than divorce" (2003, p. 47).

Judaism

Although estimates vary depending on methodology and definition, the Jewish population in the United States is estimated at 6.59 million (Sheshkin & Dashefsky, 2011). The literature examining the role of Judaism in IPV is scant, but existing research reflects similar barriers to safety for victims of IPV as those in Christianity. Cwik (1995) pointed to several factors rooted in religious beliefs and practices that serve as particular barriers for Orthodox Jewish victims of IPV include differences in gender roles and limited power for women, purity laws that regulate sexual intimacy between partners and forbid physical contact for about 12 days of the month, perpetuation of stereotypes of Jewish people as nonviolent and the denial of IPV as an issue within the community, and the discouragement of divorce and inability of women to initiate divorce proceedings.

In a study of risk factors and barriers for Orthodox Jewish IPV survivors, Ringel and Bina (2007) identified the lack of experience with social norms outside their community as an additional risk factor. The authors noted the insularity of the Orthodox Jewish community as problematic in relation to the shame and fear of divorce and as the norm within the Orthodox community to avoid talking about sex or marital issues. The authors also reported that some participants felt their rabbis were ineffective at responding to their situation, and several of the rabbis who participated in the study suggested that the psychological state of both survivors and perpetrators were to blame for the abuse.

Islam

It is estimated that there are 2 million to 3 million Muslims in the United States (Smith, 2001), with the largest subgroups being South Asian, Arab, and African American (Abugideiri, 2005). In her discussion of domestic violence in Muslim societies, Hajjar (2004) described the complex intersection between women's rights, Islamic beliefs and law, and state law. In many Muslim societies, literal interpretations of the Koran and Islamic teachings concerning gender roles, women's rights, and family relations can disempower women. Hassouneh-Phillips (2001) described how American Muslims idealized marriage and tolerated abuse and showed that beliefs about marriage, such as obedience and submission, led to conflict over leaving abusive relationships.

It is often the case in Arab and Islamic countries that IPV is treated with indifference, creating a "conspiracy of silence" (Douki, Nacef, Belhadj, Bouasker, & Ghachem, 2003; p. 168). Douki et al. (2003) explained that wife abuse may be justified by the wife's misbehavior, stressors on the husband, or religious commandments and that these efforts to justify IPV may be made by both legal authorities and health professionals. There are also financial deterrents to leaving an abusive relationship. Because of the social stigma tied to divorce and the economic burden of supporting the victims, their families may feel unable to help women leave marriages and live independently.

INTIMATE PARTNER VIOLENCE AND RELIGIOUS LEADERS

It can be helpful for clinicians to be aware of the social and faith influences on religious congregations have on clients. A number of qualitative studies have been conducted that explored IPV issues among religious leaders. In their analysis of interviews with clergy and clinicians, Ringel and Park (2008) identified several relevant interpretations of Christian religious doctrines that could perpetuate IPV, including submission of wives to husbands, forgiveness of the abuse, shame and fears of alienation from the family-based religious community, undereducated or underprepared clergy, and mistrust of clinicians from outside their faith. Cwik (1997) compared Conservative,

Reform, and Orthodox rabbis, finding that Orthodox rabbis were more likely to underestimate the prevalence of IPV in their communities and encourage survivors to stay in their marriages. Ayyub (2000) described how verses of the Qur'an are used to justify the physical abuse of wives by their husbands and that religious communities may prioritize preserving the marriage over safety of the victim.

Rotunda, Williamson, and Penfold (2004) emphasized the differences in preparedness of clergy from various faiths to respond to perpetrators and victims of IPV in their communities and the resulting potential threat to safety. Clergy preparedness and receptivity is a potential issue in any faith and is important to consider in light of the likelihood that many survivors will seek support from clergy first. Surveys of clergy members have indicated that many recognize the issue of IPV in their communities and the need for additional training and resources to address it (Brade & Bent-Goodley, 2009; Homiak & Singletary, 2007; Moon & Shim, 2010; Petersen, 2009; Rotunda et al., 2004). As a result, clergy may hesitate to advise leaving the relationship or may directly encourage survivors to stay, resulting in a "silencing" of the IPV survivor (e.g., Horne & Levitt, 2004; Levitt & Ware, 2006a, 2006b; Potter, 2007).

Qualitative research with faith leaders across religions has documented that they tended to be torn between a sense of responsibility to protect the sanctity of marriage and the responsibility to protect victims, with many seeing divorce as a last alternative to consider only after everything else has been tried (Levitt & Ware, 2006a, 2006b). The physical and emotional risks associated with IPV tended to be underestimated, and victims and perpetrators often were thought to share the blame for the situation. Religious leaders also have identified preventive strategies that can be helpful within their congregations (Ware, Levitt, & Bayer, 2003).

DEVELOPING RELIGIOUS METHODS OF COPING WITH INTIMATE PARTNER VIOLENCE

Although such obstacles may be pertinent to the experience of some survivors of IPV, religiosity and spirituality also can serve as protective factors and as sources of strength for coping (e.g., Knickmeyer et al., 2003). Several authors have demonstrated that participation in religious services and rituals is negatively correlated with perpetration of IPV (Ellison & Anderson, 2001; Ellison et al., 1999; Pournaghash-Tehrani, Ehsan, & Gholami, 2009) and positively correlated with posttraumatic symptom reduction and higher levels of social support in survivors (Watlington & Murphy, 2006). This relationship has been found within both self-reported and partner-reported IPV and when controlling for factors such as alcohol abuse and level of social support. Although understanding the exact mechanisms underlying this relationship requires further study, these authors hypothesized that these effects may result from the behavioral guidance provided by religious teachings, the support found in faith communities, and the commitment to family that is frequently found in these communities.

Gillum, Sullivan, and Bybee (2006) found that 97% of female IPV survivors interviewed in their study indicated that faith was an important resource for them. Similarly, 70% of women in Wang et al.'s (2009) sample who were both religious Christians and had left an IPV relationship credited their religion with providing them the strength to leave. These women reported that God gave them strength (66%), gave them faith that they would survive if they left (54%), helped them realize that they needed to protect themselves (52%), and helped them believe that they did not deserve the abuse (52%). Yick (2008) described two other ways in which religion promoted coping as well. Survivors drew from their faith the ability to forgive their abusers and themselves, which was experienced as a form of healing. Also, finding new religious communities or reconstructing their relationships with their faith could increase the amount of support they garnered from their faith and faith communities. Research has begun to investigate correlates between religious and spiritual supports and positive mental health outcomes (e.g., Neergaard, Lee, Anderson, & Gengler, 2007).

Recent research has explored the significance of religion and spirituality and the importance of their integration into treatment of IPV for both African American (Arnette, Mascaro, Santana, Davis, & Kaslow, 2007; Bliss, Ogley-Oliver, Jackson, Harp, & Kaslow, 2008; Brade & Bent-Goodley, 2009; Dyer, 2010; Kiely-Froude & Abdul-Karim, 2009; Paranjape & Kaslow, 2010; Potter, 2007) and Latino clients (Brabeck & Guzmán, 2008; Hancock & Ames, 2008). These studies indicated that spiritual well-being and spirituality were at times important factors in the ability to leave abusive relationships. Dyer (2010) emphasized the importance of religious leaders as resources for clinical care.

Therapists acting to increase coping strategies for women could emphasize the importance of spiritual well-being in the recovery process (Nason-Clark, 2009), focus on the religious condemnation of violence (Ringel & Park, 2008), explore biblical narratives that parallel women's situations (Nash & Hesterberg, 2009), and consider narratives that value self-care rather than just care for others (Knickmeyer et al., 2003). Both Ake and Horne (2003) and Knickmeyer et al. (2003) found that religious coping resulted in a deeper connection with God (although at times this connection included leaving one's congregation). In addition to religious resources, interventions and support from family or friends and a desire to protect oneself and one's children were identified by participants as helpful factors in leaving the relationship.

INTIMATE PARTNER VIOLENCE AND FAITH CASE STUDIES

The following case studies are meant to bring to life issues that women face when subjected to IPV within a faith context. The case studies presented are composites of stories based on a program of qualitative research investigating the intersection of faith and domestic violence in the mid-south region of the United States from the perspective of religious leaders from different faiths, perpetrators of abuse from different faiths and from a very-low-income bracket, and women who were abuse survivors and had belonged to conservative Christian religious traditions (Knickmeyer et al., 2003, 2010; Levitt et al., 2008; Levitt & Ware, 2006a, 2006b; Ware et al., 2003). Any identifying information has been altered to preserve anonymity. The studies included predominantly female victims and male perpetrators who were Christian and either Black or White. The stories here reflect common experiences that were reported in research interviews on the convergence of IPV and religion, although each case was, of course, idiosyncratic in many ways. They are presented to illustrate ways that religion and spirituality can perpetuate domestic violence and how this may be addressed. These case studies also highlight the ways religion and spirituality can offer support to survivors and allow them to make meaning of their abuse experiences.

Michelle's Story: An Intimate Partner Violence Survivor

Michelle was first drawn to Joe because he seemed strong and noble. He was a member of her church and seemed to stand up for his beliefs. She was excited to begin to date him because he was known in her community as a good Christian man. The strength of his faith made her trust him and want to develop the relationship. He spoke about his beliefs and values and how strongly their religion affected him. She recalled that he told her how special she was to him and how he cherished her, leading her to imagine only positive things in their future. They dated for just a short time before he proposed, and the couple moved forward with the wedding soon thereafter. Many of Michelle's friends were already married, and she was eager to start a family. She described their wedding as beautiful, with all friends and family there, many coming from out of state.

It was a great shock to her when things changed shortly after she and Joe were married. She noticed that he began trying to control her subtly in different ways—wanting to keep tabs on how much money she was spending, wanting to know where she was going to be each day. At first, she just thought he was looking out for her, was concerned with keeping her safe, and was trying to be a good provider. But then he started getting more and more upset if she was doing something he did not like.

A few months into the marriage, he became very upset that Michelle had spent a lot of money on a gift for a friend's baby shower. She was about two months pregnant at the time. Joe was upset that he could not reach Michelle and that her cell phone had been turned off; when he found out that she was shopping, he began yelling at her. Michelle yelled back, and that was the first time Joe initiated any violence. He grabbed Michelle, shook her, and threw her against the wall. It frightened her, but she was not physically injured.

She reported that they both felt a sense of disbelief after this event. Joe begged her to forgive him and told her the next morning that he had been praying about his anger and seeking support from God to better deal with his work-related stress. He asked her to pray with him. Michelle said that one of her religious beliefs is the value of forgiveness, and so she prayed and asked for help to open her heart to Joe and for him to do the same. She did not confide in any of her friends or family members about this event because she did not want people at church to think badly of Joe or feel concern for her. Michelle recalled feeling that she was acting in accordance with her beliefs to forgive him and work on the marriage. She was concerned she might not have been giving her husband the support he needed to adapt to the arrival of the baby and to his work stress, which might have contributed to the violence. Although things seemed to get better briefly, it was hard for Michelle to completely quiet the part of her that was now afraid of this incident recurring. She became more hesitant and careful with Joe and took steps to more actively support and please him.

The next incident of violence occurred when Sam was a new baby. Although she reported that he was a "good baby," at times he would cry at length. Michelle was not able to recall what precipitated the next violent event, because, as she said, "[Joe] was just snapping at me all the time then." Joe hit Michelle several times during that event; she reported that during the beating he chastised her and told her she had failed him as a wife, when she was supposed to be supporting him and listening to him. Michelle wanted to stay with her parents for a while after this second incident, but Joe reminded her that marriage was forever. He told her that God would condemn her if she left because she had made a promise to Him to follow Joe's lead and he did not want her to leave. She felt she had to become a better wife or she would disappoint God Himself. She reported being confused because she had faith in Joe's knowledge of religion and also had heard their preacher talking about wifely submission. She was raised to believe that a woman was supposed to follow her husband's guidance, and she held this belief herself.

After this event, Joe became more controlling, forbidding Michelle to go out of the house to see friends or to invite her family to their home. Michelle became more apprehensive about having people to the house because she worried that Joe might lose his temper. Over time, she became quite isolated. One of the only places she would see friends and receive support was at church each week. She enjoyed singing together and participating in church activities but began taking greater notice of the sermons in which the preacher talked about the sanctity of marriage and the role of submission in marriage. She felt trapped. Although she liked planning fundraisers with other women, it was uncomfortable sitting beside her husband at church each week and appearing as an ideal Christian family, wearing their best clothes and best smiles. Michelle knew that if she complained about the marriage, she would be seen as a bad wife and could lose her remaining friends. Church could quickly become an unwelcoming place for her. There was no place for the pain she was feeling inside.

One day Michelle pulled her preacher aside and inquired about the possibility of leaving a marriage if there was abuse, saying she was asking for a friend. The preacher told her that because he knew what a good marriage she and Joe had and what a good Christian Joe was, perhaps Joe could be a role model for the friend's husband and talk with him. The preacher asserted that good Christians do not divorce, because they believe that marriage is forever. He said that marriage is sometimes hard but that Michelle should encourage her friend to work through this trial and to pray to God for support; God would not abandon her. Michelle left feeling that the preacher was not someone she could turn to and that if she did talk about the abuse, she might have to leave the congregation. She felt the preacher would not believe her if he heard that Joe was abusive. She did not know where else to go because she did not have connections to other churches or other people at that point.

The beatings became more frequent, and Michelle felt she was walking on eggshells all the time. She never knew what would set Joe off. Because Joe had hurt her, she feared for Sam's safety as well. She said she read the Bible more and more. She prayed throughout each day, and this helped because she felt that God was on her side, supporting her each time there was a beating and she got through it. She would read and reread sections of scripture that gave her strength—those that talked about getting strength and perseverance from God and about forgiveness. Perhaps because she had no one else, she developed an intimate connection with God and talked to Him through the day. She still worried whether He would forgive her if she decided to leave the marriage. Sam was beginning to walk and learning to talk. She worried that because he was becoming more mobile he might become a target of Joe's anger. However, she was not sure what to do or how she could support herself and the baby on her own.

The first time she left was after a beating that resulted in a broken rib, and she took Sam with her. Her parents were away, so she hoped she could stay at their house without involving them. She knew it would pain them to hear about the abuse. Joe had told her that if she ever left him, he would kill her and take Sam. He went to Michelle's parents' house and demanded that she return home, saying that he had a gun and would shoot them. Michelle was scared that he would really hurt Sam, and so she returned home.

Michelle said that at this point she realized that the only way for her to leave was to go to a women's shelter. She called several times and spoke to people on the phone when Joe was out of the house. She sometimes called and did not say anything at all. She realized that leaving home would mean leaving her religious community as well and the friends she had known her whole life. Although she heard regularly that God wanted her to stay in the marriage, she reported a shift inside herself, and she began to feel that God was telling her that He would forgive her, that enough was enough and that it was only good to follow one's husband if he was righteous—and Joe was not. One night, 4 years after their marriage had begun, Michelle took Sam to a women's shelter. They stayed there for almost two months before they could begin their own lives. Although at first Michelle's parents were against her leaving the marriage, they changed their minds and embraced her and Sam and invited them to their home. Joe came to her parents' home threatening Michelle, and she had to seek an order of protection. Although she did visit with one of her friends from her congregation, Michelle never went back to her church, but she still feels that God has a central role in her life; she feels that He helped save her from her marriage.

Clinical Insights From Michelle's Story

Themes in Michelle's story that were common across most of the participants in this research include a strong connection to a faith community (Knickmeyer et al., 2003, 2010). For these women living in the Bible Belt, having a "church home" was the primary social support outside the family. Families went to church multiple times per week; these faith communities often house not only one's social network but also health care and child care services, which are often essential support systems. Beliefs in a wife's duty to be submissive to her husband were held deeply and complicated women's ability to leave their husbands or name or question experiences of abuse. Often at church, the women were told in various ways to suffer in silence, to become a better wife, or to pray as a method of dealing with the abuse. The women who left talked about drawing a great deal of strength, however, from their personal connection to God. Although many left their church or attended less often after leaving their marriages, their relationship with God was still central in their lives.

In terms of strategies for intervention, women found it helpful when religious leaders or others helped them to identify and integrate scripture that emphasized self-care and mutual responsibilities in marriage. The strong emphasis of scripture on forgiveness, submission, and the sanctity of marriage tended to keep women blaming themselves for the abuse instead of developing resources for leaving the marriage or putting in place enough of a break to obtain counseling and repair the marriage. Psychotherapists, pastoral counselors, and faith leaders might provide women literature on this theme to suggest alternative ways of conceptualizing abuse, and they might also provide descriptions of other women's struggles in similar situations (e.g., Knickmeyer et al., 2003, 2010). If it would be unsafe to take this literature home, psychotherapists could make it available in their office waiting rooms.

Women found it empowering when they realized that they could have a personal relationship with God outside organized religion. Psychotherapists working with women might encourage them to contemplate the questions of whether God hates abuse more than divorce, whether God thinks they are worth saving, and whether God will forgive divorce. It was in coming to their own answers to these questions that women in our research were empowered to leave their relationships. If they are interested, domestic violence survivors can learn about congregations that support women leaving abusive relationships, so they realize that there are many different interpretations of religious marital relationships and responsibilities.

Although it can be helpful to encourage religious women to examine their own religious beliefs and consider how they would like to structure their relationship with God, it is important for psychotherapists to keep in mind how difficult it is for women to leave abusive marriages when leaving could mean exile from religious communities where they and their children have formed long-standing relationships and deep commitments. An awareness of resources, such as shelters, and developing safety plans are important for any abuse victim, but these may be particularly important for religious women who may lack other sources of community. Finding shelters that are supportive of religious practices (e.g., having kosher food for Jewish women or prayer services) or are themselves faith based can make it more likely that women would use these services.

The experience of leaving can be even more complicated when the woman is a minority in terms of her racial or ethnic background, sexual orientation, disability status, or is elderly, because it can be harder to leave a community that has been a support when the dominant culture might not be supportive. It can also be more difficult to find services that would accept the woman's multiple identities. For instance, a woman may only feel comfortable in a shelter that has clients from her own background or where there are others who speak her language.

Psychotherapists and professionals working in domestic violence services may have to be sensitive to the needs of women who wish to maintain their connection with their faith community, even if this community is shared with the perpetrator. They may have to assist with plans for clients to have support within the church from family and friends. Providing written documentation of a restraining order can emphasize to pastors the need to assist in creating safety for the client.

Henry's Story: A Perpetrator of Intimate Partner Violence

Henry was arrested while fighting with Janet. He thought that she held greater responsibility for the fighting because she was pressuring him to obtain employment; he had indicated to her that he did not want to discuss that topic, yet she would not relent. He reported, "She's really good at pushing my buttons and knows how to get me going." He was invested in maintaining an image of masculinity in which his girlfriend respected him and did not question his authority, because other men in his social circle might have ridiculed him if he was seen as emasculated. He described it as especially disturbing when his girlfriend critiqued him in front of other people or did this loudly so neighbors could hear, as she was doing when he lost his temper the last time.

The neighbors called the police, and Henry was arrested. As part of his parole, he was required to attend anger management classes, and it became even harder for him to find a job while having to attend class each week. He thought a man was supposed to provide for his family, and he felt it was unjust that both he and Janet were arguing, yet only he had to attend the classes. Although he wanted to get through the classes so he could get back to finding a job, he enjoyed the classes and said that the main strategy he learned was to walk away whenever he became upset and see whether he could cool down. However, he was not sure what to do after that to resolve the conflict.

Henry did sometimes go to religious services. Although he heard religious leaders talk about how partners are not supposed to be angry at each other, it was confusing to him and did not help him respond differently in heated moments. Sometimes it just made him feel guilty, and then he would avoid going to services for a while. He would have liked to learn how to deal with conflicts in relationships, but he did not feel that was important to religious leaders, whom he saw as wealthy, self-concerned, and not understanding his life and struggles. He found it challenging to fulfill the role of being a religious family man—to pray and financially support his family—while working at minimum wage and being unable to support his children. He felt that God was withholding rewards, and he was unsure how to obtain them. He kept praying, but it seemed that God continued testing him, and Henry was unsure what to change.

He kept to himself and wanted to be independent and avoid relying on others. He wanted to be a leader in his life and not a follower. Although Henry sometimes felt alone, he would not talk with friends about his fights with his partner because he worried about receiving bad advice or becoming the topic of gossip. He believed that marriage should be forever but that it was hard to find the right woman. He believed that men are destined by God to be the leader in marriage but was not sure how this should take form, especially when many women have alternate beliefs.

Henry reported that when his girlfriend was upset with him he felt that she was questioning his authority and worth by treating him like a child and chastising him. He felt afraid that she was not seeing him as a man in those moments. He felt that he could never tell her he felt afraid of losing her admiration, because she might think even more poorly of him and not respect him anymore. He said he needed her to see him as the man in the family, so he became angry.

Even though violence was not condoned in his religious beliefs, Henry reported that it felt normal to him and to the women he knows. Henry said he had never seen any other way of settling anger and conflict; his parents used to argue behind closed doors, so he never learned how they dealt with anger, and his other relatives who did fight would resort to violence. He felt ambivalent about not having known how to help the women in abusive relationships in the past and was not sure whether they wanted help, because they often went back to the relationships; perhaps they liked the abuse or felt that it showed that they were loved.

Clinical Insights From Henry's Story

Themes in this story that were common to the perpetrators of IPV interviewed in this study included a real ambivalence about the role of a husband in their religion. Interview research with low-income perpetrators of IPV from different religious backgrounds (Levitt et al., 2008) demonstrated that religious beliefs about male leadership could be experienced as challenges to their masculinity when these men were unable to act as financial or spiritual leaders for their families. Being aggressive or angry helped to maintain their masculinity. These ideas were similar for interviewees across different faiths (e.g., Jewish, Christian, Islamic). Religious messages they received told them that they should be the providers and that women should be submissive, but this was often unclear. These roles were complicated by the fact that these men were living in poverty and did not have financial means to be breadwinners in a traditional sense. The masculinity and the dominance that their religion prescribed were threatened by their financial status as well as by partners who challenged them.

The interviewees thought that the women they abused were partially responsible for the abuse because they argued. They had trouble being empathic and realizing the difference between arguing and physical violence. Even when these men described being abusive, they often still experienced themselves as the victims of manipulation, humiliation, or hurt.

The men thought that religious leaders did not understand their needs. God was thought to be granting rewards or doling out punishment, and leaders were thought to be capriciously withholding advice on how to work this system best. They believed in God and understood that it was better to resolve conflict peaceably but did not know how, other than to leave the relationship. It might be useful for psychotherapists and faith leaders working with these men to encourage them to share religious stories in which prayer is used as a form of self-reflection and behavioral evaluation instead of as a request for rewards or help.

Psychotherapists counseling abusive men might focus on the lack of conflict resolution skills. Although the men interviewed learned from anger management groups the idea of walking away to deescalate, they could not describe what to do after this point. Developing skills in reengaging and sorting through heated topics can be an important part of treatment. Developing the ability to recognize and express emotions other than anger is also important. Although the men could admit feeling afraid of losing face in their partner's eyes, they said they would not convey this fear, because they worried that revealing this vulnerability would further compromise their masculinity. Gender-role analyses can be useful in helping men redefine what it means to be a husband or partner.

Men's discussion groups within religious contexts could be particularly useful in allowing victims to normalize their experiences of being vulnerable in relationships and learning to identify and talk about emotions that arise. These groups also could help to query notions about masculinity and being the head of the household and allow members to develop an understanding of what it means to be a strong leader in a family or to consider the idea of sharing leadership. The development of trusting relationships with other men within their religious communities might be the primary benefit as well. In the study, men reported that they had great difficulty trusting others or confiding in them about their experiences. Male counselors or mentors who can share how they resolve conflict, model owning their feelings of anxiety and fear, and provide a safe space for men to consider their religious beliefs can develop new understandings of masculinity within intimate relationships.

REFERENCES

Abugideiri, S. E. (2005, Fall). A perspective on domestic violence in the Muslim community. *Working Together—The FaithTrust Institute Newsletter, 25*, 1–4.

Abugideiri, S. E. (2012). Domestic violence. In S. Ahmad & M. M. Amer (Eds.), *Counseling Muslims: Handbook of mental health issues and interventions* (pp. 309–328). New York, NY: Routledge/Taylor Francis Group.

Ake, G. S., & Horne, S. G. (2003). Domestic violence victims and the Christian Church: Influences of patriarchal religious beliefs on religious coping. *Religion and Abuse, 5*, 5–28.

Annis, A. W., & Rice, R. R. (2001). A survey of abuse prevalence in the Christian Reformed Church. *Journal of Religion & Abuse, 3*(3/4), 7–40.

Arnette, N. C., Mascaro, N., Santana, M. C., Davis, S., & Kaslow, N. J. (2007). Enhancing spiritual well-being among suicidal African American female survivors of intimate partner violence. *Journal of Clinical Psychology, 63*, 909–924. doi:10.1002/jclp.20403

Ayyub, R. (2000). Domestic violence in the South Asian Muslim immigrant population in the United States. *Journal of Social Distress & the Homeless, 9*, 237–248. doi:10.1023/A:1009412119016

Becker, K. D., Stuewig, J., & McCloskey, L. A. (2010). Traumatic stress symptoms of women exposed to different forms of childhood victimization and intimate partner violence. *Journal of Interpersonal Violence, 25*, 1699–1715.

Black, M. C., Basile, K. C., Breiding, M. J., Smith, S. G., Walters, M. C., Merrick, M. T., . . . Stevens, M. R. (2011). *The National Intimate Partner and Sexual Violence Survey (NISVS): 2010 summary report*. Atlanta, GA: National Center for Injury Prevention and Control, Centers for Disease Control and Prevention.

Bliss, M. J., Ogley-Oliver, E., Jackson, E., Harp, S., & Kaslow, N. J. (2008). African American women's readiness to change abusive relationships. *Journal of Family Violence, 23*, 161–171. doi:10.1007/s10896-007-9138-3

Bowland, S., Biswas, B., Kyriakakis, S., & Edmond, T. (2011). Transcending the negative: Spiritual struggles and resilience in older female trauma survivors. *Journal of Religion, Spirituality & Aging, 23*, 318–337. doi:10.1080/15528030.2011.592121

Brabeck, K. M., & Guzmán, M. R. (2008). Frequency and perceived effectiveness of strategies to survive abuse employed by battered Mexican-origin women. *Violence Against Women, 14*, 1274–1294. doi:10.1177/1077801208325087

Brade, K. A., & Bent-Goodley, T. (2009). A refuge for my soul: Examining African American clergy's perceptions related to domestic violence awareness and engagement in faith community initiatives. *Social Work & Christianity, 36*, 430–448.

Brinkerhoff, M. B., Grandin, E., & Lupri, E. (1992). Religious involvement and spousal violence: The Canadian case. *Journal for the Scientific Study of Religion, 31*, 15–31. doi:10.2307/1386829

Chen, Y. Y., & Koenig, H. G. (2006). Traumatic stress and religion: Is there a relationship? A review of empirical findings. *Journal of Religion and Health, 45*, 371–381. doi:10.1007/s10943-006-9040-y

Coker, A. L., Weston, R., Creson, D. L., Justice, B., & Blakeney, P. (2005). PTSD symptoms among men and women survivors of intimate partner violence: The role of risk and protective factors. *Violence and Victims, 20*, 625–643. doi:10.1891/0886-6708.20.6.625

Copel, L. C. (2008). The lived experience of women in abusive relationships who sought spiritual guidance. *Issues in Mental Health Nursing, 29*, 115–130. doi:10.1080/01612840701792365

Cwik, M. S. (1995). Couples at risk? A feminist exploration of why spousal abuse may develop within Orthodox Jewish marriages. *Family Therapy, 22*, 165–183.

Cwik, M. S. (1997). Peace in the home? The response of rabbis to wife abuse within American Jewish congregations. *Journal of Psychology and Judaism, 21*(1), 5–81. doi:10.1023/B:JOPJ.0000011048.15596.82

Douki, S., Nacef, F., Belhadj, A., Bouasker, A., & Ghachem, R. (2003). Violence against women in Arab and Islamic countries. *Archives of Women's Mental Health, 6*, 165–171. doi:10.1007/s00737-003-0170-x

Duran, B., Oetzel, J., Parker, T., Malcoe, L. H., Lucero, J., & Jiang, Y. (2009). Intimate partner violence and alcohol, drug, and mental disorders among American Indian women in primary care. *American Indian and Alaska Native Mental Health Research, 16*(2), 11–27. doi:10.5820/aian.1602.2009.11

Dyer, J. (2010). Challenging assumptions: Clergy perspectives and practices regarding intimate partner violence. *Journal of Religion & Spirituality in Social Work, 29*, 33–48. doi:10.1080/15426430903479254

Ellison, C. G., & Anderson, K. L. (2001). Religious involvement and domestic violence among U.S. couples. *Journal for the Scientific Study of Religion, 40*, 269–286. doi:10.1111/0021-8294.00055

Ellison, C. G., Bartkowski, J., & Anderson, K. L. (1999). Are there religious variations in domestic violence? *Journal of Family Issues, 20*, 87–113. doi:10.1177/019251399020001005

Gerber, M. M., Boals, A., & Schuettler, D. (2011). The unique contributions of positive and negative religious coping to posttraumatic growth and PTSD. *Psychology of Religion and Spirituality, 3*, 298–307. doi:10.1037/a0023016

Gillum, T. L., Sullivan, C. M., & Bybee, D. I. (2006). The importance of spirituality in the lives of domestic violence survivors. *Violence Against Women, 12*, 240–250. doi:10.1177/1077801206286224

Golding, J. M. (1999). Intimate partner violence as a risk factor for mental disorders: A meta-analysis. *Journal of Family Violence, 14*, 99–132. doi:10.1023/A:1022079418229

Hajjar, L. (2004). Religion, state power, and domestic violence in Muslim societies: A framework for comparative analysis. *Law & Social Inquiry, 29*, 1–38. doi:10.1111/j.1747-4469.2004.tb00329.x

Hancock, T. U., & Ames, N. (2008). Toward a model for engaging Latino lay ministers in domestic violence intervention. *Families in Society, 89*, 623–630. doi:10.1606/1044-3894.3824

Harris, J. I., Erbes, C. R., Engdahl, B. E., Olson, R. H. A., Winkowski, A. M., & McMahill, J. (2008). Christian religious functioning and trauma outcomes. *Journal of Clinical Psychology, 64*, 17–29. doi:10.1002/jclp.20427

Hassouneh-Phillips, D. S. (2001). "Marriage is half of faith and the rest is fear Allah": Marriage and spousal abuse among American Muslims. *Violence Against Women*, 7, 927–946. doi:10.1177/10778010122182839

Homiak, K. B., & Singletary, J. E. (2007). Family violence in congregations: An exploratory study of clergy's needs. *Social Work & Christianity*, 34, 18–46.

Horne, S. G., & Levitt, H. M. (2004). Shelter from the raging wind: Religious needs of victims of intimate partner violence and faith leaders' responses. *Journal of Religion & Abuse*, 5(2), 83–97. doi:10.1300/J154v05n02_05

Horsburgh, N. (2005). Lifting the veil of secrecy: Domestic violence in the Jewish community. In N. J. Sokoloff (Ed.), *Domestic violence at the margins: Readings on race, class, gender, and culture* (pp. 206–226). Piscataway, NJ: Rutgers University Press.

Jewish Coalition Against Domestic Violence. (n.d.). *Abuse facts*. Retrieved from http://jcada.org/www/docs/4

Kelly, U. A. (2010). Symptoms of PTSD and major depression in Latinas who have experienced intimate partner violence. *Issues in Mental Health Nursing*, 31, 119–127. doi:10.3109/01612840903312020

Kiely-Froude, C., & Abdul-Karim, S. (2009). Providing culturally conscious mental health treatment for African American Muslim women living with spousal abuse. *Journal of Muslim Mental Health*, 4, 175–186. doi:10.1080/15564900903245824

Knickmeyer, N., Levitt, H. M., & Horne, S. G. (2010). Putting on Sunday's best: The silencing of battered women within Christian faith communities. *Feminism & Psychology*, 20, 94–113. doi:10.1177/0959353509347470

Knickmeyer, N., Levitt, H. M., Horne, S. G., & Bayer, G. (2003). Responding to mixed messages and double binds: Religious oriented coping strategies of Christian battered women. *Journal of Religion & Abuse*, 5(2), 55–82. doi:10.1300/J154v05n02_03

Koch, J. R., & Ramirez, I. L. (2010). Religiosity, Christian fundamentalism, and intimate partner violence among U.S. college students. *Review of Religious Research*, 51, 402–410.

Levitt, H. M., Todd-Swanger, R., & Butler, J. B. (2008). Male perpetrators' perspectives on intimate partner violence, religion, and masculinity. *Sex Roles*, 58, 435–448. doi:10.1007/s11199-007-9349-3

Levitt, H. M., & Ware, K. N. (2006a). "Anything with two heads is a monster": Religious leaders' perspectives on marital equality and domestic violence. *Violence Against Women*, 12, 1169–1190. doi:10.1177/1077801206293546

Levitt, H. M., & Ware, K. N. (2006b). Religious leaders' perspectives on marriage, divorce and intimate partner violence. *Psychology of Women Quarterly*, 30, 212–222. doi:10.1111/j.1471-6402.2006.00283.x

Lilly, M. M., & Graham-Bermann, S. A. (2009). Ethnicity and risk for symptoms of posttraumatic stress following intimate partner violence: Prevalence and predictors in European American and African American women. *Journal of Interpersonal Violence*, 24, 3–19. doi:10.1177/0886260508314335

Malley-Morrison, K. (2004). *International perspectives on family violence and abuse: A cognitive ecological approach*. New York, NY: Routledge.

McAllister, J. M., & Roberts-Lewis, A. (2010). Social worker's role in helping the church address intimate partner violence: An invisible problem. *Social Work & Christianity, 27*, 161–187.

Moon, S. S., & Shim, W. S. (2010). Bridging pastoral counseling and social work practice: An exploratory study of pastors' perceptions of and responses to intimate partner violence. *Journal of Religion & Spirituality in Social Work, 29*, 124–142. doi:10.1080/15426431003708253

Nash, S. T., & Hesterberg, L. (2009). Biblical framings of and responses to spousal violence in the narratives of abused Christian women. *Violence Against Women, 15*, 340–361. doi:10.1177/1077801208330437

Nason-Clark, N. (2004). When terror strikes at home: The interface between religion and domestic violence. *Journal for the Scientific Study of Religion, 43*, 303–310. doi:10.1111/j.1468-5906.2004.00236.x

Nason-Clark, N. (2009). Christianity and the experience of domestic violence: What does faith have to do with it? *Social Work & Christianity, 36*, 379–393.

Neergaard, J. A., Lee, J. W., Anderson, B., & Gengler, S. W. (2007). Women experiencing intimate partner violence: Effects of confiding in religious leaders. *Pastoral Psychology, 55*, 773–787. doi:10.1007/s11089-007-0078-x

Newport, F. (2011, December 23). *Christianity remains dominant religion in the United States*. Retrieved from Gallup website: http://www.gallup.com/poll/151760/christianity-remains-dominant-religion-united-states.aspx

Paranjape, A., & Kaslow, N. (2010). Family violence exposure and health outcomes among older African American women: Do spirituality and social support play protective roles? *Journal of Women's Health, 19*, 1899–1904. doi:10.1089/jwh.2009.1845

Peres, J. F., Moreira-Almeida, A., Nasello, A. G., & Koenig, H. G. (2007). Spirituality and resilience in trauma victims. *Journal of Religion and Health, 46*, 343–350. doi:10.1007/s10943-006-9103-0

Petersen, E. (2009). Addressing domestic violence: Challenges experienced by Anglican clergy in the diocese of Cape Town, South Africa. *Social Work & Christianity, 36*, 449–469.

The Pew Forum on Religion & Public Life. (2008). *U.S. religious landscape survey*. Retrieved from http://religions.pewforum.org/pdf/report-religious-landscape-study-full.pdf

Popescu, M., Drumm, R., Mayer, S., Cooper, L., Foster, T., Seifert, M., . . . Dewan, S. (2009). "Because of my beliefs that I had acquired from the church . . . ": Religious belief-based barriers for Adventist women in domestic violence relationships. *Social Work & Christianity, 36*, 394–414.

Potter, H. (2007). Battered Black women's use of religious services and spirituality for assistance in leaving abusive relationships. *Violence Against Women, 13*, 262–284. doi:10.1177/1077801206297438

Pournaghash-Tehrani, S., Ehsan, H. B., & Gholami, S. (2009). Assessment of the role of religious tendency in domestic violence. *Psychological Reports, 105*, 675–684. doi:10.2466/PR0.105.3.675-684

Ringel, S., & Bina, R. (2007). Understanding causes and responses to intimate partner violence in a Jewish Orthodox community: Survivors' and leaders' perspectives. *Research on Social Work Practice, 17*, 277–286. doi:10.1177/1049731506293079

Ringel, S., & Park, J. (2008). Intimate partner violence in the Evangelical community: Faith-based interventions and implications for practice. *Journal of Religion & Spirituality in Social Work, 27*, 341–360. doi:10.1080/15426430802345317

Rotunda, R. J., Williamson, G., & Penfold, M. (2004). Clergy response to domestic violence: A preliminary survey of clergy members, victims, and batterers. *Pastoral Psychology, 52*, 353–365. doi:10.1023/B:PASP.0000016939.21284.a3

Sheshkin, I., & Dashefsky, A. (2011). Jewish population in the United States, 2011. Retrieved from http://www.jewishdatabank.org/Reports/Jewish_Population_in_the_United_States_2011.pdf

Smith, T. W. (2001). *Estimating the Muslim population in the United States*. New York, NY: American Jewish Committee.

Todhunter, R. G., & Deaton, J. (2010). The relationship between religious and spiritual factors and the perpetration of intimate personal violence. *Journal of Family Violence, 25*, 745–753. doi:10.1007/s10896-010-9332-6

Wang, M., Horne, S., Levitt, H. M., & Klesges, L. (2009). Christian women in IPV relationships: An exploratory study in religious factors. *Journal of Psychology and Christianity, 28*, 224–235.

Ware, K. N., Levitt, H. M., & Bayer, G. (2003). May God help you: Faith leaders' perspectives of intimate partner violence within their communities. *Journal of Religion & Abuse, 5*(2), 29–54.

Watlington, C. G., & Murphy, C. M. (2006). The roles of religion and spirituality among African American survivors of domestic violence. *Journal of Clinical Psychology, 62*, 837–857. doi:10.1002/jclp.20268

World Health Organization. (2005). *WHO multi-country study on women's health and domestic violence against women: Initial results on prevalence, health outcomes and women's responses*. Geneva, Switzerland: Author.

Yick, A. G. (2008). A metasynthesis of qualitative findings on the role of spirituality and religiosity among culturally diverse domestic violence survivors. *Qualitative Health Research, 18*, 1289–1306. doi:10.1177/1049732308321772

Zinnbauer, B. J., & Pargament, K. I. (2005). Religiousness and spirituality. In R. F. Paloutzian & C. L. Park (Eds.), *Handbook of the psychology of religion and spirituality* (pp. 21–42). New York, NY: Guilford Press.

11

FAITH AND HONOR IN TRAUMA TREATMENT FOR MILITARY PERSONNEL AND THEIR FAMILIES

DAVID W. FOY AND KENT D. DRESCHER

War is a life-changing experience for all participants; for some, it is also life-threatening and challenges their religion and spirituality (R/S) at its foundations. R/S is a key factor in promoting resilience in the midst of the adversities faced by active duty service members, veterans, and their families. When faced with combat experiences involving personal injury or the deaths of fellow soldiers and civilians, warriors may experience spiritual struggles about their combat traumas, even while turning to God or a higher power for support. For many warriors, their R/S is an important resource for making meaning of their own war experiences, as well as honoring fallen friends who made the ultimate personal sacrifice. However, for some warriors, their R/S will become a casualty of their war experiences when morally injurious events are encountered in combat and spiritual "red flags" arise. *Moral injury* refers to

http://dx.doi.org/10.1037/14500-012
Spiritually Oriented Psychotherapy for Trauma, D. F. Walker, C. A. Courtois, and J. D. Aten (Editors)
Copyright © 2015 by the American Psychological Association. All rights reserved.

the psychosocial–spiritual consequence of involvement in events that violate deeply held moral beliefs.

In this chapter, we consider ways in which the relatively new concept of moral injury is useful in improving understanding of the negative spiritual consequences of combat and in tailoring spiritually based interventions to address them. We identify key R/S issues, both positive and negative, that are frequently found among military personnel who have made combat deployments. We briefly review published spiritually based interventions for combat-related trauma and its consequences before describing our own spirituality and trauma group therapy module in more detail. A case study follows that illustrates our approach to addressing combat-related changes in R/S. We next consider key characteristics of the set of published approaches that feature R/S-based interventions to address combat-related psychological dysfunction and/or attempt to alleviate R/S-related distress after combat. Finally, we propose future directions in the development of R/S-based interventions for combat-related psychological and/or spiritual problems.

RELIGION AND SPIRITUALITY AND RESILIENCE IN SERVICE MEMBERS AND THEIR FAMILIES

Resilience refers to the human ability to withstand stressful challenges and retain or regain normal functioning. Thus, individuals display resilience when they manifest positive adaptation under severely adverse circumstances. The American Psychological Association (APA) Task Force on Promoting Resilience in Response to Terrorism defined it as "the process of adapting well in the face of adversity, trauma, tragedy, threats, or even significant sources of stress" (APA, 2007, para. 1). It is generally accepted that resilience is common and derives from the basic human ability to adapt to new challenges and situations. Research has identified key factors for resilience: (a) caring relationships within and outside the family that create love and trust, provide role models, and encourage and reassure; (b) capacity to make realistic plans and implement them; (c) self-confidence; (d) communication and problem-solving skills; and (e) capacity to manage emotions (Masten, 2001).

It is notable that both intrinsic and extrinsic aspects of R/S (Maltby, 2002) are easily found among these resilience factors. For example, *intrinsic R/S* refers to the individual's deeply personal relationship with the sacred and could be represented in the self-confidence and emotional control elements of resilience (Allport & Ross, 1967). *Extrinsic R/S* involves the community aspects of membership in a religious institution, the positive aspects of which could include caring relationships with other members that provide both emotional and instrumental support, and enhanced problem-solving resources (Allport & Ross, 1967). For a resilient veteran, intrinsic spirituality might be reflected in his or her use of religious beliefs and values as a frame to interpret traumatic events and as a lens to focus his or her actions in a meaningful direction. Extrinsic spirituality might help forge strong, healthy connections within a religious community. In addition, studies in the field of positive psychology have identified specific R/S-related factors associated with resilience, including morality and self-control (Baumeister & Exline, 2000), forgiveness (McCullough, 2000), and hope (Snyder, 2000).

We recently described the results of an informal survey of marines who had returned from the war zone in Iraq. Over 500 of these marines were individually interviewed by a navy chaplain about their faith during and after their combat experiences (Foy, Drescher, & Smith, 2013). Many of the marines said their faith provided a sense of meaning to life, a sense of their own place in the world. Some made comments such as "God will not let evil triumph" that showed a belief in ultimate goodness in the world and that that goodness is worth fighting for. In terms of R/S practices during combat, prayer was the most commonly mentioned source of support; it was also described as the practice that was most helpful later with memories of combat. Often, marines mentioned the benefits of receiving encouragement during their time in the war zone from chaplains and other marines professing faith. Although combat experiences stimulated many marines toward spiritual growth, others experienced setbacks in their spirituality. Some were angry with God about the horrors they had experienced ("I can't believe in a God who would let this happen"). Others were afraid they would "never get better, never be the same as before." For a few marines there was a particular worry that they might never regain a sense of compassion after numbing themselves emotionally while serving in the war zone.

MORAL INJURY AND SPIRITUAL RED FLAGS

Under ideal circumstances one's spiritual beliefs and practices would be ready resources for coping with life crises. They would help buffer the immediate effects of severely stressful experiences, promote cognitive processing of their meaning, and facilitate finding their appropriate place in one's life narrative. Unfortunately, surviving trauma often results in shattered adaptive illusions and sustaining beliefs, along with intense emotions and arousal and an endangered sense of agency and control. Survivors may feel like strangers to themselves and the world around them. The very core or sustaining elements of the self may have been severely threatened. Thus, key aspects of survivors' R/S may become casualties of the traumatic experience, rendering them unavailable for use as coping resources.

The concept of moral injury has recently been introduced into the psychological literature to capture the distinct inner conflicts and psychospiritual consequences of exposure to or participation in traumatic events that violate deeply held moral values. Damage to one's moral compass, or moral injury, involves disruption in one's confidence and expectations about his or her own and others' capacity to behave ethically, brought about through witnessing, perpetrating, or failing to prevent immoral acts involving the suffering and/or death of others (Drescher & Foy, 2008; Litz et al., 2009). Our recent research has focused on identifying common war-related morally injurious experiences, predictable signs and symptoms of moral injury, as well as experts' recommendations for treating it (Drescher et al., 2011). Potential morally injurious experiences included (a) acts of betrayal (e.g., by leaders or fellow combatants), (b) within-ranks violence (e.g., "friendly" fire, sexual assault, fragging), and (c) incidents involving death or harm to civilians (e.g., collateral casualties). Predictable signs and symptoms included guilt and shame, existential issues (e.g., fatalism, hopelessness, sorrow), and negative self-issues (e.g., self-loathing, sense of permanent damage to self). Recommended R/S themes for interventions included forgiveness, making amends, and spiritual renewal or transformation (Drescher et al., 2011). The latter might be understood as the process of one's lived present experience becoming more consistent with one's chosen spiritual beliefs or values. Moral injury may lead to profound changes in spirituality that may be conceptualized as spiritual red flags.

The term *spiritual red flag* was first introduced in a seminal study by Pargament et al. (1998). In their original study, they identified three problematic domains or red flags in the context of religious coping with life crises: choosing inappropriate goals or ends, such as an imbalance between concerns for self and for others; using inappropriate means, such as selecting inappropriate religious strategies to cope with difficult events; and finally, experiencing religious conflict with God or other people. In their original terminology, *wrong direction*, *wrong road*, and *against the wind* were used to describe the red flags (Pargament et al., 1998). We use the term *spiritual red flag* to refer to four specific R/S-related difficulties frequently encountered by war trauma survivors during their recovery (Drescher & Foy, 2008). These obstacles may be problematic as R/S issues per se, and/or they may interfere with psychological trauma processing and recovery. The red flags we have identified are: loss of faith, negative religious coping, guilt, and lack of forgiveness.

Loss of Faith

Loss of faith may occur when a crisis-related reaction involves confusion or disillusionment about one's R/S beliefs. When a significant life crisis cannot be readily assimilated by the individual's existing cognitive interpretive framework or schema, *accommodation*, or change in the schema, ensues. Individuals may resolve such a spiritual struggle by *overaccommodation*, a process of setting aside previously held spiritual beliefs. In the short term the cognitive conflict is resolved; however, a longer term consequence is the loss of the positive coping potential found in R/S beliefs and practices. Loss of faith may also be related to other combat-related psychological disorders. For example, our early study of Vietnam combat veterans in treatment for posttraumatic stress disorder (PTSD) found that "difficulty reconciling my faith with combat experiences" was endorsed by more than 75% of respondents (Drescher & Foy, 1995). Similarly, loss of faith was found to be associated with worse mental health outcomes (i.e., greater use of mental health services) among military veterans in treatment for PTSD (Fontana & Rosenheck, 2004).

Negative Religious Coping

Negative religious coping involves questions or tensions about God's presence, power, and character; anger at God; discontent with one's faith community and/or the clergy; and punitive appraisals of negative experiences (e.g., God is punishing me for my sins; Drescher & Foy, 2008; Pargament et al., 1998). There is consistent empirical support generally for the link between negative religious coping and poorer psychological adjustment. In a meta-analysis of 49 studies of religious coping and psychological adjustment, Ano and Vasconcelles (2005) found that negative religious coping was consistently associated with negative psychological adjustment, whereas positive religious coping was related to positive psychological adjustment. However, the extent to which these findings can be applied to active duty service members or veterans is not yet well-established.

Guilt

Guilt is represented as acts of commission, acts of omission, and survivor guilt that is experienced when comrades are killed and the survivor is spared. Survivor guilt often involves unresolved issues of perceived randomness and unfairness, along with the belief that others who died were more deserving of life or had more to live for. In addition, cognitive distortions about the degree of personal culpability for tragic outcomes are often critical elements that may exacerbate and perpetuate guilt as a spiritual red flag. Guilt and reduced comfort from R/S faith have been found to be significantly related to increased use of Veterans Affairs (VA) mental health services (Fontana & Rosenheck, 2004).

Lack of Forgiveness

Lack of forgiveness is the inability to positively resolve perceptions of having forgiven others, feeling forgiven by God, and having forgiven oneself for acts of omission or commission related to life experiences with tragic outcomes. Lack of forgiveness has been found to be associated with more severe PTSD and depression among combat veterans in treatment for PTSD (Witvliet, Phillips, Feldman, & Beckham, 2004). The four red flags frequently co-occur in combinations of two or more (Drescher & Foy, 2008). In a sense, combat trauma survivors who exhibit spiritual red flags may appear to be "stuck" or "derailed" in their journey of trauma processing and recovery.

RECENT DEVELOPMENTS IN SPIRITUALLY ORIENTED INTERVENTIONS FOR COMBAT TRAUMA

What do we currently know about effective ways of alleviating moral injuries and spiritual red flags? Examination of the relevant literature should take into account both spiritually based and psychologically based interventions. There is a fairly well-developed extant literature evaluating the effectiveness of several psychological interventions designed to promote forgiveness. A meta-analysis of 14 forgiveness intervention studies found that participants receiving a process-oriented form of intervention showed significant improvements by forgiving more, increasing their positive affect and self-esteem, and reducing their negative affect (Lundahl, Taylor, Stevenson, & Roberts, 2008). Findings also favored individually administered interventions over those delivered in a group format. In addition, multiple sessions, provided over a sustained period of time, were associated with better outcomes. Most of the studies in the review were conducted with individuals reporting interpersonal betrayal, such as spousal infidelity.

The applicability of these interventions for survivors of life-threatening trauma has not been established, nor has the specific issue of self-forgiveness been addressed (Lundahl et al., 2008). However, in recent years there have been several reports of R/S-based interventions developed specifically for combat veterans. These approaches are briefly described in chronologic order of their publication. This section concludes with a detailed overview of our own spirituality and trauma group therapy module that has been in clinical use for more than a decade.

On the basis of their knowledge of combat-related spiritual struggles gained from many years of clinical experience providing psychotherapy for combat veterans with PTSD, Barton and LaPierre (1999) designed a series of 12 sessions for a group of Vietnam veterans whose combat traumas included R/S issues. The authors served as group leaders, combining their training in psychiatry (Barton) and theology (LaPierre) to lead sessions addressing R/S topics including religious upbringing, guilt, rules, stories of trauma, feeling spiritually adrift, isolation, control, forgiveness (two sessions), judgment, and meaning. Although no standard measures of group functioning or outcome were collected, the authors noted immanent spirituality improvement by the bonding between group members during the group that persisted after the group terminated.

Bormann and her colleagues (Bormann et al., 2005; Bormann, Thorp, Wetherell, & Golshan, 2008) developed and evaluated a "mantram repetition" Eastern R/S approach to improve PTSD symptoms, other indices of psychological adjustment, and spiritual well-being among veterans receiving mental health services in a VA facility. Over a series of six sessions, group members learned to use their mantram training in mindfulness to manage their PTSD symptoms and slow down their thoughts and reactions.

Decker (2007) developed a "mystical/spiritual" perspective for treating combat veterans served by the VA's community-based Vet Centers. The approach uses an individual therapy format that is focused on discovering personal meaning in the veteran's combat experiences by finding both immanent and transcendent spirituality within the tragedies of war. As might be expected from a growth-oriented approach, weekly sessions are provided over several months, with the actual length of therapy determined by the veteran's progress. Although no systematic treatment outcome data are available for the approach, it has a long anecdotal history of beneficial use within the Vet Center system.

Representing a psychological perspective, Steenkamp et al. (2011) recently developed an approach for addressing PTSD, grief, and/or combat-related moral injuries in active duty service members, termed *adaptive disclosure*. It is a manualized form of early intervention intended for use with service members on return to garrison after a combat deployment. Adaptive disclosure protocol includes six individual sessions, four of which involve exposure therapy, along with imaginal conversations with a chosen moral authority figure discussing the circumstances and judgments about the selected morally injurious experience.

In a recent randomized controlled trial of their spiritually based intervention, Harris and her colleagues (2011) developed an eight session "building spiritual strength" (BSS) group approach that focuses heavily on prayer and meditation exercises and development through the use of members' prayer logs. In addition to the three sessions dedicated to prayer and meditation, other sessions address forgiveness and conflict resolution (two sessions); theodicy, or the problem of evil; military and R/S histories; and planning for continued spiritual development. Results of the treatment outcome study showed significant reductions in PTSD symptoms in the BSS intervention group, compared with the wait-list control group. Although the BSS intervention was intended to "assist survivors in recognizing and resolving spiritual concerns," the primary focus of the controlled trial was on PTSD symptom outcome; thus, potential changes in R/S measures, such as faith service attendance and spiritual well-being, were not reported (p. 427).

SPIRITUALITY AND TRAUMA GROUP MODULE

The spirituality and trauma (ST) group module was developed to meet the needs of veterans in residential treatment for combat-related PTSD. It is a manualized eight-session group treatment in clinical use with combat veterans since 2001. It was designed as an adjunct to other empirically supported PTSD treatments, not as a primary PTSD treatment. It uses brief didactic presentations by facilitators, member-to-member interactions, as well as large and small group discussion. Detailed descriptions of the group's development and its potential for application to additional trauma populations have been provided previously (Drescher et al., 2004; Drescher, Smith, & Foy, 2007). Although the ST module was developed for a group format, the session guides and patient workbook may also be adapted for use with individuals.

The ST group module has several primary goals. One such goal is to encourage members to consider the role that a healthy personal spirituality might play in coping with traumatic events. Members' responses might include strengthening and deepening personal spiritual understandings and practices and reconnecting with their own religious or spiritual roots and traditions from childhood. New avenues of spiritual experience and expression that are more immediately relevant to members' recent experiences may also be explored. Group activities are selected to honor diversity and the inherent value of a wide range of spiritual experiences.

A second ST goal is to facilitate discussion of the meanings assigned to traumatic events. This includes identifying cognitive distortions (e.g., inappropriate survivor guilt, including self-blame) and helping members to restructure their understandings in ways that are more adaptive. It may also include finding personal explanations to the difficult existential questions of "why" and "how" these events occurred. Group sessions include sharing feedback and reflections from other group members about the personal meanings they associate with these questions.

Service members return home from combat deployments in a variety of ways. Some return to base as units with parades and fanfare, whereas others return home individually, welcomed only by family and a few friends. Many veterans express concern that civilians in the community cannot understand their experiences, and they may consequently exclude civilians as potential supports. Many veterans with PTSD subsequently develop lives characterized by alienation, distrust, and isolation. Accordingly, the third primary ST goal is to increase perceived social support, especially development of healthy family and community support systems. The ST facilitator's manual provides session-by-session clinical strategies and guidelines for implementation, using a predominantly present-centered motivation enhancement approach.

To institute a spiritual component into efforts supporting recovery from trauma, one critical ground rule is essential: The experience must be perceived by every member as safe. Safety in a clinical experience involving spirituality has two distinct components: (a) intentional awareness and acceptance of diverse spiritual experiences and (b) mutual respect for the views of others and openness to new learning. It is important for clinical staff to model these characteristics and to verbalize these ideals repeatedly. Safety is necessary for helpful discussion of sensitive and delicate issues and creates an environment that allows for honest, vulnerable self-disclosure on the part of participants.

The tone and content of conversation in the sessions should be fully inclusive so that participants can feel comfortable with, and benefit from, the experience. To participate fully, participants should experience the group as a place where feelings related to the existential impact of trauma can be expressed regardless of one's individual beliefs about religion or God. Intentional awareness of diversity means there can be no assumptions that individuals share common beliefs or religious traditions. Group leaders have to be careful in their use of language to ensure that the way they speak about spiritual issues is not heard by clients as biased or advocating a particular spiritual perspective. If leaders choose to self-disclose information about their own spiritual history, that choice should be both intentional and directly based on the clinical needs of the clients in the group.

SPIRITUALITY AND TRAUMA SESSION THEMES

A number of important themes are addressed during the course of the ST group sessions. One theme is the client's exploration of what spirituality means personally and what practices derived from spiritual traditions might assist in his or her recovery. The importance of rebuilding social connections as a means of support and a resource for living is addressed. Veterans who have experienced intense pain and loss may have wondered "why" these events occurred, but may have assumed they were alone in this. The group seeks to provide a forum in which these concerns might be discussed. Guilt and anger are powerful emotions experienced by many war veterans. Group sessions allow clients to consider whether forgiveness might be an option that would aid their recovery. A final theme that emerges during group sessions is that identification of personal values and engagement in meaningful living might enhance one's life.

Defining Spirituality Broadly

In the ST group module we define *spirituality* broadly as "connecting to something outside the self." Many people give little thought to how they define spirituality; engaging in a discussion of what each individual sees as core elements of a definition can be useful in helping that person realize that he or she can actually reconsider understandings learned in childhood. Defining spirituality as connecting to something outside the self frees each individual to define that connection for him- or herself. The ST group encourages individuals to engage in a journey of a new discovery of what spirituality might now mean for their lives.

Building Connections

The process of building connections involves increasing the number and quality of social supports both within and beyond the group. Human beings are innately social creatures. However, a primary attempt to cope with intrusive reminders of trauma is avoidance, which as it generalizes can harm relationships and distance survivors from potential support systems. Defining spirituality as "connection" fosters reconsideration of that social withdrawal and distancing process and of the role avoidance plays in creating social isolation. Because U.S. society is highly individualistic and often tends to view spirituality as an individual endeavor, the historically important community aspects of spirituality, which are evident in most religious traditions, sometimes get lost. The ST group encourages members to seek out healthy, supportive communities, whether religious or not. Examples of these communities include churches, temples, synagogues, and organizations such as Alcoholics Anonymous and other nonprofit helping organizations (e.g., service clubs, meditation groups). The group also challenges trauma survivors whose initial inclination is to pursue spirituality in total isolation to consider the possible benefits of incorporating community and relationship aspects into their personal spiritual experience.

Enhancing Spiritual Practices

ST group leaders help members enhance their spiritual practices by encouraging healthy personal behaviors and "giving back" through community service. In most traditions, spiritual practices include both reflective individual activities (e.g., meditation, prayer) as well as social practices such as service on behalf of others, worship attendance, and community singing. Recommended spiritual practice should include volunteer service and work on behalf of others. Most religious traditions encourage service as a form of spiritual practice. One of the benefits of volunteering is engagement in the lives of others, which for a person with PTSD challenges the tendency toward withdrawal and social isolation and provides evidence of shared suffering. Service for others also is a way of creating personal meaning and living a life that matters. Some trauma survivors can become quite self-focused because of the damage they perceive has been done to them. Engaging with others who also have significant needs can help to broaden a survivor's focus of attention and help them realize they are not alone and that they can actually provide benefit to others. This can have positive effects on the self-esteem of both the helper and of those who are served.

Addressing the "Why" Question

In ST we address the "why" question to help members resolve possible conflicts in their understanding of their higher power. The term *theodicy* comes from the Latin *théos díe*, meaning justification of God. The term was coined by the philosopher Leibniz, who in 1710 wrote an essay attempting to show that the existence of evil in the world does not conflict with belief in the goodness of God (Leibniz, 1890). Simply stated, theodicy poses the following question: If God is all-powerful and God is all-good, how does God allow evil to exist in the world? Historically, varied solutions have been proposed to this problem, including philosophical solutions that diminish God (i.e., God is not all-powerful, God is not all-good, God does not exist) or that diminish evil (i.e., it is a punishment for sin, it may bring about some greater good), perhaps as well as personal nonphilosophical solutions that diminish the self (e.g., self-blame, rage, loss of meaning, purpose, hope).

Cognitive dissonance theory (Festinger, 1957) posits that individuals tend to seek consistency among their thoughts or beliefs and experiences. When inconsistency exists between beliefs and experience, there is strong motivation for change, to eliminate the dissonance. In the case of a traumatic experience, the event itself cannot be changed; hence, to resolve the dissonance, survivors must struggle to adapt their beliefs and attitudes to accommodate their experience. Many trauma survivors, along with their families and friends, thus begin a lifelong struggle to make sense of these experiences.

Considering Forgiveness of Self and Others

Considering forgiveness of self and others is important in reducing guilt and reestablishing positivity in one's life direction. The ST group views forgiveness as a choice made in response to a specific event that is manifest in how one lives in the present moment. Thoresen, Harris, and Luskin (2000) defined *forgiveness* as "the decision to reduce negative thoughts, affect, and behavior, such as blame and anger, toward an offender or hurtful situation, and to begin to gain better understanding of the offense and the offender" (p. 255). For veterans with PTSD, facilitators have found it important to acknowledge that forgiveness does not include pardoning an offender, condoning or excusing an offense, forgetting an offense, or denying that an offense occurred. Rather, forgiveness involves choosing in the present moment to abandon one's right to resentment and negative judgment while nurturing undeserved qualities of compassion, generosity, and even love toward the offender (Enright & Coyle, 1998). Within a military war-zone context, forgiveness sometimes becomes an issue of tension, in that it may suggest to veterans a pressure toward forgiving an enemy that killed your friends; forgiving the government that sent you into harm's way; forgiving people who perhaps did not do their jobs effectively or who made mistakes; forgiving God, who allowed all this to happen; and forgiving the self for perceived errors, mistakes, or lack of action.

In veterans with war-zone trauma experiences, perceptions and memories of these experiences, which are colored by strong emotions such as fear, rage, grief, guilt, and shame, seem to be particularly subject to distorted thinking. The forgiveness process may be complicated by the presence of distorted thinking. Accordingly, memories of traumatic experiences should be examined carefully for distortions of belief, inappropriate assumptions or expectations, and illogical attributions about these traumatic events.

In some instances individuals have true culpability for inappropriate actions performed in a desire for retribution. Many actions, particularly those resulting in death, cannot be undone. In these instances particularly, acceptance of what has happened and one's role in it can be coupled with a commitment to live the present in ways that give expression to one's highest moral and spiritual values. Viktor Frankl, himself a trauma survivor, once said, "everything can be taken from a man but one thing: the last of the human freedoms—to choose one's attitude in any given set of circumstances, to choose one's own way" (Frankl, 1946/1984, p. 65). Ultimately, forgiveness is a free choice. One can choose to act toward self or others in ways that are compassionate and that reflect one's highest values. In the ST group, forgiveness is presented as a positive choice, one that involves action in the direction of health and wholeness, a choice that enhances supportive relationships with self and others.

Defining and Living Out Personal Values

Values are the ideas and beliefs that we hold as good, important, and worthy of our time and energy. When speaking with veterans, the things they frequently mention as valuing the most include a sense of belonging, self-respect, inner harmony, freedom, family security, health, and enjoying life. A crucial question for every person is to what degree one's values are reflected in day-to-day behavior. In other words, do we walk our talk? The ST group uses a definition of values that is consistent with that put forth by acceptance and commitment therapy (ACT) (Luoma, Hayes, & Walser, 2007). ACT frequently uses a compass metaphor to express values as a life direction rather than a destination. In the same way that a person could walk north forever without getting there, personal values are reflected in ongoing behaviors and are never fully attained.

Restoring or Finding Meaning in Life

One type of meaning is the sense of personal meaning that one derives from others. In this context, we talk about finding meaning by "being meaningful" or creating a life in which one "matters" to other people. The extreme social isolation that can accompany PTSD can severely diminish this type of meaning because the individual is no longer actively involved in the lives of other people. PTSD-related withdrawal and social isolation serve to prevent one from making a significant positive impact in the lives of other people and subsequently from receiving the positive regard and feedback that can allow the individual to feel better about self and to see life as meaningful and purpose filled. The bereavement literature has suggested two common ways in which individuals attempt to assign meaning in the face of loss. The first is by "making sense" of the loss, and the second is by "finding benefit." Loss that results from trauma is frequently experienced as both senseless and without benefit. This can make the meaning-making process extremely difficult.

Research with families in which a family member has been murdered has suggested that family members ultimately find meaning through actions (Armour, 2006). This has been called "the intense pursuit of what matters" (Armour, 2006, p. 116); a qualitative study of family members of homicide victims found that 83% of these individuals felt that this description fit their experience of coping after the death. Consistent with the goal of connection, the ST group encourages veterans to actively seek opportunities for values-consistent service. Nonprofit service agencies as well as religious and spiritual communities are frequently looking for people with time on their hands who can serve the community in significant ways. We point out that many spiritual traditions view service of others as a spiritual activity, where both the giver and receiver benefit greatly.

CASE VIGNETTE

The following is an illustrative case vignette composed of an amalgam of several cases. All names, roles, and experiences described are fictitious, so as not to endanger the confidentiality of any specific individual. Sergeant James Jones is a 26-year-old marine who recently completed a third tour of Operation Iraqi Freedom and Operation Enduring Freedom combat duty, this time in Afghanistan. James reported that he has been having problems including severe anxiety, anger, and relationship problems with his girlfriend and family. Doctors have told him that he might have a mild traumatic brain injury from a blast that occurred during his last combat tour. A recent physical altercation with another marine raised his command's attention to his adjustment problems, and Sergeant Jones was transferred to a warrior transition program for evaluation and treatment referral that could lead to a medical discharge.

In reflecting on his wartime experiences, James stated that sometime during his second combat tour "something just died inside." He no longer felt fear or anxiety; he felt like a machine. He pushed his men and himself hard and was merciless in response to insurgent attacks and ambushes. He stopped calling home and withdrew from friends during down time at the base between missions. He reported that he spent much of his third tour in Afghanistan at a remote forward operating base (FOB) where conditions were harsh and Taliban attacks were frequent. His most difficult incident happened in a convoy returning from the FOB to Bagram Airfield just 2 weeks before they were scheduled to return to the United States.

He reported that his vehicle hit an improvised explosive device that blew off the front of the Humvee. The young lance corporal sitting in the front passenger seat was blown out of the vehicle. Sergeant Jones reported that he was dazed by the blast and became fully aware again to screams of "medic." He struggled out of the vehicle, hearing heavy machine gun fire being directed at them from a ridge above. Two of his men had pulled Corporal Evans to safety, frantically trying to bind his mangled leg and apply a tourniquet to stop the bleeding. Sergeant Jones reported that he screamed at the turret gunner to direct 50-caliber fire toward the insurgents and moved around to look at the other side of the vehicle. Corporal Smith was slumped at the back of the vehicle, almost like he was sleeping. A round had entered the side of his head under his helmet, and he was dead. Corporal Evans was flown to the base hospital, where he was stabilized and later sent to Landstuhl, Germany, and then to Walter Reed National Military Medical Center. James has not seen Evans since, but heard that he lost his right leg.

During the memorial service for Corporal Smith, James found himself getting extremely angry with the presiding chaplain, and he walked away when the chaplain tried to approach him after the service. James stated that he had lost much of his religious faith earlier in the war but that this event was like the straw that broke the camel's back—it left him extremely angry with God for killing Corporal Smith. Now, the thought of going to church sends him into a rage, much to his family's dismay. Sergeant Jones is tormented by the belief that he failed his men and should have been able to keep them safe, especially when they were so close to leaving the war zone. He believes that it is horribly unfair and a harsh trick by God that Smith died when he had a beautiful wife and a baby boy who will never know him. James went to visit Smith's family to pay his respects, felt so guilty he could hardly look them in the face, and then got very drunk afterward.

James's diagnosis is combat-related PTSD, and he is receiving prolonged exposure therapy in an individual format. In addition, his psychologist suggested that James might benefit from participation in an eight-session ST group that is co-lead by the transition program's social worker and chaplain. James was initially reluctant to accept referral to the ST group, but decided that he would go for a few sessions to "give it a try."

Over time, James warmed to the experience of the ST group. As he met and spoke with other participants during group sessions, he found he had much in common with them and that their struggles were similar to his. He also appreciated that the topics each week seemed both important and were things rarely spoken of in normal conversations. Two particular sessions reportedly helped him realize that he had choices about how to deal with the pain of his losses. The session on forgiveness emphasized that forgiveness was a choice that he could make to begin to loosen his grip on his pain. He realized through the group discussion with his peers that he could consider "forgiving God" and that not everyone in the group held God accountable for the actions of the enemy. The other session that seemed to help was on meaning making. When asked to consider the "legacy" that he wanted to leave behind, he began to see that living honorably and remembering his friend would be a more suitable tribute than his own self-punishment.

After the group sessions were over, James reflected that he came away with two things from the group. First, he learned about mindfulness, and found that it was a tool that helped him focus his mind when he felt overwhelmed or stressed. Second, he decided that service to others would be a more lasting positive memorial to the loss of his friend than would wasting his own life in rage and drunkenness. James made contact with an organization called TAPS (Tragedy Assistance Program for Survivors), a group that supports military families who have lost a loved one. He has become a "Run and Remember" team member and participates in sponsored 10K and half-marathon runs. He has also become a "virtual volunteer" and shares information about TAPS activities on his social network pages. He has begun keeping a journal, with stories and positive recollections that he has about Corporal Smith from the war zone. He hopes to share this one day with Corporal Smith's son.

COMPARING RELIGION- AND SPIRITUALITY-BASED INTERVENTIONS

Key issues addressed by some or all six of the different R/S-related approaches we reviewed include effects of killing and other war horrors on combatants, guilt and shame, social isolation, forgiveness, prayer and meditation, and meaning making. Addressing military and R/S histories and identifying individual spiritual goals were also common. Number of sessions prescribed for the interventions ranged from six (Bormann et al., 2008;

Steenkamp et al., 2011), eight (Drescher et al., 2004; Harris et al., 2011), 12 (Barton & LaPierre, 1999), to an unspecified number (Decker, 2007). Although the Decker (2007) and Steenkamp et al., (2011) interventions were designed for individual therapy, the other four approaches feature a group format with weekly sessions, 90 or 120 minutes in duration.

Commendably, two groups of R/S-based intervention developers have taken steps toward empirical validation through controlled trials, comparing active intervention groups with wait-list or delayed treatment control groups. Bormann and her colleagues (2008), as well as Harris and her group (2011), used randomization of participants to treatment and control groups in their experimental designs to ensure unambiguous group outcome comparisons, showing significant improvements in PTSD symptom reduction in the active treatment groups. Although no field trials have yet been reported by the Steenkamp et al. (2011) or Drescher et al. (2004) clinical research teams, progress toward that ultimate goal has been made by both teams through the development of treatment manuals. Thus, there are currently four different R/S-based treatments with manuals that provide session guides for therapists to use in facilitating the interventions. Furthermore, group member workbooks have also been developed by the Harris and Drescher teams.

IMPLICATIONS AND FUTURE DIRECTIONS

Recent research has suggested that many veterans continue to seek mental health services to grapple with existential questions concerning the meaning of their traumatic combat experiences and to find purpose for their current lives (Fontana & Rosenheck, 2004). Clearly, there are differences between existential conflicts and psychosocial dysfunction, such that the resolution of existential issues requires respect for and understanding of active duty members' or veterans' R/S beliefs and practices, as well as consideration of their bases for moral judgments. Accordingly, trauma clinicians should include information about clients' religious backgrounds, spiritual beliefs, and practices as part of their intake assessments. Identifying R/S strengths and resources, as well as spiritual red flags, are goals for an R/S assessment. It is important that trauma clinicians do not have to share their clients' R/S beliefs and traditions to honor them and encourage the use of positive coping practices associated with them.

Negative religious coping, along with the other spiritual red flags (loss of faith, lack of forgiveness, and guilt), may be a formidable obstacle to trauma recovery. In particular, these spiritual red flags may disallow the use of positive religious and other coping practices that might otherwise promote recovery (Ano & Vasconcelles, 2005). When these red flags are significant issues, clinicians might consider referral to a member of the clergy for help in their resolution. In addition, clinicians should promote the use of those positive religious coping methods that are consistent with clients' religious backgrounds, such as seeking spiritual support from clergy or other members of their faith communities. Pargament and his colleagues (1998) provided explanations for many positive practices of Western religions. Similarly, there are positive Eastern religious practices to promote well-being, such as compassion, mindfulness, and challenging one's source of identity (Ricard, 2007).

Killing, particularly when it involves noncombatants, is a morally challenging experience for many warriors, producing profound inner conflicts. When moral challenges or inner conflicts cannot be resolved by a warrior's R/S beliefs and moral compass, inner conflicts may become moral injuries. The combat contexts in which moral injuries occur include the immediate military team or unit of which the warrior is a member, the military leaders in the member's chain of command, and the ethos of the military branch in which he or she serves. Current interventions for R/S consequences of combat are focused on the individual warrior or veteran, whereas future efforts should be set in a broader context to include consideration of the military team and its leadership and their involvement in morally challenging experiences.

Although the development of R/S-based interventions to address the psychological and spiritual consequences of combat on warriors is still in its early stages, progress has been made over the past decade. In particular, the fact that several manuals are now available describing use of R/S-based approaches for common combat-related spiritual issues, such as guilt and shame, forgiveness, and finding meaning and purpose in combat tragedies, is a major step forward. Although it is not yet accurate to describe these intervention methods as "empirically validated," it is possible to refer to them as "empirically informed" at this point. With the exception of adaptive disclosure (Steenkamp et al., 2011), none of the present R/S-based interventions are specifically designed to address moral injuries. Consequently, the extent to which the current interventions are helpful in resolving moral conflicts is not yet known. Future directions in developing R/S-based interventions should focus more on moral injuries, taking into consideration the recommendations made by combat trauma experts to address making amends, transformation, and spiritual renewal (Drescher et al., 2011).

REFERENCES

Allport, G. W., & Ross, J. M. (1967). Personal religious orientation and prejudice. *Journal of Personality and Social Psychology, 5,* 432–443. doi:10.1037/h0021212

American Psychological Association. (2007). *What is resilience?* Retrieved from PsychCentral website: http://psychcentral.com/lib/what-is-resilience/0001145

Ano, G. G., & Vasconcelles, E. B. (2005). Religious coping and psychological adjustment distress: A meta-analysis. *Journal of Clinical Psychology, 61,* 461–480. doi:10.1002/jclp.20049

Armour, M. P. (2006). Meaning making for survivors of violent death. In E. K. Rynearson (Ed.), *Violent death: Resilience and intervention beyond the crisis* (pp. 101–121). New York, NY: Routledge.

Barton, G. M., & LaPierre, L. L. (1999). The spiritual sequelae of combat as reflected by Vietnam veterans suffering from PTSD. *American Journal of Pastoral Counseling, 2*(3), 3–21. doi:10.1300/J062v02n03_02

Baumeister, R. F., & Exline, J. J. (2000). Self-control, morality, and human strength. *Journal of Social and Clinical Psychology, 19,* 29–42. doi:10.1521/jscp.2000.19.1.29

Bormann, J. E., Smith, T. L., Becker, S., Gershwin, M., Pada, L., Grudzinski, A. H., & Nurmi, E. A. (2005). Efficacy of frequent mantram repetition on stress, quality of life, and spiritual well-being in veterans: A pilot study. *Journal of Holistic Nursing, 23,* 395–414. doi:10.1177/0898010105278929

Bormann, J. E., Thorp, S., Wetherell, J. L., & Golshan, S. (2008). A spiritually based group intervention for combat veterans with posttraumatic stress disorder. *Journal of Holistic Nursing, 26,* 109–116. doi:10.1177/0898010107311276

Decker, L. R. (2007). Combat trauma: Treatment from a mystical/spiritual perspective. *Journal of Humanistic Psychology, 47*(1), 30–53. doi.org/10.1177/0022167806293000

Drescher, K. D., & Foy, D. W. (1995). Spirituality and trauma treatment: Suggestions for including spirituality as a coping resource. *National Center for PTSD Clinical Quarterly, 5*(1), 4–5.

Drescher, K. D., & Foy, D. W. (2008). When they come home: Posttraumatic stress, moral injury, and spiritual consequences for veterans. *Reflective Practice: Formation and Supervision in Ministry, 28,* 85–102.

Drescher, K. D., Foy, D. W., Kelly, C., Leshner, A., Schutz, K., & Litz, B. T. (2011). An exploration of the viability and usefulness of the construct of moral injury in war veterans. *Traumatology, 17*(1), 8–13. doi:10.1177/1534765610395615

Drescher, K. D., Ramirez, G., Leoni, J. J., Romesser, J. M., Sornborger, J., & Foy, D. W. (2004). Spirituality and trauma: Development of a group therapy module. *Group: The Journal of the Eastern Group Psychotherapy Society, 28*(4), 71–87.

Drescher, K. D., Smith, M. W., & Foy, D. W. (2007). Spirituality and readjustment following war-zone experiences. In C. R. Figley & W. P. Nash (Eds.), *Combat stress injury theory, research, and management* (pp. 486–511). New York, NY: Routledge.

Enright, R. D., & Coyle, C. T. (1998). Researching the process model of forgiveness within psychological interventions. In E. L. Worthington (Ed.), *Dimensions of forgiveness* (pp. 139–161). Radnor, PA: Templeton Foundation Press.

Festinger, L. (1957). *A theory of cognitive dissonance.* Stanford, CA: Stanford University Press.

Fontana, A., & Rosenheck, R. (2004). Trauma, change in strength of religious faith, and mental health service use among veterans treated for PTSD. *Journal of Nervous and Mental Disease, 192*, 579–584. doi:10.1097/01.nmd. 0000138224.17375.55

Foy, D. W., Drescher, K. D., & Smith, M. W. (2013). Addressing religion and spirituality in military settings and veterans' services. In K. Pargament (Ed.), *APA handbook of psychology, religion, and spirituality: Vol. 2. An applied psychology of religion and spirituality* (pp. 561–576). Washington, DC: American Psychological Association.

Frankl, V. E. (1984). *Man's search for meaning.* New York, NY: Simon & Schuster. (Original work published 1946)

Harris, J. I., Erbes, C., Engdahl, B., Thuras, P., Murray-Swank, N., Grace, D., . . . Le, T. (2011). The effectiveness of trauma focused spiritually integrated intervention for veterans. *Journal of Clinical Psychology, 67*, 425–428. doi:10.1002/jclp.20777

Leibniz, G. W. (1890). *Philosophical works* (G. M. Duncan, Trans.). New Haven, CT: Tuttle, Morehouse & Taylor.

Litz, B. T., Stein, N., Delaney, E., Lebowitz, L., Silva, C., Maguen, S., & Nash, W. P. (2009). Moral injury and moral repair in war veterans: A preliminary model and intervention strategy. *Clinical Psychology Review, 29*, 695–706. doi:10.1016/j.cpr.2009.07.003

Lundahl, B. W., Taylor, M. J., Stevenson, R., & Roberts, K. D. (2008). Process-based forgiveness interventions: A meta-analytic review. *Research on Social Work Practice, 18*, 465–478. doi:10.1177/1049731507313979

Luoma, J. B., Hayes, S. C., & Walser, R. D. (2007). *Learning ACT: An acceptance & commitment therapy skills-training manual for therapists.* Oakland, CA: New Harbinger.

Maltby, J. (2002). The Age Universal I–E Scale-12 and orientation toward religion: Confirmatory factor analysis. *The Journal of Psychology: Interdisciplinary and Applied, 5*, 555–560. doi:10.1080/00223980209605550

Masten, A. S. (2001). Ordinary magic: Resilience processes in development. *American Psychologist, 56*, 227–238. doi:10.1037/0003-066X.56.3.227

McCullough, M. E. (2000). Forgiveness as a human strength: Theory, measurement, and links to well-being. *Journal of Social and Clinical Psychology, 19*, 43–55. doi:10.1521/jscp.2000.19.1.43

Pargament, K. I., Zinnbauer, B. J., Scott, A. B., Butter, E. M., Zerowin, J., & Stanik, P. (1998). Red flags and religious coping: Identifying some religious warning signs among people in crisis. *Journal of Clinical Psychology, 54*, 77–89. doi:10.1002/(SICI)1097-4679(199801)54:1<77::AID-JCLP9>3.0.CO;2-R

Ricard, M. (2007). *Happiness: A guide to developing life's most important skill.* Boston, MA: Little, Brown & Company.

Snyder, C. R. (2000). The past and possible futures of hope. *Journal of Social and Clinical Psychology, 19*, 11–28. doi:10.1521/jscp.2000.19.1.11

Steenkamp, M. M., Litz, B. T., Gray, M. J., Lebowitz, L., Nash, W., Conoscenti, L., . . . Lang, A. (2011). A brief exposure-based intervention for service members with PTSD. *Cognitive and Behavioral Practice, 18*, 98–107. doi:10.1016/j.cbpra.2009.08.006

Thoresen, C., Harris, A., & Luskin, F. (2000). Forgiveness and health: An unanswered question. In M. McCullough, K. Pargament, & C. Thoresen (Eds.), *Forgiveness: Theory, research, and practice* (p. 334). New York, NY: Guilford Press.

Witvliet, C. V. O., Phillips, K. A., Feldman, M. E., & Beckham, J. C. (2004). Post-traumatic mental and physical health correlates of forgiveness and religious coping in military veterans. *Journal of Traumatic Stress, 17*, 269–273. doi:10.1023/B:JOTS.0000029270.47848.e5

12

RESPONDING TO THE PROBLEM OF EVIL AND SUFFERING

SUE GRAND

As we read the news and think about our global condition, the varieties of cruelty perpetrated by one human being on another (alone or in groups and even within cultures and societies) are evident: war, genocide, terrorism, torture, mass rape, and mass shootings. Brutality resurfaces throughout history, from the Roman Forum to the Inquisition, the Holocaust, Rwanda, Congo, Mali, Syria, and more local and isolated events such as those in Newtown, Connecticut. Each time one form of violence is vanquished, another appears. This mass sadism exceeds our comprehension; it breaches familiar registers of "badness," and we speak, once again, about human evil. We revisit a question that has been posed from time immemorial, without adequate answer: Do we as humans possess an innate and intractable propensity for evil? Can reason possibly come to know and prevent evil? Can goodness somehow contain and heal the more monstrous capacities of human beings? These questions have long preoccupied philosophers, ethicists, social critics, historians, and theologians.

http://dx.doi.org/10.1037/14500-013
Spiritually Oriented Psychotherapy for Trauma, D. F. Walker, C. A. Courtois, and J. D. Aten (Editors)

After World War II, these questions also became a focal point for social and clinical psychologists and psychoanalysts. Genocide became a focus of study. Exactly who are the perpetrators? What secrets lurk in their minds? As Nazis waited for the Nuremberg trials, psychologists had extraordinary access to them as objects of inquiry (see Gilbert, 1947/1995). In subsequent decades, this quest to understand has continued. Surely, the answers must be available and in the purview of depth psychology. It seems obvious: Such atrocities must emanate from a hidden deviance that lies dormant until it is unleashed by a cultural cataclysm of some sort. If this form of madness could only be identified, perhaps prevention and treatment could be formulated, hopefully leading to the end of atrocities.

After the Holocaust, psychologists joined a worldwide protest, declaring "never again," and expanded the study of evil. Yet, intensive studies of Nazi perpetrators seemed to yield nothing. There was no particular deviance or madness unique to the perpetrators (see Browning, 1992; Gilbert, 1995; Zillmer, Harrower, Ritzler, & Archer, 1995). With some psychopathic exceptions, their psyches were like those of their ordinary and nongenocidal counterparts. This raised an uncanny specter: The monstrous is latent within all of us. Perhaps the perpetrator is not our evil other, but rather a "monstrous double" (Girard, 1972). Is the genocidal perpetrator our own demonic transformation, a potentiality waiting to possess us (Rusesabagina, 2006)? Certainly, this investigation seemed to end, uncomfortably, in Arendt's (1963) formulation about the "banality" of evil. Mass atrocity has continued in Sierra Leone, Bosnia, Rwanda, and in our urban ghettos. There were chaotic social conditions. Perpetrators of evil found their permit in new ideologies and in shifting political and economic conditions. Meanwhile, the study of individual perpetrators had failed to provide enlightenment.

Psychologists shifted to an intersubjective and systemic perspective (Grand, 2000, 2010), turning to the political and cultural conditions that seem to ignite this violence. Cultural criticism was fused with depth and social psychology and evolved a psychic, social, political, and economic inquiry. Instead of individual perpetrators, the interplay between the psychic and the social became the focus of inquiry. Are there conditions that foment and liberate mass hatred while dissolving the social contract and the capacity for empathy and kindness? How does cruelty reproduce prior psychic traumas (Grand, 2010)? In general, this shift from the individual to the systemic and social has seemed a more fruitful area of study, one that might yield new models for change. These models rest on a bedrock assumption that all intrapsychic, interpersonal, and group operations are culturally embedded, including sadism and historical and intergenerational interpersonal trauma. In my view, this is a critical turn in the study of "evil"; it has been foundational to my own work.

Some difficulties exist with this evolving perspective. In displacing the focus from the individual perpetrator, the systemic approach risks reducing individual responsibility. Diffusion of responsibility can paralyze bystanders and potentiate group destructiveness. How can systemic conditions be studied without diffusing the responsibility of the individual perpetrator? If the study of group processes eclipses particular ethical subjectivities, do all humans become an unwitting mirror of mass violence, insofar as violence erases human particularity and subjectivity? Also, in the postmodern desire not to position the perpetrator as an alien "other," the systemic perspective can sometimes reach extreme positions: All of us could commit atrocities in disintegrated conditions. For me, this position is too morally relative, too exculpatory of perpetrators, too ready with forgiveness, lacking in solidarity with the victim, and too welcoming of the perpetrator into "us." But more than anything, it fails to recognize and honor what I have called the *small hero* (Grand, 2010). In every epoch of mass violence, there are those who refuse demonic transformation (see Rusesabagina, 2006), acting instead with integrity and ethical concern. These people maintain their ethical core and act on behalf of others. These heroes are in the minority, but they are not rare. They object to atrocity. They offer aid and rescue at great risk to themselves.

For many progressive psychoanalysts, there is a dread of "other-ing" the perpetrator, a dread that reflects an increasing awareness that, in extreme conditions, we do not know what we would do. And if we categorize the perpetrator as "inhuman," how can the perpetrator find redemption? But if these legitimate concerns are overemphasized, we may collapse in another direction. We can overlook the ethical hero. In the contagion of violence, these are the people who *do not*. On behalf of the other, they meet evil with courage. Given the forces of mass destruction, human hope lies in knowing them. Who are they, and how can their existence be facilitated and replicated? When these brave figures are remembered, we may find ourselves returning, once again, to the old question: How does the rescuer's psyche differ from that of the perpetrator's? Of course, we cannot ask this without maintaining our intersubjective, systemic, and cultural groundings. But when we retain our reverence for those who *do not*, a "heroic double" begins to answer Girard's (1972) monstrous double. And the capacity for individual responsibility is not upstaged by collective culpability.

This shift in perspective may allow another look at the individual perpetrator. Grounded in the ethical position and fortified with new developments in psychology and psychoanalysis, we can reexamine the inner lives of these individuals. The relational nexus that gives birth to evil can be reenvisioned as resulting from both individual and systemic responsibility. This possibility derives from the contemporary understanding of attachment and affective disorders, disorders of the self, multiple self-systems, dissociative processes, shame and guilt, the transgenerational transmission of trauma, and the familial and cultural erasure of empathic mutuality. All of these factors can be nested in the social and political forces that unleash cruelty (see Apprey, 2003). In the case study that follows, all of these factors are intertwined. They yield a patient with multiple self-states, each of which bears an ethical marker. Sometimes he is a perpetrator and sometimes a rescuer. In one self-state, he is cold, dead, cruel, and devoid of concern for others. Sometimes concern is misdirected and inverted. In other self-states, the ethical position survives: Destructiveness arouses guilt and remorse and a penitential search for punishment. At times, the perpetrator self seeks redemption and makes amends. He seeks and offers forgiveness. Links are made to the genocidal past. Victim self-states enter into dialogue with perpetrator self-states, and there is new life as a result.

In critical moments, the rescuer self has been able to recognize and contain the perpetrator self. This patient has engaged in "small" private "atrocities." These private atrocities refracted his family's exposure to mass violence. What would happen if contemporary conditions suddenly replicated those extreme historic conditions? Would he become a genocidal perpetrator? Would his rescuer self be able to restrain him and cause him to act on behalf of a victim? Would he oscillate between sadism and masochism? It is imperative to ask how the therapist reaches inside him. Is it possible to strengthen his rescuer self? Can we potentiate what Lifton (1996) called the animating function of guilt? Can we liberate him from the force of transgenerational transmission? This case study illuminates these questions. It traces the relational nexus of evil as a basis of developing a process of healing.

CASE STUDY

When David's mother was 10, she lived in Poland.[1] Her family was forced into a ghetto by the Nazis. One day, they were told to gather in the synagogue. David's mother hid, but her parents complied. The Nazis locked the Jews in the synagogue and lit it on fire. From her hiding place, David's mother listened to the screams and watched her parents and others burn. David's mother emerged at night, fled into the forest, and survived for the rest of the war with a group of partisans. After the war, she lived in a displaced persons camp and eventually settled in Argentina. There she met and married an Orthodox Jewish man. They tried to have children, but they could not conceive, so they adopted. But there was something uncanny and mysterious about this adoption. The biological mother was an unwed Christian

---

[1]The following case study is a composite, in which identifying information has been altered. However, the essence of the events and the essence of the clinical process has been preserved.

German woman. To these parents, adoption promised a renewal of life; it was a defiance of and an escape from the Nazi extermination. But this adoption was a continual evocation of the "enemy" in the country that had welcomed and "adopted" Nazi refugees. This newborn was innocent. But David was the offspring of the perpetrator in a world where the perpetrator could change his name and bide his time until renewed violence took the name of the junta. David's adoptive mother had escaped into a community of survivors, but the Nazis also found a haven in Argentina; another form of Nazism was brewing in South America (see Graziano, 1992; Hollander, 1997). For this new family, there was no transition to safety. There was no psychic space for the development of metaphor, no register for the symbolic. There were no protected generations who could begin to place the mother's memories back into history. Nazism was a continuous present; it was a psychotic contagion, and it would shape David's capacity for destructiveness.

As my patient grew up, his family observed Orthodox Jewish laws and rituals. But this was a family in which God seemed dead or absent or, at best, irrelevant. Massive trauma had hollowed out Orthodox ritual and eradicated all spirituality. For this family, Orthodoxy provided structure, community, and an important sense of continuity with the pre-Holocaust past. In shul, a collective voice was raised in a minor key of prayer; it must have felt like saying Kaddish for the 6 million. Still, this seemed to offer them little comfort in a world devoid of hope and justice. Although this family never explicitly queried God, it seemed infused with bitter despair: How could You have forsaken us? Forsaken by God in the Holocaust and again in the junta, now this religious family seemed to be saying Kaddish for God. Rituals took on a mechanized quality, void of the divine. Jewish ethics often seemed corrupted by the struggle to survive: In this family, the I–Thou relationship had been broken by trauma.

In this family, mother–child attachment would keep morphing into memory, vengeance, and retribution. This Christian German infant became the locus of his mother's Nazi projections. As an infant, David was chosen but was simultaneously hated; he owed his mother reparations. From early in life, "evil" seemed to accompany him and lurk within his cells and destroy everyone who came near him. Shortly after this adoption, his adoptive father died. An older, unmarried paternal uncle took in mother and child. The adoptive mother was a survivor. Now, she was also a grieving widow, left with what she considered a "demon" child who destroyed Jewish men.

The choice of this child, the ensuing repercussions in this family: The Nazis motifs were not metaphoric, they were real, they were terrible, and they were here and now, in present-day life and in the family. Once, this mother had been a resilient and resourceful survivor. In her early adolescence, she had been feisty, resourceful, and strong. She had survived in the Polish forests.

After the war, she became symptomatic and spiraled into mental illness. Her maternal capacity was eviscerated: Catatonic depressions alternated with paranoid assaults on David. This mother was persecuted by memory and by the presence of this small German boy. David was accused, punished, and neglected. He was often kept in a locked room with a spy-hole constructed in the door so that his parental "guards" could peer in but he could not get out. Sometimes his bedroom seemed like a prison cell. As a captive, David seemed to have an oscillating function in his mother's trauma narrative: He was a Jew held captive in the burning synagogue; he was a Nazi held captive by the Allies. When family and neighbors began to be arrested in Buenos Aires, David's prison cell acquired another function: It was as if he was an imprisoned evil interrogator for the junta and a Jew whom the junta had detained. In case he failed to grasp the meaning of his captivity, the mother would hurl these epithets at him during episodes of paranoia.

When his mother was mute, frozen, and withdrawn, David was neglected. He felt that he was responsible for killing his mother. When his mother could speak, she would say that David should be dead. There was nothing veiled about these communications. In this family, there was no register for dignity or boundaries, no room for the son's objection or disturbance. Sometimes he mirrored his mother's catatonic states. In these paralytic childhood depressions, he was considered "quiet" and "good." But when he became agitated and disturbed, he was considered "aggressive" and "out of control" and had to be locked into his room. As David grew, he only seemed more dangerous. His mother and uncle had married. When he was around 10, his mother miraculously became pregnant and gave birth to a baby girl. This biological daughter was the locus of the mother's victim identification. When David was "quiet and good" (i.e., catatonic), he would be left watching this infant. But when David was agitated and upset, this infant had to be "protected" from her "Nazi" brother. David was sent back into his "prison." David's Jewish parents were thin and dark and small. David was Aryan and soon towered over them, blond, broad, muscular, and intimidating. He looked like the men who had murdered his grandparents, and now he also looked like the men who were abducting their neighbors in Argentina.

In this family, Nazism had created splintered selves. These selves lived in psychotic dimensions of good and evil. If there were any possibility of metabolizing Holocaust memories, it was neutralized by a new epoch of terror. As a Jew, David was threatened with persecution by the junta, and as the family "Nazi," he was persecuted in his family by his own mother. Mother and child oscillated between the roles of victim and perpetrator. They tormented each other. They subjected each other to abuse and indignities; they expressed no tenderness, solidarity, or regret, and they drove each other mad. The infant "Jewish" sister was triangulated into this chaos.

In the presence of these disintegrating minds, the uncle stifled his own needs and frustrations. He labored and tried to keep the family safe. Even after he relocated the family to New York City, he never sought treatment for the mother (now his wife) or for David or David's sister. He managed to rescue them from the junta, but he seemed to collude in Holocaust dynamics: Inside the family, the Uncle was a paralyzed bystander; he acted like a "good German." Locking David in his room, the Uncle became a Capo, the "keeper" in a lunatic asylum. He endured, he worked hard, and he rescued his brother's family. He made money, and he was the caretaker of these damaged relatives.

Transgenerational Memory: Attachment, Healing, Rupture

Forty years after the adoption, this "Nazi" child arrived in my office and became my patient. Throughout his life, David had fulfilled his destiny: He had become the family's criminal. He was brutal and masochistic, he was suicidal and murderous, he was ruthless and needy, and he had a stunning capacity for exploitation and hatred. His speech was disorganized, superficial, and pressured. He could not hold a thought for a single moment. His family history emerged in random pieces at the end of sessions, and he could never answer any questions. Eventually, I interviewed his parents and acquired this family history. David had never given any conscious thought to the Holocaust or the junta. He had been drug-addicted, sex-addicted, violent, an embezzler, a forger, a liar. He had hit his aging parents and regularly stole from them as well. He had been married twice. He had moved constantly. He had promiscuous, unprotected sex and had abandoned a series of women and children all over the world. He had no idea how many offspring he had. His marriages yielded several children who had lived through his addictions; he had abandoned and neglected these children and their mothers. His uncle intervened and gave the mothers child support.

David had never worked in legitimate settings or engaged in any responsible activity. He had always been rescued and supported by his relatives. He felt entitled to that support as a form of "reparations" for his childhood victimization, even though he did not understand the full perversity of that childhood. By the time he came to treatment, he had been through drug rehab, was clean and sober, was going to Alcoholics Anonymous, and was dedicated to getting his life together. He had learned a lot in rehab. He had been diagnosed as bipolar, was taking his prescribed medication, and had moved back to New York City to repair his relations with the daughter from one of his marriages. But in New York, he was going to be in close proximity to his mother and uncle and was worried that this proximity would threaten his sobriety.

From the first, I was wary about seeing him, although he did not seem violent. I knew he would be disturbing and demanding and that he would try to trespass on my boundaries. In every encounter with David's suffering, there was always an encounter with cruelty. From the beginning of his treatment, he was obsessed with getting more money from his uncle. He cast his wealthy uncle as a controlling sadist. Throughout adulthood, David was financially rescued and supported. He spent vast and wanton sums, raged for more, and stole what the uncle would not pay. The uncle's fiscal "cruelty" was keeping David "sick" when he was trying to get "well." My patient reported screaming abuse at his uncle on a daily basis. One day, the uncle came home from the hospital after a coronary episode and was resting and on a heart monitor. David burst into his parents' apartment and screamed at him in bed, "I hate you; I hope you die." He told this story with pride in a new found "assertiveness" and "authenticity": Here was proof that the 12-step program was "working." This moment occurred in one of his earliest sessions. His account was stunning in its brutality, its cold pride, and its utter perversity. I was meant to applaud the righteousness of this "assertion" against a "bully."

This moment was one of many: In David's life, there was a perpetual inversion of victim and perpetrator. He could never identify the actual perpetrators in his history but experienced their shadow everywhere. Like most bullies, he experienced himself as an innocent victim. His assertions were a matter of self-protection and justice. He felt like the fiscal prisoner of his uncle, even though the uncle was the victim of David's thefts. He thought he was entitled to his reparations, but he was fulfilling his Nazi destiny: He was a brute kicking the infirm. This uncle had lost his own brother and taken in his brother's wife and infant. He had married David's mother and formally adopted David. He rescued them first from penury and then again from the junta. He had lost his own relatives in Argentina, and then he lost his homeland. By now, he was elderly, fragile, and depressed. He had failed to protect David in childhood and in fact had helped to imprison him at times. He was far from perfect and deserved some anger, in modulation. But he did not deserve such rough brutality, and David was not an innocent victim.

I immediately confronted David's assaultiveness as unacceptable behavior. My patient was self-righteous and insistent, and I fought with him. I did not know whether I wanted to treat him. But then something emerged that would recurrently reassure me: He stopped his pressured speech for a moment. He listened and said that he wanted to act better. He admitted that he had hit his aging parents. One of his 12 steps was to make amends to those he had hurt during his addiction. In moving back to New York, this was his intention; he hoped to receive their forgiveness. I highlighted this need to make amends and tried to explore the possibilities of mutual forgiveness. But these questions touched on mass trauma: The Nazis never made amends; they escaped and recycled cruelty in Argentina. How would it be possible for this family to explore forgiveness? To speak about amends and forgiveness touched on massive trauma.

David was unable to focus and returned to his self-righteous insistence that he was defending himself against victimization. I said that I thought this family's illness was driven by the Holocaust and by the terrors in Argentina. No one had ever suggested that before. From the first, I cast their familial trouble in psychic, social, and ethical terms. I tried to nest his individual responsibility in systemic conditions. I took a leap I do not usually take so quickly. I said,

> In this family, your mother is the Jewish "corpse" who didn't survive the Polish massacre, and you have been the family Nazi. When you were a child, they kept you in a prison cell. When the disappearances started, you must have somehow felt that they were you. It must have been terrible to feel so lonely and evil.

I feared this might precipitate further disorganization or an increase in self-hatred. What it produced was a miraculous moment of organization in which David's thoughts and speech cohered. For the first time he had a narrative for this story, for the self-destruction, and for the abusiveness. He even had a new way to think about his family. For the next 6 months, he still spoke compulsively about rescue and money. It was a rare moment when I could get him to make links to history. But in the transference, I set firm boundaries about aggressive demands and intrusions; I was empathic, but I confronted this bullying. His speech gradually became more cogent and his mind more clear.

He liked it when I labeled and contained the bully. He was learning to label it. In his own behavior he recognized the verbal assaults he had received from mother. I said,

> Your mother was a victim, and she is very wounded from the war and from the death of your father. But it doesn't legitimize the ways she tormented you, especially since you were a child. Your own wounds don't justify how you treat others.

Gradually, we developed a warmer and more respectful bond that was grounded in greater ethics and empathy. We began to notice similarities between us. In the winter, we were both tea drinkers. One day, he gave me a gift: a box of tea. I accepted it with gratitude and we had a miraculous moment: He was a loving son with a responsive mother. A few weeks later, he came in with a cold. I decided to offer him a cup of tea. I left the session, heated the kettle, and brought him a mug with one of his tea bags. Now he was a needy child with a nurturing mother. He was not evil, and his analyst–mother was neither a corpse nor destructive. Attachment and object constancy were coming into view.

As he sipped his tea, he began to tell me more about an episode of sexual abuse in his childhood. He had referred to it in bits, but now he was telling me the whole story. The abuse was committed by a much-loved male friend of his parents, also a survivor. When David tried to tell his uncle at the time of the incident, his uncle did not believe him. For the first time in treatment, David cried. I said,

> You felt the abuser loved you, and then he used you. It was a terrible betrayal by all of them. Your mother lost so many people, they probably couldn't bear to believe this, because then they would have to lose this man too. They were the "Jews"; you were the "German." You felt that they could sacrifice you.

He let this sink in and continued crying. But while he was all there, I was getting distracted. I smelled something burning. At first, it was faint, and then it got stronger. I must have left the gas on under the kettle; something might catch fire. I did not want to leave David during this breakthrough, but our survival seemed to require quick action. I rushed into the kitchen that is adjacent to my office. The stove was not lit; everything was still. Nothing was on fire. I returned to the session and tried to pick up where we left off. But burning still seemed to permeate the air. In my countertransference, I was having an olfactory hallucination. I realized that I was David's mother at 10 years old: I was smelling her parents' bodies burning in the Polish synagogue.

This experience was stunning in its somatic reality. The smell continued throughout the rest of the session. It did not evaporate, even when I knew what it was. I never told my patient about it. I felt that I could endure it, hold it inside me, subject it to translation, turn it into memory, and discretely place it into our intersubjective history. I did not want to recapitulate the uncle and mother who could not attend to the son's molestation. I wanted to be the mother who could contain her own historic wound and attend to her son. It would have seemed like madness to tell David about my hallucination; he was already in a hallucinatory relationship with his mother. He had suffered enough from transgenerational transmission and from the crippling "narcissistic identification" (Faimberg, 2005) he had formed with this mother.

In general, I think analysts should metabolize their own countertransference in private, and then use it as an internal map for creativity in the treatment. With David, psychic fusion and invasion had reached extremes, and I expected my countertransference to mirror those extremities. I did not expect my sensorium to be consumed by history. Still, I thought I could turn my sensorium into symbolization, into history, by myself, for my "child." If I could manage this, we might heal his disorganized attachment pattern, and he might form his first secure maternal bond.

But the Nazis set fire to this emergent bond. In retrospect, I wish I had told him about the way that history seized me. When I suddenly left the session, I had said, "I think I left the kettle on." I certainly seemed pressured. When I returned, I was shaken and absent, but I was trying to "move on."

Now, I was enacting another analogue of history. I was mother, trying to move away to another country, where life was banal, innocuous, and safe. We know that there was no other safe country to flee to: The junta was waiting. The junta was layered onto Nazi memories and produced the ultimate "dead mother" (Green, 1986). David could always sense that which was inchoate, ominous, and malignant. Growing up, he lived in this kind of primal, traumatic transmission, but there was no one to label or interpret this phenomenon. There was no witnessing or translation or ego-organizing function. There was only primary process, the psychotic sensorium of disorganized minds, a new regime of terror, and a caretaker uncle who could not know what he was seeing inside his family. Perhaps it would have been better if I had acknowledged and labeled this hallucinatory episode. Perhaps this would have placed primal experience into secondary process.

In this session of the "burning," the Nazis returned to disrupt human bonds. Here we were: good mother, good infant. Nurturance was bountiful; there was tea for both of us. Briefly, we were linked in grief, compassion, and mutual concern. We were finding a narrative for sexual abuse, and trauma was being placed into history. My patient's mind was cogent and clear. The Polish massacre was memory. The Nazis were terrible, but they were dead. Metaphorically, we had reached a safer country. But just when "evil" was excised with our growing intimacy, it reemerged with unexpected force. The scent of burning was visceral. It was dangerous, and it was going to consume us. I left my patient in the midst of his suffering. I returned, but like his mother, something in me was damaged. The executioners had returned.

Given our eventual rupture, what would have happened if I had labeled and interpreted this enactment? If only I could have linked this enactment to what happened with his mother, we might have repaired our attachment, and our impasse might have been averted. I have thought of this, and I think the idea has some merit. But I also want to say, "Wait." I was paralyzed by this uncanny experience. It seized every cell of my body. I was able to label it, privately, for myself. But I felt that I could not speak it. This was a recurrent predicament for me in this treatment. Every major breakthrough was characterized by repellent and disorganizing forms of countertransference that occupied my body. Metabolizing countertransference such as this takes me weeks or sometimes months, and sometimes it never happens. Meanwhile, a part of me becomes mute and dead. I continue speaking and conducting analysis. But part of me becomes the "corpse" mother–self who did not survive the massacre. When I do not "return," neither does my patient: Whatever material we were processing seems to disappear into an unmarked grave. Once I was able to refer to these experiences, David had already fled to another country.

Often enough, we were in a simultaneous state of recovery and healing. It looked like we were going to make it. He could always tell when I was coming back from one of these episodes. I was less quiet and distant. I was more authentically empathic toward his pain but also more firm and challenging about his abusiveness. I confronted the lies, stealing, rages, and bullying. He could be evasive and defensive, but generally he was responsive and receptive. What he wanted more than anything was intimate, reliable love from a woman. If he wanted love, he knew he had to learn to act loving. He had been working on this with his parents and with his sister in New York. He was more accepting of his mother's illness. He made amends to his mother for hitting her, stealing from her, and screaming at her. The mother apologized for her inability to mother—she was too "sick" from the "war." This family had profound moments of mutual recognition and forgiveness. But these moments were broken up by a compulsive return to the destructive patterns that caused the original wounds. No one can speak about the ultimate problems of forgiveness: the Nazis, the Junta, the abandonment by God. Nonetheless, David stopped vilifying his uncle. He began to remember his uncle's warmth and kindness in his early childhood. With the rise of the junta, the uncle became mechanical and wooden and masked; his focus was on the terror outside their home. When my patient screamed at him now, he expressed remorse. With his sister, David tried to be a kinder brother.

Meanwhile, David was inexplicably drawn back to Argentina. In his travel back and forth to Buenos Aires, he met a new woman. The girlfriend was sober, warm, and affectionate, and David hoped that she was "the one." He liked her and was willing to give their relationship a try. David had more insight into his bad choices, into the ways that he destroyed prior relationships. If he was going to form a bond with his new love, he had to stay with her for more extended periods and give them time to be together. He wanted to live in Buenos Aires, but decided to stay there for 3 months at a time and return to New York for extended visits. He had considerable guilt about leaving.

For all his life, David had been forming bonds and breaking them. He was constantly moving and setting up new homes. He had been reenacting loss and dislocation. He repeated his own adoption, and sometimes his behavior mimicked the forced adoptions perpetrated by the junta. He impregnated women and had children scattered all over the world. Married twice, he had one son in Chile and one son in New York. He abandoned both of their mothers. He took in animals when he needed company. Then he abandoned them when he was high or dropped them when relocating.

After being in treatment, David was less impulsive and more ambivalent. He was trying to create some consistency with old and new attachments. But he could not think about why the only woman for him was thousands of miles from his other relationships. And he could not reflect on the pull of Argentina. He was obsessed with the new girlfriend and afraid she would be unfaithful while he was away. I could not inquire into the meaning of this relocation, the "unfaithfulness," or the complex Jew–Nazi–junta history of Buenos Aires. He blocked my inquiries and obsessed like a vulnerable teenager in love. He could not imagine continuity, whole families, enduring bonds between generations. He could not talk about the disruption in our relationship, although he wanted to e-mail me and see me "when he comes in." He was not interested in maintaining phone contact, even when I offered it. But there was something new happening for David: He spent months in therapy considering what to do. With regard to the girlfriend, he tried to separate reality from fantasy, and he was less abusive about the imagined "unfaithfulness." He was concerned about how his relocation would affect others. Meanwhile, he was coming and going for extended periods.

In all of this there was the legitimacy of wanting a new life in a world in which he was much more at home. He really did seem saner in South America, although the reason was mysterious. The junta had ended. Had he finally found the sanctuary there, which his mother had hoped for? Did he need this distance from a toxic mother? Maybe I overvalued continuity and undervalued the new relationship he found. When he was there, he did not feel so edgy, anxious, chaotic, hostile, or deprived. He did not feel "evil." In Buenos Aires there was an intact Jewish community, and somehow he lived as a "good Jew" who belongs to other Jews. Somehow in Buenos Aires there were only good Jews among Jews. He never spoke about the Nazis who fled to South America or about the virulent antisemitism of his youth. When he was away, he seemed to shed his Aryan identity and had a legitimate distance from the provocations of the parental home. Perhaps he could also protect his aging parents from himself. It was obvious that he was healthier in Argentina. He decided to go. In these sessions no one was evil, but relationships seemed tragic. Closeness was not broken up by destructiveness but was still ruptured by too much loss. I felt sorry that I would not continue seeing David and finish what we had begun. I was glad I got to know him, and that surprised me. I just relaxed into trusting him; I did not feel so wary about the Nazi self. His parents were old and fragile—they had been making amends, and then there was another parting.

Mystery, Impossibility, and Excess

Together, we experienced grief. I think we might have parted without reviving the Nazi self. Then this self seized us by the throat. David had two dogs. He was going to the vet to put the dogs to sleep. Why, I asked, are they sick? No. He was going away and what was he supposed to do with them? He would not pay for a kennel, even though he had wasted enormous sums on material possessions. It is difficult to convey the cold brutality of his tone. His dogs were disposable objects. Inconvenient, they could be excised from existence. They were props from an old life when he was alone. Now, they were in his way. They were helpless and dependent, and he was going to euthanize them. I was horrified, and there was no way I could hide it. I said, "They're living creatures, and they're helpless. You're going to kill them because they're inconvenient?" He was flippant and defensive, but I would not have it. I said,

> This is the Nazi, shooting Jews, burning them in pits, sending them to the gas. You will never be well or have real love in your life if your new relationship is based on killing trusting creatures because they're inconvenient. Life is sacred. You put dogs to sleep when they are too ill to live, because they need you to do it. These dogs are healthy; they're just in your way. You are going to get very sick from feeling evil if you do this. Don't do this.

Needless to say, I do not usually have such eruptions, and rarely tell my patients what to do. I had a visceral reaction, a sense of ethical shock and revulsion. This ethical sense was rooted in our shared Jewish tradition, as is stated in Deuteronomy: "See I have set before thee this daily life and good, death and evil . . . choose life" (Deuteronomy 30:15–19). This tradition had become bankrupt in David's traumatic legacy, but it had always been central to my consciousness and to my clinical practice. I could not be a bystander to the wanton killing of an innocent. To me, this is the lesson of the Holocaust: We cannot remain passive and silent in these moments. In some sense, I also needed to believe that David would feel evil if he did this. I needed to believe that this would revive his penitential masochism—I could not bear to think of him without guilt or remorse. And I did not want to think about the Nazis who moved to Argentina and escaped justice. I could not think about the full clinical effect of what I was saying. He agreed not to put the dogs to sleep that day.

Then I asked him about what he had done with animals before. The session only grew more chilling. He told me things he had not spoken of previously. Once, when he was high and his son was little, a puppy scratched his child. David became enraged, locked the puppy in the garage, and let it starve to death while listening to it whine and howl. He had a sense of righteous satisfaction and cruelty because the puppy had "abused" his son. He sounded like an agent of the junta purging innocents identified as terrorists. He sounded like a Gestapo agent purging the Jewish defilement. He had reenacted the persecutory confusion he had received from his mother. He was projecting evil onto the innocent and construing his sadism as "justice." Part of him was an animal lover and had felt ashamed. But in another self-state he had never questioned that behavior until then, when he saw my reaction.

Then his memories went back to his childhood. In this memory, he was about 11. His mother was in another catatonic state, but David was not in his corresponding "quiet and good" catatonic depression. He had been locked in his room. The uncle was going to work. His mother let David out of his room so she could go back to bed while David "watched" his infant "Jewish" sister.

Liberated from his "cell," David was even more agitated. Most Holocaust survivors are overprotective of children and grandchildren. Most refugees of the junta have anxiety about children "disappearing." Leaving the agitated "Nazi" boy alone with the helpless "Jewish" infant seemed like an unconscious invitation to evil. Or perhaps it was a throwback to more naive times before the war. Or it was some hope for decency in the maelstrom of "evil." In this family context, it was another psychotic register.

Whenever he was left alone in this state with this baby sister, he would plant a smothering "kiss" on her lips and start sucking the breath out of her body. The limbs of the infant struggled as she started to turn blue. David would stop just before the baby suffocated. No one ever discovered this, and no one ever knew. After two or three episodes, David awakened to a sense of horror and guilt. He stopped. He saved himself, and he saved his sister. In this moment part of him knew "the self may be turned into a friend of the spirit if one is capable of developing a persistent perception of the non-self, of the anxiety and dignity, of fellow beings" (Heschl, 1955, p. 399). He told the uncle he would not watch his sister again. His struggle with evil took place in the zone of what I call *catastrophic loneliness* (Grand, 2000), and his rescuer self remained secret, sacrificial, and unrecognized. Refusing to watch his sister, he was assailed for his selfishness and locked back in his room.

He told this story with a sense of shame and horror. His affect was appropriate, and there was no confusion about his culpability. This was the darkest core of his Holocaust self. He was a rescuer, a hero, and a murderer. He had almost killed his own projected Nazi baby-self, he was almost a Nazi killing Jewish children, and then he revived those lost Jewish children. He suckled at the grim breast of genocide. He reenacted the lethal "kiss" of his own maternal symbiosis, and he reenacted the ability to survive that lethal kiss. I was awed at his truthfulness, honored by his trust, and repelled by what lived inside of him. Were there more stories, worse stories, which he still had not told me? Could I bear to hear them? Could he bear to tell them? In another epoch of terror, who would he become? If cruelty were licensed, would he become the torturer in the "blue room" of torture and interrogation? Would he seize on some genocidal ideology? Or would his rescuer self interrupt his violence and allow him to empathize with and save another victim?

I said that these incidents had confirmed his sense of evil and increased his penitential masochism, his self-destructiveness, and his need for forgiveness. But I also pointed to his heroic strength at age 11: He stopped himself, alone, without adult help or intervention. He saved the baby from himself, even though he faced false accusations and unjust punishment. He had chosen life, empathy, and ethical action. He had acted heroically to save the innocent, despite all the abuse and neglect he had experienced. Anointed as the family "Nazi," he had refused that role, alone, at a critical moment. But even as I affirmed this, I had an uncanny suspicion: It felt as though there was another baby who died by his hands. Would either of us ever know what was real? With David, material reality was elusive; it was lost to the psychotic trespass of the past. Bonding was continually ruptured by malignance, and every moment of lucidity was infused with doubt. His interpersonal transactions were a plea for attention, and they were a tissue of lies. Who knew what had actually happened with those infants or whether anything had actually happened at all? I have heard the confessions of pedophiles and murderers, but I have never felt this personally disorganized by a patient.

At the end of the session, he agreed not to put the dogs to sleep that day. It was the obvious and necessary thing to say to his therapist. He knew I was appalled by what I found inside him. He knew what he had to do to restore our relationships and to keep me. I thought I had brought him back from the brink. He seemed to feel a bit safer. I had stopped him from killing the dogs as he had once stopped himself from smothering his sister. In childhood, there was no one to protect him from destructiveness. There was no one to cherish his heroic attempts at goodness. His sister would never know that he had almost killed her and that he had saved her. Now, with the dogs, he had me to tell and me to help him. He did not need to live in the zone of catastrophic loneliness.

During the war, there had been no one to protect his grandparents and his mother. There were only perpetrators and passive bystanders. In reacting to his intention to put the dogs to sleep, I refused to function as a passive bystander. I simply could not do it. This allowed a fuller memory to emerge. Still, I did not know whether I had really protected David or whether his reassurance was mere simulation. I know I tried to revive our shared Jewish ethics. I did not know whether he would tell me the truth about what he had done with the dogs. There was nothing else I could have done at this juncture. If he was merely in a state of false compliance, there was no hope of authenticity between us. I think I reassured one self-state in him while silencing another. He felt heard as a rescuer, in his capacity for concern. But he also felt seen and known as a murderer. Neither of us had real faith in the triumph of his heroic self.

After this session, I was gripped by nausea. Over the weekend, I dreaded the next session. I thought I had stomach flu and fantasized about canceling David's appointment. On Monday, I vomited a few minutes before his session. I managed to sit in my chair, but I could barely speak. I did not know what I would do if he had sent the dogs "to the gas." At the end of the session, he told me that he had not done it and that he was looking for someone to adopt them. Of course, I was relieved, and this allowed me to go on being a therapist. I said, "The dog is baby David. Your biological mother couldn't care for you, but you deserved a family who could really love you. You didn't get that. Maybe you can give that to your dogs." At another moment I said, "Your mother adopted you, but you must have felt that she really wanted you to die." My patient seemed to make the link between these adoptions. He seemed to understand that you cannot begin a healthy new life by killing a helpless creature. Or that is what I wanted to think. But I never knew whether to believe him. I could not refer to the baby whom he had allowed to live. To speak about that rescuer self was also to speak to a monster.

It was hard enough that day simply to sit in my chair. I was comforted when I believed that he did not put the dogs to sleep. But he knew when to lie, and this was the only thing to say to me. Shortly thereafter he announced that the vet had said that one dog was sick and should be put to sleep, so that is what he did. The other one was healthy and had been adopted. I am an animal person, and I know how hard it is to find a home for an elderly dog. I have never heard of this happening so easily or so quickly. I never queried this story, because I just could not do it. We never talked again about the sister he almost killed. We never talked about whether he was lying or telling me the truth about the dog. I never returned to the Nazi self, and I never wanted to know what else that part of him had done. Somehow, I knew that there were other stories. He knew that I could not bear to hear them. I am an analyst who specializes in the problems of destructiveness, and I treat transgenerational trauma, but with this patient, I simply could not do it. I was ashamed of my cowardice. Before this confession I had wanted him to stay. Now I just wanted him to go.

Was this the only way we could part? We worked together for a few more sessions after the dog "adoption," and he left for 3 months. He did not want phone sessions or any contact with me. He deposited the Nazi self with me and departed to be a good Jew among other Jews. But he also departed to a country of ex-Nazis who had worked for the junta. I knew what no one else knew. Perhaps he could be "good" there because his sense of "evil" was deposited in me, here, or because I also knew about his rescuer self. Perhaps he could feel more "good" there because "evil" had been so much more extreme there. I think we were both relieved to be far away from each other. After that, he came and went from treatment. He would make appointments by e-mail then break them when he was in New York. Our meetings became more and more infrequent. When he would come there was a repetitive pattern: I saw some decency, earnestness, and good intentions. There was some warmth, mutuality, human kindness, and trust between us. Bonding would begin. We would both know he was leaving. At that moment, he felt quite human.

Our separation seemed inevitable, but tragic. Attachments are disrupted by loss and dislocation but not by cruelty. Then, there was another revelation just before he left, when there was no time to discuss or contain it. In Buenos Aires, he had adopted more animals that might have to be left or destroyed if he had to move back to New York. He and his new girlfriend were not using birth control. He had impregnated women all over the world. He may have had to leave another woman and child. I said, "You were a hurt and abandoned child. You have hurt and abandoned so many animals and children. Isn't it enough? Living creatures are not disposable props, to be used when convenient and then cast aside." I could only take an ethical position; I am not much good at interpretation. Every time he left, he provoked this protest from me. He aroused this nausea and then he went. Perhaps this contained his destructiveness and helped him leave the sense of evil in New York. Maybe he had used my containment to live a better life while he was away. As he left, he always reassured me that he was not going to "do it." I know that he had seen the disturbance in my eyes. I know that I had seen the sadism in his. I am never sure what the Nazi self is actually doing in Argentina.

FINAL REFLECTIONS

This case is a disturbing one. If only I could have stayed with the Nazi self, perhaps it would have been more available to healing. But the confrontation with evil is repellent and disorganizing, and it can easily overwhelm the therapist. Then, too, the sense of evil predominated; it made it hard to really put the rescuer self in the foreground. But if we think about it, it is the rescuer self who is the miraculous subject in this case. Whether that rescuer self was evoked in my countertransference or lived out in his protection of his baby sister, that self kept faith with Jewish ethics. It was the surviving trace of the I–Thou relationship that transcends atrocity and helps to protect us from further atrocity. Given the conditions of his childhood, one would easily expect him to become and remain a perpetrator. The "small hero" is the surprise, and in retrospect, I wish I had made that my focus. No doubt, it is possible to ameliorate the destructiveness inside such a patient. But in critical moments, it is their ethical self that needs fortification. As I suggested at the beginning of this chapter, it is the ethical self that needs more attention. Perhaps this self is less fascinating and less compelling than the perpetrator self, more easily eclipsed in psychotherapy. But this work is going to be essential to stopping mass violence. It is difficult to know how to encounter these contradictory self-states. Unfortunately, there are no clear answers. What I do know is that this case contains hope as well as destruction.

Inside of David were multiple self-states, each of them in a different ethical position. There was a perpetrator inside him, a genocidal potential, which might engage in mass atrocity. But there were other heroic self-states too. Deprived, assaulted, neglected, full of rage and psychotic wounds, bereft of attachment, and bearing his family's Nazi projections, he was left alone with a Jewish infant. His family seemed to be tempting him to murder, and yet he did not. Who was this David, and how could this heroic self-state be potentiated? If temptation awakened him in a murderous culture, would the small hero restrain him again? What types of psychic and cultural supports would help him resist the license to kill? What types of psychic and cultural interventions would heal the Nazi introject inside him? Can we think about demonic transformations in terms of psyche and culture, attachment disorders, empathic failures, dysregulated affect, the projection and internalization of badness, and the transgenerational transmission of trauma? Can we think about demonic transformations as the foreclosure of the heroic self? This case leaves these questions open and invites further study and discussion.

REFERENCES

Apprey, M. (2003). Repairing history: Reworking trans-generational trauma. In D. Moss (Ed.), *Hating in the first person plural* (pp. 3–29). New York, NY: Other Press.

Arendt, H. (1963). *Eichmann in Jerusalem: A report on the banality of evil.* New York, NY: Penguin Books.

Browning, C. (1992). *Ordinary men: Reserve Police Battalion 101 and the final solution in Poland.* New York, NY: HarperCollins.

Faimberg, H. (2005). *The telescoping of generations.* London, England: Routledge.

Gilbert, G. M. (1995). *Nuremberg diary.* Washington, DC: De Capo Press. (Original work published 1947)

Girard, R. (1972). *Violence and the sacred.* Baltimore, MD: Johns Hopkins University Press.

Grand, S. (2000). *The reproduction of evil: A clinical and cultural perspective.* Hillsdale, NJ: Analytic Press.

Grand, S. (2010). *The hero in the mirror: From fear to fortitude.* New York, NY: Routledge.

Graziano, F. (1992). *Divine violence: Spectacle, psychosexuality and radical Christianity in the Argentine Dirty War.* Boulder, CO: Westview Press.

Green, A. (1986). *On private madness* (K. Aubertin, Trans.). London, England: Hogarth Press.

Heschl, A. (1955). *God in search of man.* New York, NY: Farrar, Straus & Giroux.

Hollander, N. C. (1997). *Love in a time of hate.* New Brunswick, NJ: Rutgers University Press.

Lifton, R. J. (1996). Dreaming well: On death and history. In D. Barret (Ed.), *Trauma and dreams* (pp. 125–140). Cambridge, MA: Harvard University Press.

Rusesabagina, P. (2006). *An ordinary man: An autobiography.* New York, NY: Penguin Books.

Zillmer, E. A., Harrower, M., Ritzler, B. A., & Archer, R. P. (1995). *The quest for the Nazi personality: A psychological investigation of Nazi war criminals.* Hillsdale, NJ: Erlbaum.

AFTERWORD: REFLECTIONS AND FUTURE DIRECTIONS

DONALD F. WALKER, CHRISTINE A. COURTOIS, AND JAMIE D. ATEN

In our introduction to this volume, we began with a prayer attributed to Job: "Though He slay me, yet will I trust in Him" (Job 13:15, King James Version). This prayer, and the biblical story of Job, reflects trauma work in many ways. Psychotherapy with traumatized clients inherently involves perseverance in the midst of great pain, a belief that things will get better, and a necessary commitment to working through long-standing problems resulting from traumatic events for both psychotherapists and clients. In this afterword, we reflect on the material that has been presented throughout this volume and consider the future state of practice and research in this area. We have organized this discussion into three broad areas: (a) key take-home points from research, (b) key take-home points from clinical experience, and (c) recommendations to advance research and practice in the field.

http://dx.doi.org/10.1037/14500-014
Spiritually Oriented Psychotherapy for Trauma, D. F. Walker, C. A. Courtois, and J. D. Aten (Editors)

TAKE-HOME POINTS FROM RESEARCH

Spiritually oriented treatment for trauma is still in its early stages. Within this specialty niche of practice, some areas of research have been more thoroughly investigated than others. For example, the meaning making for trauma model presented by Slattery and Park (Chapter 6) has a substantial amount of research behind it. This model builds on previous work in the trauma literature emphasizing damage to systems of meaning resulting from trauma by also highlighting the process by which meaning making occurs after trauma. Not all meaning-making efforts are successful in reducing distress. In her previous research, Park distinguished between the process of meaning making, in the form of a search for meaning, versus the product of meaning making (see Chapter 6, this volume). Slattery and Park noted that the development of posttraumatic stress disorder (PTSD) among survivors of trauma is dependent on how they resolve discrepancies between global and appraised meaning and how they attempt to do so. The meaning-making model for trauma is useful in understanding survivors' attempts to resolve traumatic events and for organizing trauma psychotherapy to do so.

Another area in which relatively more research has been done is that of changes in faith following traumatic events (Chapter 7). In particular, a substantial body of work has been completed in understanding changes related to religion and spirituality after childhood abuse. As expected, faith is typically damaged after abuse and survivors' faith sometimes increases after abuse. Furthermore, in some instances aspects of faith are damaged, whereas other aspects of religion and spirituality are used to cope with and make meaning of child abuse. When child abuse damages faith, survivors' relationship with God and their participation in organized religion are typical areas of injury. However, when survivors experience simultaneous damage to faith and increases in faith, the typical pattern is of a decrease in involvement in organized religion while simultaneously drawing closer to God and engaging more frequently in spiritual practices. Understanding the processes involved in such changes in faith after abuse helps inform the process of assessing spiritual impact after abuse, as well as actual treatment.

The role of spirituality and religion in maintaining and resolving intimate partner violence (IPV) is another area that has received relatively greater attention in research (for reviews, see Chapter 10, this volume; Stephens & Walker, in press). Studies have repeatedly demonstrated that aspects of religious faith—including religious values that encourage the submission of women over gender equality, prohibit divorce, and encourage forgiveness in all circumstances, regardless of repentance on the part of the offender—all play a role in maintaining IPV. Clergy and members of religious congregations have also been found to assist in maintaining IPV by reinforcing these kinds of religious messages. On the positive side, a survivor's relationship with God is often a significant source of comfort and support in leaving an abusive relationship and recovering from IPV. Knowing the kinds of religious messages that have served to maintain abusive relationships can assist psychotherapists in confronting distorted religious values when treating survivors of IPV. But when counseling IPV survivors, psychotherapists can also encourage clients to rely on their relationship with God as well as supportive spiritual practices.

TAKE-HOME POINTS FROM CLINICAL EXPERIENCE

Although work in this area is still in its infancy, we are encouraged by several areas of clinical practice in spiritually oriented psychotherapy for trauma. First, the field as a whole has moved beyond the simple recognition that considering spiritual issues for trauma survivors is essential to considering ways to do trauma therapy comprehensively. As a result, there are currently some promising models to build on. As we noted in the introduction to this volume, psychotherapists have three broad choices of models for the inclusion of spiritual issues in psychotherapy. First, they may choose to use a secular psychotherapy model for a spiritual goal, but not explicitly incorporate spiritual content. Second, psychotherapists may also engage spiritual models for psychotherapy that are devoid of secular content entirely. Finally, psychotherapists may also use spiritual interventions within secular treatment models. To date, there are some emerging models from the last two perspectives.

Spiritual Interventions Without Secular Content

Several spiritually oriented psychotherapy models for trauma use spiritual interventions outside of a secular treatment. The most frequently used models were developed specifically to address moral injury and other spiritual struggles stemming from combat. Foy and Drescher (Chapter 11, this volume) reviewed six different treatments, four of which involved group formats to address spiritual problems related to combat. Across groups, discussion and exploration of meaning is a frequently used intervention, particularly when exploring the problem of evil and theodicy.

Independent of combat-related traumas, Murray-Swank (2003) developed *Solace for the Soul: A Journey Toward Wholeness*, an eight-session, spiritually integrated manualized treatment for adult survivors of childhood sexual abuse. This treatment manual explores God images early in treatment, encourages journaling about spiritual struggles, and facilitates spiritual openness and exploration. It has been found to be effective in two case studies (Murray-Swank & Pargament, 2005).

Spiritual Interventions in the Context of Secular Evidence-Based Practices

Other promising spiritually oriented psychotherapy models for trauma have been developed in the context of secular evidence-based treatment models. In Chapter 7, we presented several case studies involving the use of spiritually oriented trauma-focused cognitive behavior therapy (SO–TF–CBT; Walker, Reese, Hughes, & Troskie, 2010). In addition to multiple case studies demonstrating the effectiveness of this model, Walker and his research team at the Child Trauma Institute at Regent University are conducting ongoing outcome studies comparing the effectiveness of SO–TF–CBT with that of secular TF–CBT in resolving spiritual issues stemming from abuse as well as reducing posttraumatic symptoms in children and teens.

Murray-Swank and Waelde (2013) presented a model for addressing spiritual themes in the context of secular cognitive processing therapy (CPT; Resick & Schnicke, 1996). Their adaptation of the original treatment calls for therapists to address four core spiritual themes in sexual trauma therapy: (a) spiritual safety and trust, (b) spiritual power and control, (c) spiritual self-esteem, and (d) spiritual intimacy and connection. Although their discussion of these themes did not include modification to specific CPT treatment modules, their work represents a promising start to the development of a spiritually oriented form of CPT.

Effective Spiritual Components Across Treatment Models

As discussed throughout this book, there are several spiritual treatment components that should be emphasized in helping clients to resolve traumatic events. First, open discussion of spiritual struggles appears to be an important element of holistic recovery from trauma. Spiritual health overlaps with emotional and mental health, and we question the degree to which someone can fully process past traumatic events without resolving, at least to some extent, any spiritual struggles related to trauma. In helping clients to process questions related to where God was when the trauma occurred, and why evil exists, it appears helpful for psychotherapists to take a supportive stance and encourage open discussion. Attempting to answer such questions for clients, or challenging their views, at least initially, appears to hold more potential for damage to the therapeutic relationship and clients' recovery.

Second, whenever possible, maintaining their relationship with God appears to be important in resolving traumatic events for clients with pre-existing faith. In multiple case studies, clients have reported struggling with where God was after the trauma while also simultaneously leaning on their relationship with God in resolving the experience. In other cases, a relationship with God served as a protective factor explicitly involved in resolving the traumatic experience, without questioning where God was during the trauma.

Third, addressing God images appears to be an important factor in resolving spiritual damage stemming from abuse. Frawley-O'Dea (Chapter 8) and authors in other chapters emphasized the importance of therapeutic relationships that give clients new experiences for relating to God. These are excellent examples of addressing distorted God images from a psychodynamic perspective. In addition, several case studies highlighted the importance of actively confronting distorted cognitions related to God images from a cognitive behavioral perspective.

Fourth, to the extent that clients engage in them, spiritual practices in general appear to be important. In particular, prayer, reference to the sacred writings from one's own faith tradition, and acceptance and forgiveness (when clients are ready and not in physical danger) appear, across the chapters of this volume, to have enhanced clients' recovery from trauma. Many clients report praying as part of their process of resolving spiritual struggles related to trauma. Others use prayer for comfort, for assistance in coping with anxiety, and to simply maintain a connection with God or their higher power. Some clients appear to be helped by referring to passages in sacred texts that give them encouragement or comfort. Finally, a number of authors wrote in case studies that part of the process of healing from trauma, particularly from various kinds of abuse, involved acceptance of the limitations of the person who harmed them and forgiveness to some degree. We would never encourage survivors to forgive when they are not ready to do so, and we would not attempt reconciliation in instances in which it could be harmful. However, we are also not prepared to stand in the way of survivors who choose to let go of anger and pain for their own peace. Doing so appears to have helped a number of clients, as reported in case studies throughout the book.

RECOMMENDATIONS TO ADVANCE RESEARCH AND PRACTICE IN THE FIELD

In this section, we propose a series of recommendations to advance work in the area of spirituality, religion, and trauma. We have organized this material into two broad areas: (a) the development of a comprehensive framework of spiritually oriented psychotherapy for trauma and (b) psychotherapist approaches to resolving problems related to evil and suffering in trauma psychotherapy.

Toward a Comprehensive Framework in Spiritually Oriented Psychotherapy for Trauma

We are excited to be part of the model building in this developing area of clinical practice. We believe that such conceptual models should focus on spiritually oriented psychotherapy in the areas of (a) spiritual interventions that are separate from secular content and (b) spiritual interventions in the context of secular evidence-based practice. With respect to the former, we encourage trauma psychotherapists to consider spiritual interventions across religious faith traditions. For example, across different religious traditions, many survivors of traumatic events have reported an increase in prayer in an effort to draw near to God after trauma. There are myriad ways to pray, but we are unaware of any protocols to help survivors of different traumatic events to organize their efforts to pray in ways that are therapeutic for them.

Many trauma survivors have reported damage to their image of and their personal relationship with God. Although there are published manuals for helping clients to resolve discrepancies between their God image and their God concept (e.g., Moriarty & Hoffman, 2008), no manualized protocols of this kind have been adapted for trauma survivors specifically. Sophisticated attempts to do so would incorporate knowledge of treatment issues that arise when working with survivors of specific traumatic events, findings on meaning making and the impact of traumatic events on specific dimensions of survivors' relationship with God, and findings on changes in faith after traumatic events. Of course, in developing spiritually oriented interventions, researchers need not limit themselves to these two examples.

We also encourage the incorporation of spiritual interventions in the context of secular evidence-based treatment for trauma. For example, as we noted earlier, SO–TF–CBT for children and adolescents (Walker et al., 2010) fits within this category. Due in part to the proliferation of secular evidence-based trauma models in the past decade, we believe that this area has great promise. For example, research has repeatedly demonstrated the efficacy of CPT for both combat-related PTSD and for IPV. Independent of these two psychotherapy models, substantial work has demonstrated the spiritual effects of combat in the form of moral injury as well as the debilitating spiritual injuries from IPV. Researchers should consider engaging in the difficult task of applying such research to the clinical treatment of IPV to develop spiritually oriented forms of CPT for combat-related PTSD and IPV.

As we noted earlier in this chapter, Murray-Swank and Waelde (2013) provided a helpful discussion of spiritual themes to consider. Additional work needs to be done in modifying specific treatment modules within CPT that focus on spiritual issues and practices but remain broad enough to accommodate clients from various religious traditions. When such conceptual work is complete, outcome studies evaluating the effectiveness of such spiritually oriented CPT models against their secular counterparts are sorely needed. Of course, CPT is not the only evidence-based treatment model treatment model that could also benefit from the use of spiritual interventions.

Courtois's complex trauma processing framework (e.g., Courtois, Ford, & Briere, 2012) is another evidence-based practice for trauma that has great promise for addressing spiritual issues. Indeed, in this volume, Van Deusen and Courtois (Chapter 2) as well as Walker et al. (Chapter 7) presented cases involving a complex trauma processing framework that effectively used spiritual interventions in treatment over time to address spiritual damage from child abuse. Clinical research is needed to further elucidate the effectiveness of this framework.

Psychotherapist Approaches to Addressing Evil and Suffering in Practice

Further research is sorely needed on how psychotherapists approach issues related to evil and suffering and the resulting spiritual and emotional outcomes for clients. In addition, research is needed that addresses therapists' understanding of defining evil across different religious traditions, or the study of theodicy. At this point, little is known about the impact of different approaches to understanding and dealing with theodicy and psychotherapeutic outcome. Additional research and conceptual models are needed to describe ways of approaching suffering across psychotherapeutic orientations. It is probable that each psychotherapy system has a different way of helping people resolve these questions.

From a research perspective, some conceptual overlap exists between theodicy and previous attempts to understand the impact of spiritual struggles on mental health (see Exline, 2013, for a review). As a result, clinical and counseling psychology already has a language related to the problem of evil and a conceptual framework with which to begin these undertakings. However, this area of investigation has been considered almost exclusively from a paradigm in which psychology informs spirituality and theology. In moving forward in developing conceptual frameworks to serve clients with trauma histories, greater dialogue needs to occur between the disciplines of psychology and theology in which theological understandings of the problem of evil inform psychotherapeutic approaches to addressing theodicy in trauma.

CONCLUSION

It is a daunting and humbling task to provide psychotherapy in so intensely personal a realm as personal faith in the context of trauma. Many times, there are no words to describe the horrors that clients have faced and the challenges of remaining present in the midst of enormous pain. It is our personal belief that God frequently meets us and our clients in those places of agony in people's hearts for which there are no words. Thank you for being willing to be a person who works in such places. Our thoughts and prayers are with you and your clients as we conclude this book.

REFERENCES

Courtois, C. A., Ford, J. D., & Briere, J. (2012). *Treating complex trauma: A sequenced, relationship based approach.* New York, NY: Guilford Press.

Exline, J. J. (2013). Religious and spiritual struggles. In K. I. Pargament, J. J. Exline, & J. W. Jones (Eds.), *APA handbook of psychology, religion, and spirituality: Vol. 1. Context, theory, and research* (pp. 459–475). Washington, DC: American Psychological Association.

Moriarty, G., & Hoffman, L. (2008). (Eds.) *The God image handbook for spiritual counseling and psychotherapy: Research, theory and practice.* New York, NY: Haworth Press.

Murray-Swank, N. A. (2003). *Solace for the soul: An evaluation of a psycho-spiritual intervention for female survivors of sexual abuse* (Unpublished doctoral dissertation). Bowling Green State University, Bowling Green, OH.

Murray-Swank, N. A., & Pargament, K. I. (2005). God, where are you? Evaluating a spiritually integrated intervention for sexual abuse. *Mental Health, Religion & Culture, 8,* 191–203. doi:10.1080/13694670500138866

Murray-Swank, N. A., & Waelde, L. C. (2013). Spirituality, religion, and sexual trauma: Integrating research, theory, and clinical practice. In K. I. Pargament (Ed.), *APA handbook of psychology, religion, and spirituality: Vol. 2. An applied psychology of religion and spirituality* (pp. 335–354). Washington, DC: American Psychological Association.

Resick, P. A., & Schnicke, M. (1996). *Cognitive processing therapy for rape victims: A treatment manual.* Newbury Park, CA: Sage.

Stephens, R., & Walker, D. F. (in press). White Evangelical and Fundamentalist churches. In A. Johnson (Ed.), *Religion and men's violence against women.* New York, NY: Springer.

Walker, D. F., Reese, J. B., Hughes, J. P., & Troskie, M. J. (2010). Addressing religious and spiritual issues in trauma-focused cognitive behavior therapy with children and adolescents. *Professional Psychology: Research and Practice, 41,* 174–180. doi:10.1037/a0017782

INDEX

and spiritual/emotional reactions to
    disasters, 195–197
Disaster Response Network, 198
Disasters, as collective experience, 190
Disaster trauma, 190
Disclosure(s)
    adaptive, 239
    behavioral, 119–121
    nondisclosure, 120
    overdisclosure, 114
    of psychotherapists' religious beliefs,
        113–118
    self-, 65–66
Disorganized attachment style, 21–22,
    32
Disparaging labels, 30–31
Dispiritedness, 134
Dissociation
    from complex trauma, 34
    and faith development, 41–42
Divine struggles, 8
Doubt, existential, 92–93
Douki, S., 216
Doxey, C., 151
Dual relationships, 64–65
Dynes, R. R., 191

Early postimpact phase (disaster
    recovery), 191–192
Earned secure attachment style, 32
Eastern Body Western Mind (Judith), 35
Edmondson, D., 129, 153
Edwards, C. E., 177
Eisenberg, A., 109
Emergency phase (disaster recovery),
    191
Emotional care. *See* Spiritual and emo-
    tional care
Emotional dysregulation, 33–34
Emotional reactions
    to assessments, 78
    to disasters, 195–197
Emotional transparency, of psycho-
    therapists, 67
Empathy
    in assessments, 80
    of psychotherapists, 63
Environment, safe, 57
Erikson, E. H., 31, 38

Ethical issues, 10
    application of evidence-based
        approaches, 70–71
    boundaries, 64–68
    for disaster spiritual/emotional care,
        198–200
    psychotherapists' competence, 58–62
    psychotherapists' willingness to treat,
        62–63
    safety and risk management, 68–69
    with trauma-informed care, 56–57
Ethical positions, 255–256, 270
Evans-Campbell, T., 192
Everly, G. S., 133
Evidence-based approaches, 70–71
Evil, 11–12, 253–271
    addressing of, by psychotherapists,
        279
    case study of, 256–271
    resistance against, 255–256
    source of, 254–255
    in theodicy, 243
Existential anxiety and doubt, 92–93
Exline, J. J., 8
Exposure-related work, 47
Extrinsic religion/spirituality, 234–235

Faith
    damage to, from trauma, 148–150
    loss of, 69, 236–237
    as protective factor, 150–151
Faith development
    and complex trauma, 35–38
    and dissociation, 41–42
Falsetti, S. A., 110
Fassinger, R. E., 109
Feltey, K. M., 153
Ferguson, L. J., 179
Foa, E. B., 129
Ford, J. D., 33, 48
Forgiveness
    interventions to promote, 238
    lack of, as spiritual red flag, 237–238
    in spiritual assessment, 93–94
    in spirituality and trauma group
        module, 243–244
    and trauma recovery, 277
Forward focus (term), 142
Fowler, J. W., 35–38, 42

understanding of trauma by, 6
willingness of, to treat, 62–63
Psychotherapy
    failure of, address religious issues,
        104–105
    including religious content in, 105,
        111–113
    spirituality in. *See* Spirituality in
        psychotherapy
PTSD. *See* Posttraumatic stress disorder
Purpose, spiritual, 90–91

Qur'an, 147

RCI-10 (Religious Commitment Inven-
    tory), 95
Reconnection, in treatment, 49–52
Redemption, 50
Reinert, D. F., 177
Relational development, of God images,
    173–176
Relationships. *See also* Relationship
    with God
    and dissociation, 34
    dual, 64–65
    multiple, 64–65
    of sexual abuse survivors with God,
        176–178
Relationship with God
    empowered, 150–151
    and intimate partner violence, 222
    trauma and damage to, 148–150
    and trauma recovery, 276–277
Religion
    addressing of, in education programs,
        104
    benefits and harms of, 18–19
    changes in. *See* Changes in spiritu-
        ality and religion following
        trauma
    defining, 8, 211–212
    as experienced by psychotherapists,
        5–6
    extrinsic, 234–235
    and intimate partner violence,
        214–216
    intrinsic, 234–235
    as justification for abusive behaviors,
        110, 111, 117
    maintaining connection to, 155

misuse of, 69
outcomes affected by, 194–195
and persecution, 19–20
as play, 173–174
as protective factor, 217–218
use of, for coping, 110–111
well-being harmed by, 68
Religious assessment. *See* Spiritual
    assessment
Religious behaviors
    decreased, due to trauma, 149–150
    increased, due to disasters, 192
    positive impact of, 151
Religious beliefs
    disclosure of psychotherapists',
        113–118
    as diversity variable, 17–18
    as hindrance to survivors' treatment,
        117
    rigidity of, 89–90
Religious Commitment Inventory
    (RCI-10), 95
Religious communities
    disaster planning for, 202
    disaster response by, 191–192
    and posttraumatic recovery, 196
    survivors' relationships with, 91
Religious holidays, 119–120
Religious interventions. *See also* Spiri-
    tual interventions
    and coping, 111
    as evidence-based approach, 70–71
    for military personnel and families,
        247–248
    praying as, 118
    and working alliance, 118–119
Religious issues, in trauma treatment,
    110–113
Religious jewelry, 120, 121
Religious Problem-Solving Scale, 95
Religious resources, 84
Religious struggles, 8
Religious symbols, 120–121
Remembrance, in treatment, 46–49
Resilience, 234–235
Resources
    religious, 84
    spiritual, 84
    for spiritual and emotional care,
        197–198

Resources, *continued*
  for women leaving abusive
        marriages, 223
Restoration phase (disaster recovery),
      192
Rice, A., 194
Richards, P. S., 78–79
Ringel, S., 215–216
Risk management, 68–69
Rituals, 51
Rodin, Auguste, 173–174
Roman Catholic sex scandal, 179–180
Ronan, K. R., 189
Rosenfeld, G. W., 112
Rossetti, S. J., 148–149
Rothbaum, B. O., 129
Rotunda, R. J., 217
Ryan, P. L., 152

Safety
  in communities, 50–51
  creating, in communities, 50–51
  creating, in therapy environment, 57
  as ethical issue, 68–69
Santangelo, L. K., 192
Schneider, R. Z., 153
Schuster, M. A., 192
Secondary reactions, of psychothera-
      pists, 62
Secure attachment style, 21, 32
Seguin, M. H., 109
Self, W. R., 191
Self-directing spiritual coping style, 89
Self-disclosure, by psychotherapists,
      65–66
Self-judgment, 91
Senselosing (term), 196
Sensemaking (term), 196
Service, acts of, 242–243
Sexual abuse, 11, 169–186
  case studies of, 39–41, 170–172
  by clergy members, 179–181
  and impact of religious behaviors, 151
  and relational development of God
        images, 148–149, 173–176
  and spirituality, 152
  spirituality in psychotherapy with
        survivors of, 181–186
  and survivors' relationship with God,
        176–178

Shafranske, E. P., 5
Shame
  after combat, 236
  and spiritual assessment, 92
Shengold, L., 176–177
Smith, B. W., 194
Social media sites, 66–67
Social support, 240
*Solace for the Soul: A Journey Toward
      Wholeness*, 275–276
Somatization, 34
Sorsoli, L., 152
SO–TF–CBT. *See* Spiritually oriented
      trauma-focused cognitive behav-
      ior therapy
Soul, defining, 35
"Soul murder," 35, 176–177
Spiritual and emotional care
  ethical guidelines for, 198–200
  practicing, in disaster response,
        200–205
  resources for, 197–198
Spiritual assessment, 77–100
  case study of, 96–100
  creating safe context for, 79–81
  and differential diagnosis, 20
  of issues relevant to trauma work,
        85–94
  multidimensional strategy for, 81–83
  and outcome measures, 94–96
  over course of therapy, 154–155
  process of conducting, 83–85
  rationale for conducting, 78–79
  in spiritually oriented trauma-
        focused cognitive behavior
        therapy, 26
Spiritual behaviors
  enhancing, 242–243
  and trauma recovery, 277
Spiritual communities
  disaster planning for, 202
  disaster response by, 191–192
Spiritual coping style, 88–89
Spiritual crisis, 85–87
Spiritual identity and purpose, 90–91
Spiritual interventions. *See also* Reli-
      gious interventions
  across treatment models, 276–277
  in case studies, 99–100
  categorization of, 24–25

ABOUT THE EDITORS

Donald F. Walker, PhD, directs the Child Trauma Institute, an interdisciplinary research center devoted to understanding the role of religious faith in recovery from childhood abuse, treating survivors of child abuse, and training professionals in addressing spiritual issues in treatment. Dr. Walker also teaches in the PsyD program in clinical psychology at Regent University. As a professor, he teaches courses on trauma and clinical child psychology and supervises students at all levels of the program. He is a member of the Society for the Psychology of Religion and Spirituality, and the Division of Trauma Psychology (American Psychological Divisions 36 and 56, respectively). He is also the founder and executive director of Tidewater Child and Family Behavioral Health Center, PLLC, in Virginia Beach, Virginia. He is a clinical child psychologist and treats children, teens, and families.

Christine A. Courtois, PhD, ABPP, is a board certified counseling psychologist in independent practice in Washington, DC, and national clinical trauma consultant at Elements Behavioral Health/Promises. Dr. Courtois has published three books in conjunction with Dr. Julian Ford on the topic of complex trauma and its treatment. She lectures widely and is currently chairing a committee on developing treatment guidelines for posttraumatic stress disorder for the American Psychological Association. She is the recipient of a number of professional awards, among them the American Psychological Association Award for Distinguished Contributions to Psychology as a Professional Practice and the International Society for Traumatic Stress Studies Sarah Haley Award for Clinical Excellence.

Jamie D. Aten, PhD, is the founder and codirector of the Humanitarian Disaster Institute and Dr. Arthur P. Rech and Mrs. Jean May Rech Associate Professor of Psychology at Wheaton College, Wheaton, Illinois. Dr. Aten's interests include the psychology of religion and disasters, disaster spiritual and emotional care, and faith-based relief and development. He has received over $2 million in external funding to study disasters, trauma, and faith issues around the globe and has been recognized with the American Psychological Association's Division 36 (Society for the Psychology of Religion and Spirituality) Margaret Gorman Early Career Award and Mutual of America Merit Finalist Award. He is also the coeditor or author of seven books.